Revenue Statistics in Latin America and the Caribbean

1990-2014

Estadísticas tributarias en América Latina y el Caribe

1990-2014

This work is published under the responsibility of the Secretary-General of the OECD. The opinions expressed and arguments employed herein do not necessarily reflect the official views of OECD member countries or of the United Nations Economic Commission for Latin America and the Caribbean (UN-ECLAC), the Inter-American Center of Tax Administrations (CIAT) or the Inter-American Development Bank (IDB), its Board of Directors, or the countries they represent.

El presente trabajo se publica bajo la responsabilidad del Secretario General de la OCDE. Las opiniones expresadas y los argumentos utilizados en el mismo no reflejan necesariamente el punto de vista oficial de los países miembros de la OCDE, ni de la Comisión Económica para América Latina y el Caribe de las Naciones Unidas (CEPAL-UN) o aquellas del Centro Interamericano de Administraciones Tributarias (CIAT), ni del Banco Interamericano de Desarrollo (BID), de su Directorio Ejecutivo ni de los países que representan.

This document and any map included herein are without prejudice to the status of or sovereignty over any territory, to the delimitation of international frontiers and boundaries and to the name of any territory, city or area.

Tanto este documento como cualquier mapa que se incluya en él no conllevan perjuicio alguno respecto al estatus o la soberanía de cualquier territorio, a la delimitación de fronteras y límites internacionales, ni al nombre de cualquier territorio, ciudad o área.

Please cite this publication as:
OECD/ECLAC/CIAT/IDB (2016), *Revenue Statistics in Latin America and the Caribbean 2016*, OECD Publishing, Paris.
http://dx.doi.org/10.1787/rev_lat-2016-en-fr

Por favor, cite esta publicación de la siguiente manera:
OCDE/CEPAL/CIAT/BID (2016), Estadísticas tributarias en América Latina y el Caribe 2016, OECD Publishing, Paris.
http://dx.doi.org/10.1787/rev_lat-2016-en-fr

ISBN 978-92-64-25191-5 (print/impresa)
ISBN 978-92-64-25193-9 (PDF)

The compilation of data for this publication was completed in December 2015. On 7 January 2016 Argentina's National Institute of Statistics and Census published an official decree (*https://www.boletinoficial.gob.ar/pdf/linkQR/QlFlS1dmVmpOWXMrdTVReEh2ZkU0dz09*) temporarily suspending the publication of certain data in the National Statistics System. The nominal GDP series for Argentina used in this publication was obtained on 13 December 2015 through the official website of Argentina's National Institute of Statistics and Census (*http://www.indec.mecon.ar/*). As a consequence of the decree and the potential for future revisions of the GDP data, the tax to GDP ratio figures for Argentina should be treated with caution.

La recopilación de datos para esta publicación finalizó en diciembre de 2015. El 7 de enero 2016 el Instituto Nacional de Estadísticas y Censos de la República de Argentina publicó un boletín oficial (*https://www.boletinoficial.gob.ar/pdf/linkQR/QlFlS1dmVmpOWXMrdTVReEh2ZkU0dz09*) mediante el cual suspende temporalmente la publicación de ciertos datos en el Sistema Nacional de Estadísticas. En el caso de Argentina, la serie del PIB nominal utilizada en esta publicación se obtuvo el 13 de diciembre 2015 a través del sitio web oficial del Instituto Nacional de Argentina de Estadística y Censos (*http://www.indec.mecon.ar/*). Como consecuencia del decreto y la posibilidad de futuras revisiones de los datos del PIB, las cifras de impuestos en relación al PIB de Argentina deben ser tratadas con precaución.

Corrigenda to OECD publications may be found on line at: *www.oecd.org/publishing/corrigenda*.
Las erratas de las publicaciones de la OCDE se encuentran en línea en *www.oecd.org/publishing/corrigenda*.

Foreword

Revenue Statistics in Latin America and the Caribbean is a joint publication by the OECD Centre for Tax Policy and Administration, the OECD Development Centre, the United Nations Economic Commission for Latin America and the Caribbean (ECLAC), the Inter-American Centre of Tax Administrations (CIAT) and the Inter-American Development Bank (IDB). It presents detailed, internationally comparable data on tax revenues for 22 Latin American and Caribbean economies, two of which are OECD members. Its approach is based on the well-established methodology of the OECD Revenue Statistics database, which has become an essential reference source for OECD member countries. Comparisons are also made with the average for OECD economies.

The term "taxes" in this publication is confined to compulsory, unrequited payments to general government. As outlined in the Interpretative Guide to the Revenue Statistics, taxes are "unrequited" in the sense that benefits provided by government to taxpayers are not normally in proportion to their payments. The OECD methodology classifies a tax according to its base: income, profits and capital gains (classified under heading 1000), payroll (heading 3000), property (heading 4000), goods and services (heading 5000) and other taxes (heading 6000). Compulsory social security contributions paid to general government are treated as taxes, and classified under heading 2000. Much greater detail on the tax concept, the classification of taxes and the accrual basis of reporting is set out in the Interpretative Guide in Annex A.

Extending the OECD methodology to Latin America and the Caribbean countries makes possible comparisons of tax systems on a consistent basis both across this region and between them and OECD countries. However, in a few cases this methodology is different from the approach used by ECLAC, CIAT and IDB. In these cases the differences are noted in the text and in the tables, either with a footnote or an extra row. The report provides an overview of the main taxation trends in Latin America and the Caribbean. It examines changes in both the level and the composition of taxation plus the attribution of tax collection by sub-level of government between 1990 and 2014.

Presentación

La publicación *Estadísticas tributarias en América Latina y el Caribe* ha sido elaborada conjuntamente por el Centro de Política y Administración Tributaria de la OCDE, el Centro de Desarrollo de la OCDE, la Comisión Económica de las Naciones Unidas para América Latina y el Caribe (CEPAL), el Centro Interamericano de Administraciones Tributarias (CIAT) y el Banco Interamericano de Desarrollo (BID). Esta publicación presenta datos detallados comparables a escala internacional sobre los ingresos tributarios de 22 economías latinoamericanas y caribeñas, 2 de las cuales son miembros de la OCDE. Su enfoque se basa en la metodología consagrada de la base de datos Revenue Statistics de la OCDE, que se ha convertido en un referente esencial para los países miembros de la OCDE. Se presentan también comparaciones con la media de la OCDE.

En la presente publicación, el término "impuestos" se circunscribe exclusivamente a los pagos obligatorios sin contraprestación efectuados al gobierno general. Tal y como lo subraya la Guía de interpretación de Revenue Statistics, los impuestos carecen de contraprestación en el sentido en que, normalmente, las prestaciones proporcionadas por el gobierno a los contribuyentes no guardan relación directa con los pagos realizados por estos. La metodología de la OCDE clasifica los impuestos según la base sobre la que recaen: renta, utilidades y ganancias del capital (categoría 1000); nomina (categoría 3000); propiedad (categoría 4000); bienes y servicios (categoría 5000); y otros impuestos (categoría 6000). Las contribuciones obligatorias a la seguridad social abonadas al gobierno general se tratan aquí como impuestos (categoría 2000). Para mayor detalle sobre el concepto de impuesto, su clasificación y su registro según el criterio de devengo, véase la Guía de interpretación que figura en el Anexo A.

Aplicar la metodología de la OCDE a América Latina y el Caribe posibilita la comparación de sistemas tributarios a partir de una base coherente en la región, entre los países latinoamericanos, y con los países de la OCDE. Sin embargo, en algunas ocasiones, esta metodología difiere de la empleada por la CEPAL, el CIAT y el BID; en esos casos, las diferencias se han indicado en el texto y los cuadros, sea con una nota a pie de página, o en una línea adicional.

El informe ofrece un panorama general de las principales tendencias en materia tributaria en América Latina y en el Caribe. A tal efecto, examina los cambios registrados entre 1990 y 2014 en el nivel y la composición de la tributación, así como en la atribución de la recaudación tributaria a los diversos subsectores de gobierno.

Acknowledgements

Revenue Statistics in Latin America and the Caribbean has been jointly produced by the Organisation for Economic Co-operation and Development (OECD) Centre for Tax Policy and Administration, the OECD Development Centre, the United Nations Economic Commission for Latin America and the Caribbean (ECLAC), the Inter-American Centre of Tax Administrations (CIAT) and the Inter-American Development Bank (IDB). The staff from these organisations with responsibility for producing the publication were: Juan Carlos Benitez and René Orozco of the OECD Development Centre under the supervision of the Director Mario Pezzini and the Head of the Latin American and Caribbean Unit Angel Melguizo; Maurice Nettley and Emmanuelle Modica of the OECD Centre for Tax Policy and Administration under the supervision of the Director Pascal Saint-Amans, Deputy Director Grace Perez-Navarro and the Head of the Tax Policy and Tax Statistics Division David Bradbury; Juan Pablo Jiménez and Michael Hanni of the Economic Development Division of UN-ECLAC under the supervision of the Director Daniel Titelman and the Chief of the Fiscal Affairs Unit Ricardo Martner; Julio Alberto López from the CIAT Tax Studies and Research Directorate, under the supervision of Director, Miguel Eduardo Pecho; Michael Stephen Anthony Browne and Agnes Rojas under the supervision of Principal Technical Leader in Fiscal Economics Alberto Barreix and Senior Fiscal Economist Gerardo Reyes-Tagle of the IDB.

The authors would like to thank other staff at the OECD Development Centre, the OECD Centre for Tax Policy and Administration and the IDB for their invaluable help in completing this fifth edition of the publication. Elizabeth Nash and Delphine Grandrieux from the OECD Development Centre's Communications and Publications team ensured the production of the publication, in both paper and electronic form.

Finally, the Centre for Tax Policy and Administration, the Development Centre of the OECD, as well as CEPAL and the IDB are also very grateful to our colleagues working in national entities with whom we have consulted regularly. These institutions include the finance ministries and national tax agencies of Argentina, Bahamas, Barbados, Bolivia, Brazil, Chile, Colombia, Costa Rica, Dominican Republic, Ecuador, El Salvador, Guatemala, Honduras, Jamaica, Mexico, Nicaragua, Panama, Paraguay, Peru, Trinidad and Tobago, Uruguay and Venezuela, the Ministry of Economy and Production of Argentina, the Central Bank of Barbados and the Central Reserve Bank of Peru. In addition, CIAT would like to thank their Network of Tax Studies and Research.

Agradecimientos

La publicación *Estadísticas tributarias en América Latina y el Caribe* ha sido elaborada conjuntamente por el Centro de Política y Administración Tributaria de la Organización para la Cooperación y el Desarrollo Económicos (OCDE), el Centro de Desarrollo de la OCDE, la Comisión Económica de las Naciones Unidas para América Latina y el Caribe (CEPAL), el Centro Interamericano de Administraciones Tributarias (CIAT) y el Banco Interamericano de Desarrollo (BID). Las personas de esas organizaciones responsables de redactar la presente publicación han sido: Juan Carlos Benitez y René Orozco del Centro de Desarrollo de la OCDE, bajo la supervisión del director, Mario Pezzini y del Jefe de la Unidad de América Latina y el Caribe Angel Melguizo; Maurice Nettley y Emmanuelle Modica del Centro de Política y Administración Tributaria de la OCDE, bajo la supervisión del director, Pascal Saint-Amans, sub-directora Grace Perez-Navarro y el Jefe de la División de Políticas y Estadísticas Tributarias David Bradbury; Juan Pablo Jiménez y Michael Hanni de la División de Desarrollo Económico de la CEPAL, bajo la supervisión del director Daniel Titelman y del jefe de la Unidad de Asuntos Fiscales Ricardo Martner; Julio Alberto López de la Dirección de Estudios e Investigaciones Tributarias del CIAT, bajo la supervisión del Director, Miguel Eduardo Pecho; Michael Stephen Anthony Browne y Agnes Rojas bajo la supervisión del Líder Técnico Principal en Economía Fiscal Alberto Barreix y el Economista Fiscal Senior Gerardo Reyes-Tagle del BID.

Los autores desean agradecer a otras personas del Centro de Desarrollo de la OCDE, del Centro de Política y Administración Tributaria de la OCDE y BID su incalculable contribución a la finalización de la quinta edición de esta publicación. Elizabeth Nash y Delphine Grandrieux, del equipo de Comunicaciones y Publicaciones del Centro de Desarrollo de la OCDE, que aseguraron la producción de la publicación, tanto física como en formato electrónico.

Por último, el Centro de Política y Administración Tributaria, el Centro de Desarrollo de la OCDE, la CEPAL y el BID hacen partícipes de nuestro agradecimiento a nuestros colegas de entidades nacionales, a los que hemos consultado con frecuencia. Entre esas instituciones, se cuentan los ministerios de finanzas y las agencias tributarias nacionales de Argentina, Bahamas, Barbados, Bolivia, Brasil, Chile, Colombia, Costa Rica, Ecuador, El Salvador, Guatemala, Honduras, Jamaica, México, Nicaragua, Panamá, Paraguay, Perú, República Dominicana, Trinidad y Tobago, Uruguay y Venezuela, así como el Ministerio de Economía y Producción de Argentina, el Banco Central de Barbados (CBB) y el Banco Central de Reserva del Perú. Asimismo, CIAT también desea agradecer La Red de Estudios e Investigaciones Tributarias.

Table of contents

Índice de materias

LIST OF TABLES/ÍNDICE DE CUADROS

Chapter 1/Capítulo 1

Tax revenue trends, 1990-2014/Tendencias tributarias, 1990-2014

Chapter 2/Capítulo 2

Special Feature/Sección especial

Chapter 3/Capítulo 3

Tax levels and tax structures, 1990-2014/Niveles impositivos y estructuras tributarias, 1990-2014

LIST OF FIGURES/ÍNDICE DE GRÁFICOS

Chapter 1/Capítulo 1

Tax revenue trends, 1990-2014/Tendencias tributarias, 1990-2014

Chapter 2/Capítulo 2

Special Feature/Sección especial

Executive summary

Tax revenues as a proportion of national incomes in Latin American and Caribbean (LAC) countries have, with the exception of the financial crisis in 2009, risen almost continuously between 1990 and 2014. In the group of 22 LAC countries covered by the Report the average tax to GDP ratio rose from 21.5% in 2013 to 21.7% in 2014 compared with 21.4% in 2012 and 20.8% in 2011.

Although tax to GDP ratios have been increasing, the LAC average of 21.7% is still well below the OECD average of 34.4%. In some LAC countries, there is scope for further tax base broadening and measures to modernise tax policy and administrations to support domestic resource mobilisation as their GDP per capita grows.

There are wide national variations in the tax to GDP ratios across both OECD and LAC countries. In 2014, the LAC countries covered by the Report range from 12.6% in Guatemala to 33.4% in Brazil. The corresponding range amongst OECD countries was from 19.5% in Mexico to 50.9% in Denmark.

Countries with higher levels of GDP per capita are more likely to have higher tax to GDP ratios. This relationship is generally reflected in the revenue data for the LAC countries in this publication.

Between 1990 and 2014, the LAC average tax to GDP ratio rose more quickly than the OECD average – by 7.1 percentage points compared with 2.3 percentage points. Tax to GDP ratios have been increasing in LAC countries as these countries have undertaken tax reforms and modernised their tax systems and administrations, particularly with respect to income taxes and VAT. However, high levels of informality and relatively narrow tax bases still remain a challenge in LAC countries, with both factors contributing to lower tax to GDP ratios in comparison to OECD countries.

There have also been substantial increases in the share of tax revenues from income and profits as well as the share of VAT, two important sources of revenue for LAC countries. The share of specific consumption taxes (mainly excises and import duties) has nearly halved, a decline related to global trade liberalisation.

The Report provides internationally comparable data on tax levels and tax structures for the group of 22 countries across the LAC region. Using the same methodology as the OECD Revenue Statistics database, it presents cross-country comparisons between LAC economies and between LAC and OECD economies. The LAC countries covered are Argentina, Bahamas, Barbados, Bolivia, Brazil, Chile, Colombia, Costa Rica, Dominican Republic, Ecuador, El Salvador, Guatemala, Honduras, Jamaica, Mexico, Nicaragua, Panama, Paraguay, Peru, Trinidad and Tobago, Uruguay and Venezuela. The tax to GDP ratio for Mexico is different in this publication from the figures presented in ECLAC and CIAT publications because this publication also includes fees levied on hydrocarbon production as tax revenues.

The Report also contains a Special Feature, which depicts changes in revenues from non-renewable natural resources in some LAC countries between 2013 and 2014 and presents estimates for this source of revenue in 2015. In 2014, the sharp decline in commodity prices resulted in a significant reduction in hydrocarbon-related revenues by

0.7 percentage points of GDP and for 2015 the expected drop is estimated at 2.1 percentage points of GDP. This impact is substantial on revenues that are not classified as taxes and are not included in the tax to GDP ratios. Likewise, mining revenues were affected by the decrease in commodity prices causing these revenues to fall by 0.1 percentage of GDP in 2014. The estimated drop for 2015 is similar to the previous year. In some countries, increases in mining production coupled with currency depreciations have resulted in relatively stable non-tax revenues. On the other hand, corporate income tax revenues in the sector have fallen sharply as profit margins tightened.

Key findings

Tax to GDP ratios

- The average tax burden in the group of 22 LAC countries increased from 21.5% in 2013 to 21.7% in 2014. This followed a rise of 1.5 percentage points over the four years between 2010 and 2013, reversing the decline from 20.6% to 19.9% between 2008 and 2009.
- There is a wide variation across countries. The tax to GDP ratios in LAC countries range from 12.6% (Guatemala) and 14.1% (Dominican Republic) to 32.2% (Argentina) and 33.4% (Brazil).
- The difference between the OECD average tax to GDP ratio and that for the 22 LAC countries fell from 18 to 13 percentage points between 1990 and 2008. The gap has remained steady at 13 percentage points since 2008.
- VAT revenues were responsible for the vast majority of the increase in average LAC tax burden from 14.6% to 17.2% between 1990 and 2000. After 2000, revenues from personal and corporate income taxes became the more important driver and about half of the growth from 17.2% to 21.7% is attributed to these revenues.
- All of the LAC countries showed increases in their tax to GDP ratio between 1990 and 2014, though there is considerable variation between individual LAC countries. The countries with the largest increases were Bolivia (20.6 percentage points) and Argentina (19.8 percentage points). These are followed by Colombia, Ecuador and Paraguay which displayed increases of 11-12 percentage points, whereas the increases in Jamaica and Venezuela were 1.2 and 0.1 percentage points respectively.

Tax structures

- Following strong growth over the past twenty years, general consumption taxes (mainly VAT and sales taxes) accounted for 31.2% of tax revenues in the LAC countries in 2013 compared with 20.2% in OECD countries) whereas the share of specific consumption taxes declined to 18.3% (in OECD it is 10.5%).
- Taxes on income and profits accounted for 27.4% of revenues on average in the LAC countries and social security contributions represented 16.6% (in OECD the corresponding figures are 33.7% and 26.1% respectively).

Tax revenues attributed to local governments

- The share of tax revenues collected by local governments is small in most LAC countries and has not increased, reflecting the relatively weak taxing powers of sub-central levels of government compared with OECD countries.

Resumen ejecutivo

Los ingresos fiscales como proporción del PIB han aumentado en los países de América Latina y el Caribe (ALC), con excepción de la crisis financiera en 2009, de forma casi ininterrumpida entre 1990 y 2014. Con referencia al grupo de los 22 países ALC analizados en el informe, la tasa media de recaudación tributaria en términos porcentuales del PIB se elevó del 21.5% registrado en 2013 hasta un 21.7% en 2014, frente al 21.4% referenciado en 2012 y el 20.8% en 2011.

Pese a que el coeficiente de impuestos frente a PIB en estos países ha ido en aumento, el promedio del 21.7% en la región ALC se sitúa aún muy por debajo de la media de los países de la OCDE, que alcanza un 34.4%. En algunos países ALC quedan retos por enfrentar como la ampliación de la base imponible, la adopción de medidas de modernización de la administración y política tributarias para favorecer la movilización de recursos internos a medida que el PIB per cápita crece.

Existen amplias diferencias nacionales en lo concerniente al cociente impuestos/PIB que registran tanto los países de la OCDE como los países de la región ALC. En 2014, el cociente correspondiente a los países ALC incluidos en el informe oscilaba entre el 12.6% de Guatemala y el 33.4% de Brasil, mientras que la registrada entre los países de la OCDE iba del 19.5% de México al 50.9% de Dinamarca.

Aquellos países con los niveles más elevados de PIB per cápita son más propensos a presentar los coeficientes más altos de impuestos con respecto al PIB, correlación que se corrobora en términos generales en los datos sobre los ingresos de los países ALC reflejados en el presente documento.

Entre 1990 y 2014, el promedio de recaudación tributaria en términos porcentuales del PIB en los países ALC aumentó más rápidamente que el de los países OCDE (las cifras indican un aumento de 7.1 puntos porcentuales en los países ALC frente a los 2.3 registrados en los países OCDE). Esta evolución en los países ALC responde a la implementación de reformas fiscales y a la modernización de sus administraciones y sistemas tributarios, en particular por lo que respecta a los impuestos sobre la renta y al IVA. No obstante, el elevado nivel de informalidad existente y unas bases imponibles relativamente bajas siguen representando un reto al que se enfrentan los países ALC, contribuyendo ambos factores a rebajar la recaudación sobre PIB en comparación con los países de la OCDE.

En las últimas dos décadas se observa un aumento significativo en la recaudación por impuestos sobre la renta personal (IRPF), por el impuesto de sociedades (IS) y por el impuesto sobre el valor añadido (IVA), todas ellas importantes fuentes de ingresos para los países ALC. En cambio, la proporción de los impuestos específicos sobre el consumo (principalmente impuestos especiales y derechos de importación) se ha reducido casi a la mitad, una disminución imputable a la liberalización del comercio mundial.

El informe presenta datos internacionalmente comparables sobre las estructuras y niveles tributarios correspondientes al referido grupo de 22 países a través de ALC. Utilizando la misma metodología que la base de datos Estadísticas tributarias de la OCDE, ofrece comparaciones por países entre las economías latinoamericanas, entre ellas, y respecto a economías de la OCDE. En concreto, los países ALC objeto de análisis son: Argentina, Bahamas, Barbados, Bolivia, Brasil, Chile, Colombia, Costa Rica, República Dominicana, Ecuador, El Salvador, Guatemala, Honduras, Jamaica, México, Nicaragua, Panamá, Paraguay, Perú, Trinidad y Tobago, Uruguay y Venezuela. Las cifras correspondientes a la proporción de impuestos/PIB de México presentes en esta publicación difieren de las reportadas en las publicaciones de la CEPAL y del CIAT, dado que este documento incluye también los impuestos sobre la producción de hidrocarburos como ingresos fiscales.

El informe incluye, asimismo, un apartado especial que alude a los cambios en relación con los ingresos procedentes de recursos naturales no renovables en algunos países ALC entre 2013 y 2014, así como estimaciones para 2015. En el 2014, la fuerte caída de los precios de las materias primas a nivel internacional se tradujo en un descenso promedio de 0.7 puntos del PIB en los ingresos procedentes de hidrocarburos y para el 2015 se espera una caída de 2.1 puntos del PIB. Este impacto se ha hecho patente fundamentalmente en aquellos ingresos que no reciben la consideración de impuestos y que no se incluyen en las ratios de impuestos frente a PIB. De manera similar, los ingresos mineros se vieron afectados por la caída de los precios de las materias primas y en el 2014 la caída fue en torno a 0.1 puntos del PIB, cifra similar a la estimada para el 2015. Por un lado, en algunos países, el aumento de la producción minera, aunado a diversas devaluaciones monetarias, ha dado origen a unos ingresos extra fiscales relativamente estables; por otro, la recaudación por el impuesto de sociedades en dicho sector ha registrado un brusco descenso con motivo de los estrechos márgenes de beneficio.

Principales conclusiones

Recaudación tributaria en términos porcentuales del PIB

- La carga impositiva media en el grupo de 22 países ALC se elevó del 21.5% en 2013 al 21.7% en 2014. Este resultado se da después de haber registrado un aumento de 1.7 puntos porcentuales durante un período de cuatro años que se extiende de 2010 a 2013, revirtiendo el descenso del 20.6% al 19.9% registrado entre los años 2008 y 2009.
- Existe una amplia variación entre los países de la región. En 2014 los impuestos con respecto al PIB en los países de ALC abarcan desde el 12.6% en Guatemala y el 14.1% en República Dominicana, hasta el 32.2% en Argentina y el 33.4% en Brasil.
- La diferencia entre la tasa media de recaudación tributaria en términos porcentuales del PIB de la OCDE y la correspondiente a los 22 países ALC de referencia se redujo de 18 a 13 puntos porcentuales entre 1990 y 2008, habiendo permanecido estable en 13 puntos desde 2008.
- La recaudación por IVA fue el factor responsable, en su mayor parte, del aumento del 14.6% al 17.2% de la carga impositiva media en los países ALC durante la década 1990-2000. A partir de entonces el IRPF y el IS se convirtieron en el principal motor, atribuyéndose a dichas modalidades recaudatorias alrededor de la mitad del aumento de la recaudación del 17.2% al 21.7%.
- Todos los países de la región ALC experimentaron un aumento en sus respectivos índices de impuestos frente a PIB entre 1990 y 2014, si bien existe igualmente una considerable disparidad de un país ALC a otro en esta medida. Los países que registraron mayores incrementos fueron: Bolivia (con 20.6 puntos porcentuales) y Argentina (con 19.8 puntos porcentuales). Seguidos por Colombia, Ecuador

y Paraguay que registraron un aumento de entre 11 y 12 puntos porcentuales, mientras que el aumento correspondiente a Jamaica y Venezuela se situó en 1.2 y 0.1 puntos porcentuales, respectivamente.

Estructuras fiscales

- Tras un fuerte crecimiento a lo largo de los últimos veinte años, los impuestos generales sobre el consumo (principalmente el IVA y los impuestos sobre las ventas) representaron un 31.2% de los ingresos fiscales en los países ALC en 2013 frente al 20.2% de los países de la OCDE. En cambio, la proporción de los impuestos específicos sobre el consumo (como los impuestos especiales o los impuestos sobre el comercio internacional) se redujeron hasta un 18.3% (frente al 10.5% en la OCDE).
- En los países ALC, los impuestos sobre ingresos y utilidades, que incluyen IRPF e IS, representaron en promedio, el 27.4% de la recaudación. Asimismo, las cotizaciones a la seguridad social supusieron el 16.6% (en la OCDE, las cifras correspondientes se sitúan, respectivamente, en un 33.7% y 26.1%).

Ingresos fiscales atribuidos a las administraciones locales

- La proporción de ingresos fiscales recaudada por las administraciones locales es reducida y no ha registrado aumento alguno en la mayoría de los países ALC, hecho éste que deja constancia de la capacidad impositiva relativamente limitada que ostentan las autoridades locales frente a lo que ocurre en los países de la OCDE.

CHAPTER 1

TAX REVENUE TRENDS, 1990-2014

CAPÍTULO 1

TENDENCIAS TRIBUTARIAS, 1990-2014

The compilation of data for this publication was completed in December 2015. On 7 January 2016 Argentina's National Institute of Statistics and Census published an official decree (https://www.boletinoficial.gob.ar/pdf/linkQR/QlFlS1dmVmpOWXMrdTVReEh2ZkU0dz09) temporarily suspending the publication of certain data in the National Statistics System. The nominal GDP series for Argentina used in this publication was obtained on 13 December 2015 through the official website of Argentina's National Institute of Statistics and Census (www.indec.mecon.ar/). As a consequence of the decree and the potential for future revisions of the GDP data, the tax to GDP ratio figures for Argentina should be treated with caution.

La recopilación de datos para esta publicación finalizó en diciembre de 2015. El 7 de enero 2016 el Instituto Nacional de Estadísticas y Censos de la República de Argentina publicó un boletín oficial (https://www.boletinoficial.gob.ar/pdf/linkQR/QlFlS1dmVmpOWXMrdTVReEh2ZkU0dz09) mediante el cual suspende temporalmente la publicación de ciertos datos en el Sistema Nacional de Estadísticas. En el caso de Argentina, la serie del PIB nominal utilizada en esta publicación se obtuvo el 13 de diciembre 2015 a través del sitio web oficial del Instituto Nacional de Argentina de Estadística y Censos (www.indec.mecon.ar/). Como consecuencia del decreto y la posibilidad de futuras revisiones de los datos del PIB, las cifras de impuestos en relación al PIB de Argentina deben ser tratadas con precaución.

CHAPTER 1

TAX REVENUE TRENDS, 1990-2014

1.1. Tax ratios

The tax to GDP ratio is a key indicator reflecting the current collection of funds through taxation by a country in order to finance public goods and services and to invest in infrastructure. Raising revenue through taxes is an important factor in ensuring a country's economic emergence (OECD, 2014). The appropriate level of taxation gives governments the capacity to make the investments necessary to achieve growth. It also enables emerging countries to develop their political autonomy and build effective and accountable States. Many developing countries recognise that tax revenues provide more predictable revenue streams than the often uncertain and more volatile non- tax revenues from oil and commodities that some countries have come to rely on.

Tax ratios in 2014

Table 1.1. **Total tax revenue as percentage of GDP**

	1990	2000	2008	2009	2010	2011	2012	2013	2014
Argentina	12.4	18.0	24.7	25.6	26.7	27.6	29.2	30.6	32.2
Bahamas	12.3	15.2	17.2	16.5	16.1	18.9	18.0	17.1	17.5
Barbados[1]	23.2	30.2	31.1	30.5	30.6	32.4	33.1	29.5	30.4
Bolivia[1, 2]	8.1	16.4	25.3	25.9	23.3	26.2	27.6	28.9	28.7
Brazil	25.4	29.5	33.8	32.4	32.4	33.3	33.3	33.6	33.4
Chile	17.0	18.8	21.4	17.2	19.5	21.2	21.5	20.0	19.8
Colombia	9.0	14.6	18.8	18.6	18.0	18.9	19.7	20.0	20.3
Costa Rica	16.1	18.2	22.7	21.2	20.8	21.3	21.3	22.6	22.5
Dominican Republic	7.8	11.7	14.3	12.7	12.3	12.3	13.1	13.9	14.1
Ecuador	7.1	10.1	14.0	14.9	16.3	17.3	19.3	19.2	19.0
El Salvador	10.5	12.1	15.1	14.4	15.1	15.4	16.1	17.0	16.5
Guatemala	9.0	12.4	12.9	12.2	12.4	12.7	12.8	13.0	12.6
Honduras	16.2	15.3	18.9	17.1	17.3	16.9	17.8	18.3	19.8
Jamaica[1]	23.0	22.8	25.0	24.8	25.0	24.5	24.6	25.0	24.2
Mexico[3,4]	15.5	16.5	20.7	17.2	18.5	19.5	19.5	19.7	19.5
Nicaragua	..	13.0	16.8	16.9	18.0	18.8	19.5	19.9	20.3
Panama	14.7	17.4	17.4	18.0	18.9	18.6	19.4	19.4	18.1
Paraguay[1]	5.4	14.5	14.6	16.1	16.5	16.8	17.7	16.4	17.1
Peru	12.1	14.6	19.0	16.9	17.8	18.5	18.8	18.4	18.8
Trinidad and Tobago	23.4	21.4	29.5	28.4	27.5	26.7	27.4	27.4	28.3
Uruguay	19.6	21.6	26.1	25.8	26.0	26.4	26.7	27.2	27.0
Venezuela[1]	18.1	13.6	14.1	14.3	11.8	13.5	14.2	14.8	18.2
Unweighted average:									
LAC (22)[5]	14.6	17.2	20.6	19.9	20.0	20.8	21.4	21.5	21.7
OECD (34)[6]	32.1	34.2	33.6	32.7	32.8	33.3	33.8	34.2	34.4

Note: The figures exclude local government revenues for Argentina (but include provincial revenues), Bahamas, Barbados, Bolivia, Costa Rica (up to 1997), Dominican Republic, Ecuador, El Salvador, Honduras, Jamaica, Nicaragua, Panama (up to 1998), Paraguay (up to 2004, 2013 and 2014), Peru (up to 2004) and Venezuela as the data are not available.

1. The data are estimated from 2011 to 2014 (Venezuela), for 2013 and 2014 (Bolivia and Paraguay) and for 2014 (Barbados and Jamaica).
2. In ECLAC data the excise tax on hydrocarbons is treated as non-tax revenues.
3. In ECLAC and CIAT data, fees levied on hydrocarbon production are treated as non-tax revenues.
4. The data are estimated for 2014 including expected revenues for state and local governments.
5. Represents a group of 22 Latin American and Caribbean countries, the average is calculated using calendar year data, except for Bahamas and Trinidad and Tobago where fiscal year data are used. Chile and Mexico are also part of the OECD (34) group.
6. Calculated by applying the unweighted average percentage change for 2014 in the 30 countries providing data for that year to the overall average tax to GDP ratio in 2013.

StatLink http://dx.doi.org/10.1787/888933337517

Tax revenues as a proportion of gross domestic product (GDP) in Latin America and the Caribbean (LAC) have increased considerably during the last 25 years to reach 21.7% in 2014. Both Table 1.1 and Figure 1.1 show how revenues, including social security contributions, for these LAC countries have, with the exception of 2009, risen almost continuously between 1990 and 2014. They increased by more than seven percentage points over that period. This growth in the relative importance of tax revenues is a reflection of favourable macroeconomic conditions, changes in tax system design and strengthening of tax administrations. This trend contrasts with that in the OECD area where the ratio has been relatively stable reaching 34.4% in 2014 just 2.3 percentage points above its corresponding level in 1990.

Tax to GDP ratios in LAC countries increased in each year of the last five years following the global financial crisis. In 2014 the LAC tax ratio was 0.2 percentage points higher than the previous year. The crisis resulted in the fall in economic activity and commodity prices that led to a decrease of the LAC average by 0.7 percentage points between 2008 and 2009. At the same time, the OECD tax ratio registered a decrease of 1.4 percentage points over two years. After the crisis the trends of the OECD and LAC averages aligned closely rising continuously since 2009. The OECD area recovered to its pre-crisis tax-to-GDP level of 34.2% in 2013. In 2014 the tax ratios in both areas rose by 0.2 percentage points. However this conceals a range of different situations across LAC countries as 6 countries out of 22 recorded a decrease in 2013 and 11 countries in 2014.

Figure 1.1. **Total tax revenues as percentage of GDP in Latin America and the Caribbean and OECD, 1990-2014**

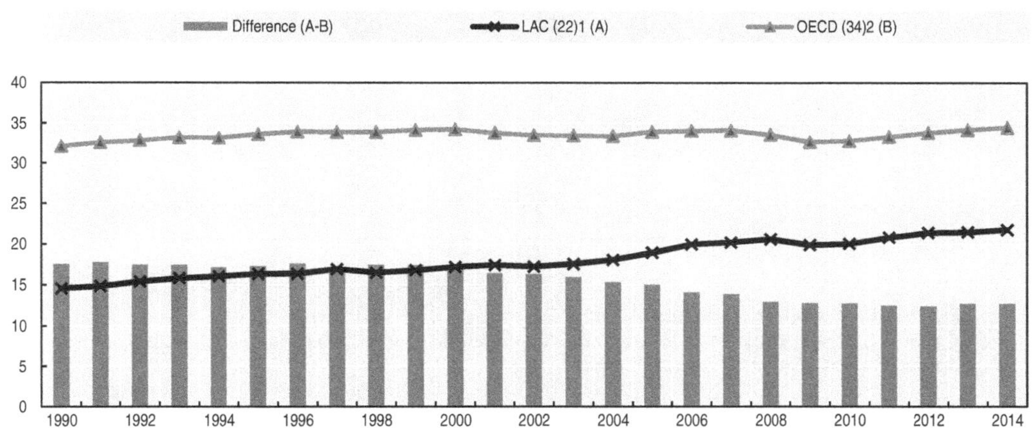

1. Represents a group of 22 Latin American and Caribbean countries. These are Argentina, Bahamas, Barbados, Bolivia, Brazil, Chile, Colombia, Costa Rica, Dominican Republic, Ecuador El Salvador, Guatemala, Honduras, Jamaica, Mexico, Nicaragua, Panama, Paraguay, Peru, Trinidad and Tobago, Uruguay and Venezuela. Chile and Mexico are also part of the OECD (34) group.

2. Represents the unweighted average for OECD member countries.

Source: Table 3.1.

StatLink http://dx.doi.org/10.1787/888933337625

The LAC countries convergence process towards the OECD tax to GDP ratio has been halted since 2008 and the gap has remained steady from then on. The tax to GDP ratio gap between LAC countries and the OECD average decreased from 18 percentage points in 1990 down to 13 percentage points in 2008. The trend has stabilised since then and in 2014, the gap amounted to 12.7 percentage points.

The differences between the average tax to GDP ratio for LAC countries in this Report and that for the OECD reflect the fact that higher income countries tend to have higher tax to GDP ratios. The level of income of a country or its level of development is often measured using the GDP per capita. As observed in Figure 1.2 there is a clear positive correlation between the GDP per capita and tax to GDP ratios for the LAC countries as well as for the OECD countries. The OECD countries are to the top right hand of the figure, representing countries that are comparatively wealthier and also collect higher tax revenues. The LAC countries are scattered with the vast majority in the lower left quadrant of the figure, displaying countries that are poorer and mobilising less tax revenues. Some of the LAC countries Argentina, Barbados, Brazil and Trinidad and Tobago are at the lower end of the cluster of OECD countries.

Figure 1.2. **GDP per capita in PPP (USD) and tax to GDP ratios in Latin American and Caribbean countries and the OECD**

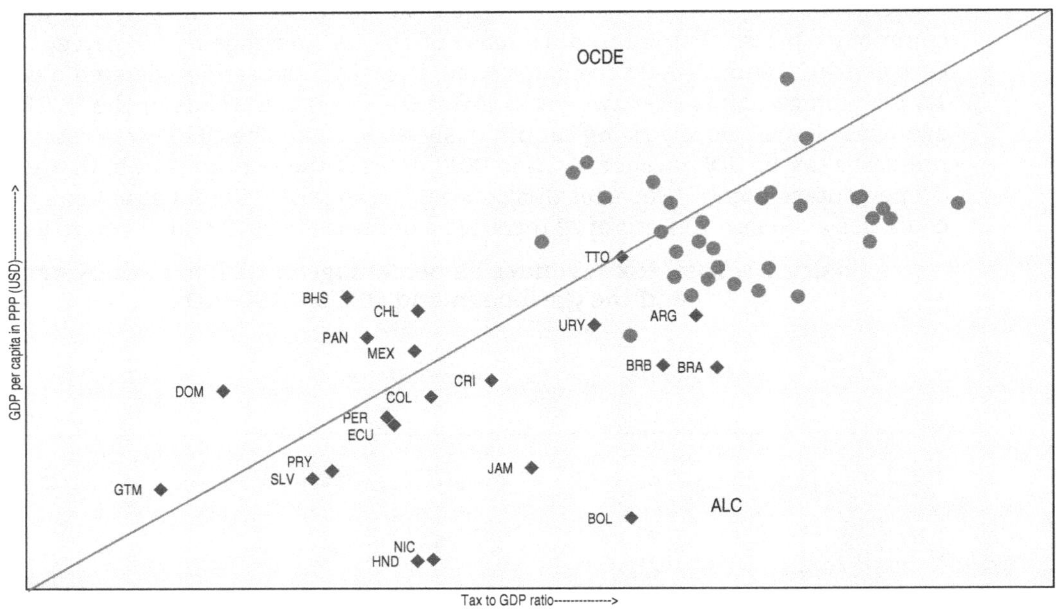

Note: The y axis is in logarithmic scale.

Source: GDP per capita in PPP indicator is from the World Economic Outlook, October 2015, International Monetary Fund. Tax to GDP ratios from Table 3.1.

StatLink http://dx.doi.org/10.1787/888933337636

There is a wide range between the highest and lowest tax to GDP ratios across countries in LAC. Tax to GDP ratios in the region range from 12.6% in Guatemala to 33.4% in Brazil. In the same way, the characteristics of the OECD economies show a wide variation. In 2014, the OECD tax to GDP ratios ranged from 19.5% in Mexico[1] to 50.9% in Denmark (OECD, 2015a). The implications of these wide ranges are that differences in tax to GDP ratios between OECD and LAC should be interpreted with caution given that they include economies that are widely different in character.

Eight LAC countries displayed a tax to GDP ratio higher than the regional average. Argentina (32.2%), Barbados (30.4%) and Brazil (33.4%) rank well above the LAC average. Another five countries above the LAC average in their ranking order are Bolivia, Trinidad and Tobago, Uruguay, Jamaica and Costa Rica. The group of countries with tax ratios below the LAC average ranges from Guatemala (12.6%) and Dominican Republic (14.1%) to Colombia and Nicaragua both at 20.3%.

Evolution of tax ratios

There is considerable variation in trends over time for individual LAC countries as shown in Table 1.1. The countries with the largest increases between 1990 and 2014 were Bolivia (20.6 percentage points) and Argentina (19.8). The majority of the countries showed increases of between 3 and 8 percentage points. Colombia, Ecuador and Paraguay displayed higher increases by around 11-12 percentage points whereas Jamaica and Venezuela showed increases of 1.2 and 0.1 percentage points respectively.

The background to the rise in tax revenues that started in the early 1990s was the period of macroeconomic instability occurring in LAC countries during the previous decade. During the 1980s, countries ran large fiscal imbalances and at the same time some recoursed to alternative ways to finance their spending (borrowing or printing money). This caused rapid inflation across the region, which eroded the real value of their tax revenues. As a result, the reforms in the 1990s focused on fighting this inflation and imposing fiscal discipline. Most LAC governments responded by both cutting public expenditure and implementing policies aimed at increasing tax revenues with budget management and fiscal balance improving considerably. On the revenue side of the equation, tax policy and administration reforms contributed considerably in achieving this goal. As part of that, the impact of inflation on revenues forced policy makers to find ways to render tax systems less vulnerable to inflationary episodes by shortening collection lags and indexing tax liabilities.

Significant efforts were undertaken to modernise the tax administrations and tax systems over the last 25 years. Over that period, new information technology systems were implemented, the structure of tax administrations were rationalised, tax collection systems became more efficient and staff gained in expertise (IDB, 2013). In addition LAC countries made significant changes to simplify their tax systems by broadening their tax bases. They reduced the number of exemptions and tax incentives granted to certain activities and sectors principally to incentivise foreign investment that did, however, not prove always successful. Tax reforms included the introduction or development of simplified regimes for small taxpayers and the taxation of property based on presumed incomes. In addition, during the past half decade various income tax reforms were introduced in LAC, which have included rate hikes and increases in the tax base. These measures have had a positive effect thanks to the expansion of taxation to all labour and capital income, including dividends (Colombia, Dominican Republic, Guatemala, El Salvador, Nicaragua, Panama, Peru). Additionally, they have also included the establishment of minimum taxes, taxes on financial transactions, the gradual reduction in real terms in the threshold at which the top marginal personal income rate is levied and additional controls on transfer prices (ECLAC, 2013; ECLAC, 2014).

The introduction of VAT was the most significant tax reform in Latin America and the Caribbean in the 1980s and early 1990s. Subsequent reforms relating to the tax have concentrated on extending and strengthening it by increasing the tax rate and widening the tax base. In the 1990s the VAT to GDP ratio increased by 2.3 percentage points and then by a further 1.5 points up to 2014 (Figure 1.3). Between 2000 and 2014, the increase in revenue from taxes on income and profits – mainly corporate income tax – by 2.1 percentage points of GDP became a more important contributor than VAT to the rise in tax revenues. One of the elements that contributed to this result was the commodity prices' boom period following 2003, which was very important for some countries in the region. Changes in revenue from taxes on goods and services, taxes on income and profits and social security contributions have contributed to the recovery in tax-to-GDP ratios since 2010. These increases in tax revenues are partly due to the recovery of LAC economic activity (ECLAC-OECD, 2012).

Figure 1.3. **Changes in total tax revenue, revenues from taxes on income and profits and revenues from VAT as percentage of GDP between 1990 and 2000 and between 2000 and 2014 in LAC countries (in percentage points)**

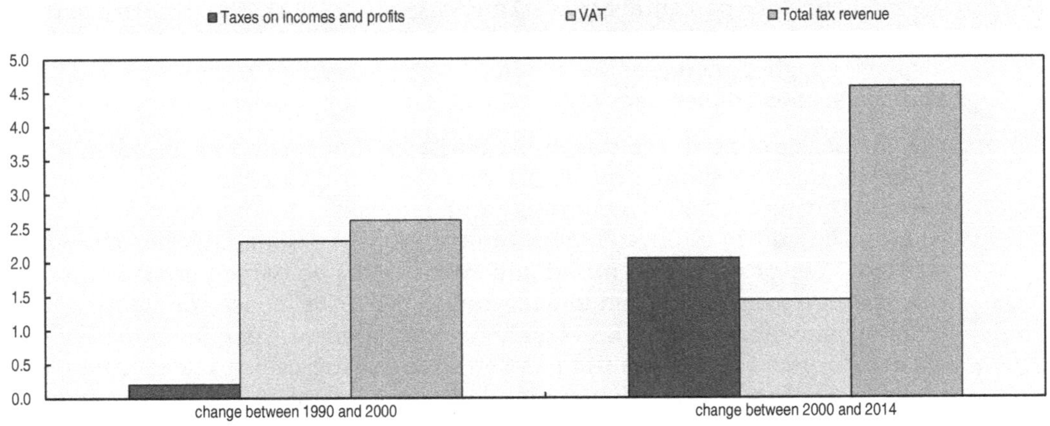

Source: Tables 3.1, 3.4, 3.16 and tables in Chapter 4.

StatLink http://dx.doi.org/10.1787/888933337641

Factors influencing tax to GDP ratios

Tax to GDP ratios are influenced by many factors both domestic and international, and both economic and structural. Economic factors that influence tax to GDP ratios include GDP per capita, openness to trade, the extent of the informal economy, whether the country is considered "resource-rich" and the importance of agriculture in the economy. Socio demographic determinants are also key such as the level of education or the level of female participation in the labour force. In addition, foreign governments have an impact by setting competitive tax rates or engaging in aggressive tax practices such as transfer pricing. All of these factors can promote or undermine a country's ability to raise revenues (Mascagnani, Moore and McCluskey, 2014). The structure of tax collection also plays a role: the power of tax administrations, level of corruption and tax morale (or willingness of people to pay taxes) are all strongly linked to the level of tax revenues (OECD, 2014). Finally, geographic location and historical factors can also have an influence on tax to GDP ratios: for example landlocked countries are less able to impose taxes on goods and services at the port of entry than coastal countries.

The extent of the State participation in financing social security is another important factor underlying the level of tax ratios in the LAC region. From the 1980s onwards, many LAC countries have privatised healthcare, pension and social security to greater or lesser degrees (ECLAC, 2010). Chile, El Salvador and Mexico for example have shifted their public pension programme to a mostly privately fully funded pension system. In Colombia and Peru, the private and public programmes compete and employees opt for one of them (OECD, 2015b). This regional position contrasts with the substantial public provision of these services, and the corresponding requirement for revenue receipts, in many OECD countries, particularly in Europe. On the other hand, Argentina, Brazil and Uruguay, like many OECD countries, follow a model where the public and private systems are complementary. In these three countries substantial reforms were undertaken to extend the coverage of social security systems to those previously excluded. This has also been instrumental in the increase of tax revenues (ECLAC, 2014).

There are also high levels of informality that exclude many from paying taxes in LAC countries (OECD, 2008 and Gómez Sabaini et al. 2010). In Latin America,[2] the rate of informality[3] was around 55% on average in 2013 (OECD/IDB/WB, 2014). Bolivia, Guatemala, Honduras, Nicaragua, Paraguay and Peru have the highest rates of informality exceeding 65% and Brazil, Chile, Costa Rica and Uruguay have rates of informality less than 40%. These levels were even higher in the 1990 and pushed governments to introduce simplified tax systems for small taxpayers that were to some extent successful in integrating informal workers into the formal sector. These simplified systems vary greatly in design depending on the type of taxpayers covered and the actual capacity of tax administrations (ECLAC, 2014).

1.2. Tax structures

The monitoring of the structures of tax systems in individual countries in addition to level of total revenues provides insights into how governments choose to collect their revenues. It also helps to understand the country's social and political system. Tax structures are the result of social and political choices reflecting the balance of economic and political interests in the country. Analysing the breakdown in tax revenues by sub-categories of taxes can help gain insight into tax policy priorities, the effects of tax reforms or the aftermath of economic events.

Evolution of tax structures

At the same time as tax levels have been rising in LAC countries, the tax structure (defined as the share of major taxes in total tax revenue) also changed significantly between 1990 and 2014. Table 1.2 illustrates the several trends on "tax mix" that emerge from the data. The most important trends are those related to consumption taxes and taxes on income and profits.

Consumption taxes

In 2014, consumption taxes (mainly VAT, excises, import and export duties) represented the largest share of the total tax revenue for LAC countries generating about half of their tax revenues. This proportion remained fairly stable over the period but within the total, the share of general consumption taxes (mainly VAT) increased considerably by 10 percentage points between 1990 and 2014, while specific consumption taxes (excises, import and export duties) saw their share decline by 14 percentage points over the same period.

These two opposing trends within consumption taxes reflect the rising importance of VAT and the diminishing role of specific consumption taxes. Although VAT was adopted early by the economies of the region (most countries had already introduced it in some form by the late 1970s), its expansion in revenue terms has been relatively recent. From the early 1990s, it has represented a growing source of revenue for LAC countries and has been consolidated by the implementation of cumulative adjustments to the tax base and statutory rates, as well as the strengthening of tax administrations. The reforms also focused on the simplification of tax systems, with most countries reducing the number of items with zero or reduced rates, moving towards single-rate VAT schemes in several cases.

Table 1.2. **Tax structures in a group of Latin American and Caribbean countries**[1]

	1990	2000	2010	2011	2012	2013	2014
Taxes on income and profits	23.3	22.4	26.4	27.3	27.5	27.4	27.9
Social security contributions	13.4	15.2	15.8	15.6	15.9	16.6	16.4
Payroll taxes	0.5	0.8	0.6	0.6	0.6	0.6	0.6
Property taxes	4.2	2.9	3.2	3.2	3.3	3.4	3.3
General consumption taxes	20.9	30.4	31.6	31.4	31.1	31.2	31.3
Specific consumption taxes	32.1	25.5	19.5	19.1	18.9	18.3	17.8
Other taxes[2]	5.6	2.8	2.9	2.8	2.7	2.6	2.8
Total	**100**	**100**	**100**	**100**	**100**	**100**	**100**

1. Represents the percentage shares of major tax categories in total tax revenue. The group of 22 countries is listed in Table 1.1.
2. Including certain taxes on goods and services (heading 5200) and stamp taxes.

StatLink http://dx.doi.org/10.1787/888933337523

In 2014, about 30% of the total tax revenues in LAC countries came from VAT alone. However there is a wide disparity within the region. All of the countries operate a VAT regime except Bahamas. The shares of VAT in these countries range from 11.6% in Trinidad and Tobago to 47.4% in Venezuela as shown in Figure 1.4. Bahamas has introduced a VAT in July 2014 (VAT revenue receipts will first be reflected in 2015). The low shares of VAT revenue in Costa Rica, Jamaica, Mexico, Panama, and Trinidad and Tobago reflect the higher reliance on taxes on income and profits in the tax structure in these countries. The wide discrepancy across countries is also the result of differences in the design of the VAT: the rates and tax bases vary widely in the region. For example Mexico does not apply VAT on food, medicines as well as numerous other products resulting in a relatively narrow tax base. ECLAC (2014) suggests that the tax loss from these particular exemptions could range between 1.1% and 2.5% of GDP, according to experts.

Figure 1.4. **Revenue from taxes on income and profits and revenue from VAT as a proportion of total tax revenue in LAC countries, 2014**

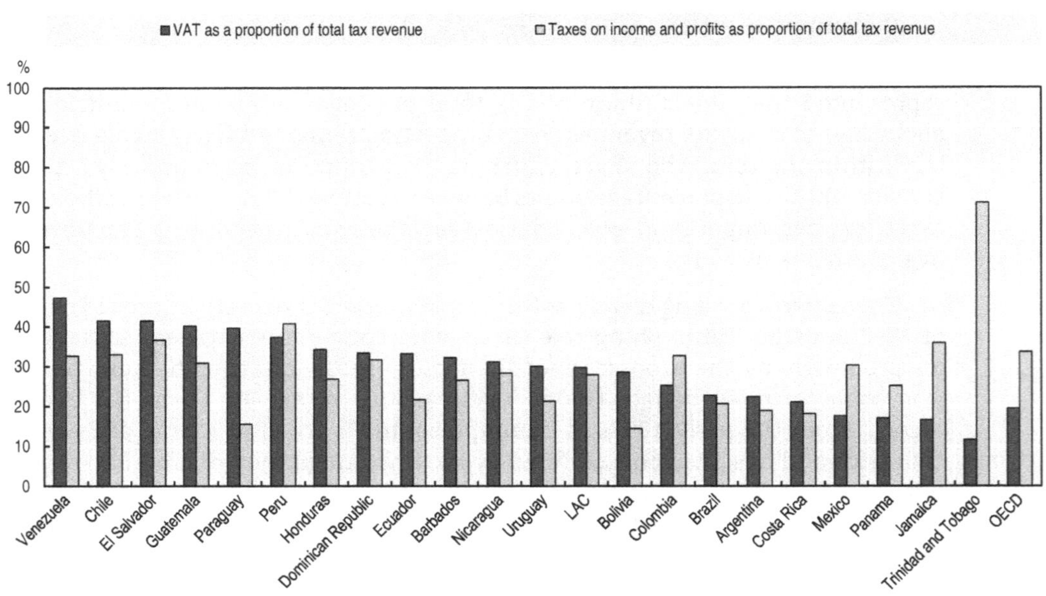

Note: For OECD, the data for 2013 are used. Bahamas is not included as there is no revenue from personal or corporate income taxes.

Source: Table 3.4 and tables in Chapter 4.

StatLink http://dx.doi.org/10.1787/888933337656

In contrast, the decline in the share of specific consumption taxes is associated with the processes of trade liberalisation. This generated a consequent reduction in import tariffs and the elimination of taxes on exports in a considerable number of LAC countries. One important exception is Argentina where taxes on exports were re-established in 2002; however the current government is planning to abolish these taxes on certain agricultural products. Additionally, the range of goods and services subject to excises in LAC countries has been narrowed to focus mainly on products and services with a relatively inelastic demand, such as alcoholic beverages, fuel and derivatives and tobacco.

Taxes on income and profits and social security contributions

At the same time, the share of revenues on taxes on incomes and profits grew from 23% to 28% of total tax revenues between 1990 and 2014, mainly as a result of much higher collection levels in the late 2000s. It actually peaked over the years from 2008 to 2009 at a level of 27.9% before declining to 26.4% in 2010, due to the impact of the global crisis. It has subsequently increased to the level of 27.9% in 2014 (Table 3.5).

Corporate income tax shares are generally much larger than those from personal income tax in this group of LAC countries except in Barbados, Jamaica and Uruguay (Figure 1.5). Trinidad and Tobago has the highest share of corporate income tax with more than half of tax revenues being generated from this source. It is important to note that most of it is collected from the oil and gas companies. In the other LAC countries, the share of corporate income tax revenues ranges from 8% (Barbados) to 30% (Peru). Bahamas is the only country not to operate an income tax (corporate or personal) regime. Corporate income tax revenue has grown at a faster pace than revenue from personal income tax over the past 25 years. This growth reflects the sizeable increase in revenues from companies in the natural-resources sector. It was also the result of the implementation of tax policies reducing tax incentives in free trade zones, the introduction of minimum taxes for corporate income tax, reforms in international taxation and other agreements between countries to fight tax evasion (ECLAC, 2014).

On the other hand the share of personal income tax remains low in LAC countries despite some countries having implemented reforms to expand their tax base. After the crisis some progress was made to set up flat rates on capital income previously exempt and implement progressive rates on labour income (ECLAC, 2014), however the share of personal income tax in LAC countries remains modest as more than half of the countries shown in Figure 1.5 generate less than 10% of their tax revenue from this source. The personal income tax shares range from 0.6% (Bolivia) to 19% (Jamaica) of total tax revenue. Previous OECD studies (OECD, 2008 and Daude et al., 2010) suggest that the share of labour income in GDP is substantially low in LAC countries and its distribution means that there are relatively fewer taxpayers, given the concentration of income earners at low income levels. Only 10% of the population in Latin America are registered taxpayers (IDB, 2013). Moreover, several studies (IDB, 2015; ECLAC, 2014; ECLAC, 2010 and Gómez Sabaini et al., 2010) mention two additional factors: the high income tax gap in LAC countries and a more limited taxable base that is comprised primarily of wages, given the tax privileges granted to returns on capital. Besides the narrow tax bases, personal income taxes suffer from high levels of evasion. IDB (2013) explains that "about half of potential revenue from personal income tax is lost through evasion".

The share of social security contributions in total tax revenues increased by 3.0 percentage points over the last 25 years to account for 16.4% in 2014 (Table 3.7). This reflects two major factors working simultaneously. Firstly, rising personal incomes have had an upward impact on the amounts collected. But this is partially counter-balanced, and sometimes more than off-set, by the varying processes of full or partial privatisation that occurred in many countries in the region as explained previously in the tax ratios section. In countries with public or mixed schemes, including Barbados, Brazil, Costa Rica, Ecuador, Nicaragua, Panama, Paraguay and Uruguay, social-security contributions still have a significant weight (more than 20% of total tax revenues). In Colombia and Peru where the private and public programmes compete, social security contributions as a share of total tax revenue amount to around 11-13%. In Argentina, the figures reflect the introduction of funded schemes in 1994 and their subsequent nationalisation in 2008.

Figure 1.5. **Revenue from corporate income tax and personal income tax as a proportion of total tax revenue in selected LAC countries, 2014**

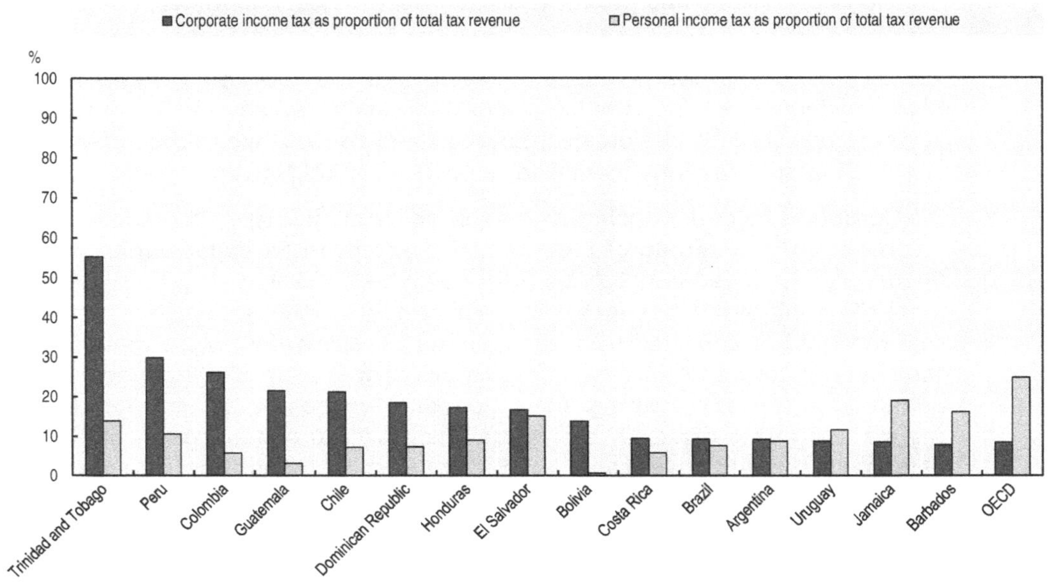

Note: For OECD, the data for 2013 are used. The share of taxes on income and the share of taxes on profits may not add up to the total share of taxes on incomes and profits due to unallocable revenue. Only countries that could allocate 75% or more of revenue of taxes on incomes and profits into the sub categories taxes on income and taxes on profits are shown in the figure above.

Source: Tables in Chapter 4.

StatLink http://dx.doi.org/10.1787/888933337663

Comparison with the OECD

Relative to the OECD, LAC countries exhibit a relatively low direct-tax take counterbalanced by high indirect-tax receipts (see Figure 1.6). In particular, LAC countries rely heavily on taxes on goods and services, which make up about half of overall tax revenues compared with around 30% in OECD economies. In comparison less than 45% of tax revenues in LAC countries come from the combination of taxes on income and profits and social security contributions compared with around 60% in OECD economies. This greater reliance on indirect taxes implies a more regressive tax system.

In 2013, the average ratio of the combined tax revenue from income and profits and social security contributions to GDP in the LAC countries was around 10% and this represents half the ratio in OECD countries. As a result, these taxes play a secondary role as a source of revenue in LAC countries compared with the OECD area. The share of social security contributions in total tax revenues was about 10 percentage points lower in LAC countries than in the OECD (16.6% compared with 26.1%). As noted above, the tendency towards a privately-oriented provision of social security in many countries in the LAC region explains some of the differences for this category. The corresponding figures for taxes on income and profits were 6 percentage points lower (27.4% compared with 33.7%).

Corporate income taxes as a share of total tax revenue are about 8.5% in the OECD area lower than in all of the group of LAC countries except in Bahamas and Barbados. Revenues from personal income taxes contributed as much as to 25% of the aggregate tax collection in the OECD area in 2013, while this category has a considerably lower share in LAC countries.

As a counterpart to the lower share of direct taxes, general consumption taxes represent a higher proportion of total tax collection than in the OECD. In 2013, this category accounted for 31% of the total tax revenues in the region whereas the corresponding figure in the OECD area is only 20%. However, the ratio of general consumption taxes to GDP in the countries of LAC (6.6%) is slightly lower to that of the OECD (6.8%).

Figure 1.6. **Tax structures in LAC and the OECD, 2013**

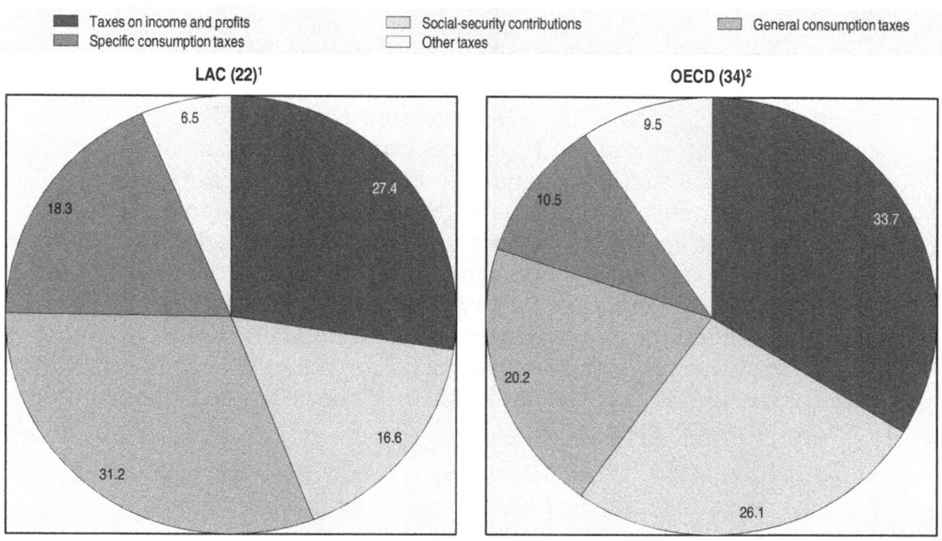

1. Represents a group of 22 Latin American and Caribbean countries listed in Table 1.1. Chile and Mexico are also part of the OECD (34) group.
2. Represents the unweighted average for OECD member countries.
Source: Tables 3.2 and 3.3 to 3.15.

StatLink http://dx.doi.org/10.1787/888933337676

Finally, taxes on immovable property and payroll (comprised within the category "Other taxes" in Figure 1.6) are not important sources of revenues for LAC countries. The difficulties that sub-national governments have in collecting their own taxes are exemplified by the weak revenue-generating capacity of property taxes, which are generally the main source of revenue for local governments in the region (Brossio and Jiménez, 2012). The share of payroll taxes has been negligible over the whole period, partly because these types of schemes are not very well developed in LAC countries. Nevertheless, it must be pointed out that missing data at the sub-national level makes the analysis of this category difficult. The shares of property and payroll taxes as a proportion of total tax revenue in the LAC countries are similar on average to those in OECD countries.

1.3. Taxes by level of government

Since the mid-1980s the LAC countries have generally experienced reforms involving the transfer of government functions from the central government to sub-national entities. In the first stage, this wave of decentralisation mainly focused on strengthening the democratic role of local authorities. This has been followed by a gradually increasing trend towards a higher share of public expenditure being executed at sub-national level.

In contrast, the scope of the sub-national tax policies in the region has been relatively modest. The available data suggests that most LAC countries have not been concentrating on the strengthening of the revenues received by the sub-national entities. Between 1995 and 2013, the share of revenue raised by sub-national levels of government declined by

0.7 points in Argentina and rose by 0.4 to 1.2 percentage points in Brazil, Colombia and Mexico. In the other countries where trends in sub-national revenue data are available, the share changed by less than one percentage point. At the same time the share of social security funds has fallen in nearly half of 22 LAC countries sometimes due to full or partial privatisation. The largest changes were in Colombia and El Salvador (by around 11 and 4 percentage points respectively). The largest increases in the share of social security funds were in Honduras and Nicaragua (both around 8 percentage points) (see Table 1.3).

There are two statistical issues to be taken into account when comparing the attribution of revenues for these LAC countries with that of OECD members. First, the revenues of both groups have been attributed to the different levels of government according to the revised guidelines set out in to the final version of the 2008 System of National Accounts (SNA). This means that revenues are generally attributed to the level of government that exercises the authority to impose the tax or has the final discretion to set and vary the tax rate. This has implications for situations where one level of government collects tax revenues and transfers them in whole or in part to other levels. Regional examples of this type of mechanism are the Co-participation Law in Argentina, federal participations in Mexico mandated in the Fiscal Co-ordination Law, and participation funds in Brazil defined in Article 159 of the Constitution. The second issue is that the data for some of the LAC countries are affected by the lack of tax-revenue statistics at sub-national level.

Not-withstanding these points, the attribution of tax revenues appears to be highly skewed towards central or federal entities with sub-national activities relying more heavily on a system of transfers from upper to lower levels of administration compared with OECD members. In all but one of the LAC countries, receipts by central governments accounted for about two thirds or more of the total collected whereas the corresponding figure for OECD countries was about 60%. Brazil is a notable exception with less than 50% of revenues attributed to the Federal administration, and where a large part of the VAT (ICMS – imposto sobre operações relativas à circulação de mercadorias e prestação de serviços de transporte interestadual e intermunicipal e de comunicação) is collected at the sub-national state level. To a lesser extent, Argentina has a significant collection at state level, which is explained in part by the provincial sales tax (impuesto sobre los ingresos brutos).

These figures reflect the fact that sub-national governments in LAC countries tend to have a relatively narrow range of taxes under their jurisdiction. The taxes most frequently assigned to sub-national entities are property taxes, motor-vehicle licenses, taxes on specific services and municipal fees and the revenue generation potential of these instruments is relatively limited compared with the tax bases under central jurisdiction, such as VAT and income taxes. In OECD member countries, sub-national entities on average tend to have much broader potential tax bases. A substantial proportion of the revenue collection for sub-national governments in OECD countries is through income taxes and profits (representing more than a third of the total collected amount at sub-national level). In contrast, none of the LAC countries with available data recorded any collection of income taxes by sub-national governments.

Low tax revenues at the sub-national levels in LAC countries also result from the lack of administrative and technical capacity to collect high level of tax revenues. For example property taxes - that are considered as the recommended source of revenue at the sub-national level- require sophisticated systems and information since the collection of this revenue is expensive. In addition appropriate property registers are lacking and when they exist they are rarely updated (IDB, 2012). As a result, tax authoritities have little access to accurate valuations of lands and buildings and real estate registries are often reluctant to share this information. Property tax also suffers from other endemic issues that are common characteristics of developing countries such as high levels of informality. Buildings are constructed without permits, properties are not registered and reported prices of some real estate transactions are falsificated. As property tax is one of the most controversial taxes with citizens and has high political costs, local tax officials are often unwilling to invest the appropriate resources to levy this revenue (IDB, 2015).

Table 1.3. **Attribution of tax revenues to sub-sectors of general government as percentage of total tax revenue[1]**

	Central government			State or regional government			Local government			Social security funds		
	1995	2000	2013	1995	2000	2013	1995	2000	2013	1995	2000	2013
Federal countries	59.0	66.4	60.6	17.5	17.8	16.8				23.4	15.8	22.6
Argentina	44.7	47.8	42.6	26.8	25.3	25.8	3.7	3.4	5.9	24.8	23.5	25.6
Brazil	80.1	80.7	80.1	2.1	2.0	3.1	1.1	0.8	1.2	16.6	16.5	15.5
Mexico	94.6	94.6	93.4							5.4	5.4	6.6
Venezuela	53.2	56.5	54.2	15.9	15.3	16.5	7.7	6.9	7.5	22.9	21.1	21.3
OECD[2,3]												
Regional countries	63.2	68.6	73.3	5.5	5.6	4.2	8.6	9.4	10.8	22.7	16.4	11.7
Colombia[4]	50.4	49.0	22.3	4.8	7.6	13.7	8.5	9.1	9.9	35.8	33.8	34.0
OECD[5]												
Unitary countries												
Bahamas	89.1	88.1	84.1							10.9	11.9	15.9
Barbados	85.3	84.3	80.1							14.7	15.7	19.9
Bolivia	100.0	92.2	95.1							0.0	7.8	4.9
Chile	89.9	87.8	87.0				6.5	7.9	7.3	3.6	4.4	5.7
Costa Rica	66.2	65.3	58.8					2.1	3.0	33.8	32.6	38.1
Dominican Republic	99.3	99.0	99.6							0.7	1.0	0.4
Ecuador	73.9	87.7	75.0							26.1	12.3	25.0
El Salvador	86.3	84.8	89.7							14.1	16.6	10.3
Guatemala	83.8	83.6	82.9				0.6	0.9	1.4	15.6	15.5	15.7
Honduras	90.1	89.4	81.9							9.9	10.6	18.1
Jamaica	100.0	99.3	94.3				0.0	0.7	1.6	0.0	0.0	4.1
Nicaragua	84.1	80.1	76.1							15.9	19.9	23.9
Panama	62.0	61.1	64.3				0.0	2.1	1.5	38.0	36.8	34.2
Paraguay	100.0	82.7	80.0				0.0	0.0	2.7	0.0	17.3	17.4
Peru	88.2	87.7	85.7				0.0	0.0	3.1	11.8	12.3	11.3
Trinidad and Tobago	94.5	91.7	92.4				2.4	1.9	1.4	3.1	6.4	6.2
Uruguay	62.0	62.5	69.3				7.8	7.9	3.9	30.1	29.6	26.8
OECD[2,6]	65.8	66.4	63.2				10.8	11.0	12.0	23.1	22.3	24.6

1. The figures exclude local government revenues for Argentina (but include provincial revenues), Bahamas, Barbados, Bolivia, Costa Rica (up to 1997), Dominican Republic, Ecuador, El Salvador, Honduras, Jamaica, Nicaragua, Panama (up to 1998), Paraguay, Peru (up to 2004) and Venezuela as the data are not available.
2. Chile and Mexico are also part of the OECD group.
3. Represents the unweighted average for OECD federal member countries.
4. Colombia is constitutionally a unitary country with high autonomy of its territorial entities.
5. Represents Spain, which is constitutionally a non-federal country with a highly decentralised political structure.
6. Represents the unweighted average for OECD unitary countries.

StatLink http://dx.doi.org/10.1787/888933337531

1.4. Comparative figures / 1.4. Gráficos comparativos

Figure 1.7. Total tax revenues as percentage of GDP, 2014[1]
Gráfico 1.7. Total de recaudación tributaria como porcentaje del PIB, 2014[1]

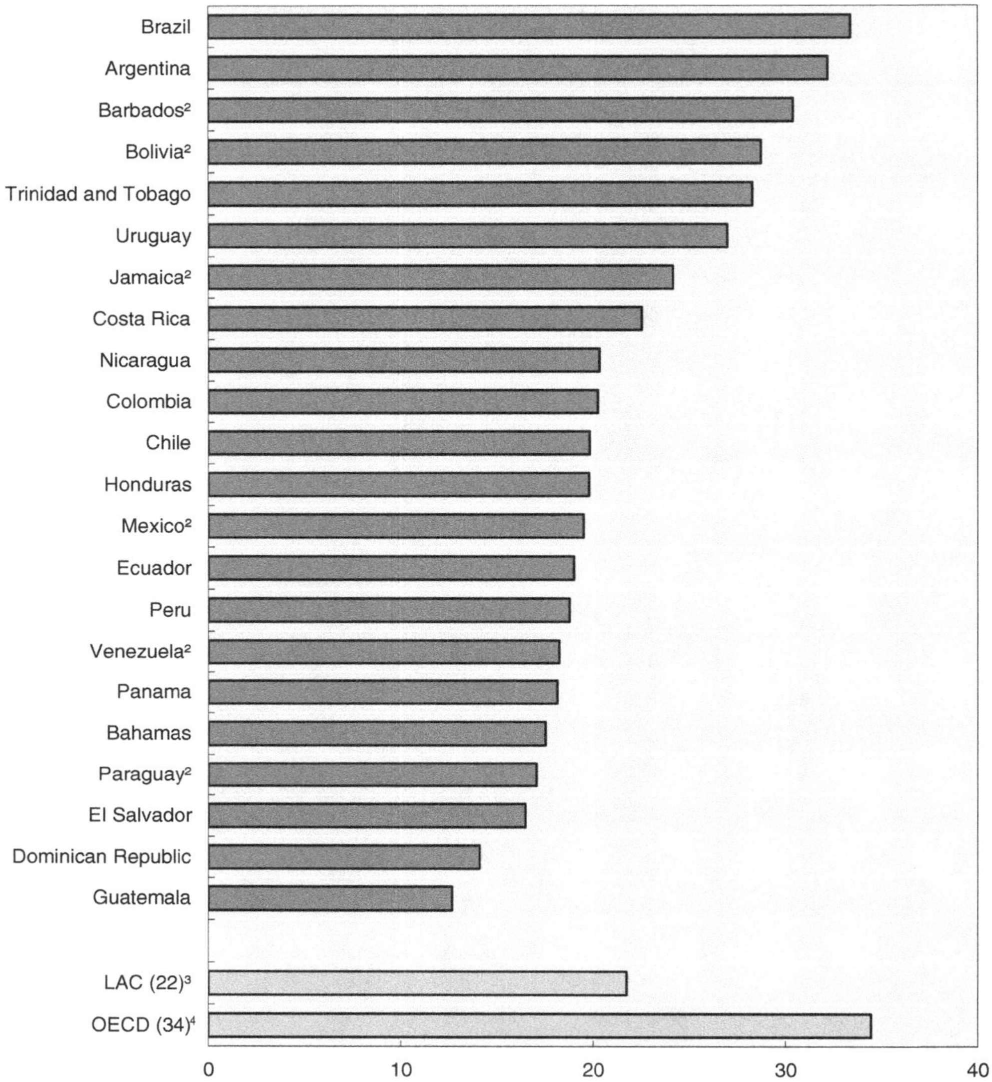

1. Countries have been ranked by their total tax revenue to GDP ratios.
1. Los países han sido ordenados según el ratio total de ingresos tributarios como porcentaje de PIB.
2. The data are estimated.
2. Datos estimados.
3. Represents the unweighted average for a group of 22 Latin American and Caribbean countries. Chile and Mexico are also part of the OECD (34) group.
3. Representa el promedio no ponderado para un grupo de 22 países de América Latina y el Caribe. Chile y México son también parte del grupo OCDE (34).
4. Represents the unweighted average for OECD member countries.
4. Representa el promedio no ponderado para los países miembros de la OCDE.

Source: Table 3.1/Cuadro 3.1.

StatLink http://dx.doi.org/10.1787/888933337745

Figure 1.8. **Changes in tax to GDP ratios in selected Latin American countries, 1990- 2014[1]**

Gráfico 1.8. **Cambios en la recaudación tributaria como porcentaje del PIB en países seleccionados de América Latina, 1990-2014[1]**

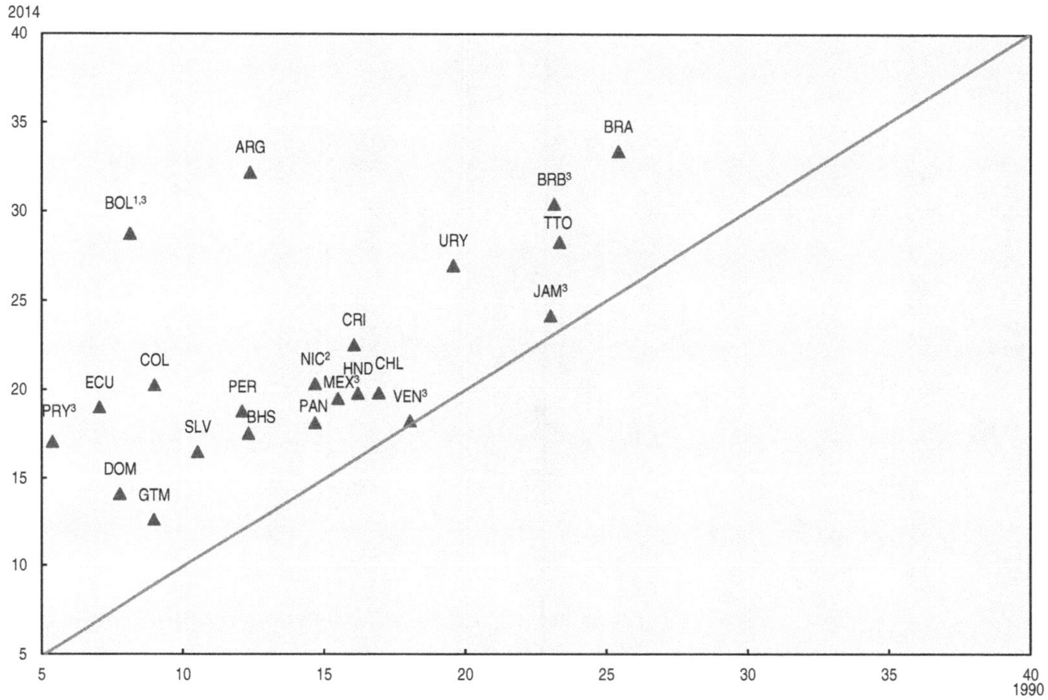

1. In ECLAC and CIAT data, fees levied on hydrocarbon production are treated as non tax revenues.
1. En los datos de CEPAL y CIAT, los derechos sobre la producción de hidrocarburos son tratados como ingresos no tributarios.
2. Figures for 1991 are used.
2. Se utilizan datos para el 1991.
3. The data are estimated for 2014.
3. Datos estimados para el 2014.

Source: Table 3.1/Cuadro 3.1.

StatLink http://dx.doi.org/10.1787/888933337758

Figure 1.9. **Changes in tax to GDP ratios in selected Latin American countries, 1990-2000**[1]

Gráfico 1.9. **Cambios en la recaudación tributaria como porcentaje del PIB en países seleccionados de América Latina, 1990-2000**[1]

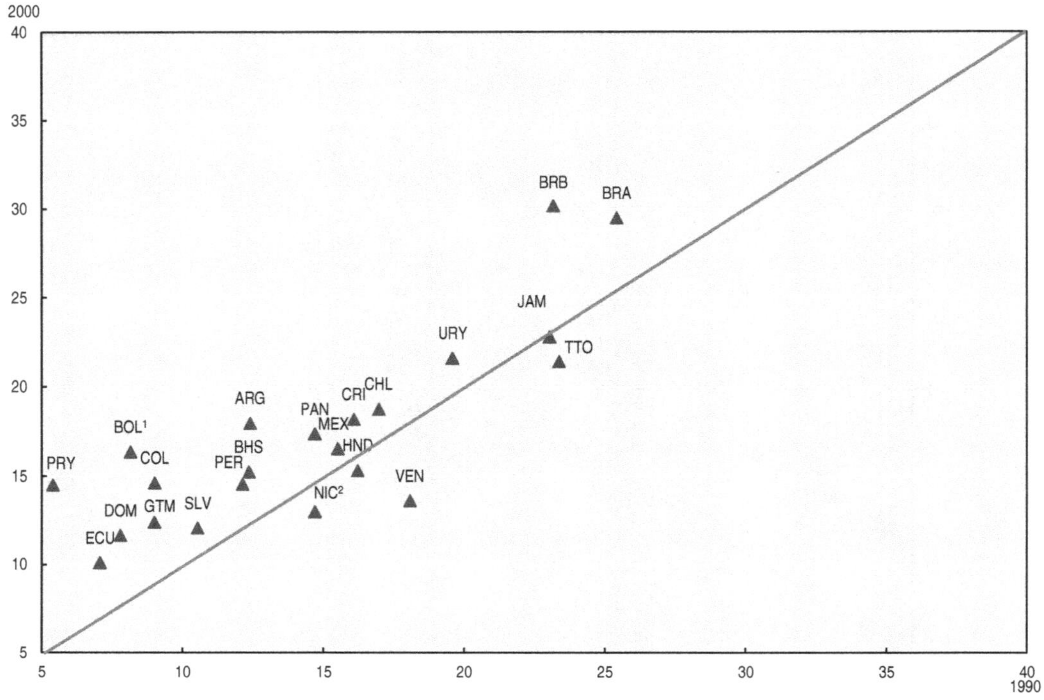

1. In ECLAC and CIAT data, fees levied on hydrocarbon production are treated as non tax revenues.

1. En los datos de CEPAL y CIAT, los derechos sobre la pròducción de hidrocarburos son tratados como ingresos no tributarios.

2. Figures for 1991 are used.

2. Se utilizan datos para el 1991.

Source: Table 3.1/Cuadro 3.1.

StatLink http://dx.doi.org/10.1787/888933337766

Figure 1.10. **Changes in tax to GDP ratios in selected Latin American countries, 2000-2014[1]**

Gráfico 1.10. **Cambios en la recaudación tributaria como porcentaje del PIB en países seleccionados de América Latina, 2000-2014[1]**

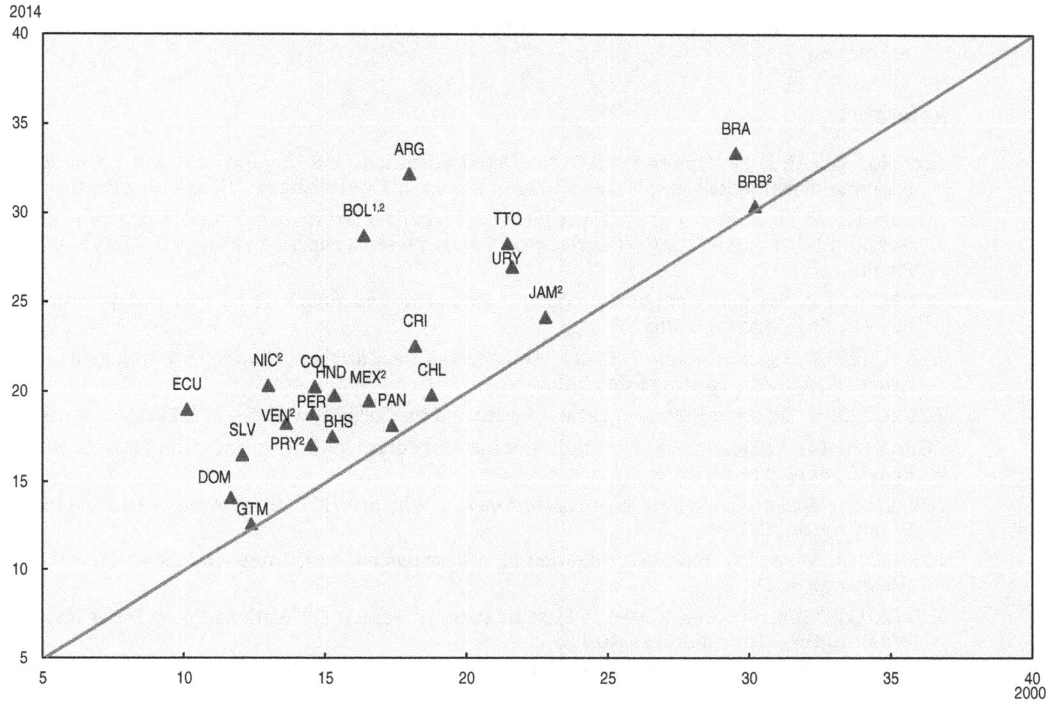

1. In ECLAC and CIAT data, fees levied on hydrocarbon production are treated as non tax revenues.

1. En los datos de CEPAL y CIAT, los derechos sobre la producción de hidrocarburos son tratados como ingresos no tributarios.

2. The data are estimated for 2014.

2. Datos estimados para el 2014.

Source: Table 3.1/Cuadro 3.1.

StatLink http://dx.doi.org/10.1787/888933337778

Notes

1. This figure is different from the ones presented in ECLAC and CIAT publications because of the inclusion of fees levied on hydrocarbon production as tax revenues.
2. Average of 19 countries Argentina, Bolivia, Brazil, Chile, Colombia, Costa Rica, Republica Dominicana, Ecuador, Guatemala, Honduras, Jamaica, Mexico, Nicaragua, Panama, Peru, Paraguay, El Salvador, Uruguay and Venezuela.
3. Informality is defined as the percentage of non-contributors to pension systems over total employed.

References

Brossio, G. and J.P. Jiménez (2012), *Decentralization and Reform in Latin America: Improving Intergovernmental Relations*, Edward Elgar, in press, Cheltenham, UK and Northampton, MA.

Daude, C., A. Melguizo and A. Neut (2010), "Fiscal Policy in Latin America: Countercyclical and Sustainable at Last?", *OECD Development Centre Working Paper* No. 291, OECD Development Centre, Paris.

ECLAC (2014), *Tax policy in Latin America. Assessment and guidelines for a second generation of reforms*, ECLAC, Santiago de Chile.

ECLAC (2013), *Fiscal Panorama of Latin America and the Caribbean: Tax Reform and Renewal of the Fiscal Covenant*, ECLAC, Santiago de Chile.

ECLAC (2011), *Economic Survey of Latin America and the Caribbean 2010-2011*, ECLAC, Santiago de Chile.

ECLAC (2010), "La Hora de la igualdad. Brechas por cerrar, caminos por abrir", (LC/G.2432(SES.33/3)), ECLAC, Santiago de Chile.

IDB (2015), *Decentralizing Revenue in Latin America Why and How*, Inter-American Development Bank, Washington, DC.

IDB (2013), *More than revenues, Taxation as a development tool*, Inter-American Development Bank, Washington, DC.

IDB (2012), "Sub-national Revenue Mobilization in Peru", *IDB Working Paper Series* No. IDB-WP-299, Washington, United States, IDB

Gómez Sabaini, J.C., J.P. Jiménez and A. Podestá (2010), "Evasión y equidad en América Latina", *Project documents*, No. 309 (LC/W.309/ Rev.1), Santiago, Chile, ECLAC.

Mascagnani, G., M. Moore and R. McCluskey (2014), *Tax revenue mobilisation in developing countries issues and challenges*, European Union, Brussels, www.europarl.europa.eu/RegData/etudes/etudes/join/2014.433849/EXPO-DEVE_ET%282014%29433849_EN.pdf.

OECD (2015a), *Revenue Statistics 1965-2014*, OECD Publishing, Paris, http://dx.doi.org/10.1787/rev_stats-2015-en-fr.

OECD (2015b), *Revenue Statistics in Latin America and the Caribbean 1990-2013*, OECD Publishing, Paris, http://dx.doi.org/10.1787/rev_lat-2015-en-fr.

OECD (2014), *Development Cooperation Report 2014: Mobilising Resources for Sustainable Development*, OECD Publishing, Paris, http://dx.doi.org/10.1787/dcr-2014-en.

OECD (2008), *Latin American Economic Outlook 2009*, OECD Publishing, Paris, http://dx.doi.org/10.1787/leo-2009-en.

OECD/ECLAC (2012), *Latin American Economic Outlook 2013: SME Policies for Structural Change*, OECD Publishing, Paris, http://dx.doi.org/10.1787/leo-2013-en.

OECD/IDB/World Bank (2014), *Pensions at a Glance: Latin America and the Caribbean*, OECD Publishing, Paris, http://dx.doi.org/10.1787/pension_glance-2014-en.

CAPÍTULO 1

TENDENCIAS TRIBUTARIAS, 1990-2014

1.1. Niveles de recaudación

El ingreso tributario como proporción del PIB es un indicador clave que refleja los ingresos disponibles en un país recolectados a través de los impuestos y que permiten financiar bienes y servicios públicos así como las inversiones en infraestructura. Recaudar ingresos por medio de los impuestos es un factor importante para asegurar el desarrollo económico (OCDE, 2014). Un nivel apropiado de impuestos da a los gobiernos la capacidad de realizar las inversiones necesarias que garanticen el crecimiento. Así mismo, permite a las economías emergentes asegurar su autonomía política y construir estados efectivos y transparentes. La mayoría de las economías en desarrollo reconocen que los ingresos tributarios representan ingresos más estables y predecibles que los ingresos no tributarios, como los derivados del petróleo y matrerías primas, que tienden a ser mucho más volátiles.

Niveles de recaudación en el 2014

Los ingresos tributarios como proporción del producto interno bruto (PIB) han aumentado considerablemente en América Latina y el Caribe en los últimos 25 años, representando el 21.7% del PIB en el 2014. Tanto el cuadro 1.1 como el gráfico 1.1 plasman cómo los ingresos de los países latinoamericanos y caribeños, incluyendo las contribuciones a la seguridad social, han venido incrementándose, con la excepción del 2009, desde 1990. Entre 1990 y 2014 los ingresos en promedio se han incrementado por 7.1 puntos porcentuales. Este crecimiento de la importancia relativa de los ingresos tributarios es reflejo de unas condiciones macroeconómicas favorables, así como de los cambios en el diseño de los sistemas tributarios y del fortalecimiento de las administraciones tributarias. Esta tendencia contrasta con la registrada en las economías de la OCDE, donde la proporción ha permanecido relativamente estable, ya que en 2014, arrojaba un valor del 34.4% del PIB, menos de un 2.3 puntos porcentuales por encima de su nivel de 1990.

Los ingresos tributarios como proporción del PIB en América Latina y el Caribe han aumentado cada año durante el último quinquenio, desde la crisis financiera del 2009. En el 2014 la recaudación tributaria como porcentaje del PIB fue 0.2 puntos porcentuales superior a la del año anterior. La crisis resulto en una caída de la actividad económica y de los precios de las materias primas que llevó a la reducción de los ingresos tributarios en la región por 0.7 puntos porcentuales entre el 2008 y el 2009. En el mismo periodo, los ingresos tributarios como proporción del PIB en la OCDE registraron una disminución de 1.4 puntos porcentuales. Desde la crisis, las tendencias de las economías de ALC y OCDE se han alineado relativamente, incrementándose continuamente desde el 2009. El promedio de las economías de la OCDE regreso a su nivel previo a la crisis del 34.2% en el 2013. En el 2014 los ingresos tributarios como proporción del PIB se incrementaron por 0.2 puntos porcentuales en ambas regiones. Sin embargo el promedio esconde heterogeneidades entre las economías latinoamericanas y caribeñas ya que en el 2013 solo 6 economías registraron una contracción en su ingreso tributario como proporción del PIB, mientras que en el 2014 este se contrajo en 11 de las 22 economías.

Cuadro 1.1. **Total de recaudación tributaria como porcentaje del PIB**

	1990	2000	2008	2009	2010	2011	2012	2013	2014
Argentina	12.4	18.0	24.7	25.6	26.7	27.6	29.2	30.6	32.2
Bahamas	12.3	15.2	17.2	16.5	16.1	18.9	18.0	17.1	17.5
Barbados[1]	23.2	30.2	31.1	30.5	30.6	32.4	33.1	29.5	30.4
Bolivia[1,2]	8.1	16.4	25.3	25.9	23.3	26.2	27.6	28.9	28.7
Brasil	25.4	29.5	33.8	32.4	32.4	33.3	33.3	33.6	33.4
Chile	17.0	18.8	21.4	17.2	19.5	21.2	21.5	20.0	19.8
Colombia	9.0	14.6	18.8	18.6	18.0	18.9	19.7	20.0	20.3
Costa Rica	16.1	18.2	22.7	21.2	20.8	21.3	21.3	22.6	22.5
Ecuador	7.1	10.1	14.0	14.9	16.3	17.3	19.3	19.2	19.0
El Salvador	10.5	12.1	15.1	14.4	15.1	15.4	16.1	17.0	16.5
Guatemala	9.0	12.4	12.9	12.2	12.4	12.7	12.8	13.0	12.6
Honduras	16.2	15.3	18.9	17.1	17.3	16.9	17.8	18.3	19.8
Jamaica[1]	23.0	22.8	25.0	24.8	25.0	24.5	24.6	25.0	24.2
México[3,4]	15.5	16.5	20.7	17.2	18.5	19.5	19.5	19.7	19.5
Nicaragua	..	13.0	16.8	16.9	18.0	18.8	19.5	19.9	20.3
Panamá	14.7	17.4	17.4	18.0	18.9	18.6	19.4	19.4	18.1
Paraguay[1]	5.4	14.5	14.6	16.1	16.5	16.8	17.7	16.4	17.1
Perú	12.1	14.6	19.0	16.9	17.8	18.5	18.8	18.4	18.8
República Dominicana	7.8	11.7	14.3	12.7	12.3	12.3	13.1	13.9	14.1
Trinidad y Tobago	23.4	21.4	29.5	28.4	27.5	26.7	27.4	27.4	28.3
Uruguay	19.6	21.6	26.1	25.8	26.0	26.4	26.7	27.2	27.0
Venezuela[1]	18.1	13.6	14.1	14.3	11.8	13.5	14.2	14.8	18.2
Promedio simple:									
ALC (22)[5]	14.6	17.2	20.6	19.9	20.0	20.8	21.4	21.5	21.7
OCDE (34)[6]	32.1	34.2	33.6	32.7	32.8	33.3	33.8	34.2	34.4

Nota : Las cifras excluyen los ingresos de gobiernos locales en Argentina (pero incluye ingresos de las provincias), Bahamas, Barbados, Bolivia, Costa Rica (hasta 1997), República Dominicana, Ecuador, El Salvador, Honduras, Jamaica, Nicaragua, Panamá (hasta 1998), Paraguay (hasta 2004, 2013 y 2014), Perú (hasta 2004) y Venezuela dado que los datos no están disponibles.

1. Datos estimados desde el 2011 hasta el 2014 (Venezuela), 2013 y 2014 (Bolivia y Paraguay) y 2014 (Barbados y Jamaica).
2. En los datos de CEPAL, el Impuesto Directo sobre Hidrocarburos (IDH) es considerado como regalía en los ingresos no tributarios.
3. En los datos de CEPAL y CIAT, los derechos sobre la producción de hidrocarburos son tratados como ingresos no tributarios.
4. Los datos estimados incluyen ingresos esperados a nivel estatal y local para el 2014.
5. Representa un grupo de 22 países de América Latina y el Caribe, para el promedio se utiliza año calendario, excepto para Barbados y Trinidad y Tobago donde el año fiscal se utiliza. Chile y México son también parte del grupo OCDE (34).
6. Calculado aplicando el promedio no ponderado en el cambio porcentual para el 2014 en los 30 países con datos disponibles para ese año en el total de ingreso tributario en porcentaje del PIB.

StatLink http://dx.doi.org/10.1787/888933337549

Gráfico 1.1. **Total de recaudación tributaria como porcentaje del PIB en América Latina y el Caribe y la OCDE, 1990-2014**

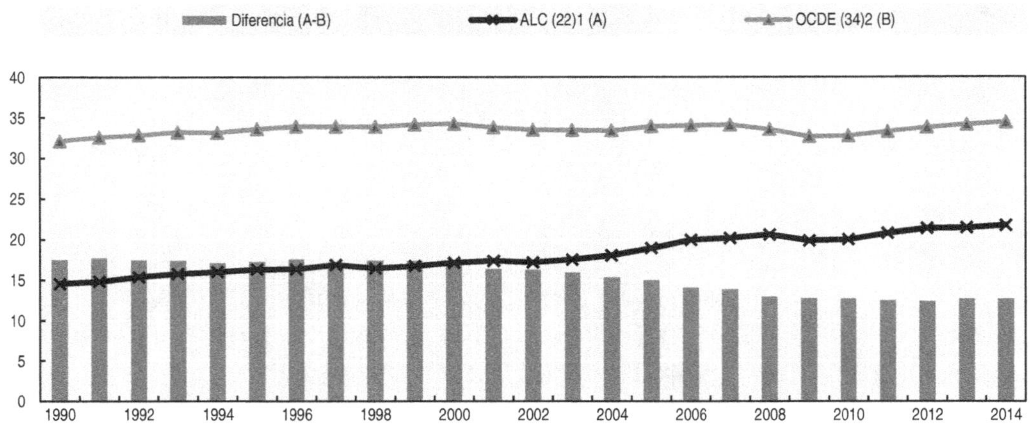

1. Representa un grupo de 22 países de América Latina y el Caribe. Estos son Argentina, Bahamas, Barbados, Bolivia, Brasil, Chile, Colombia, Costa Rica, República Dominicana, Ecuador, El Salvador, Guatemala, Honduras, Jamaica, México, Nicaragua, Panama, Paraguay, Perú, Trinidad y Tobago, Uruguay y Venezuela. Chile y México son también parte del grupo OCDE (34).

2. Representa el promedio no ponderado de los países miembros de la OCDE.

Fuente: Cuadro 3.1.

StatLink http://dx.doi.org/10.1787/888933337684

El proceso de convergencia entre los niveles de recaudación como porcentaje del PIB entre ALC y OCDE se ha detenido desde el 2008 y la brecha entre ambas regiones se ha mantenido estable. La brecha entre la proporción de los impuestos en relación con el PIB entre las economías de América Latina y el Caribe y las economías de la OCDE se redujo de 18 puntos porcentuales en 1990 a 13 puntos en el 2008. Desde entonces, esta tendencia se ha mantenido relativamente estable y en el 2014 la brecha fue de 12.7 puntos porcentuales.

Las diferencias en el promedio de ingresos tributarios como proporción del PIB entre la región de América Latina y el Caribe y el de la OCDE se puede explicar en gran parte por el alto nivel de ingreso que presentan las economías desarrolladas. El nivel de ingreso de una economía o su nivel de desarrollo, se miden comúnmente utilizando el PIB per cápita en paridad de poder adquisitivo (PPP). Como se observa en el gráfico1.2 existe una clara y positiva correlación entre la recaudación tributaria como porcentaje del PIB y el PIB per cápita para las economías de América Latina y el Caribe y para las economías de la OCDE. Las economías de la OCDE se encuentran en la parte superior derecha del gráfico, representando economías con un mayor nivel de ingreso, pero también un mayor nivel de recaudación tributaria. Por su parte, las economías de América Latina y el Caribe se presentan en la parte inferior izquierda, representando economías con un ingreso y una recaudación relativamente baja. Algunas de las economías de la región de ALC como Argentina, Barbados, Brasil y Trinidad y Tobago se encuentran en la parte baja de las economías de la OCDE.

Gráfico 1.2. **PIB per cápita en PPA (USD) y recaudación tributaria como porcentaje del PIB para América Latina y el Caribe y la OCDE, 2014**

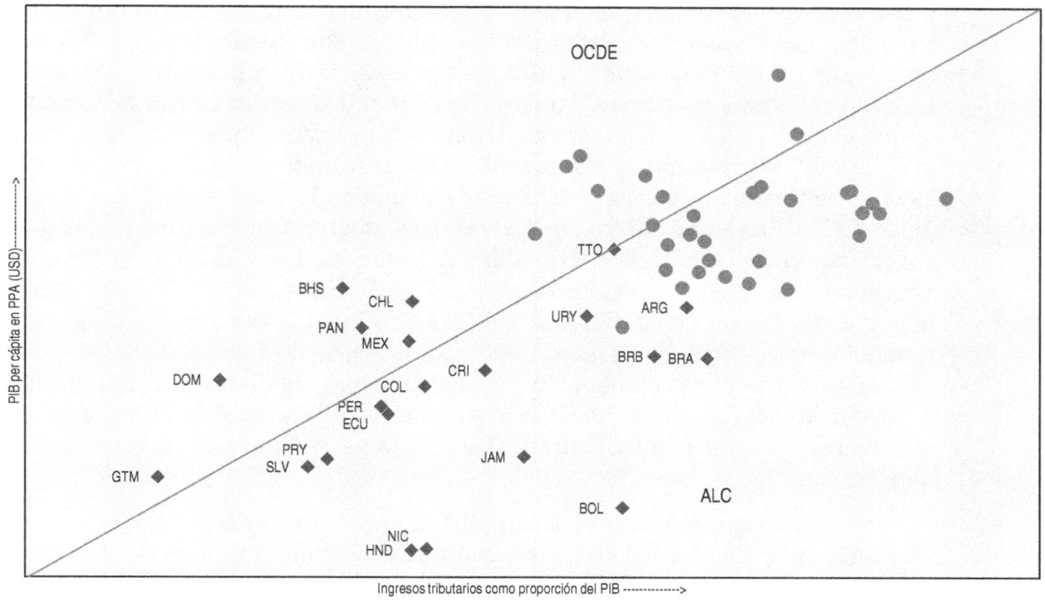

Nota: El eje Y esta en escala logarítmica.
Fuente: para el PIB per cápita se utilizó World Economic Outlook, Octubre 2015, Fondo Monetario Internacional. Recaudación tributaria como porcentaje de PIB de Cuadro 3.1.

StatLink http://dx.doi.org/10.1787/888933337695

Existe una amplia variación en la recaudación de impuestos en relación con el PIB entre los países de la ALC. Este cociente varía entre el 12.6% de Guatemala y el 33.4% de Brasil. Del mismo modo, las características de las economías de la OCDE muestran una gran disparidad. Así, en 2014, la proporción de los impuestos en el PIB en el seno de la OCDE oscilaba desde un 19.5% en México[1] al 50.9% en Dinamarca (OCDE, 2015a). Las implicaciones de estas variaciones regionales indican que los promedios se deben utilizar con reservas debido a que se incluyen economías con características considerablemente diferentes.

Ocho de las economías de ALC registraron ingresos tributarios como proporción del PIB superiores al promedio regional. Argentina (32.2%), Barbados (30.4%) y Brasil (33.4%) se sitúan considerablemente por encima del promedio regional. Las otras cinco economías con un ingreso tributario superior al promedio, ordenadas de forma descendente, son Bolivia, Trinidad y Tobago, Uruguay, Jamaica y Costa Rica. Las economías con un nivel inferior al promedio varían desde Guatemala (12.6%) o República Dominicana (14.1%) hasta Colombia y Nicaragua, ambos con 20.3%.

Evolución de los niveles de recaudación

Existe una considerable disparidad entre las tendencias de los diversos países considerados a lo largo del tiempo. Los países que mayores incrementos registraron entre 1990 y 2014 fueron Bolivia (20.6 puntos porcentuales) y Argentina (19.8). La mayoría de las economías presentaron incrementos entre 3 y 8 puntos porcentuales. Colombia, Ecuador y Paraguay mostraron incrementos entre 11-12 puntos porcentuales, mientras que Jamaica y Venezuela incrementos entre 1.2 y 0.1 puntos porcentuales, respectivamente.

El contexto en el que se produjo el incremento de los ingresos tributarios registrado a partir de los años 1990 fue el periodo de inestabilidad macroeconómica que vivieron los países latinoamericanos en la década anterior. Durante los años 1980, los países de la región padecieron fuertes desequilibrios fiscales y, al mismo tiempo, algunos recurrieron a vías alternativas para financiar su gasto (tomando préstamos o imprimiendo moneda), lo que generó una inflación que se extendió rápidamente por toda la región y erosionó el valor real de los ingresos tributarios. Como resultado de ello, las reformas de los años 1990 se centraron en controlar dicha inflación y en imponer disciplina fiscal. La mayor parte de los gobiernos latinoamericanos reaccionaron tanto recortando el gasto público como instaurando políticas destinadas a incrementar la recaudación, obteniendo así una notable mejora de la gestión presupuestaria y el saldo fiscal. En la parte recaudatoria de la ecuación, las reformas fiscales y de las administraciones tributarias contribuyeron notablemente a alcanzar ese objetivo. Como parte de este proceso, el impacto de la inflación en los ingresos obligó a los responsables de dictar políticas (policy-makers) a buscar soluciones para hacer que el sistema fuera menos vulnerable a episodios inflacionistas, tales como disminuir los plazos para el pago de impuestos e indexar las obligaciones tributarias.

Esfuerzos significativos se han realizado en los últimos 25 años para modernizar las administraciones y los sistemas tributarios. Durante ese periodo, se implementaron nuevos sistemas de tecnologías de la información junto con la racionalización de las administraciones tributarias, sistemas de recaudación más eficientes y empleados públicos más capacitados (BID, 2013). Adicionalmente, las economías de la región simplificaron el sistema tributario e incrementaron la base imponible. Se redujo el número de exenciones e incentivos fiscales que se otorgaban a ciertas actividades o sectores, principalmente para fomentar la inversión extranjera directa, los cuales no siempre fueron exitosos. Otras reformas fiscales incluyeron la introducción o el desarrollo de regímenes simplificados para pequeños contribuyentes y la imposición patrimonial sobre la base de ingresos presuntos. Además, en el último quinquenio se han impulsado varias reformas del impuesto sobre la renta en América Latina y el Caribe, donde ha predominado el efecto positivo de ampliaciones de las bases imponibles del impuesto debido a la extensión de la tributación al conjunto de ingresos del trabajo y de las rentas de capital, incluida la aplicación de impuestos a dividendos (Colombia, Guatemala, El Salvador, Nicaragua, Panamá, Perú, República Dominicana). Además de otras medidas que han incluido la introducción de impuestos mínimos, la reducción de exenciones, y gastos deducibles, la gradual reducción del umbral de ingreso al cual es aplicada la máxima tasa marginal y cierto control de los precios de transferencia (CEPAL, 2013; CEPAL, 2014).

La reforma fiscal más significativa en América Latina y el Caribe en los años ochentas y principios de los años noventa vino constituida por la introducción del IVA. Las subsiguientes reformas relacionadas con este impuesto se han centrado en extenderlo y reforzarlo mediante la suba de la tasa impositiva y la ampliación de la base tributaria. En la década de los noventa, el IVA como porcentaje del PIB aumentó 2.3 puntos porcentuales y, posteriormente, 1.5 puntos más hasta 2014. Entre 2000 y 2014, el incremento de los ingresos tributarios procedentes de los impuestos sobre la renta y utilidades (principalmente, el impuesto sobre las utilidades de las sociedades), fue cercano a 1.7 puntos porcentuales del PIB, e hizo de este tributo el principal motor del aumento de los ingresos tributarios, por delante del IVA. Uno de los elementos que contribuyó a este resultado fue el periodo de auge de los precios de las materias primas que se inició tras 2003, que resultó particularmente importante para algunos países de la región. Los cambios en los ingresos tributarios de bienes y servicios, impuestos sobre la renta y las contribuciones a la seguridad social han contribuido a la recuperación en los ingresos tributarios como proporción del PIB en ALC desde el 2010. Estos incrementos en los ingresos tributarios son en parte debidos a la recuperación económica de las economías latinoamericanas y caribeñas.

Gráfico 1.3. **Cambio en el total de los ingresos tributarios, ingresos sobre el impuesto sobre la renta e ingresos provenientes del IVA como porcentaje del PIB entre 1990 y 2000 y entre 2000 y 2014 en países de ALC (puntos porcentuales)**

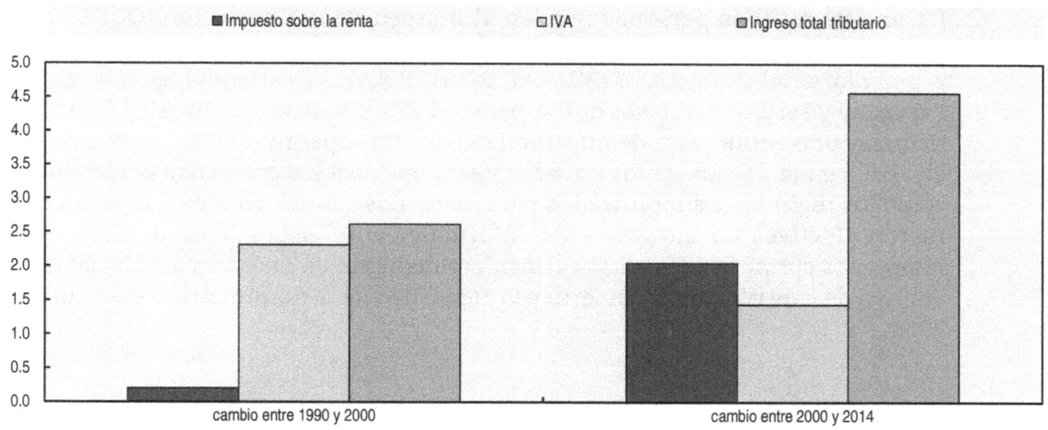

Fuente: Cuadros 3.1, 3.4, 3.16 y cuadros del Capítulo 4.

StatLink http://dx.doi.org/10.1787/888933337702

Factores que influyen los ingresos tributarios como proporción del PIB

Los ingresos tributarios como proporción del PIB se ven influenciados por múltiples factores tanto domésticos como internacionales, así como económicos y estructurales. Dentro de los factores económicos que influyen se puede incluir el PIB per cápita, la apertura económica, la informalidad, los recursos naturales y la importancia de la agricultura en la economía. Los factores socio demográficos, como el nivel de educación o la participación de las mujeres en el mercado laboral, también pueden ser determinantes para los ingresos tributarios. Adicionalmente, los gobiernos extranjeros pueden influir en el nivel de recaudación, si se dan prácticas competitivas o agresivas de imposición entre los países, como la fijación de precios de transferencia. Todos estos factores puede promover o perjudicar la habilidad de una economía para recaudar ingresos (Mascagnani, Moore y McCluskey, 2014). La estructura impositiva también tiene un impacto importante en los niveles de recaudación, así como el poder de la administración tributaria, el nivel de corrupción y la moral tributaria, (o la voluntad de pagar impuestos) entre otros (OCDE, 2014). Finalmente, la ubicación geográfica y los factores históricos pueden también ser determinantes en el nivel de ingresos tributarios como proporción del PIB, por ejemplo países sin acceso al mar tienen menos capacidad para recaudar impuestos sobre bienes y servicios que economías con acceso.

La participación del Estado en el financiamiento de la seguridad social es otro factor determinante de los niveles de ingresos tributarios como proporción del PIB. De los años 1980 en adelante, muchos países latinoamericanos privatizaron, en mayor o menor medida, los servicios de atención sanitaria, educación y seguridad social (CEPAL, 2010). Chile, El Salvador y México por ejemplo se han desplazado de un sistema de pensiones mayoritariamente financiado por el sector público a un sistema mayoritariamente financiado por el sector privado. En Colombia y Perú, los programas público y privado compiten entre ellos y los empleados deciden entre uno de los dos (OCDE, 2015b). Esta característica regional contrasta con la provisión sustancialmente pública de esos servicios, y la consiguiente necesidad de ingresos fiscales, en múltiples países de la OCDE, en particular en Europa. Por otra parte, Argentina, Brazil y Uruguay, como muchas economías de la OCDE, siguen un modelo en donde el sistema público y privado es complementario. En estas tres economías se llevaron a cabo reformas estructurales para extender la cobertura de la seguirá social. Estos cambios también han determinado el incremento en los niveles de ingresos tributarios como proporción del PIB (CEPAL, 2014).

También existen elevados niveles de informalidad en América Latina y el Caribe que hacen que muchas personas queden al margen de la imposición (OCDE, 2008; Gómez Sabaini et al., 2010). En la región[2], la tasa de informalidad[3] fue de alrededor de 55% en promedio en el 2013 (OCDE/BID/BM, 2014). Bolivia, Guatemala, Honduras, Nicaragua, Paraguay y Perú tienen tasas que superan el 65% mientras que Brasil, Chile, Costa Rica, y Uruguay presentan tasas de informalidad que no superan el 40%. Estos niveles eran más elevados en la década de los noventa y empujaron a los gobiernos a introducir medidas como los regímenes simplificados para pequeños contribuyentes que hasta cierto punto fueron efectivos en integrar a los informales en el sector formal. En la región, estos regímenes simplificados varían considerablemente en cuanto a su diseño dependiendo del tipo de contribuyente cubierto y la capacidad de la administración tributaria (CEPAL, 2014).

1.2. Estructuras impositivas

El seguimiento y análisis de las estructuras de los sistemas impositivos de los países aunado a los niveles del recaudo tributario proveen información valiosa del cómo eligen recaudar los gobiernos de los países. Esta información también ayuda a comprender el sistema político y social imperante en los países dado que las estructuras tributarias son el resultado de elecciones sociales y políticas y reflejan el balance de los intereses económicos y políticos del país. Asimismo, el análisis del desglose de los ingresos tributarios por subcategoría de impuesto contribuye a la mejor comprensión de las políticas impositivas y los efectos que las reformas tributarias y los sucesos económicos tienen en el recaudo tributario.

Evolución de las estructuras tributarias

A medida que los niveles impositivos han ido aumentando en América Latina y el Caribe, la estructura impositiva (esto es, la proporción de las principales categorías de impuestos respecto al total de ingresos tributarios) ha venido transformándose significativamente entre 1990 y 2014.El cuadro 1.2 plasma las diversas tendencias registradas en la "combinación tributaria" (tax mix) que se desprenden de los datos. Las tendencias más destacadas se han observado en relación con los impuestos sobre el consumo y los impuestos sobre la renta y las utilidades.

Impuestos sobre consumo

En 2014, la proporción de los impuestos sobre el consumo de bienes y servicios (especialmente el IVA, y los específicos e impuestos a las exportaciones e importaciones) representaron la fuente más importante del recaudo total, generando aproximadamente la mitad los ingresos tributarios. Esta proporción permaneció bastante estable durante el periodo de referencia, pero el peso de los impuestos generales sobre el consumo aumentó considerablemente en 10 puntos porcentuales entre 1990 y 2014, mientras que la incidencia de los impuestos específicos sobre el consumo (selectivos e impuestos a las exportaciones e importaciones) cayó 14 puntos durante el mismo periodo.

Estas dos tendencias antagónicas en el seno de los impuestos sobre el consumo reflejan la creciente incidencia del IVA y la pérdida de importancia de los impuestos específicos sobre el consumo. Aunque el IVA fue introducido tempranamente en las economías de la región (la mayoría de los países ya lo habían adoptado de alguna forma a finales de los años 1970), su expansión en términos de ingresos tributarios es relativamente reciente. Desde principios de los años 1990, este impuesto ha venido constituyendo una fuente creciente de ingresos para los países de ALC y se ha consolidado mediante sucesivas ampliaciones de la base tributaria y de las tasas impositivas oficiales, así como también a través del fortalecimiento de las administraciones tributarias. Las reformas se han enfocado también en la simplificación de los sistemas tributarios, con la mayoría de los países reduciendo el número de bienes con tasa cero o reducida, encaminándose así a un sistema de tasa única del IVA en muchos casos.

Cuadro 1.2. **Estructuras impositivas en un grupo de países de América Latina y del Caribe**[1]

	1990	2000	2010	2011	2012	2013	2014
Impuestos sobre ingresos y ganancias	23.3	22.4	26.4	27.3	27.5	27.4	27.9
Contribuciones a la seguridad social	13.4	15.2	15.8	15.6	15.9	16.6	16.4
Impuesto sobre la nómina	0.5	0.8	0.6	0.6	0.6	0.6	0.6
Impuestos a la propiedad	4.2	2.9	3.2	3.2	3.3	3.4	3.3
Impuestos generales al consumo	20.9	30.4	31.6	31.4	31.1	31.2	31.3
Impuestos específicos	32.1	25.5	19.5	19.1	18.9	18.3	17.8
Otros impuestos[2]	5.6	2.8	2.9	2.8	2.7	2.6	2.8
Total	**100**	**100**	**100**	**100**	**100**	**100**	**100**

1. Representa los porcentajes de las mayores categorías del recaudo tributario total. El grupo de 22 países está listado en el Cuadro 1.1.
2.Incluye algunos impuestos sobre bienes y servicios (encabezado 5200) y timbres.

StatLink http://dx.doi.org/10.1787/888933337556

En 2014, el 30% del recaudo tributario total en los países de ALC provino únicamente del IVA. No obstante, existe una disparidad importante en la región. La proporción del IVA en los países va desde 11.6% en Trinidad y Tobago hasta 47.4% en Venezuela, como lo muestra el gráfico 1.4. Bahamas no tenía un régimen de IVA vigente para los años analizados e introdujo este impuesto en Julio 2014, por lo que sus ingresos se verán reflejados en el año 2015. Por otra parte, la baja participación del IVA dentro de los ingresos totales en Jamaica, México, Panamá y Trinidad y Tobago reflejan su mayor dependencia en impuestos sobre ingresos y ganancias. De igual forma, la amplia discrepancia entre países es también el resultado de las diferencias en el diseño del IVA: las tasas y bases impositivas varían mucho en la región. Por ejemplo, México no grava con IVA a los alimentos, medicamentos y varios otros productos, lo que resulta en una base impositiva estrecha. La CEPAL 2014 estima que la pérdida en la recaudación por estas exenciones es de entre 1.1% y 2.5% del PIB.

Por el contrario, el declive del peso de los impuestos específicos sobre el consumo tiene que ver con los procesos de liberalización del comercio. Lo anterior propició la reducción de los derechos de aduanas sobre las importaciones y supresión de los impuestos sobre las exportaciones en numerosos países latinoamericanos y caribeños. Una importante excepción es Argentina, donde los impuestos sobre las exportaciones se reestablecieron en 2002, aunque cabe destacar que el gobierno actual tiene previsto la eliminación de gravámenes sobre ciertos productos agropecuarios. Además, se ha acotado el conjunto de bienes y servicios sujetos a impuestos selectivos, que hoy se limitan principalmente a productos y servicios con una demanda relativamente inelástica, tales como bebidas alcohólicas, combustible y derivados, y tabaco.

Gráfico 1.4. Recaudacion de impuestos sobre la renta y ganancias y del IVA como proporción de los ingresos totales en países de ALC, 2014

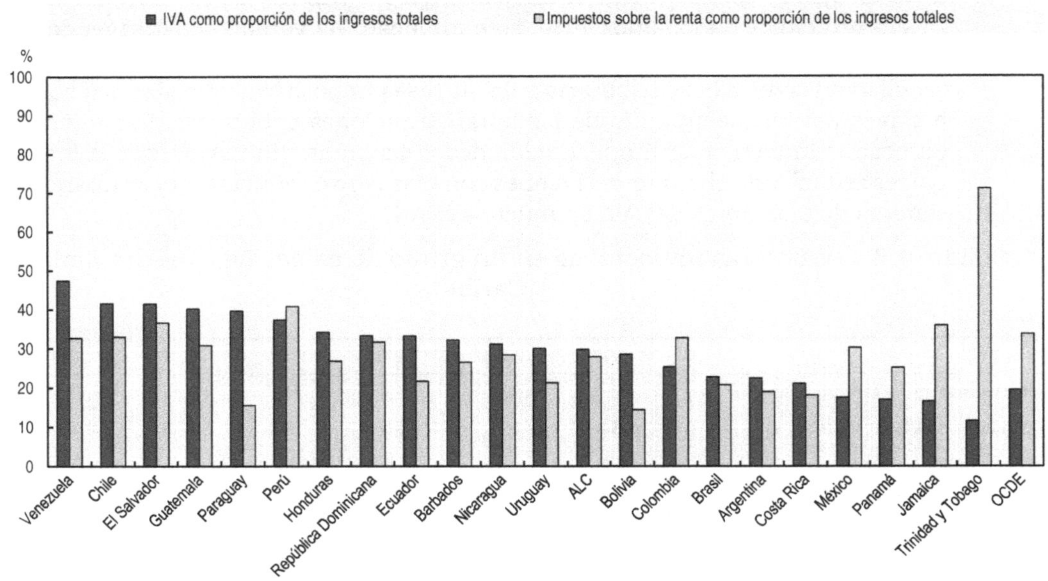

Nota: Para la OCDE se utilizan los datos de 2013. Bahamas no está incluido ya que no hay ingresos procedentes de impuestos sobre la renta personales o a sociedades.

Fuente: Cuadro 3.4 y cuadros en el Capítulo 4.

StatLink http://dx.doi.org/10.1787/888933337716

Impuestos sobre la renta y utilidades y contribuciones a la seguridad social

Al mismo tiempo, los ingresos procedentes de la renta y las utilidades han crecido, pasando del 23% al 28% del total de ingresos tributarios entre 2000 y 2014, principalmente como resultado de niveles de recaudación mucho más elevados a finales de los años 2000. El peso de los impuestos sobre la renta y utilidades en el total de la recaudación llegó a su cúspide entre 2008 y 2009 a un nivel de 27.9% antes de caer hasta 26.4% en 2010 debido al impacto de la crisis global. Desde entonces ha vuelto a crecer hasta 27.9% en 2014 (Cuadro 3.5).

La participación del impuesto sobre la renta de las sociedades es superior a la del impuesto sobre la renta personal para los países de ALC, exceptuando los casos de Barbados, Jamaica y Uruguay (Gráfico 1.5). Trinidad y Tobago cuenta con la proporción más grande del impuesto sobre las utilidades de sociedades, donde más de la mitad del recaudo total proviene de esta fuente. Para este último, es importante hacer notar que provienen del pago del impuesto de compañías de petróleo y gas. En los otros países de ALC, la proporción del impuesto a las utilidades de sociedades varía desde un 8% (Barbados) hasta 30% (Perú). Bahamas es el único país que no cuenta con un régimen de impuesto a la renta o utilidades (sobre sociedades o personas). El incremento general de esta categoría refleja el notorio crecimiento de los ingresos generados por la tributación de las sociedades, especialmente aquellas que se dedican a la explotación de recursos naturales. Así como de la implementación de políticas tributarias tendientes a la reducción de los incentivos otorgados a las zonas de libre comercio, la introducción de impuestos mínimos a las utilidades de sociedades, las reformas en materia de tributación internacional y los acuerdos entre países para combatir la evasión de los contribuyentes (CEPAL, 2014).

Por otra parte, la proporción del impuesto a la renta de personas permanece bajo en los países de ALC a pesar que varios países implementaron reformas con el fin de expandir la base del impuesto. Asimismo, luego de la crisis, se avanzó mediante la implantación de tasas proporcionales sobre los ingresos del capital, previamente exentos, y la implementación de tasas más progresivas sobre las rentas del trabajo (CEPAL 2014). No obstante, la proporción del impuesto a la renta de personas en los países de ALC sigue siendo modesta puesto que más de la mitad de los países mostrados en el gráfico 1.5 generan menos del 10% de su ingreso tributario de esta fuente. La proporción del impuesto a la renta de personas varía de entre 0.6% (Bolivia) hasta 19% (Jamaica) del recaudo tributario total. Estudios previos de la OCDE (OCDE, 2008 y Daude et al., 2010) sugieren que la proporción de los ingresos provenientes del trabajo como porcentaje del PIB, son sustancialmente inferiores en los países de ALC y su distribución implica que los contribuyentes son relativamente menores, dada la concentración de población con bajos niveles de ingreso. Únicamente el 10% de la población son contribuyentes registrados en Latino América (BID, 2013). Además, varios estudios (BID, 2015; CEPAL, 2014; CEPAL, 2010 y Gómez Sabaini et al., 2010) mencionan dos factores adicionales, la amplia brecha en los ingresos en los países de ALC y una base tributaria más limitada que está compuesta fundamentalmente por salarios dados los beneficios impositivos otorgados a las ganancias de capital. Aunado a su base estrecha, el impuesto a la renta de personas padece niveles de evasión elevados. BID, 2013 señala que "se pierde cerca de la mitad del recaudo potencial del impuesto a la renta de personas por la evasión".

Gráfico 1.5. **Recaudación del impuesto a las utilidades de sociedad y del impuesto a la renta de personas como proporción del recaudo tributario total en países seleccionados de ALC, 2014**

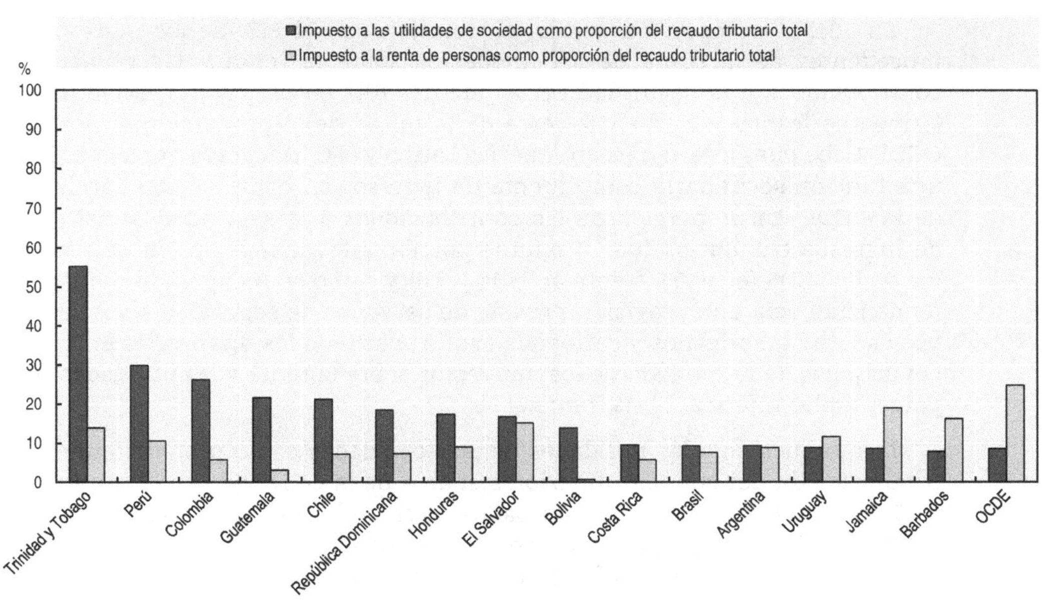

Nota: Para la OCDE se utilizan los datos de 2013. Es posible que la proporción de impuestos sobre la renta de las personas y sobre las utilidades de sociedades no sumen el porcentaje total de los impuestos sobre los ingresos y ganancias debido a la existencia de ingresos no clasificables. La gráfica únicamente muestra aquellos países para los cuales fue posible clasificar el 75 por ciento o más del impuesto entre las subcategorías de impuesto a la renta de personas e impuesto a las utilidades de sociedades.

Fuente: Cuadros en el Capítulo 4.

StatLink http://dx.doi.org/10.1787/888933337725

Las contribuciones a la seguridad social como proporción del recaudo tributario total incrementaron 3 puntos porcentuales durante los últimos 25 años y representaron el 16.4% en 2014 (Cuadro 3.7). Esto refleja dos factores que se dan de forma simultánea. En primer lugar, el incremento de las rentas personales ha empujado al alza las cantidades recaudadas. Pero este efecto se ha visto contrarrestado y, a menudo, más que compensado, por los variados procesos de privatización total o parcial registrados en numerosos países de la región explicados anteriormente. En algunos países con esquemas públicos o mixtos, incluyendo a Barbados, Brasil, Costa Rica, Ecuador, Nicaragua, Panamá, Paraguay y Uruguay, las contribuciones a la seguridad social continúan teniendo un peso significativo (más del 20% de los ingresos tributarios totales). En Colombia y Perú donde los programas públicos y privados compiten, las contribuciones a la seguridad social representan niveles cercados al 11-13%. En Argentina, las cifras reflejan la introducción de sistemas de capitalización en 1994 y su posterior nacionalización en 2008.

Comparación con la OCDE

En relación con la OCDE, América Latina y el Caribe registra una incidencia de los impuestos directos relativamente baja, compensada por ingresos fiscales elevados en concepto de impuestos indirectos (véase el gráfico 1.6). En concreto, América Latina y el Caribe depende acusadamente de los impuestos sobre los bienes y servicios, que representan aproximadamente la mitad de los ingresos tributarios totales, en comparación con el 30% en el caso de las economías de la OCDE. A título comparativo, obsérvese que, en América Latina y el Caribe, cerca del 45% de los ingresos tributarios procede de la suma de los impuestos sobre la renta y las utilidades y de las contribuciones a la seguridad social, frente al 60% en la OCDE. Esta mayor dependencia de los impuestos indirectos puede acarrear que el sistema tributario sea más regresivo.

En 2013, la proporción media, en relación con el PIB, de los ingresos tributarios procedentes de la suma de los impuestos sobre la renta y las utilidades y de las contribuciones a la seguridad social fue del 10% en el grupo seleccionado de países latinoamericanos y caribeños, cerca de la mitad de la proporción en los países de la OCDE. Cabe pues inferir que, en América Latina y el Caribe, esos impuestos desempeñan una función secundaria como fuente de ingresos en comparación con las economías de la OCDE. La proporción de las contribuciones a la seguridad social sobre el total de ingresos tributarios fue 10 puntos porcentuales menor en los países ALC que en los de la OCDE (el 16.6% frente al 26.1%). Tal y como se ha apuntado anteriormente, la tendencia hacia una provisión privada de servicios de seguridad social en numerosos países latinoamericanos y caribeños explica parte de las diferencias en esta categoría. Por su parte, la proporción de los impuestos sobre la renta y las utilidades fue 6 puntos porcentuales inferior (27.4% frente al 33.7%).

Los impuestos a las utilidades de las sociedades como proporción de los ingresos tributarios totales son 8.5% inferiores el área de la OCDE que en el grupo de países de ALC, exceptuando a Bahamas y Barbados. El recaudo del impuesto a la renta de personas contribuyó 25% al agregado total de recaudo tributario en el área de la OCDE en 2013, mientras que esta categoría fue considerablemente menor en los países de ALC.

Como contrapartida de la menor importancia de los gravámenes directos, los impuestos generales sobre los bienes y servicios representan una mayor proporción de la recaudación tributaria total que en los países de la OCDE. En 2013, esta categoría supuso en la región el 31% del total de los ingresos tributarios mientras la cifra correspondiente en la zona de la OCDE fue sólo del 20%. Sin embargo, el peso de los impuestos generales sobre bienes y servicios como proporción del PIB es ligeramente inferior en los países de ALC (6.6%) frente al de los países de la OCDE (6.8%).

Gráfico 1.6. **Estructuras impositivas en América Latinay el Caribe y la OCDE, 2013**

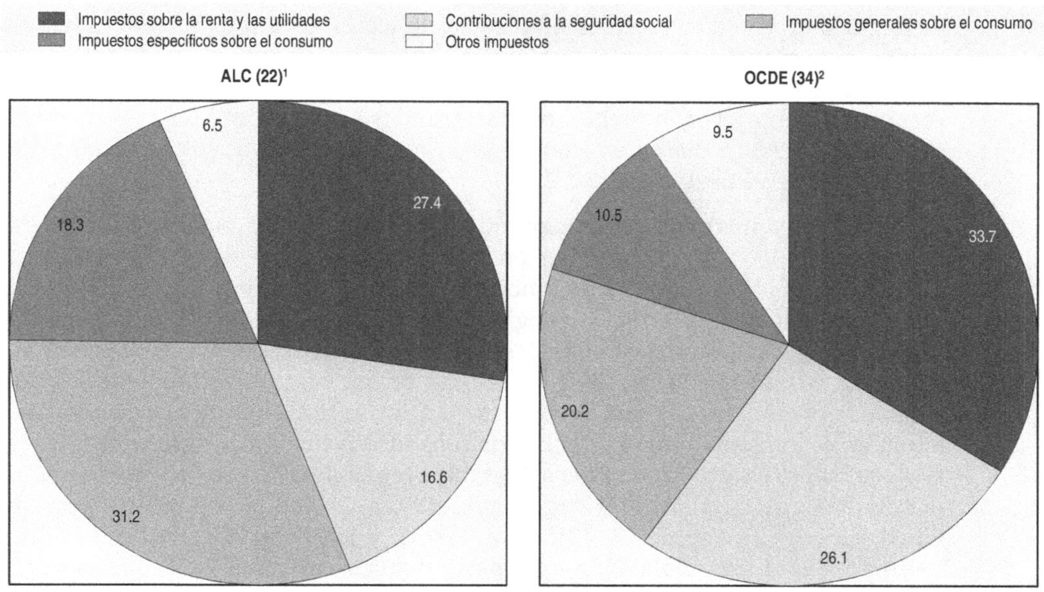

1. Representa un grupo de 22 países de América Latina y el Caribe. Los países se encuentran detallados en la Cuadro 1.1. Chile y México también forman parte del grupo de la OCDE (34).

2. Representa el promedio simple para los países miembros de la OCDE.

Fuente: Cuadros 3.2 y 3.5-3.15.

StatLink http://dx.doi.org/10.1787/888933337733

Por último, los impuestos sobre la propiedad inmueble y la nómina (incluidos en "Otros impuestos" en el gráfico 1.6) no constituyen importantes fuentes de ingresos para los países latinoamericanos y caribeños. Las dificultades que encuentran los gobiernos subnacionales para recaudar sus propios tributos quedan ejemplificadas por la escasa capacidad de generar ingresos que tienen los impuestos sobre la propiedad, que suelen ser la principal fuente de entradas de los gobiernos locales de la región (Brossio y Jiménez, 2012). Por su parte, los impuestos sobre la nómina han sido insignificantes durante todo el periodo, en parte porque este tipo de mecanismos, no está muy desarrollado en América Latina y el Caribe. Sin embargo, conviene señalar que la falta de datos a escala subnacional dificulta el análisis de estas categorías. Las proporciones de los impuestos sobre la propiedad y la nómina en la recaudación tributaria total de los países latinoamericanos y caribeños son similares, en promedio, a las de los países de la OCDE.

1.3. Impuestos por nivel de gobierno

Desde mediados de los años ochentas, los países de ALC han experimentado de forma generalizada reformas que implican la transferencia de funciones gubernamentales desde el gobierno central a entidades subnacionales. En su primera fase, la ola de descentralización se centró principalmente en reforzar el carácter democrático de las autoridades locales. A esto siguió una creciente tendencia a que, paulatinamente, una parte cada vez mayor del gasto público se ejecutase a escala subnacional.

Pese a ello, el alcance de las políticas tributarias subnacionales de la región ha permanecido relativamente modesto. Los datos disponibles parecen apuntar que la mayoría de los países de ALC no se han ocupado de reforzar los ingresos que reciben las instancias subnacionales. Entre 1995 y 2013, la fracción de ingresos recaudada por los niveles de gobierno subnacional descendió de 0.7 puntos en Argentina y creció entre 0.4 y 1.2 puntos porcentuales en Brasil, Colombia y México. En los otros países para los que se dispone de datos sobre las tendencias en los ingresos subnacionales, la proporción varió menos de un punto porcentual. Al mismo tiempo, la proporción de los fondos de seguridad social cayó en casi la mitad de los 22 países de ALC estudiados, a veces debido a su privatización total o parcial. Los cambios más grandes en este ámbito se registraron en Colombia y El Salvador (con descensos de casi 11 y 4 puntos porcentuales, respectivamente). Los incrementos más grandes en la proporción de contribuciones a la seguridad social se dieron en Honduras y Nicaragua (en ambos casos cerca de 8 puntos porcentuales) (véase la cuadro 1.3).

A fin de comparar la atribución de los ingresos en los países de ALC con la de los miembros de la OCDE, cabe tener en cuenta previamente dos cuestiones estadísticas. En primer lugar, los ingresos de ambos grupos se han atribuido a los diferentes niveles de gobierno de acuerdo con lo recogido en la versión final 2008 del Sistema de Cuentas Nacionales (SCN), según el cual, los ingresos se atribuyen por lo general al nivel de gobierno que ejerce la facultad de aplicar el impuesto o que puede a su discreción establecer y modificar la tasa del impuesto. Esto tiene claras implicaciones para aquellas situaciones en que un nivel de gobierno recauda los ingresos tributarios y los transfiere, en todo o en parte, a otros niveles. Ejemplos regionales de este tipo de mecanismos son la Ley de Coparticipación de Argentina; el Fondo General de Participación de México establecido en la Ley de Coordinación Fiscal; y los Fondos de Participación de Brasil definidos en el artículo 159 de la Constitución de este país. La segunda cuestión está relacionada con el hecho de que los datos para algunos países de ALC se ven afectados por la falta de estadísticas de ingresos tributarios en la esfera subnacional.

Considerando las dos aclaraciones anteriores, la atribución de los ingresos tributarios en América Latina y el Caribe, en comparación con la OCDE, parece estar muy orientada hacia las entidades centrales o federales, mientras que las actividades subnacionales dependen más claramente de las transferencias que reciben de niveles superiores de la Administración. En todos los países de ALC, menos en uno, las entradas de los gobiernos centrales representaron cerca de dos tercios o más de la recaudación total, mientras los países de la OCDE arrojan un resultado aproximado del 60%. Brasil constituye la notable excepción a la regla, ya que atribuye menos del 50% a la Administración federal, entre otras, porque en este país una gran parte del IVA (ICMS – imposto sobre operações relativas à circulação de mercadorías e prestação de serviços de transporte interestadual e intermunicipal e de comunicação) se recauda en la esfera subnacional. Aunque en menor medida, Argentina cuenta también con una significativa recaudación a nivel estatal, que se explica en parte por la existencia del impuesto sobre los ingresos brutos, un impuesto provincial sobre las ventas.

Todo lo anterior pone de manifiesto que los gobiernos subnacionales de los países de ALC tienden a tener competencia sobre un abanico de impuestos restringido. Los impuestos que más frecuentemente se atribuyen a las instancias subnacionales son aquellos que gravan la propiedad, las licencias de vehículos automotores, las tasas por servicios específicos, así como ciertas tasas municipales, y no cabe duda de que el potencial de generación de ingresos de esos instrumentos es relativamente limitado en comparación con las bases tributarias atribuidas a los órganos centrales, tales como el IVA o los impuestos sobre la renta. En los países miembros de la OCDE, las entidades subnacionales tienden a disponer en promedio de bases tributarias potenciales mucho más amplias. De hecho, una proporción sustancial de la recaudación tributaria de los gobiernos subnacionales de los países de la OCDE se obtiene de los impuestos sobre la renta, que representan más de un tercio de la cantidad total recaudada. Por el contrario, ninguno de los países de ALC para los que se dispone de datos registra recaudación alguna en concepto de impuestos sobre la renta por parte de los gobiernos subnacionales.

Cuadro 1.3. **Atribución de los ingresos tributarios en los sub-sectores del gobierno general como porcentaje del ingreso tributario total**[1]

	Gobierno central			Gobierno estatal o regional			Gobierno local			Fondos de seguridad social		
	1995	2000	2013	1995	2000	2013	1995	2000	2013	1995	2000	2013
Países federales												
Argentina	59.0	66.4	60.6	17.5	17.8	16.8				23.4	15.8	22.6
Brasil	44.7	47.8	42.6	26.8	25.3	25.8	3.7	3.4	5.9	24.8	23.5	25.6
México	80.1	80.7	80.1	2.1	2.0	3.1	1.1	0.8	1.2	16.6	16.5	15.5
Venezuela	94.6	94.6	93.4							5.4	5.4	6.6
OCDE[2,3]	53.2	56.5	54.2	15.9	15.3	16.5	7.7	6.9	7.5	22.9	21.1	21.3
Países regionales												
Colombia[4]	63.2	68.6	73.3	5.5	5.6	4.2	8.6	9.4	10.8	22.7	16.4	11.7
OCDE[5]	50.4	49.0	22.3	4.8	7.6	13.7	8.5	9.1	9.9	35.8	33.8	34.0
Países unitarios												
Bahamas	89.1	88.1	84.1							10.9	11.9	15.9
Barbados	85.3	84.3	80.1							14.7	15.7	19.9
Bolivia	100.0	92.2	95.1							0.0	7.8	4.9
Chile	89.9	87.8	87.0				6.5	7.9	7.3	3.6	4.4	5.7
Costa Rica	66.2	65.3	58.8					2.1	3.0	33.8	32.6	38.1
Ecuador	73.9	87.7	75.0							26.1	12.3	25.0
El Salvador	86.3	84.8	89.7							14.1	16.6	10.3
Guatemala	83.8	83.6	82.9				0.6	0.9	1.4	15.6	15.5	15.7
Honduras	90.1	89.4	81.9							9.9	10.6	18.1
Jamaica	100.0	99.3	94.3				0.0	0.7	1.6	0.0	0.0	4.1
Nicaragua	84.1	80.1	76.1							15.9	19.9	23.9
Panamá	62.0	61.1	64.3				0.0	2.1	1.5	38.0	36.8	34.2
Paraguay	100.0	82.7	80.0				0.0	0.0	2.7	0.0	17.3	17.4
Perú	88.2	87.7	85.7				0.0	0.0	3.1	11.8	12.3	11.3
República Dominicana	99.3	99.0	99.6							0.7	1.0	0.4
Trinidad y Tobago	94.5	91.7	92.4				2.4	1.9	1.4	3.1	6.4	6.2
Uruguay	62.0	62.5	69.3				7.8	7.9	3.9	30.1	29.6	26.8
OCDE[2,6]	65.8	66.4	63.2				10.8	11.0	12.0	23.1	22.3	24.6

1. Las cifras excluyen los ingresos de gobiernos locales en Argentina (pero incluye ingresos de las provincias), Bahamas, Barbados, Bolivia, Costa Rica (hasta 1997), República Dominicana, Ecuador, El Salvador, Honduras, Jamaica, Nicaragua, Panamá (hasta 1998), Paraguay, Perú (hasta 2004) y Venezuela dado que los datos no están disponibles.
2. Chile y México son también parte del grupo OCDE.
3. Representa el promedio no ponderado para los países federales miembros de la OCDE.
4. Colombia es constitucionalmente un país unitario con una estructura política descentralizada.
5. Representa a España, que es constitucionalmente un país no federal con una estructura política altamente descentralizada.
6. Representa el promedio no ponderado para los países unitarios miembros de la OCDE.

StatLink http://dx.doi.org/10.1787/888933337568

El bajo recaudo tributario a niveles subnacionales en los países de ALC es también resultado de una baja capacidad administrativa y técnica. Por ejemplo, los impuestos a la propiedad – que se consideran como la fuente recomendada de ingresos a niveles subnacionales – requieren de sistemas sofisticados de información que elevan el costo del recaudo de este tributo. Aunado a ello, los registros de propiedad apropiados son escasos y cuando existen su actualización es poco frecuente (BID, 2012). Como resultado, las autoridades tributarias tienen acceso restringido a valuaciones precisas y actualizadas de tierras y edificios. Aunado a ello, los registros de bienes y raíces a menudo se rehúsan a compartir esta información. El impuesto a la propiedad también sufre de otros problemas característicos y endémicos de países en desarrollo, como los altos niveles de informalidad. Los edificios son construidos sin permisos, las propiedades no son registradas y los montos de las transacciones de bienes y raíces registradas son muchas veces falsificadas. Dado que el impuesto a la propiedad es uno de los más controvertidos con los ciudadanos y tienen costos políticos elevados, las autoridades subnacionales son muchas veces reacios a invertir los recursos necesarios para gravar esta fuente de ingresos tributarios (BID, 2015).

Notas

1. Esta cifra difiere de las presentadas en las publicaciones de CEPAL y CIAT debido a la inclusión de derechos sobre la producción de hidrocarburos como ingresos tributarios.
2. Promedio simple de 19 economías Argentina, Bolivia, Brasil, Chile, Colombia, Costa Rica, República Dominicana, Ecuador, Guatemala, Honduras, Jamaica, México, Nicaragua, Panamá, Perú, Paraguay, El Salvador, Uruguay y Venezuela.
3. Se define la informalidad como el porcentaje de no contribuyentes a un sistema de pensiones sobre el total de ocupados.

Referencias

Brossio, G. and J.P. Jiménez (2012), *Decentralization and Reform in Latin America: Improving Intergovernmental Relations*, Edward Elgar, in press, Cheltenham, UK and Northampton, MA.

BID (2015), *Descentralizando los ingresos fiscales en América Latina, por qué y cómo*, Banco Interamericano de Desarrollo, Washington, DC.

BID (2013), *Recaudar no basta, los impuestos como herramienta de desarrollo*, Banco Interamericano de Desarrollo, Washington, DC.

BID (2012), "Sub-national Revenue Mobilization in Peru", *IDB Working Paper Series* No. IDB-WP-299, Washington, DC, BID.

CEPAL (2014), *Política Tributaria en América Latina: Agenda para una segunda generación de reformas*, CEPAL, Santiago de Chile.

CEPAL (2013), *Panorama Fiscal de América Latina y el Caribe: reformas tributarias y renovación del pacto fiscal*, CEPAL, Santiago de Chile.

CEPAL (2011), *Estudio Económico de América Latina y el Caribe 2010-2011*, CEPAL, Santiago de Chile.

CEPAL (2010), "La Hora de la igualdad. Brechas por cerrar, caminos por abrir", LC/G.2432(SES.33/3)), CEPAL, Santiago de Chile.

Daude, C., A. Melguizo and A. Neut (2010), "Fiscal Policy in Latin America: Countercyclical and Sustainable at Last?", *OECD Development Centre Working Paper* No. 291, OECD Development Centre, Paris.

Gómez Sabaini, J.C., J.P. Jiménez y A. Podestá (2010), "Evasión y equidad en América Latina", *Documentos de proyectos*, No. 309 (LC/W.309/ Rev.1), Santiago, Chile, CEPAL.

Mascagnani, G., M. Moore and R. McCluskey (2014), *Tax revenue mobilisation in developing countries issues and challenges*, European Union, Brussels, www.europarl.europa.eu/RegData/etudes/etudes/join/2014/433849/EXPO-DEVE_ET(2014)433849_EN.pdf.

OCDE (2015a), *Revenue Statistics 1965-2014*, OECD Publishing, Paris, http://dx.doi.org/10.1787/rev_stats-2015-en-fr.

OCDE (2015b), *Estadísticas tributarias en América Latina y el Caribe* 1990-2013, OECD Publishing, Paris, http://dx.doi.org/10.1787/rev_lat-2015-en-fr.

OCDE (2014), *Development Cooperation Report 2014: Mobilising Resources for Sustainable Development*, OECD Publishing, Paris, http://dx.doi.org/10.1787/dcr-2014-en.

OCDE (2008), *Perspectivas económicas de América Latina 2009*, OECD Publishing, Paris, http://dx.doi.org/10.1787/leo-2009-en.

OCDE/CEPAL (2012), Perspectivas Económicas en América Latina 2013: políticas de pymes para el cambio estructural, OECD Publishing, Paris, http://dx.doi.org/10.1787/leo-2013-en.

OCDE/BID/Banco Mundial (2014), *Pensions at a Glance: Latin America and the Caribbean*, OECD Publishing, Paris, http://dx.doi.org/10.1787/pension_glance-2014-en.

CHAPTER 2

SPECIAL FEATURE

Fiscal revenues from non-renewable natural resources in Latin America and the Caribbean

CAPÍTULO 2

SECCIÓN ESPECIAL

Ingresos fiscales provenientes de recursos naturales no renovables en América Latina y el Caribe

The compilation of data for this publication was completed in December 2015. On 7 January 2016 Argentina's National Institute of Statistics and Census published an official decree (https://www.boletinoficial.gob.ar/pdf/linkQR/QlFlS1dmVmpOWXMrdTVReEh2ZkU0dz09) temporarily suspending the publication of certain data in the National Statistics System. The nominal GDP series for Argentina used in this publication was obtained on 13 December 2015 through the official website of Argentina's National Institute of Statistics and Census (www.indec.mecon.ar/). As a consequence of the decree and the potential for future revisions of the GDP data, the tax to GDP ratio figures for Argentina should be treated with caution.

La recopilación de datos para esta publicación finalizó en diciembre de 2015. El 7 de enero 2016 el Instituto Nacional de Estadísticas y Censos de la República de Argentina publicó un boletín oficial (https://www.boletinoficial.gob.ar/pdf/linkQR/QlFlS1dmVmpOWXMrdTVReEh2ZkU0dz09) mediante el cual suspende temporalmente la publicación de ciertos datos en el Sistema Nacional de Estadísticas. En el caso de Argentina, la serie del PIB nominal utilizada en esta publicación se obtuvo el 13 de diciembre 2015 a través del sitio web oficial del Instituto Nacional de Argentina de Estadística y Censos (www.indec.mecon.ar/). Como consecuencia del decreto y la posibilidad de futuras revisiones de los datos del PIB, las cifras de impuestos en relación al PIB de Argentina deben ser tratadas con precaución.

SPECIAL FEATURE

Fiscal revenues from non-renewable natural resources in Latin America and the Caribbean

SPECIAL FEATURE
Fiscal revenues from non-renewable natural resources in Latin America and the Caribbean

Key findings

Trends in fiscal revenues from non-renewable natural resources for 2014

- A sharp decline in international oil prices resulted in a significant reduction of hydrocarbon-related revenues in the region, which fell from an average of 7.3% of GDP in 2013 to 6.6% of GDP in 2014. Non-tax revenues bore the brunt of the decline, falling sharply in Ecuador and Venezuela (Bolivarian Republic of).
- Mining revenues were similarly affected by falling prices, dropping to 0.5% of GDP on average from 0.6% of GDP in 2013. A rise in mining production in some countries coupled with currency depreciations served to stabilise non-tax revenues. Tax revenues, derived mainly from corporate income taxes, fell sharply as profit margins in the sector tightened.

Estimated non-renewable natural resources revenues for 2015

- The global supply-side and demand-side factors that reduced commodities prices in 2014 continued in 2015, intensifying the decline in the region's non-renewable natural resource revenues. Hydrocarbon revenues are estimated to have returned to their pre-boom level, falling from an average of 6.6% of GDP in 2014 to 4.5% of GDP. Mining revenues are also projected to have declined, but not to the same extent (from 0.5% of GDP to 0.4% of GDP).

Non-renewable natural resource revenues in this Special Feature refer to tax (income tax, sector specific taxes and certain excise taxes) and non-tax revenues (royalties, dividends) derived from hydrocarbon production and commercialisation and from mining. They do not include tax withholdings or payments made by companies on behalf of their employees or investors, nor do they include payments of consumption taxes (namely the value-added tax, where applicable).

2.1. Trends in fiscal revenues from non-renewable natural resources for 2014

Non-renewable natural resources revenues in Latin America and the Caribbean fell both in absolute terms and relative terms in 2014 reflecting the strong impact of plunging international commodities prices for a number of the region's principal raw material products. After posting a 10.0% increase to USD 263 billion in 2013, they declined 9.5% in 2014 to USD 238 billion (Figure 2.1).[1] At the regional level a decline in hydrocarbon revenues, provoked by a collapse in oil prices in the second half of the year, was the principal driver of the overall trend. The region's mining revenues also crept down, but their decline played a secondary role given their relatively smaller participation in overall non-renewable natural resource revenues in the region.

Unlike in 2013 (see last year's Special Feature), non-renewable natural resources revenues registered a fairly generalised decline relative to GDP across countries and commodities revenues in 2014 (Table 2.1). Hydrocarbon revenues fell on average 0.7 percentage points of GDP, with higher than average declines recorded in Colombia, Ecuador and Venezuela (Bolivarian Republic of). Mining revenues fell in nearly all countries (0.1 percentage points of GDP on average) as international prices continued to fall from their 2011 highs. Larger declines were registered among the region's larger producers, with Brazil, Chile and Peru all experiencing a contraction of around 0.3 percentage points of GDP.

Figure 2.1. **Non-renewable natural resources revenues, 2014**

USD billion and percentages of GDP

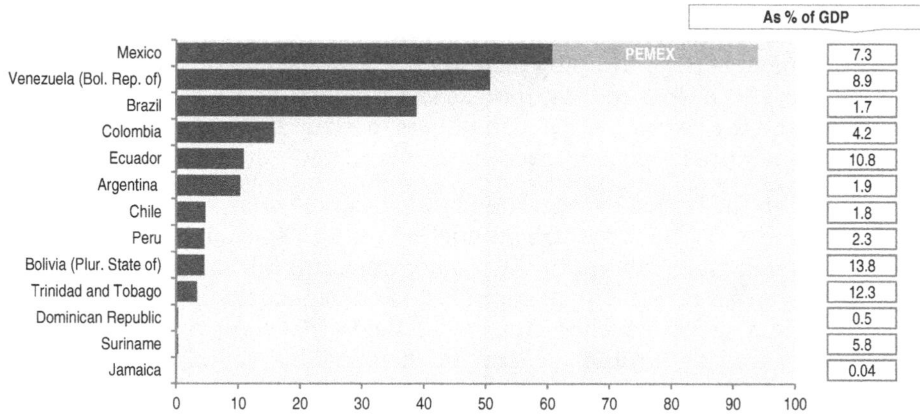

Source: Economic Commission for Latin America and the Caribbean (ECLAC).

StatLink http://dx.doi.org/10.1787/888933337782

Table 2.1. **Public revenues from non-renewable natural resources, by country and commodity, 2013-14**

Percentage of GDP

Country	Total			Hydrocarbons[1]			Mining		
	2013 (r)	2014 (p)	Δ	2013 (r)	2014 (p)	Δ	2013 (r)	2014 (p)	Δ
Argentina	1.8	1.9	0.1	1.7	1.8	0.1	0.1	0.1	0.0
Bolivia (Plur. State of)	14.2	13.8	-0.4	13.5	13.1	-0.4	0.7	0.7	0.0
Brazil	2.2	1.7	-0.5	1.8	1.6	-0.2	0.4	0.1	-0.3
Chile	2.1	1.8	-0.3	..	..	..	2.1	1.8	-0.3
Colombia	5.1	4.2	-1.0	4.8	3.9	-0.9	0.4	0.3	-0.1
Dominican Republic	0.6	0.5	-0.1	..	..	..	0.6	0.5	-0.1
Ecuador	12.1	10.8	-1.3	12.1	10.8	-1.3	..	..	..
Jamaica	0.1	0.0	-0.1	..	..	..	0.1	0.0	-0.1
Mexico	8.0	7.3	-0.8	7.8	7.0	-0.8	0.2	0.2	0.0
Peru	2.8	2.3	-0.5	1.9	1.6	-0.3	0.9	0.7	-0.3
Suriname	6.2	5.8	-0.4	5.5	5.0	-0.6	0.6	0.9	0.2
Trinidad and Tobago	11.7	12.3	0.5	11.7	12.3	0.5	..	..	..
Venezuela (Bol. Rep. of)	12.2	8.9	-3.3	12.2	8.9	-3.3	..	..	..
Latin America and the Caribbean	**6.1**	**5.5**	**-0.6**	**7.3**	**6.6**	**-0.7**	**0.6**	**0.5**	**-0.1**

1. Hydrocarbons includes revenues from upstream (exploration and production) and downstream (refining and commercialization) activities.

Note: (r) and (p) refer to "revised" and "preliminary", respectively. Figures may not add due to rounding. Regional averages of hydrocarbon and mining revenues do not sum to the regional average of total non-renewable natural resources revenues as each represents a simple average of available data.

Source: Economic Commission for Latin America and the Caribbean (ECLAC).

StatLink http://dx.doi.org/10.1787/888933337575

Hydrocarbons

Trends in hydrocarbon-related revenues in 2014 were strongly marked by developments in the global oil market. International oil prices fell by roughly 50% between June and the end of the year, reaching levels last seen in the depths of the global economic and financial crisis of 2009.[2] Nevertheless, for the year as a whole the decline was a more modest 7.5%. At the global level this dynamic was driven by both demand and supply factors. In the first case, growth in global oil consumption slumped in 2014, relative to 2013, reflecting declining consumption in OECD countries as well as muted growth in consumption in emerging markets (IEA, 2015). In the second case, key factors include the surprising increase in OPEC production during the year, bolstered by a recovery in output in Iraq; increased non-OPEC production, especially in the United States; and the decision of OPEC members to maintain production despite the emergence of an imbalance in global supply and demand (IMF, 2015a).

Within the region hydrocarbon production registered relatively little change in 2014 with respect to 2013. Crude oil production rose 0.4%, though with significant divergence among countries (Table 2.2). Output continued to fall in a number of major producers – namely Argentina (1.3%), Mexico (3.7%) and Venezuela (Bolivarian Republic of) (3.8%) – reflecting a secular decline from older fields that have passed their peak production levels as well as limited investment in preceding years. In Colombia the dip (2.0%) was largely due to lower production by EcoPetrol, the largest operator in the country, whose output was impacted by blockades that delayed work as well as a number of infrastructure related limitations (EcoPetrol, 2015). In contrast, oil output rose sharply in Brazil (11.4%) and Ecuador (5.7%) as production ramped up following significant investment, especially in Brazil.

Table 2.2. **Hydrocarbon production, by country, 2013-14**

Thousands of barrels daily and billions of cubic meters

Country	Crude oil (thousand barrels daily)			Marketed natural gas (Billions cubic meters)		
	2013	2014	%	2013	2014	Δ
Argentina	525	519	-1.3	36. 9	36. 9	-0.1
Bolivia (Plur. State of)	n.a.	n.a.	..	20. 5	21.1	3.0
Brazil	2 024	2 255	11.4	19.	20.4	7.0
Colombia	1 008	988	-2.0	10. 2	10.0	-2.0
Ecuador	526	557	5.7	0.5	0.6	12.2
Mexico	2 522	2 429	-3.7	52. 4	50.5	-3.6
Peru	63	69	10.4	11. 6	12.9	11.1
Suriname	17	17	1.2	n.a.	n.a.	..
Trinidad and Tobago	81	81	0.0	42. 8	42. 1	-1.8
Venezuela (Bol. Rep. of)	2 789	2 683	-3.8	21. 8	21. 9	0.3
Latin America and the Caribbean	**9 556**	**9 597**	**0.4**	**215. 8**	**216. 2**	**0.2**

Source: Economic Commission for Latin America and the Caribbean (ECLAC), based on OPEC (2015) and Staatsolie (2014, 2015).

StatLink http://dx.doi.org/10.1787/888933337586

Natural gas production rose only marginally in 2014 (0.2%), reflecting a mix of declining output among major producers and strong growth among smaller producers (Table 2.2). Gas production among the three largest producers in the region – Argentina, Mexico and Trinidad and Tobago – continued to show little dynamism in 2014. In Bolivia (Plurinational State of) and Brazil production increased, but at much lower growth rates than in previous years (with 2010-13 average annual growth of 12.9% and 16.7%, respectively). Gas production rebounded in Peru (11.1%), after posting a decline in 2013.

As a result of these trends, public revenues from hydrocarbons gave ground in 2014, falling on average 0.7 percentage points of GDP in 2014 (Table 2.3). At the regional level this decline was centred on non-tax revenues, which are predominately composed of royalties and dividends paid by state oil companies to their governments. Tax revenues, in contrast, held relatively stable relative to GDP, reflecting to some extent one-off increases in Trinidad and Tobago and Venezuela (Bolivarian Republic of). Nevertheless, there was significant variation among countries, reflecting differences in exchange rates, production volumes, production costs and other country specific factors.

Table 2.3. **Public revenues from hydrocarbons, by country and type of revenue, 2013-14**

Percentage of GDP

Country	Total			Tax revenues			Non-tax revenues		
	2013 (r)	2014 (p)	Δ	2013 (r)	2014 (p)	Δ	2013 (r)	2014 (p)	Δ
Argentina	1.7	1.8	0.1	1.3	1.4	0.1	0.4	0.4	0.0
Bolivia (Plur. State of)	13.5	13.1	-0.4	9.4	9.2	-0.2	4.1	3.9	-0.2
Brazil	1.8	1.6	-0.2	0.9	0.9	0.0	1.0	0.7	-0.3
Colombia	4.8	3.9	-0.9	1.7	1.4	-0.3	3.0	2.5	-0.5
Ecuador	12.1	10.8	-1.3	0.0	0.0	0.0	12.1	10.8	-1.3
Mexico	7.8	7.0	-0.8	4.8	4.5	-0.4	3.0	2.6	-0.4
Peru	1.9	1.6	-0.3	0.9	0.8	-0.1	1.0	0.8	-0.2
Suriname	5.5	5.0	-0.6	2.6	2.3	-0.3	2.9	2.6	-0.3
Trinidad and Tobago	11.7	12.3	0.5	9.8	10.9	1.1	1.9	1.4	-0.5
Venezuela (Bol. Rep. of)	12.2	8.9	-3.3	1.2	2.0	0.8	11.0	6.9	-4.0
Latin America and the Caribbean	**7.3**	**6.6**	**-0.7**	**3.3**	**3.3**	**0.1**	**4.0**	**3.3**	**-0.8**

Note: (r) and (p) refer to "revised" and "preliminary", respectively. Tax revenues refer to corporate income taxes (Argentina, Bolivia (Plurinational State of), Brazil (Petrobras), Colombia, Peru, Suriname (Staatsolie), Trinidad and Tobago and Venezuela (Bolivarian Republic of)), export duties (Argentina), excise taxes on hydrocarbon production (Bolivia (Plurinational State of) and Mexico) and excise taxes on hydrocarbon products (Argentina, Bolivia (Plurinational State of), Brazil, Colombia, Mexico and Peru). Non-tax revenues principally refer to production levies and dividends (Argentina: national and subnational royalties; Bolivia (Plurinational State of): royalties; Brazil: royalties, special state participation, signing bonuses, occupation and retention fees and dividends from Petrobras; Colombia: royalties and dividends from EcoPetrol; Ecuador: non-financial public sector revenues from export sales of petroleum; Mexico: PEMEX revenues; Peru: royalties; Suriname: dividends from Staatsolie; Trinidad and Tobago: royalties; and Venezuela (Bolivarian Republic of): royalties, dividends from PDVSA and extraordinary non-tax petroleum revenues.) Figures may not add due to rounding.
Source: Economic Commission for Latin America and the Caribbean (ECLAC).

StatLink http://dx.doi.org/10.1787/888933337594

Argentina was one of two countries in the region that saw an increase in hydrocarbon revenues during the year. Tax revenues rose (0.1 percentage points of GDP) following strong growth in the excise tax on fuels, which made up roughly half of total hydrocarbon revenues. Exploration and production related tax revenues grew in line with GDP, with higher corporate income tax receipts offsetting a decline in those from export duties. In the latter falling export volumes (10%) and a reduction in the tax rate for periods when the international price of crude oil is below USD 80 a barrel contributed to the decline. Non-tax revenues, principally comprising royalties, surged in nominal terms as a result of a nearly 50% devaluation of the Argentine peso, but held steady as a share of GDP.

In the Plurinational State of Bolivia, hydrocarbon revenues fell relative to GDP (0.4 percentage points of GDP) as production slowed and the country's currency, which maintains a crawling peg to the US dollar, registered no year-on-year change in value.

Tax revenues declined modestly (0.2 percentage points of GDP), with a rise in corporate income tax payments offsetting relatively stagnant receipts, in absolute terms, from the Direct Tax on Hydrocarbons. Non-tax revenues, which include royalties and the national government's participation in profits, likewise registered a decline in relative terms (0.2 percentage points of GDP).

Rising oil and gas production in Brazil, as well as a 9% depreciation of the Real, softened the blow of lower prices on hydrocarbon revenues, which registered a smaller than average decline of 0.2 percentage points of GDP in 2014. The year was marked, however, by the revelation that Petrobras, the country's principal producer, was involved in a large-scale corruption scandal. Tax revenues largely held steady, with a strong gain in receipts of the ICMS on fuels offsetting a decline in corporate income tax payments by Petrobras. The fall in non-tax revenues (0.3 percentage points of GDP) was largely due to the comparison with an exceptionally high level in 2013 caused by signing bonus revenues associated with the pre-sale oil concession auction held in October of that year. Revenues from royalties and the State's special participation in sales revenues, which together represented roughly 40% of total hydrocarbon revenues, rose in line with higher production volumes.

Falling prices and production volumes weighed on hydrocarbon revenues in Colombia, which fell 0.9 percentage points of GDP. The decline in tax revenues (0.3 percentage points of GDP) resulted from a near 20% decline in corporate tax payments by the sector. Non-tax revenues fell sharply (0.5 percentage points of GDP) due to an 18% reduction in dividend payments by EcoPetrol, which accounted for nearly 40% of hydrocarbon revenues in 2014. In dollarised Ecuador, oil revenues fell sharply (1.3 percentage points of GDP) despite rising production (5.7%) and export (10.3%) volumes.

Hydrocarbon revenues in Mexico fell in line with the regional average (0.8 percentage points of GDP), as prices and production volumes fell. Tax revenues fell 0.4 percentage points of GDP primarily due to a sharp decline in the federal government's participation in the market value of production. This was offset to some extent by a reduction in the fiscal drag associated with the Special Production and Services Tax (IEPS) on gasoline and diesel – which serves as a subsidy depending on international prices levels (from -0.5% of GDP in 2013 to -0.1% of GDP in 2014). Non-tax revenues comprising PEMEX's revenues dropped 0.4 percentage points of GDP as a result of falling production volumes, rising production costs and the weaker price from Mexican crude oil (PEMEX, 2015).

In Peru, hydrocarbon revenues dipped (0.3 percentage points of GDP) despite solid gains in natural gas production (11.1%). Tax revenues registered a slight decline (0.1 percentage points of GDP) in 2014, as strong corporate income tax payments – especially in the first half of the year – were offset by a decline in revenues from the excise tax on fuels. Non-tax revenues, comprising entirely of royalties, dropped 0.2 percentage points of GDP reflecting declining prices and a relatively modest, as compared to its peers, depreciation of the Nuevo Sol. Revenues in Suriname also dropped (0.6 percentage points of GDP) as corporate income tax payments and dividends of Staatsolie, the state-owned oil firm, declined.

Oil and gas revenues in Trinidad and Tobago, in contrast with the region's other producers, registered a modest increase (0.5 percentage points of GDP). This was largely due to a strong rise in tax revenues (1.1 percentage points of GDP) thanks to a one-off boost in corporate income tax receipts as the government liquidated outstanding petroleum subsidies to Petrotrin, the state-owned oil firm, which in turn had been delaying its tax payments (Government of the Republic of Trinidad and Tobago, 2014). Non-tax revenues, principally royalties on oil and dividends from state-owned energy companies, fell in line with lower prices and stagnant production (0.5 percentage points of GDP).

The Bolivarian Republic of Venezuela registered the most significant decline in hydrocarbon revenue in the region, relative to GDP, during 2014, falling 3.3 percentage points of GDP. A sharp decline in so-called extraordinary non-tax revenues – whose composition is largely unknown – was largely responsible for this result, pulling down overall non-tax revenues by 4.0 percentage points of GDP. Tax revenues proved to be more buoyant, rising 0.8 percentage points of GDP, boosted by a largely one-off surge in corporate income tax payments by Petróleos de Venezuela S.A. stemming from the devaluation of the currency in 2013 and the sale of a 40% stake in its newly created gold mining subsidiary to the Central Bank (PDVSA, 2015).

Mining

The decline in mining revenues in Latin America and the Caribbean, as in the case of those stemming from hydrocarbons, can largely be attributed to a continuing decline in commodities prices. The minerals and metals price index of the CEPALSTAT database reveals that the decline in prices for the region's principal minerals and metal commodities intensified in 2014, falling 10.6% compared to a drop of 6.2% in 2013.[3] Demand-side factors continued to dominate international prices, in particular owing to the economic slowdown in East Asia. Between 2002 and 2014, China alone was the principal driver of growth in the global consumption of base metals. By 2014 that country accounted for half of global base metal consumption (IMF, 2015b). Unsurprisingly, the IMF (2015b) suggests that 60% of the variance in international base metals prices can be explained by fluctuations in China's industrial production.

Supply-side factors played a secondary role in determining the prices of minerals and metals. While rapid growth in East Asia during the 2000s boosted prices and stimulated significant investment, the long lag times from concept to actual production meant that many new projects were only beginning to come online in recent years. There were sizable increases in mine production in Bolivia (Plurinational State of) (zinc), Brazil (iron ore), Chile (silver), Colombia (coal), Dominican Republic (gold), Mexico (copper, zinc, coal) and Peru (lead, silver) (Table 2.4). In the Dominican Republic the increase in gold production (36.6%) was due to the ramping up of operations of a new gold mine in the country. Likewise, in Chile the rise in silver production (33.9%) was a result of the commencement of operations at Codelco's new Ministro Hales mine.

Table 2.4. Minerals and metals prices and production, by selected commodities and countries, 2013-14

Thousands of metric tons, thousands of kilograms and percentages

Minerals and metals	Market price (2014-2013%)	Country	MIne production		
			2013	2014	%
Copper (TMT)	-6.3	Chile	5 851.1	5 793.1	-1.0
		Mexico	409.2	452.4	10.6
		Peru	1 375.6	1 379.6	0.3
Iron ore (TMT)	-26.7	Brazil	316.8	345.8	9.2
Silver (TKg)	-20.0	Bolivia (Plur. State of)	1 287.0	1 341.0	4.2
		Chile	1 173.8	1 571.8	33.9
		Mexico	4 860.9	4 729.4	-2.7
		Peru	3 674.3	3 777.8	2.8
Zinc (TMT)	13.1	Bolivia (Plur. State of)	407.3	445.7	9.4
		Mexico	420.9	449.1	6.7
		Peru	1 351.3	1 318.7	-2.4
Bauxite (TMT)	1.1	Jamaica	9 573.4	9 579.4	0.1
Tin (TMT)	-1.8	Bolivia (Plur. State of)	19.3	19.8	2.6
		Brazil	23.7	23.1	-2.4
		Peru	43.0	42.9	-0.2
Lead (TMT)	-7.1	Bolivia (Plur. State of)	82.1	76.0	-7.5
		Mexico	200.4	196.7	-1.8
		Peru	266.5	278.5	4.5
Gold (TKg)	5.3	Chile	51.3	46.0	-10.3
		Colombia	55.7	57.0	2.3
		Dominican Republic	13.8	18.9	36.6
		Mexico	98.0	98.2	0.2
		Peru	151.5	140.0	-7.6
		Suriname	10.0	9.7	-3.4
Coal (TMT)	-17.1	Colombia	85 496.0	88 578.0	3.6
		Mexico	13 065.4	13 435.0	2.8

Note: TMT = thousand metric tons; TKg = thousand kilograms. Market price refers to change in annual monthly average prices.

Source: Economic Commission for Latin America and the Caribbean (ECLAC), based on data from CEPALstat (prices), Ministry of Economy and Public Finances of the Plurinational State of Bolivia (2015), DNPM (2014, 2015), Ministry of Mining of Chile (2015), Ministry of Mines and Energy of Colombia (2015), Barrick Gold (2015), Jamaica Bauxite Institute (2015), INEGI (2015), Ministry of Energy and Mines of Peru (2014, 2015) and IAMGOLD (2015).

StatLink http://dx.doi.org/10.1787/888933337608

Mining revenues in the region continued to fall in 2014, though to a lesser extent than in 2013 (0.1 percentage points of GDP compared to -0.4 percentage points). A decrease in tax revenues was largely responsible for the overall decline, falling by 0.1 percentage points of GDP on average (Table 2.5). Corporate income tax receipts were particularly impacted, reflecting shrinking profit margins due to lower revenues and rising operating costs. Non-tax revenues – principally royalty payments – held steady as rising production and currency depreciations offset declines in prices.

Table 2.5. **Public revenues from mining, by country and type of revenue, 2013-14**

Percentage of GDP

Country	Total			Tax revenues			Non-tax revenues		
	2013 (r)	2014 (p)	Δ	2013 (r)	2014 (p)	Δ	2013 (r)	2014 (p)	Δ
Argentina	0.1	0.1	0.0	0.1	0.1	0.0	0.0	0.0	0.0
Bolivia (Plur. State of)	0.7	0.7	0.0	0.2	0.1	-0.1	0.5	0.6	0.1
Brazil	0.4	0.1	-0.3	0.3	0.0	-0.3	0.1	0.0	0.0
Chile	2.1	1.8	-0.3	1.8	1.6	-0.2	0.3	0.3	0.0
Colombia	0.4	0.3	-0.1	0.2	0.1	-0.1	0.2	0.2	0.0
Dominican Republic	0.6	0.5	-0.1	0.6	0.4	-0.1	0.1	0.1	0.0
Jamaica	0.1	0.0	-0.1	0.0	0.0	0.0	0.1	0.0	-0.1
Mexico	0.2	0.2	0.0	0.2	0.2	0.0	0.0	0.0	0.0
Peru	0.9	0.7	-0.3	0.7	0.5	-0.2	0.2	0.2	0.0
Suriname	0.6	0.9	0.2	0.1	0.4	0.3	0.5	0.5	-0.1
Latin America and the Caribbean	**0.6**	**0.5**	**-0.1**	**0.4**	**0.3**	**-0.1**	**0.2**	**0.2**	**0.0**

Note: (r) and (p) refer to "revised" and "preliminary", respectively. Tax revenues refer to corporate income taxes (Argentina, Bolivia (Plurinational State of), Brazil (Vale), Chile, Colombia, Dominican Republic, Mexico, Jamaica, Peru and Suriname (IAMGOLD)), export duties (Argentina; Chile: Impuesto Ley N°13.196) and other sector specific taxes (Chile: specific tax on mining; Dominican Republic: annual minimum mining tax and net mining profits tax; Peru: special mining tax (IEM)). Non-tax revenues principally refer to production levies (Bolivia (Plurinational State of): royalties; Brazil: CFEM (Financial Compensation for the Exploration of Mineral Resources), TAH (Taxa Anual por Hectare) and the TFRM (Taxa de fiscalizacao de recursos minerarios) in Minas Gerais; Chile: dividends from CODELCO; Colombia: royalties; Dominican Republic: net smelter royalty; Jamaica: bauxite levy and bauxite royalties; Mexico: mining duties; Peru: royalties and GEM (Gravámen Especial a la Minería); Suriname: royalties (IAMGOLD)). Figures may not add due to rounding.

Source: Economic Commission for Latin America and the Caribbean (ECLAC).

StatLink http://dx.doi.org/10.1787/888933337617

In Argentina mining revenues registered little change relative to GDP in 2014. While corporate income tax payments by the sector fell sharply (30%), this was largely compensated for by a rise in export duty receipts (52.2%) in line with the devaluation of the currency and the introduction of a new optional special prepayment regime. Likewise, overall mining receipts in the Plurinational State of Bolivia changed little relative to GDP during the year, with a decline in tax revenues – caused by a 52% decline in corporate tax payments – being offset by an increase in non-tax revenues associated with greater mine production.

The sharp decline in the price of iron ore (26.7%) significantly impacted mining revenues in Brazil, which fell 0.3 percentage points of GDP in 2014. Tax revenues declined due to lower corporate tax payments, reflecting both a decline in the sector's profits, but also the exceptionally high level in 2013 when Vale S.A. made a significant one-off payment as a result of a settlement with the Brazilian government. Non-tax revenues slid in line with the price of iron ore, with receipts from the Financial Compensation for the Exploration of Mineral Resources (CFEM, a royalty) declining 28%.

In Chile, a sharp contraction in mining tax revenues (0.2 percentage points of GDP) drove overall mining revenues down. In particular, tax payments by Codelco, the state-owned mining company, fell markedly, including a 19% decline in corporate income payments and a 36% decline in payments of the specific tax on mining (which is calculated on net income). The company is currently executing a significant investment programme that aims to boost production and lower operating costs, the latter having risen sharply in recent years. Tax revenues from the private-sector, in contrast, posted a more moderate decline, falling 3.2%.

The decline in mining revenues in Colombia (0.1 percentage points of GDP) was caused by a contraction in tax payments by the sector. In particular, corporate income tax receipts more than halved (56%). Non-tax revenues, in contrast, registered little change as a modest rise in coal production –the principal generator of royalty payments – offset lower prices in part. In the Dominican Republic the decline in mining revenues (0.1 percentage points of GDP) was also centred on tax revenues. A sharp decline in the annual minimum mining tax, which is calculated as the difference between the State's minimum participation in mining revenues and current period tax payments by sector, drove the overall trend.

Mining revenues in Jamaica from the bauxite/alumina industry fell to near zero in the 2014 fiscal year, despite a 2.6% increase in production. Non-tax revenues evaporated (0.1 percentage points of GDP) as bauxite levy payments by the sector hit zero as a result of substantial concessions granted by the government. In Mexico, mining revenues held relatively stable relative to GDP in 2014 due to the introduction of the new fiscal regime for the sector enacted in late 2013. Corporate income tax receipts rose 35% as a result of the enlargement of the tax base thanks to a reduction in deduction rates and the repeal of the tax consolidation regime. Mining production duties, which after the reform of 2013 are calculated on net income, fell sharply (52%) as lower prices and higher taxes squeezed profit margins.

In Peru, the decline in mining revenues (0.3 percentage points of GDP) was principally caused by a decrease in tax revenues (0.2 percentage points of GDP). In particular, corporate tax receipts fell 32% over the year. Non-tax revenues registered little change relative to GDP, although royalty payments were down 11% following falling prices and lower production of some minerals and metals (table 4). Suriname was the only country in the region that saw its mining revenues rise in 2014 (0.2 percentage points of GDP). Higher tax revenues (0.3 percentage points of GDP), thanks to an increase in corporate income tax payments of IAMGOLD (Canada), offset a decline in non-tax revenues (0.1 percentage points of GDP).

2.2. Estimated non-renewable natural resources revenues for 2015

ECLAC estimates that public revenues from non-renewable natural resources in Latin America and the Caribbean fell sharply in 2015, relative to GDP, reflecting the continued weakness in international commodities prices. Oil prices, which had fallen sharply in the second half of 2014, continued to give ground in 2015, falling an estimated 47% compared to the average price from the previous year (Figure 2.2). Supply-side factors that drove prices down in 2014, particularly the imbalance between global demand and supply of oil, continued unabated in 2015. Prices of minerals and metals accelerated their decline during the year (23%), with particularly notable decreases for copper (20%) and iron ore (44%), as Chinese demand waned.

Hydrocarbon revenues in Latin America and the Caribbean are estimated to have returned to their pre-boom levels in 2015, falling 2.1 percentage points of GDP on average to 4.5% of GDP (Figure 2.3). A number of countries are projected to have experienced even greater declines that have challenged public finances, including the Bolivia (Plurinational State of) (4.6 percentage points of GDP), Ecuador (3.8), Suriname (2.4), Trinidad and Tobago (4.0) and Venezuela (Bolivarian Republic of) (2.3). Mining revenues likewise are projected to have declined in 2015, but for the majority of the region's producers this latest reduction is likely to have been marginal (on average -0.1 percentage points of GDP). Chile is the lone exception, where the government estimates a decline of 0.5 percentage points of GDP for the year.

In response to these trends, a number of the region's countries enacted policy measures during the year aimed to spur activity in the extractive sector. At the end of 2014 the government of Argentina further modified tax rates for hydrocarbon exports and adopted a new sliding scale for certain hydrocarbon products, including crude oil, to bolster the competitiveness of domestic producers. Under the new system, exporters will pay a rate of only 1% when the price of Brent crude is below USD 79, compared with rates of up to 13% under the regime that had been adopted earlier in 2014. In February, the government announced the creation of the Crude Oil Production Stimulus Program (Programa de Estimulo a la Producción de Petróleo Crudo), through which the federal government will pay production and export subsidies, up to USD 6 per barrel, during the 2015 calendar year.

Figure 2.2. **Commodities price forecasts, 2011-17**

Index 100 = 2005

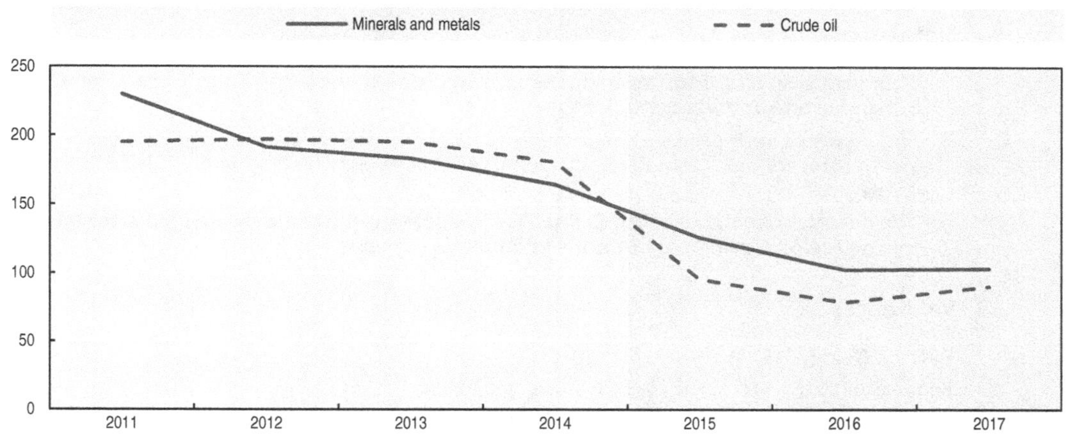

Source: Economic Commission for Latin America and the Caribbean (ECLAC), based on data from IMF (2015c).

StatLink http://dx.doi.org/10.1787/888933337797

Figure 2.3. **Non-renewable natural resource revenues, 2000-15**

Percentage of GDP

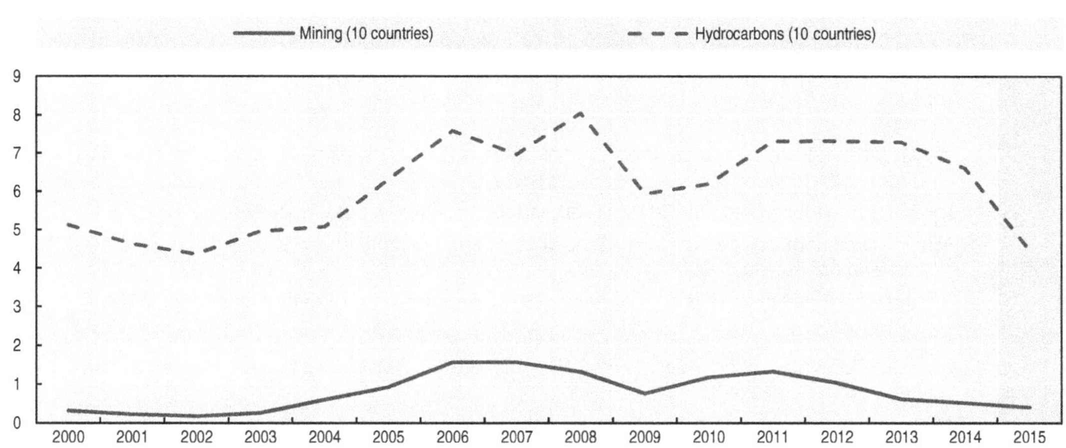

Note: Mining includes: Argentina, Bolivia (Plurinational State of), Brazil, Chile, Colombia, Dominican Republic, Jamaica, Mexico, Peru and Suriname. Hydrocarbons include: Argentina, Bolivia (Plurinational State of), Brazil, Colombia, Ecuador, Mexico, Peru, Suriname, Trinidad and Tobago and Venezuela (Bolivarian Republic of). The values for 2015 are based on available official government estimates from 2016 public budget reports. When official estimates are not available, annual revenues by instrument are estimated using monthly data (for the first three quarters of the year). When monthly data are not available, typically for corporate tax payments by industry, revenues are estimated by applying the year-on-year change for the most representative commodity price for the given revenue instrument expressed in national currency terms to 2014 revenues.

Source: Economic Commission for Latin America and the Caribbean (ECLAC).

StatLink http://dx.doi.org/10.1787/888933337806

The government of Ecuador presented a portfolio of 25 new mining exploration areas as well as 17 oil blocks in October as part of an effort to attract greater investment in exploration and production during the period 2016-20. The Bolivian Chamber of Deputies approved a law creating the Promotion Fund for Investment in Hydrocarbon Exploration in November. The law stipulates that a portion of the revenues generated by the Direct Hydrocarbons Tax (IDH) are to be deposited into the fund to finance investment incentives as a way of promoting greater investment and increasing the country's reserves and production of hydrocarbons.

Notes

1. This year's Special Feature includes four additional countries (Dominican Republic, Jamaica, Suriname and Trinidad and Tobago).
2. For example, spot prices – the prevailing market price for current transactions – of WTI (West Texas Intermediate) and Brent crude fell 48% between the last week of June 2014 and the end of the year.
3. The overall price index of the CEPALSTAT database is a trade weighted (2010 base year) of prices for the region's principal minerals and metals exports.

References

Barrick Gold (2015), *Annual Report 2014*.

Ecopetrol (2015), SEC form 20-F for fiscal year 2014.

DNPM (2015), *Informe Mineral 2°/2014*, National Department of Mineral Production of Brazil.

DNPM (2014), *Informe Mineral 2°/2013*, National Department of Mineral Production of Brazil.

Government of the Republic of Trinidad and Tobago (2014), *Review of the Economy 2014*.

IAMGOLD (2015), *Annual Report 2014*.

IEA (International Energy Agency) (2015), Oil Market Report, accessed at: https://www.iea.org/oilmarketreport/omrpublic/.

IMF (2015a), "Commodity Special Feature", World Economic Outlook, International Monetary Fund, April.

IMF (2015b), "Commodity Special Feature", World Economic Outlook, International Monetary Fund, October.

IMF (2015c), *Commodity Price Forecasts*, accessed at www.imf.org/external/np/res/commod/index.aspx.

INEGI (2015), Banco de Información Económica (BIE), Instituto Nacional de Estadística y Geografía, accessed at: www.inegi.org.mx/sistemas/bie/.

Jamaica Bauxite Institute (2015), *Total bauxite production data*, accessed at: www.jbi.org.jm/.

Ministry of Economy and Public Finances of the Plurinational State of Bolivia (2015), *Memoria de la economía boliviana 2014*.

Ministry of Energy and Mines of Peru (2015), *Reporte Anual Producción Minera 2014*.

Ministry of Energy and Mines of Peru (2014), *Reporte Anual Producción Minera 2013*.

Ministry of Mines and Energy of Colombia (2015), "Anexos Minas", Memorias al Congreso de la República 2014-2015.

Ministry of Mining of Chile (2015), *Anuario de la minería de Chile 2014*.

OPEC (2015), *Annual Statistical Bulletin 2015*, Organization of the Petroleum Exporting Countries.

PDVSA (2015), *Annual Report 2014*, Petróleos de Venezuela, S.A.

Pemex (2015), SEC form 20-F for fiscal year 2014, Petróleos Mexicanos.

Staatsolie (2015), *Annual Report 2014*.

Staatsolie (2014), *Annual Report 2013*.

SECCIÓN ESPECIAL

Ingresos fiscales provenientes de recursos naturales no renovables en América Latina y el Caribe

SECCIÓN ESPECIAL
Ingresos fiscales provenientes de recursos naturales no renovables en América Latina y el Caribe

Principales conclusiones

Tendencias en ingresos fiscales provenientes de recursos naturales no renovables para 2014

- El pronunciado descenso en los precios internacionales del petróleo provocó en la región una importante rebaja en los ingresos relacionados con los hidrocarburos, que cayeron de un promedio del 7.3% del PIB en 2013 al 6.6% del PIB en 2014. Los ingresos no tributarios se llevaron la peor parte de esta reducción, con un notorio descenso en Ecuador y Venezuela (República Bolivariana de).
- Los ingresos derivados de la minería se vieron igualmente afectados por el descenso en los precios y cayeron al 0.5% del PIB, en promedio, del 0.6% del PIB en 2013. El aumento de la producción minera en algunos países, sumado a las depreciaciones de la moneda, sirvió para estabilizar los ingresos no tributarios. Los ingresos tributarios, derivados principalmente del impuesto sobre la renta o ganancias de sociedades, registraron un gran descenso ante la reducción de los márgenes de beneficio en el sector.

Ingresos estimados provenientes de recursos naturales no renovables para 2015

- Los factores de oferta y demanda que incidieron en los precios de los productos básicos en 2014 se mantuvieron en 2015, intensificando la rebaja en los ingresos provenientes de recursos naturales no renovables de la región. Se estima que los ingresos provenientes de los hidrocarburos han regresado al promedio registrado antes del auge, bajando de un promedio del 6.6% del PIB en 2014 al 4.5% del PIB en 2015. También se estima que los ingresos derivados de la minería han descendido, aunque no en la misma medida (del 0.5% del PIB al 0.4% del PIB).

Los ingresos provenientes de recursos naturales no renovables en esta Sección especial se refieren a ingresos tributarios (impuesto sobre la renta, impuestos específicos del sector y ciertos impuestos indirectos) e ingresos no tributarios (regalías y dividendos pagados por las empresas estatales a sus respectivos gobiernos) derivados de la producción y comercialización de hidrocarburos y de la minería. No incluyen retenciones impositivas ni pagos realizados por empresas en nombre de sus empleados o inversionistas, y tampoco incluyen pagos de impuestos sobre el consumo (específicamente el impuesto sobre el valor añadido, cuando corresponda).

2.1. Tendencias en ingresos fiscales provenientes de recursos naturales no renovables para 2014

Los ingresos provenientes de recursos naturales no renovables en América Latina y el Caribe cayeron tanto en términos absolutos como relativos en 2014 como resultado del fuerte impacto del descenso de los precios internacionales de los "commodities" para varios de los principales productos de la región. Tras aumentar un 10.0% a 263.000 millones de dólares en 2013, en 2014 se redujeron un 9.5% a 238.000 millones de dólares (véase el gráfico 2.1).[1] A nivel regional, el principal impulsor de esta disminución fue el descenso de los ingresos provenientes de los hidrocarburos debido a un colapso en los precios del petróleo en la segunda mitad del año. Los ingresos de la región derivados de la minería también fueron menores, pero este descenso jugó un papel secundario en virtud de su participación relativamente más pequeña en el total de ingresos provenientes de recursos naturales no renovables en la región.

Gráfico 2.1. **Ingresos provenientes de recursos naturales no renovables, 2014**

En miles de millones de dólares y porcentajes del PIB

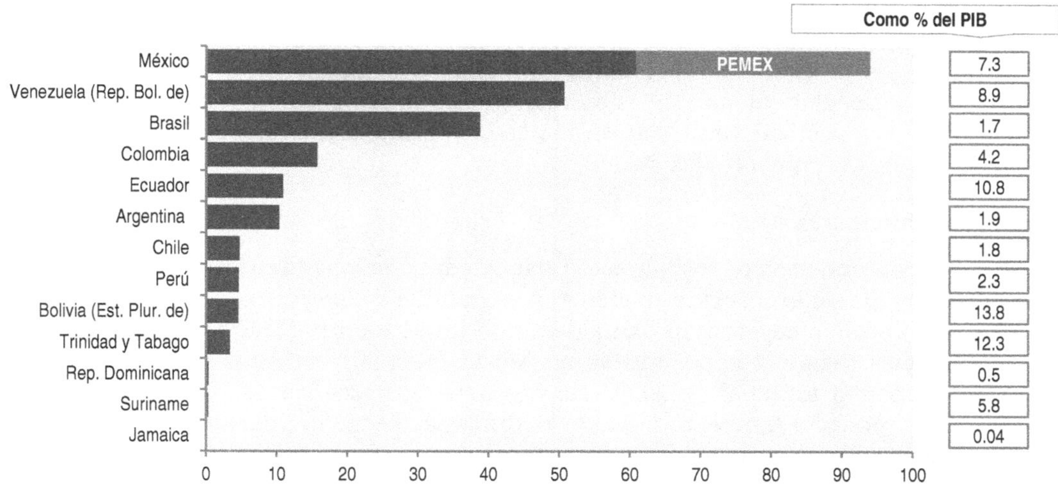

Fuente: Comisión Económica para América Latina y el Caribe (CEPAL).

StatLink http://dx.doi.org/10.1787/888933337812

Cuadro 2.1. **Ingresos públicos provenientes de recursos naturales no renovables, por país y producto básico, 2013-14**

En porcentajes del PIB

País	Total			Hidrocarburos[1]			Minería		
	2013 (r)	2014 (p)	Δ	2013 (r)	2014 (p)	Δ	2013 (r)	2014 (p)	Δ
Argentina	1.8	1.9	0.1	1.7	1.8	0.1	0.1	0.1	0.0
Bolivia (Est. Plur. de)	14.2	13.8	-0.4	13.5	13.1	-0.4	0.7	0.7	0.0
Brasil	2.2	1.7	-0.5	1.8	1.6	-0.2	0.4	0.1	-0.3
Chile	2.1	1.8	-0.3	..	..	..	2.1	1.8	-0.3
Colombia	5.1	4.2	-1.0	4.8	3.9	-0.9	0.4	0.3	-0.1
Ecuador	12.1	10.8	-1.3	12.1	10.8	-1.3	..	..	..
Jamaica	0.1	0.0	-0.1	..	..	..	0.1	0.0	-0.1
México	8.0	7.3	-0.8	7.8	7.0	-0.8	0.2	0.2	0.0
Perú	2.8	2.3	-0.5	1.9	1.6	-0.3	0.9	0.7	-0.3
Republica Dominicana	0.6	0.5	-0.1	..	..	..	0.6	0.5	-0.1
Suriname	6.2	5.8	-0.4	5.5	5.0	-0.6	0.6	0.9	0.2
Trinidad y Tabago	11.7	12.3	0.5	11.7	12.3	0.5	..	..	..
Venezuela (Rep. Bol. de)	12.2	8.9	-3.3	12.2	8.9	-3.3	..	..	..
América Latina y el Caribe	**6.1**	**5.5**	**-0.6**	**7.3**	**6.6**	**-0.7**	**0.6**	**0.5**	**-0.1**

1. Los hidrocarburos incluyen ingresos provenientes de actividades preliminares (exploración y producción) y actividades de ejecución (refinería y comercialización).

Nota: (r) y (p) se refieren a "revisada" y "preliminar", respectivamente. Las cifras pueden no sumar exactamente debido al redondeo. Los promedios regionales de los ingresos derivados de los hidrocarburos y la minería no se suman al promedio regional del total de ingresos provenientes de recursos naturales no renovables, ya que cada uno representa un promedio simple de los datos disponibles.

Fuente: Comisión Económica para América Latina y el Caribe (CEPAL).

StatLink http://dx.doi.org/10.1787/888933337845

A diferencia de lo ocurrido en 2013 (véase la Sección especial del año pasado), en 2014 los ingresos provenientes de recursos naturales no renovables registraron un descenso bastante generalizado en relación al PIB en distintos países (véase el cuadro 2.1). Los ingresos provenientes de los hidrocarburos descendieron en promedio 0.7 puntos porcentuales del PIB, con reducciones mayores al promedio en Colombia, el Ecuador y Venezuela (República Bolivariana de). Los ingresos derivados de la minería cayeron en casi todos los países (0.1 puntos porcentuales del PIB en promedio) a medida que los precios internacionales continuaron bajando de las elevadas cifras de 2011. Los descensos más grandes se registraron en los productores más importantes de la región – el Brasil, Chile y el Perú –, que experimentaron una contracción en torno a los 0.3 puntos porcentuales del PIB.

Hidrocarburos

La tendencia de los ingresos relacionados con los hidrocarburos en 2014 estuvo muy marcadapor lo acaecido en el mercado mundial del petróleo. Los precios internacionales del petróleo cayeron aproximadamente un 50% entre junio y fin de año, y llegaron a niveles registrados por última vez en los peores momentos de la crisis económica y financiera mundial de 2009.[2] No obstante, el descenso de 7.5% para todo el año fue más modesto.A nivel mundial, esta dinámica se vio impulsada por factores tanto de la demanda como de la oferta. En el primer caso, el crecimiento del consumo mundial de petróleo se desplomó en 2014 en comparación con 2013, como consecuencia de la menor demanda en los países de la Organización de Cooperación y Desarrollo Económicos (OCDE) y el lento crecimiento del consumo en los mercados emergentes (AIE, 2015). En el segundo caso, los factores claves incluyeron el sorpresivo incremento de la producción en la Organización de Países Exportadores de Petróleo (OPEC) durante el año, reforzado por la recuperación de la extracción en Iraq; el aumento en la producción de los países que no pertenecen a la OPEP, sobre todo en los Estados Unidos; y la decisión de los países miembros de la OPEP de mantener la producción pese al desequilibrio entre la demanda y la oferta mundial (FMI, 2015a).

Cuadro 2.2. **Producción de hidrocarburos, por país, 2013-14**

En miles de barriles diarios y miles de millones de metros cúbicos

País	Petróleo crudo (Miles barriles por día)			Gas natural comercializado (Mil millones de metros cúbicos)		
	2013	2014	%	2013	2014	Δ
Argentina	525	519	-1.3	36. 9	36. 9	-0.1
Bolivia (Est. Plur. de)	n.a.	n.a.	..	20. 5	21. 1	3.0
Brasil	2 024	2 255	11.4	19.	20. 4	7.0
Colombia	1 008	988	-2.0	10.2	10.0	-2.0
Ecuador	526	557	5.7	0.5	0.6	12.2
México	2 522	2 429	-3.7	52. 4	50. 5	-3.6
Perú	63	69	10.4	11. 6	12. 9	11.1
Suriname	17	17	1.2	n.a.	n.a.	..
Trinidad y Tabago	81	81	0.0	42. 8	42. 1	-1.8
Venezuela (Rep. Bol. de)	2 789	2 683	-3.8	21. 8	21. 9	0.3
América Latina y el Caribe	**9 556**	**9 597**	**0.4**	**215. 8**	**216. 2**	**0.2**

Fuente: Comisión Económica para América Latina y el Caribe (CEPAL), sobre la base de la Organización de Países Exportadores de Petróleo (OPEP, 2015) y Staatsolie (2014, 2015).

StatLink http://dx.doi.org/10.1787/888933337852

En la región, la producción de hidrocarburos registró relativamente pocos cambios en 2014 con respecto a 2013. La producción de petróleo crudo aumentó un 0.4%, aunque con importantes diferencias entre un país y otro (véase el cuadro 2.2). La extracción de varios grandes productores – como la Argentina (1.3%), México (3.7%) y Venezuela (República Bolivariana de) (3.8%) – continuó descendiendo a causa de yacimientos antiguos que han superado sus niveles máximos de producción y las escasas inversiones de los últimos años. En Colombia, el descenso (2.0%) se debió principalmente a una menor producción de EcoPetrol, el principal operador del país, cuyas actividades de extracción se vieron afectadas por bloqueos que demoraron los trabajos, así como por diversas limitaciones relacionadas con la infraestructura (EcoPetrol, 2015). A diferencia de los casos anteriores, la extracción de petróleo registró un marcado incremento en el Brasil (11.4%) y el Ecuador (5.7%) debido a las grandes inversiones realizadas, sobre todo en el primer país.

La producción de gas natural en la región registró un aumento mínimo en 2014 (0.2%) como consecuencia de una mezcla en el descenso de la extracción por parte de los grandes productores y el sólido crecimiento de los productores más pequeños (véase el cuadro 2.2). La producción de gas por parte de los tres productores más grandes de la región (Argentina, México y Trinidad y Tobago) siguió mostrando poco dinamismo en 2014. En Bolivia (Estado Plurinacional de) y Brasil la producción aumentó, pero a tasas mucho más bajas que las de los años anteriores (el crecimiento anual medio en el período 2010-13 fue del 12.9% y el 16.7%, respectivamente). Tras registrar un descenso en 2013, la producción de gas en el Perú se recuperó (11.1%).

Cuadro 2.3. **Ingresos públicos provenientes de los hidrocarburos, por país y tipo de ingreso, 2013-14**

En porcentajes del PIB

País	Total			Ingresos tributarios			Ingresos no tributarios		
	2013 (r)	2014 (p)	Δ	2013 (r)	2014 (p)	Δ	2013 (r)	2014 (p)	Δ
Argentina	1.7	1.8	0.1	1.3	1.4	0.1	0.4	0.4	0.0
Bolivia (Est. Plur. de)	13.5	13.1	-0.4	9.4	9.2	-0.2	4.1	3.9	-0.2
Brasil	1.8	1.6	-0.2	0.9	0.9	0.0	1.0	0.7	-0.3
Colombia	4.8	3.9	-0.9	1.7	1.4	-0.3	3.0	2.5	-0.5
Ecuador	12.1	10.8	-1.3	0.0	0.0	0.0	12.1	10.8	-1.3
México	7.8	7.0	-0.8	4.8	4.5	-0.4	3.0	2.6	-0.4
Perú	1.9	1.6	-0.3	0.9	0.8	-0.1	1.0	0.8	-0.2
Suriname	5.5	5.0	-0.6	2.6	2.3	-0.3	2.9	2.6	-0.3
Trinidad y Tabago	11.7	12.3	0.5	9.8	10.9	1.1	1.9	1.4	-0.5
Venezuela (Rep. Bol. de)	12.2	8.9	-3.3	1.2	2.0	0.8	11.0	6.9	-4.0
América Latina y el Caribe	**7.3**	**6.6**	**-0.7**	**3.3**	**3.3**	**0.1**	**4.0**	**3.3**	**-0.8**

Nota: (r) y (p) se refieren a "revisada" y "preliminar", respectivamente Los ingresos tributarios se refieren a impuestos sobre la renta o ganancias de sociedades (Argentina, Bolivia (Estado Plurinacional de), Brasil (Petrobras), Colombia, Perú, Suriname (Staatsolie), Trinidad y Tobago y Venezuela (Republica Bolivariana de)), derechos de exportación (Argentina), impuestos indirectos sobre la producción de hidrocarburos (Bolivia (Estado Plurinacional de) y México) e impuestos indirectos sobre los productos de hidrocarburos (Argentina, Bolivia (Estado Plurinacional de), Brasil, Colombia, México y Perú). Los ingresos no tributarios se refieren principalmente a dividendos y gravámenes sobre la producción (Argentina: regalías nacionales y subnacionales; Bolivia (Estado Plurinacional de): regalías; Brasil: regalías, participación especial del Estado, bonos de suscripción, tasas de ocupación y retención, y dividendos de Petrobras; Colombia: regalías y dividendos de EcoPetrol; Ecuador: ingresos del sector público no financiero derivados de las ventas de exportación del petróleo; México: ingresos de Petróleos Mexicanos (PEMEX); Perú: regalías; Suriname: dividendos de Staatsolie; Trinidad y Tobago: regalías, y Venezuela (República Bolivariana de): regalías, dividendos de Petróleos de Venezuela, S.A. (PDVSA) e ingresos no tributarios extraordinarios derivados del petróleo.) Las cifras pueden no sumar exactamente debido al redondeo.
Fuente: Comisión Económica para América Latina y el Caribe (CEPAL).

StatLink http://dx.doi.org/10.1787/888933337869

Como resultado de estas tendencias, los ingresos públicos provenientes de los hidrocarburos sufrieron una contracción en 2014 y en promedio cayeron 0.7 puntos porcentuales del PIB (véase el cuadro 2.3). A nivel regional, este descenso se centró en los ingresos no tributarios, que se componen, principalmente, de regalías y dividendos pagados por las empresas petroleras estatales a sus respectivos gobiernos. Los ingresos tributarios, por su parte, se mantuvieron relativamente estables con relación al PIB, a causa, en cierta medida, de incrementos únicos en Trinidad y Tobago y Venezuela (República Bolivariana de). Se registraron, no obstante, importantes variaciones de un país a otro a causa de las diferencias en los tipos de cambio, los volúmenes y costos de producción, y otros factores específicos de cada país.

Argentina de los únicos países de la región que registró un incremento en los ingresos provenientes de los hidrocarburos durante el año. Los ingresos tributarios aumentaron (0.1 puntos porcentuales del PIB) debido al sólido crecimiento del impuesto indirecto a los combustibles, que conformó aproximadamente la mitad del total de los ingresos provenientes de los hidrocarburos. Los ingresos tributarios relacionados con la exploración y la producción aumentaron de conformidad con el PIB, y los ingresos más elevados del impuesto a la renta o ganancias de sociedades compensaron la caída en lo ingresado por los derechos de exportación. En el último caso, la caída de los volúmenes de exportación (10%) y la reducción en el tipo impositivo en períodos en que el precio internacional del petróleo crudo se ubicó por debajo de los 80 dólares el barril contribuyeron al descenso. Los ingresos no tributarios, sobre todo los que comprenden regalías, repuntaron en términos nominales como resultado de una devaluación del peso argentino de casi 50%, pero se mantuvieron constantes como porcentaje del PIB.

En el Estado Plurinacional de Bolivia, los ingresos provenientes de los hidrocarburos se redujeron con relación al PIB (0.4 puntos porcentuales del PIB). Esta reducción se explica por una desaceleración en la producción y a que la moneda del país, que mantiene una paridad móvil con el dólar, no registró una variación interanual en términos de valor. Los ingresos tributarios decrecieron ligeramente con relación al PIB (0.2 puntos porcentuales del PIB), pese a un ligero incremento del impuesto sobre la renta a sociedades que compensó en términos absolutos, la caída del Impuesto Directo a los Hidrocarburos (IDH). Los ingresos no tributarios, que incluyen regalías y la participación del gobierno nacional en los beneficios, también registraron un descenso con relación al PIB (0.2 puntos porcentuales del PIB).

El aumento en la producción de petróleo y gas en Brasil, así como la depreciación del 9% del real, aminoraron el efecto del descenso de precios en los ingresos provenientes de los hidrocarburos, que en 2014 registraron una rebaja inferior al promedio, de 0.2 puntos porcentuales del PIB. El año estuvo marcado, no obstante, por la noticia de que Petrobras, el principal productor del país, estaba involucrado en un gran escándalo de corrupción. Los ingresos tributarios básicamente se mantuvieron estables; la sólida ganancia derivada de los ingresos del impuesto a la circulación de mercaderías y servicios (ICMS) sobre los combustibles compensó el descenso en los pagos de impuesto a la renta o ganancias de las sociedades por parte de Petrobras. La caída de los ingresos no tributarios (0.3 puntos porcentuales del PIB) en gran parte se debió a la comparación con el nivel excepcionalmente alto de 2013 a causa de los ingresos de los bonos de suscripción asociados con la subasta de la concesión petrolera del presal, realizada en octubre de ese año. Los ingresos derivados de regalías y la participación especial del Estado en los ingresos por ventas, que juntos representaron alrededor del 40% del total de ingresos provenientes de los hidrocarburos, aumentaron de conformidad con los mayores volúmenes de producción.

El descenso en los precios y los volúmenes de producción incidió en los ingresos provenientes de los hidrocarburos en Colombia, que bajaron 0.9 puntos porcentuales del PIB. La reducción de los ingresos fiscales (0.3 puntos porcentuales del PIB) se debió a un descenso de casi el 20% en los pagos del impuesto a la renta o ganancias de las sociedades en el sector. Los ingresos no tributarios registraron un marcado descenso (0.5 puntos porcentuales del PIB) debido a una reducción del 18% en los pagos de dividendos por parte de EcoPetrol al gobierno, lo que representó casi el 40% de los ingresos provenientes de los hidrocarburos en 2014. En un Ecuador dolarizado, los ingresos provenientes del petróleo bajaron mucho (1.3 puntos porcentuales del PIB), pese al aumento en los volúmenes de producción (5.7%) y exportación (10.3%).

Los ingresos provenientes de los hidrocarburos en México descendieron de conformidad con el promedio regional (0.8 puntos porcentuales del PIB) en virtud de la rebaja de los precios y los volúmenes de producción. Los ingresos tributarios cayeron 0.4 puntos porcentuales del PIB, principalmente debido a una notoria menor participación del gobierno federal en el valor de mercado de la producción. Esto se vio compensado, en cierta medida, por una reducción de la carga fiscal excesiva asociada al impuesto especial sobre producción y servicios (IEPS) a la gasolina y el diésel, que sirve como subsidio en coyunturas de precios internacionales elevados (del -0.5% del PIB en 2013 al -0.1% del PIB en 2014). Los ingresos no tributarios que incluyen los ingresos de PEMEX (Petróleos Mexicanos) se redujeron 0.4 puntos porcentuales del PIB como consecuencia del descenso de los volúmenes de producción, el incremento de los costos de producción y el menor precio del petróleo mexicano (PEMEX, 2015).

En Perú, los ingresos provenientes de los hidrocarburos bajaron (0.3 puntos porcentuales del PIB), pese a las sólidas ganancias en la producción de gas natural (11.1%). Los ingresos tributarios registraron un leve descenso (0.1 puntos porcentuales del PIB) en 2014, al tiempo que los fuertes pagos del impuesto a la renta o ganancias de las sociedades – sobre todo en la primera mitad del año – compensaron por una baja en los ingresos provenientes del impuesto indirecto a los combustibles. Los ingresos no tributarios, enteramente compuestos de regalías, cayeron 0.2 puntos porcentuales del PIB a causa del descenso de precios y una relativamente modesta depreciación del nuevo sol, en comparación a otros países de la región. Los ingresos también bajaron en Suriname (0,6 puntos porcentuales del PIB) al reducirse los pagos del impuesto a la renta o ganancias de las sociedades y dividendos de Staatsolie, la empresa petrolera estatal.

En Trinidad y Tobago, a diferencia de lo ocurrido con los otros productores de la región, los ingresos provenientes del petróleo y el gas en 2014 registraron un modesto ascenso (0.5 puntos porcentuales del PIB). Principalmente, esto se debió al notorio aumento en los ingresos tributarios (1.1 puntos porcentuales del PIB) gracias a un impulso único en los ingresos del impuesto a la renta o ganancias de las sociedades cuando el gobierno liquidó los subsidios de petróleo pendientes a Petrotrin, la empresa petrolera estatal, que, a su vez, estaba atrasada en el pago de impuestos (Gobierno de la República de Trinidad y Tobago, 2014). La reducción de los ingresos no tributarios, principalmente regalías sobre el petróleo y dividendos de empresas estatales de energía, se mantuvo en línea con una caída en los precios mundiales del petróleo y un estancamiento de la producción (0.5 puntos porcentuales del PIB).

La República Bolivariana de Venezuela registró el descenso más importante en los ingresos provenientes de los hidrocarburos, en relación con el PIB, en la región durante 2014, con una caída de 3.3 puntos porcentuales del PIB. El marcado descenso en los denominados ingresos no tributarios extraordinarios (cuya composición es ampliamente desconocida) fue, en gran parte, responsable de este resultado e hizo que los ingresos no tributarios globales bajaran 4.0 puntos porcentuales del PIB. Los ingresos tributarios se mostraron más activos y aumentaron 0.8 puntos porcentuales del PIB, impulsados en gran parte por un alza única en los pagos del impuesto a la renta o ganancias de las sociedades por parte de Petróleos de Venezuela S.A. como consecuencia de la devaluación de la moneda en 2013 y de la venta al Banco Central de una participación del 40% en su filial de minería de oro recién creada (PDVSA, 2015).

Minería

El descenso de los ingresos derivados de la minería en América Latina y el Caribe, como en el caso de aquellos que provienen de los hidrocarburos, en gran medida puede atribuirse a una continua rebaja en los precios de los "commodities". El índice de precios de minerales y metales de la base de datos CEPALSTAT da cuenta de que los precios para los principales productos básicos de metales y minerales de la región han intensificado su descenso en 2014 y se han reducido un 10.6% en comparación con la rebaja del 6.2% verificada en 2013.[3] Los precios internacionales siguieron estando dominados por factores vinculados a la demanda, en especial la desaceleración económica en Asia oriental. Entre 2002 y 2014, China sola fue el principal promotor del crecimiento del consumo global de metales comunes. En 2014, el país representaba la mitad del consumo mundial de metales comunes (FMI, 2015b). No resulta sorprendente que el FMI (2015b) indique que el 60% de la diferencia en los precios internacionales de los metales comunes pueda explicarse por las fluctuaciones en la producción industrial de China.

Los factores vinculados a la oferta jugaron un papel secundario en la determinación de los precios de los minerales y los metales. Mientras que el rápido crecimiento de Asia oriental en la década de 2000 hizo aumentar los precios y estimuló grandes inversiones, los extensos tiempos que van desde la idea hasta la producción real han supuesto que muchos nuevos proyectos solo se hayan comenzado a concretar en los últimos años. Se registraron cuantiosos aumentos en la producción minera tanto en Bolivia (Estado Plurinacional de) (zinc), como en el Brasil (mineral de hierro), Chile (plata), Colombia (carbón), México (cobre, zinc, carbón), el Perú (plomo, plata) y la República Dominicana (oro) (véase el cuadro 2.4). El aumento en la producción de oro en la República Dominicana (36.6%) se debió al refuerzo de las operaciones de una nueva mina de oro en el país. De modo similar, el incremento de la producción de plata en Chile (33.9%) fue consecuencia del inicio de las operaciones en la nueva mina Ministro Hales de Codelco.

Los ingresos derivados de la minería en la región continuaron cayendo en 2014, aunque en una proporción más pequeña que en 2013 (0.1 puntos porcentuales del PIB frente a 0.4 puntos porcentuales). La rebaja en los ingresos tributarios explica en gran medida el descenso global, con una reducción de 0.1 puntos porcentuales del PIB en promedio (véase el cuadro 2.5). Los ingresos del impuesto a la renta o ganancias de las sociedades se vieron especialmente afectados a causa de un estrechamiento de los márgenes de beneficio debido a los menores ingresos y los crecientes costos operativos. Los ingresos no tributarios – principalmente pagos de regalías – se mantuvieron constantes, en tanto las crecientes depreciaciones de la moneda y el incremento de la producción compensaron los descensos de los precios.

Cuadro 2.4. Precios y producción de minerales y metales, por productos básicos y países seleccionados, 2013-14

En miles de toneladas métricas, miles de kilogramos y porcentajes

Minerales y metales	Precio de mercado (2014-2013 %)	País	Producción minera		
			2013	2014	%
Cobre (MTM)	-6.3	Chile	5 851.1	5 793.1	-1.0
		México	409.2	452.4	10.6
		Perú	1 375.6	1 379.6	0.3
Mineral de hierro (MTM)	-26.7	Brasil	316.8	345.8	9.2
Plata (MKg)	-20.0	Bolivia (Est. Plur. de)	1 287.0	1 341.0	4.2
		Chile	1 173.8	1 571.8	33.9
		México	4 860.9	4 729.4	-2.7
		Perú	3 674.3	3 777.8	2.8
Zinc (MTM)	13.1	Bolivia (Est. Plur. de)	407.3	445.7	9.4
		México	420.9	449.1	6.7
		Perú	1 351.3	1 318.7	-2.4
Bauxita (MTM)	1.1	Jamaica	9 573.4	9 579.4	0.1
Estaño (MTM)	-1.8	Bolivia (Est. Plur. de)	19.3	19.8	2.6
		Brasil	23.7	23.1	-2.4
		Perú	43.0	42.9	-0.2
Plomo (MTM)	-7.1	Bolivia (Est. Plur. de)	82.1	76.0	-7.5
		México	200.4	196.7	-1.8
		Perú	266.5	278.5	4.5
Oro (MKg)	5.3	Chile	51.3	46.0	-10.3
		Colombia	55.7	57.0	2.3
		México	13.8	18.9	36.6
		Perú	98.0	98.2	0.2
		República Dominicana	151.5	140.0	-7.6
		Suriname	10.0	9.7	-3.4
Carbón (MTM)	-17.1	Colombia	85 496.0	88 578.0	3.6
		México	13 065.4	13 435.0	2.8

Nota: MTM = miles de toneladas métricas; MKg = miles de kilogramos. "Precio de mercado" hace referencia al cambio en los precios medios mensuales anuales.
Fuente: Comisión Económica para América Latina y el Caribe (CEPAL), sobre la base de datos CEPALstat (precios), Ministerio de Economía y Finanzas Públicas del Estado Plurinacional de Bolivia (2015), Departamento Nacional de Producción Mineral del Brasil (DNPM) (2014, 2015), Ministerio de Minería de Chile (2015), Ministerio de Minas y Energía de Colombia (2015), Barrick Gold (2015), Jamaica Bauxite Institute (2015), Instituto Nacional de Estadística y Geografía de México (INEGI) (2015), Ministerio de Energía y Minas del Perú (2014, 2015) e IAMGOLD (2015).

StatLink http://dx.doi.org/10.1787/888933337879

Cuadro 2.5. **Ingresos públicos derivados de la minería, por país y tipo de ingreso, 2013-14**

En porcentajes del PIB

País	Total			Ingresos tributarios			Ingresos no tributarios		
	2013 (r)	2014 (p)	Δ	2013 (r)	2014 (p)	Δ	2013 (r)	2014 (p)	Δ
Argentina	0.1	0.1	0.0	0.1	0.1	0.0	0.0	0.0	0.0
Bolivia (Est. Plur. de)	0.7	0.7	0.0	0.2	0.1	-0.1	0.5	0.6	0.1
Brasil	0.4	0.1	-0.3	0.3	0.0	-0.3	0.1	0.0	0.0
Chile	2.1	1.8	-0.3	1.8	1.6	-0.2	0.3	0.3	0.0
Colombia	0.4	0.3	-0.1	0.2	0.1	-0.1	0.2	0.2	0.0
República Dominicana	0.6	0.5	-0.1	0.6	0.4	-0.1	0.1	0.1	0.0
Jamaica	0.1	0.0	-0.1	0.0	0.0	0.0	0.1	0.0	-0.1
México	0.2	0.2	0.0	0.2	0.2	0.0	0.0	0.0	0.0
Perú	0.9	0.7	-0.3	0.7	0.5	-0.2	0.2	0.2	0.0
Suriname	0.6	0.9	0.2	0.1	0.4	0.3	0.5	0.5	-0.1
América Latina y el Caribe	**0.6**	**0.5**	**-0.1**	**0.4**	**0.3**	**-0.1**	**0.2**	**0.2**	**0.0**

Nota: (r) y (p) se refieren a "revisada" y "preliminar", respectivamente Los ingresos tributarios se refieren a impuestos de sociedades (Argentina, Bolivia (Estado Plurinacional de), Brasil (Vale), Chile, Colombia, México, Jamaica, Perú, República Dominicana y Suriname (IAMGOLD)), derechos de exportación (Argentina; Chile: Impuesto Ley N°13.196) y otros impuestos específicos del sector (Chile: impuesto específico a la minería; Perú: impuesto especial a la minería (IEM); República Dominicana: impuesto mínimo anual minero e impuesto a los beneficios netos de la minería). Los ingresos no tributarios se refieren principalmente a gravámenes sobre la producción (Bolivia (Estado Plurinacional de): regalías; Brasil: Compensación Financiera por la Exploración de Recursos Minerales (CFEM), Tasa Anual por Hectárea (TAH) y tasa de fiscalización de recursos minerales (TFRM) en Minas Gerais; Chile: dividendos de CODELCO; Colombia: regalías; República Dominicana: neto regalía de retorno de fundición; Jamaica: gravamen sobre la bauxita y regalías sobre la bauxita; México: derechos de minería; Perú: regalías y Gravamen Especial a la Minería (GEM); Suriname: regalías (IAMGOLD)). Las cifras pueden no sumar exactamente debido al redondeo.
Fuente: Comisión Económica para América Latina y el Caribe (CEPAL).

StatLink http://dx.doi.org/10.1787/888933337885

En Argentina, los ingresos derivados de la minería registraron pocos cambios con relación al PIB en 2014. Mientras que los pagos del impuesto a la renta o ganancias de las sociedades por parte del sector se redujeron notoriamente (30%), esto fue compensado, principalmente, por un incremento en los ingresos de derechos de exportación (52.2%) de conformidad con la devaluación de la moneda y la implementación de un nuevo sistema de prepago especial opcional. Los ingresos globales derivados de la minería también registraron pocos cambios en el Estado Plurinacional de Bolivia con relación al PIB durante el año, con un descenso en los ingresos tributarios – causado por una reducción del 52% en los pagos de impuesto a la renta o ganancias de las sociedades – que se compensó con un aumento en los ingresos no tributarios asociados con una mayor producción minera.

El pronunciado descenso en el precio del mineral de hierro (26.7%) tuvo gran incidencia en los ingresos derivados de la minería en el Brasil, que se redujeron 0.3 puntos porcentuales del PIB en 2014. Los ingresos tributarios bajaron debido al descenso en los pagos del impuesto a la renta o ganancias de las sociedades, como consecuencia tanto de una rebaja en los beneficios del sector, como del nivel excepcionalmente alto de 2013, cuando Vale S.A. efectuó un importante pago único a raíz de un acuerdo con el gobierno brasileño. Los ingresos no tributarios bajaron de conformidad con el precio del mineral de hierro, y los ingresos derivados de la Compensación Financiera por la Exploración de Recursos Minerales (CFEM) (una regalía) se redujeron un 28%.

Chile exhibió una marcada contracción en los ingresos tributarios derivados de la minería (0.2 puntos porcentuales del PIB). En especial, los pagos de impuestos realizados por Codelco, la empresa minera propiedad del Estado, registraron un notorio descenso, incluida una reducción del 19% en los pagos del impuesto a la renta o ganancias de las sociedades y una rebaja del 36% en los pagos de impuestos específicos a la minería (que se calculan sobre los ingresos netos). Actualmente, la empresa se encuentra llevando adelante un importante programa de inversión con el que pretende incentivar la producción y reducir los costos operativos, que han aumentado mucho en los últimos años. Los ingresos tributarios provenientes del sector privado, por su parte, registraron un descenso más moderado del 3.2%.

La reducción de los ingresos derivados de la minería en Colombia (0.1 puntos porcentuales del PIB) se debió a una contracción en los pagos de impuestos por parte del sector. En particular, los ingresos del impuesto a la renta o ganancias de las sociedades se redujeron más de la mitad (56%). En oposición, los ingresos no tributarios mostraron pocos cambios, ya que un modesto incremento de la producción de carbón – el principal generador de pagos por regalías – compensó, en parte, los precios más bajos. En la República Dominicana, el descenso de los ingresos derivados de la minería (0.1 puntos porcentuales del PIB) también se centró en los ingresos tributarios. El marcado descenso en los impuestos mínimos anuales derivados de la minería, que se calculan como la diferencia entre la participación mínima del Estado en los ingresos derivados de la minería y los pagos de impuestos del período actual por parte del sector, impulsó la tendencia global.

Los ingresos derivados de la minería en Jamaica, procedentes de la industria de la bauxita/alúmina, cayeron casi a cero durante el ejercicio fiscal 2014, pese a un incremento del 2.6% en la producción. Los ingresos no tributarios se evaporaron (0.1 puntos porcentuales del PIB) cuando los pagos de gravámenes sobre la bauxita por parte del sector llegaron a cero como resultado de importantes concesiones otorgadas por el gobierno. En México los ingresos derivados de la minería se mantuvieron relativamente estables en relación con el PIB en 2014 debido a la implementación del nuevo sistema fiscal para el sector, promulgado a fines de 2013. Los ingresos del impuesto a la renta o ganancias de las sociedades se elevaron un 35% como resultado de la ampliación de la base imponible gracias a una reducción en las tasas de descuento y la derogación del régimen de consolidación fiscal. Los derechos de producción minera, que tras la reforma de 2013 se calculan sobre los ingresos netos, registraron un marcado descenso (52%), en tanto que los precios más bajos y los impuestos más altos redujeron los márgenes de beneficio.

En Perú, el descenso en los ingresos derivados de la minería (0.3 puntos porcentuales del PIB) se debió principalmente a una rebaja en los ingresos tributarios (0.2 puntos porcentuales del PIB). En particular, los ingresos del impuesto a la renta o ganancias de las sociedades cayeron un 32% durante el año. Los ingresos no tributarios registraron pocos cambios con relación al PIB, aunque los pagos de regalías descendieron un 11% tras la caída de los precios y el descenso de la producción de algunos minerales y metales (véase el cuadro 2.4). Suriname fue el único país de la región que registró un incremento en los ingresos derivados de la minería en 2014 (0.2 puntos porcentuales del PIB). El incremento de los ingresos tributarios (0.3 puntos porcentuales del PIB), gracias al aumento de los pagos del impuesto a la renta o ganancias de las sociedades por parte de IAMGOLD (Canadá), compensó el descenso en los ingresos no tributarios (0.1 puntos porcentuales del PIB).

2.2. Ingresos estimados provenientes de recursos naturales no renovables para 2015

La CEPAL estima que los ingresos públicos provenientes de recursos naturales no renovables en América Latina y el Caribe registraron una pronunciada caída en 2015, con relación al PIB, a causa de la continua debilidad de los precios internacionales de los productos básicos. Los precios del petróleo, que habían registrado un marcado descenso en la segunda mitad de 2014, continuaron bajando en 2015 y se estima que se redujeron un 47% en comparación con el precio medio del año anterior (véase el gráfico 2.2). Los factores vinculados a la oferta que impulsaron los precios a la baja en 2014, en especial el desequilibrio entre la oferta y la demanda mundial de petróleo, continuaron con la misma intensidad en 2015. Los precios de los minerales y metales aceleraron su descenso durante el año (23%), con reducciones particularmente notorias en el caso del cobre (20%) y el mineral de hierro (44%), ante el debilitamiento de la demanda china.

Gráfico 2.2. **Predicciones del precio de los productos básicos, 2011-17**

Índice 100 = 2005

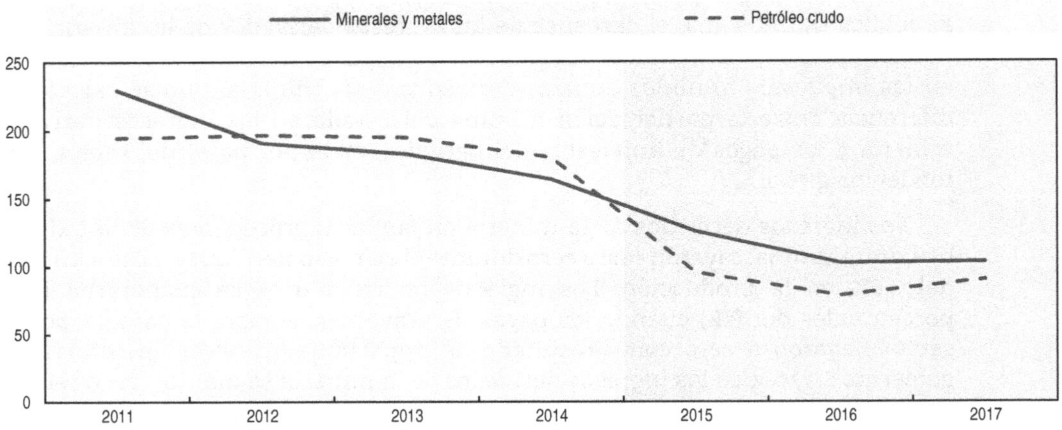

Fuente: Comisión Económica para América Latina y el Caribe (CEPAL), sobre la base de datos del Fondo Monetario Internacional (FMI) (2015c).

StatLink http://dx.doi.org/10.1787/888933337828

Se estima que los ingresos provenientes de los hidrocarburos en América Latina y el Caribe han regresado en 2015 a los niveles que registraban previo al auge, cayendo 2.1 puntos porcentuales del PIB en promedio, al 4.5% del PIB (véase el gráfico 2.3). Se prevé que varios países han experimentado descensos incluso mayores que han supuesto un desafío para las finanzas públicas, entre ellos, Bolivia (Estado Plurinacional de) (4.6 puntos porcentuales del PIB), el Ecuador (3.8), Suriname (2.4), Trinidad y Tobago (4.0) y Venezuela (República Bolivariana de) (2.3). Asimismo, se prevé que los ingresos derivados de la minería han descendido en 2015, pero es probable que esta reducción haya sido mínima para la mayoría de los productores de la región (0.1 puntos porcentuales del PIB en promedio). Chile es la única excepción, ya que el gobierno estima un descenso de 0.5 puntos porcentuales del PIB para el año.

En respuesta a estas tendencias, varios países de la región promulgaron medidas de políticas durante el año, dirigidas a incentivar la actividad en el sector extractivo. A fines de 2014, el Gobierno de Argentina modificó los tipos impositivos para las exportaciones de hidrocarburos y adoptó una nueva escala móvil para determinados productos de hidrocarburos, incluido el petróleo crudo, para fomentar la competitividad de los productores nacionales. En virtud de este nuevo sistema, los exportadores pagarán una tasa de solo el 1% cuando el precio del petróleo crudo Brent sea inferior a 79 dólares, en comparación con tasas de hasta el 13% bajo el sistema que se había adoptado en 2014. En febrero, el gobierno anunció la creación del Programa de Estímulo a la Producción de Petróleo Crudo, mediante el cual el gobierno federal pagará subsidios a la producción y a la exportación, de hasta 6 dólares por barril, durante el año civil 2015.

Gráfico 2.3. **Ingresos provenientes de recursos naturales no renovables, 2000-15**

En porcentajes del PIB

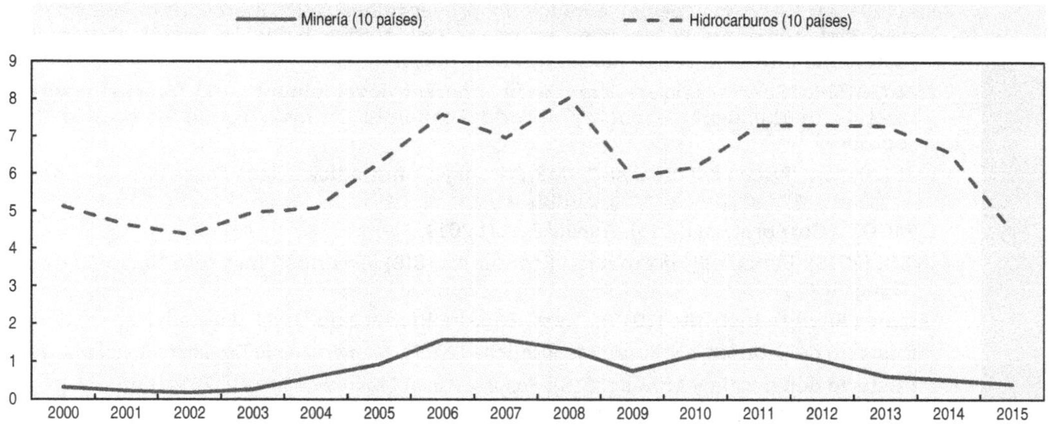

Nota: La minería incluye: Argentina, Bolivia (Estado Plurinacional de), Brasil, Chile, Colombia, Jamaica, México, Perú, República Dominicana y Suriname. Hidrocarburos incluye: Argentina, Bolivia (Estado Plurinacional de), Brasil, Colombia, Ecuador, México, Perú, Suriname, Trinidad y Tobago y Venezuela (República Bolivariana de). Los valores de 2015 se basan en estimaciones oficiales disponibles de los gobiernos registradas en los informes de presupuesto público de 2016. En los casos en que no hay estimaciones oficiales disponibles, los ingresos anuales por instrumento se estiman usando datos mensuales (para los primeros tres trimestres del año). Cuando no se dispone de datos mensuales, para los pagos de impuesto a la renta o ganancias de las sociedades por sector, por lo general los ingresos se estiman aplicando el cambio interanual para el precio del producto básico más representativo para el instrumento de ingreso en cuestión, expresado en moneda nacional a ingresos de 2014.

Fuente: Comisión Económica para América Latina y el Caribe (CEPAL).

StatLink http://dx.doi.org/10.1787/888933337836

En octubre, el Gobierno de Ecuador presentó una cartera de 25 nuevas áreas de exploración minera, así como 17 bloques petroleros, como parte de una iniciativa que busca atraer más inversiones en exploración y producción durante el período 2016-20. En noviembre, la Cámara de Diputados del Estado Plurinacional de Bolivia aprobó una ley que crea el Fondo de Promoción para la Inversión en Exploración y Explotación Hidrocarburífera. En la ley se estipula que una parte de los ingresos generados a través del Impuesto Directo a los Hidrocarburos deben depositarse en el Fondo para financiar iniciativas de inversión, como forma de promover las inversiones y aumentar las reservas y la producción de hidrocarburos del país.

Notes

1. En la Sección especial de este año se incluyen cuatro países adicionales: Jamaica, República Dominicana, Suriname y Trinidad y Tobago.
2. Por ejemplo, los precios al contado – el precio de mercado para las transacciones actuales – del crudo WTI (West Texas Intermediate) y Brent bajaron un 48% entre la última semana de junio de 2014 y el fin de año.
3. El índice general de precios de la base de datos CEPALSTAT es un índice de precios ponderado en función del comercio (año base 2010) para las exportaciones de los principales minerales y metales de la región.

Referencias

AIE (2015), *Oil Market Report* [en línea], Agencia Internacional de la Energía, https://www.iea.org/oilmarketreport/omrpublic/.

Barrick Gold (2015), *Annual Report 2014.*

DNPM (2015), *Informe Mineral 2°/2014*, Departamento Nacional de Producción Mineral del Brasil.

DNPM (2014), *Informe Mineral 2°/2013*, Departamento Nacional de Producción Mineral del Brasil.

Ecopetrol (2015), *Reporte Integrado de Gestión Sostenible*, 2014, Bogotá.

FMI (2015a), "Sección especial: evolución y proyecciones de los mercados de materias primas, con especial atención a la inversión en una era de precios bajos del petróleo", Perspectivas de la economía mundial, Fondo Monetario Internacional, abril.

FMI (2015b), "Special feature: commodity market developments and forecasts, with a focus on metals in the world economy", World Economic Outlook, Fondo Monetario Internacional, octubre.

FMI (2015c), "Prices & Forecasts", IMF Primary Commodity Prices Forecasts [en línea], www.imf.org/external/np/res/commod/index.aspx.

IAMGOLD Corporation (2015), *Annual Report 2014.*

INEGI (2015), Banco de Información Económica (BIE) [en línea], Instituto Nacional de Estadística y Geografía, www.inegi.org.mx/sistemas/bie/.

Jamaica Bauxite Institute (2015), "Total Bauxite Production Data" [en línea], www.jbi.org.jm/.

Ministerio de Economía y Finanzas Públicas (2015), *Memoria de la Economía Boliviana, 2014*, La Paz.

Ministerio de Energía y Minas (2015), *Reporte Anual Producción Minera 2014*, Lima.

Ministerio de Energía y Minas (2014), *Reporte Anual Producción Minera 2013*, Lima.

Ministerio de Minas y Energía (2015), "Anexos minas", Memorias al Congreso de la República 2014 – 2015, Bogotá.

Ministerio de Minería (2015), *Anuario de la minería de Chile 2014*, Santiago.

OPEP (2015), *Annual Statistical Bulletin 2015*, Organización de Países Exportadores de Petróleo.

PDVSA (2015), *Informe de Gestión Anual 2014*, Petróleos de Venezuela, S.A.

PEMEX (2015), *Petróleos Mexicanos. Informe Anual 2014*, Petróleos Mexicanos, Ciudad de México.

Staatsolie (2015), *Annual Report 2014.*

Staatsolie (2014), *Annual Report 2013.*

Trinidad y Tobago, Gobierno de (2014), *Review of the Economy 2014.*

CHAPTER 3

TAX LEVELS AND TAX STRUCTURES, 1990-2014

CAPÍTULO 3

NIVELES IMPOSITIVOS Y ESTRUCTURAS TRIBUTARIAS, 1990-2014

The compilation of data for this publication was completed in December 2015. On 7 January 2016 Argentina's National Institute of Statistics and Census published an official decree (https://www.boletinoficial.gob.ar/pdf/linkQR/QlFlS1dmVmpOWXMrdTVReEh2ZkU0dz09) temporarily suspending the publication of certain data in the National Statistics System. The nominal GDP series for Argentina used in this publication was obtained on 13 December 2015 through the official website of Argentina's National Institute of Statistics and Census (www.indec.mecon.ar/). As a consequence of the decree and the potential for future revisions of the GDP data, the tax to GDP ratio figures for Argentina should be treated with caution.

La recopilación de datos para esta publicación finalizó en diciembre de 2015. El 7 de enero 2016 el Instituto Nacional de Estadísticas y Censos de la República de Argentina publicó un boletín oficial (https://www.boletinoficial.gob.ar/pdf/linkQR/QlFlS1dmVmpOWXMrdTVReEh2ZkU0dz09) mediante el cual suspende temporalmente la publicación de ciertos datos en el Sistema Nacional de Estadísticas. En el caso de Argentina, la serie del PIB nominal utilizada en esta publicación se obtuvo el 13 de diciembre 2015 a través del sitio web oficial del Instituto Nacional de Argentina de Estadística y Censos (www.indec.mecon.ar/). Como consecuencia del decreto y la posibilidad de futuras revisiones de los datos del PIB, las cifras de impuestos en relación al PIB de Argentina deben ser tratadas con precaución.

Chapter 3 / Capítulo 3

3.1. Comparative tables, 1990-2014

In all of the following tables a (..) indicates not available or not applicable. The main series in this volume cover the years 1990 to 2014.

Figures referring to 1991-94 and 1996 in Table 3.1 and figures relating to 1991-99, 2001-04 and 2006-07 in Tables 3.4 to 3.16 have been omitted because of lack of space. Complete series are, however, available on line at www.latameconomy.org and on the OECD iLibrary.

3.1. Cuadros comparativos, 1990-2014

En todos los cuadros siguientes, (..) indica no aplicable o dato indisponible. Las principales series de datos de esta sección cubren el periodo que va de 1990 a 2014.

Las cifras relativas a 1991-94 y a 1996 en Cuadro 3.1 y las cifras relativas a 1991-99, 2001-04 y 2006-07 en Cuadros 3.4 hasta 3.16 a se han omitido por falta de espacio. Sin embargo, las series completas están disponibles en línea en www.latameconomy.org y en OECD iLibrary.

Table 3.1. Total tax revenue as percentage of GDP, 1990-2014
Cuadro 3.1. Total de ingresos tributarios en porcentaje del PIB, 1990-2014

	1990	1995	1997	1998	1999	2000	2001	2002	2003	2004
Argentina	12.4	16.9	17.2	17.6	17.7	18.0	17.5	16.7	19.6	22.0
Bahamas	12.3	14.4	14.3	14.5	13.8	15.2	14.9	12.8	13.5	13.5
Barbados[1]	23.2	27.2	30.5	29.0	28.9	30.2	31.2	29.6	31.2	31.2
Bolivia[1,2]	8.1	12.3	13.6	14.7	13.6	16.4	15.3	15.6	14.9	16.1
Brazil / Brasil	25.4	26.5	26.2	26.7	28.0	29.5	30.6	31.4	30.9	31.8
Chile	17.0	18.4	19.1	18.8	18.1	18.8	19.0	19.0	18.7	19.1
Colombia	9.0	13.8	15.6	15.0	15.0	14.6	16.3	16.2	16.7	17.5
Costa Rica	16.1	16.3	17.9	18.3	17.7	18.2	19.3	19.8	19.8	19.6
Dominican Republic / República Dominicana	7.8	10.0	11.0	11.0	11.3	11.7	12.9	13.0	11.3	11.9
Ecuador	7.1	7.9	8.3	8.8	8.7	10.1	11.5	12.3	11.4	11.4
El Salvador	10.5	13.0	12.1	12.1	12.0	12.1	12.1	12.9	13.1	13.0
Guatemala	9.0	10.4	11.4	11.5	12.3	12.4	12.7	13.7	13.5	13.4
Honduras	16.2	18.1	16.0	18.7	19.4	15.3	15.4	15.6	16.2	17.0
Jamaica[1]	23.0	24.7	22.4	21.1	22.2	22.8	21.6	22.1	25.0	24.7
Mexico / México[3,4]	15.5	14.9	15.6	14.8	15.5	16.5	16.8	16.2	17.1	16.8
Nicaragua	..	10.9	12.3	13.0	12.8	13.0	12.6	13.3	14.7	15.3
Panama / Panamá	14.7	17.1	17.1	16.5	17.2	17.4	16.3	15.8	15.7	15.4
Paraguay[1]	5.4	13.6	12.7	12.6	14.2	14.5	14.2	13.4	11.6	13.1
Peru / Perú	12.1	15.9	16.7	16.4	15.0	14.6	15.2	14.7	15.5	15.7
Trinidad and Tobago / Trinidad y Tobago	23.4	23.3	22.3	16.6	19.9	21.4	23.5	21.9	22.2	22.9
Uruguay	19.6	21.0	21.9	22.0	21.6	21.6	22.0	21.1	21.5	22.7
Venezuela[1]	18.1	12.8	17.6	12.9	13.8	13.6	12.2	11.2	11.9	13.3
Unweighted average / Promedio simple										
LAC / ALC[5]	**14.6**	**16.3**	**16.9**	**16.5**	**16.8**	**17.2**	**17.4**	**17.2**	**17.5**	**18.1**
OECD / OCDE[6]	**32.1**	**33.6**	**33.9**	**33.9**	**34.2**	**34.2**	**33.8**	**33.5**	**33.5**	**33.4**

	2005	2006	2007	2008	2009	2010	2011	2012	2013	2014
Argentina	22.1	22.2	23.0	24.7	25.6	26.7	27.6	29.2	30.6	32.2
Bahamas	13.8	15.6	16.3	17.2	16.5	16.1	18.9	18.0	17.1	17.5
Barbados[1]	29.5	30.5	30.2	31.1	30.5	30.6	32.4	33.1	29.5	30.4
Bolivia[1,2]	21.6	24.0	24.4	25.3	25.9	23.3	26.2	27.6	28.9	28.7
Brazil / Brasil	32.7	32.5	33.1	33.8	32.4	32.4	33.3	33.3	33.6	33.4
Chile	20.7	22.0	22.8	21.4	17.2	19.5	21.2	21.5	20.0	19.8
Colombia	18.1	19.1	19.1	18.8	18.6	18.0	18.9	19.7	20.0	20.3
Costa Rica	20.1	20.6	22.0	22.7	21.2	20.8	21.3	21.3	22.6	22.5
Dominican Republic / República Dominicana	13.8	14.0	15.0	14.3	12.7	12.3	12.3	13.1	13.9	14.1
Ecuador	11.7	12.4	12.8	14.0	14.9	16.3	17.3	19.3	19.2	19.0
El Salvador	13.9	15.1	15.2	15.1	14.4	15.1	15.4	16.1	17.0	16.5
Guatemala	13.1	13.8	13.9	12.9	12.2	12.4	12.7	12.8	13.0	12.6
Honduras	16.9	17.6	19.0	18.9	17.1	17.3	16.9	17.8	18.3	19.8
Jamaica[1]	23.3	24.1	24.9	25.0	24.8	25.0	24.5	24.6	25.0	24.2
Mexico / México[3,4]	17.7	17.9	17.6	20.7	17.2	18.5	19.5	19.5	19.7	19.5
Nicaragua	16.1	17.1	17.3	16.8	16.9	18.0	18.8	19.5	19.9	20.3
Panama / Panamá	15.2	16.8	17.4	17.4	18.0	18.9	18.6	19.4	19.4	18.1
Paraguay[1]	13.8	14.2	13.9	14.6	16.1	16.5	16.8	17.7	16.4	17.1
Peru / Perú	16.5	17.9	18.5	19.0	16.9	17.8	18.5	18.8	18.4	18.8
Trinidad and Tobago / Trinidad y Tobago	26.7	30.4	26.4	29.5	28.4	27.5	26.7	27.4	27.4	28.3
Uruguay	23.8	25.4	25.0	26.1	25.8	26.0	26.4	26.7	27.2	27.0
Venezuela[1]	15.9	16.3	16.8	14.1	14.3	11.8	13.5	14.2	14.8	18.2
Unweighted average / Promedio simple										
LAC / ALC[5]	**19.0**	**20.0**	**20.2**	**20.6**	**19.9**	**20.0**	**20.8**	**21.4**	**21.5**	**21.7**
OECD / OCDE[6]	**33.9**	**34.1**	**34.1**	**33.6**	**32.7**	**32.8**	**33.3**	**33.8**	**34.2**	**34.4**

Note: The figures exclude local government revenues for Argentina (but include provincial revenues), Bahamas, Barbados, Bolivia, Costa Rica (up to 1997), Dominican Republic, Ecuador, El Salvador, Honduras, Jamaica, Nicaragua, Panama (up to 1998), Paraguay (up to 2004, 2013 and 2014), Peru (up to 2004) and Venezuela as the data are not available.

1. The data are estimated from 2011 to 2014 (Venezuela), for 2013 and 2014 (Bolivia and Paraguay) and for 2014 (Barbados and Jamaica).
2. In ECLAC data the excise tax on hydrocarbons is treated as non-tax revenues.
3. In ECLAC and CIAT data, fees levied on hydrocarbon production are treated as non-tax revenues.
4. The data are estimated for 2014 including expected revenues for state and local governments.
5. Represents a group of 22 Latin American and Caribbean countries, the average is calculated using calendar year data, except for Bahamas and Trinidad and Tobago where fiscal year data are used. Chile and Mexico are also part of the OECD (34) group.
6. Calculated by applying the unweighted average percentage change for 2014 in the 30 countries providing data for that year to the overall average tax to GDP ratio in 2013.

Nota : Las cifras excluyen los ingresos de gobiernos locales en Argentina (pero incluye ingresos de las provincias), Bahamas, Barbados, Bolivia, Costa Rica (hasta 1997), República Dominicana, Ecuador, El Salvador, Honduras, Jamaica, Nicaragua, Panamá (hasta 1998), Paraguay (hasta 2004, 2013 y 2014), Perú (hasta 2004) y Venezuela dado que los datos no están disponibles.

1. Datos estimados desde el 2011 hasta el 2014 (Venezuela), 2013 y 2014 (Bolivia y Paraguay) y 2014 (Barbados y Jamaica).
2. En los datos de CEPAL, el Impuesto Directo sobre Hidrocarburos (IDH) es considerado como regalía en los ingresos no tributarios.
3. En los datos de CEPAL y CIAT, los derechos sobre la producción de hidrocarburos son tratados como ingresos no tributarios.
4. Los datos estimados incluyen ingresos esperados a nivel estatal y local para el 2014.
5. Representa un grupo de 22 países de América Latina y el Caribe, para el promedio se utiliza año calendario, excepto para Barbados y Trinidad y Tobago donde el año fiscal se utiliza. Chile y México son también parte del grupo OCDE (34).
6. Calculado aplicando el promedio no ponderado en el cambio porcentual para el 2014 en los 30 países con datos disponibles para ese año en el total de ingreso tributario en porcentaje del PIB.

StatLink http://dx.doi.org/10.1787/888933337920

Table 3.2. Tax revenue of main headings as percentage of GDP, 2014
Cuadro 3.2. Ingresos tributarios en las principales partidas en porcentaje del PIB, 2014

	1000 Income & profits / Renta & utilidades	2000 Social security / Seguridad social	3000 Payroll / Nómina	4000 Property / Patrimonio	5000 Goods and services / Bienes & servicios	6000 Others / Otros
Argentina	6.1	7.0	0.0	2.9	15.9	0.3
Bahamas	0.0	2.9	0.0	1.2	11.6	1.8
Barbados[1]	8.1	6.1	0.0	1.3	14.6	0.4
Bolivia[1]	4.2	1.4	0.0	0.2	18.4	4.7
Brazil / Brasil	6.9	8.7	0.9	1.9	13.9	1.0
Chile	6.5	1.4	0.0	0.9	11.0	0.0
Colombia	6.6	2.5	0.3	2.1	7.6	1.1
Costa Rica	4.1	7.7	1.0	0.4	9.1	0.2
Dominican Republic / República Dominicana	4.5	0.1	0.0	0.6	9.0	0.0
Ecuador	4.1	4.7	0.0	0.0	10.1	0.1
El Salvador	6.0	1.8	0.0	0.1	8.6	0.0
Guatemala	3.9	1.8	0.0	0.2	6.7	0.1
Honduras	5.3	3.0	0.0	0.5	10.9	0.0
Jamaica[1]	8.7	0.9	0.0	0.4	13.3	0.8
Mexico / México[2]	6.0	3.1	0.3	0.3	9.8	0.3
Nicaragua	5.8	4.9	0.0	0.1	9.5	0.0
Panama / Panamá	4.6	6.4	0.3	0.8	5.4	0.7
Paraguay[1]	2.7	4.1	0.0	0.2	10.0	0.1
Peru / Perú	7.7	2.1	0.0	0.4	8.3	0.4
Trinidad and Tobago / Trinidad y Tobago	20.1	1.7	0.0	0.4	5.9	0.2
Uruguay	5.7	7.6	0.0	1.8	11.8	0.0
Venezuela[1]	6.0	0.9	0.0	0.0	11.1	0.3
Unweighted average / Promedio simple						
LAC / ALC[3]	**6.1**	**3.7**	**0.1**	**0.8**	**10.6**	**0.6**
OECD / OCDE[2,4]	**11.5**	**9.1**	**0.4**	**1.9**	**11.0**	**0.2**

Note: The figures exclude local government revenues for Argentina (but include provincial revenues), Bahamas, Barbados, Bolivia, Costa Rica (up to 1997), Dominican Republic, Ecuador, El Salvador, Honduras, Jamaica, Nicaragua, Panama (up to 1998), Paraguay (up to 2004, 2013 and 2014), Peru (up to 2004) and Venezuela as the data are not available.

1. The data are estimated.
2. The data for 2013 are used for 3000, 4000, 5000 and 6000.
3. Represents a group of 22 Latin American and Caribbean countries. Chile and Mexico are also part of the OECD (34) group.
4. Represents the unweighted average for OECD member countries.

Nota : Las cifras excluyen los ingresos de gobiernos locales en Argentina (pero incluye ingresos de las provincias), Bahamas, Barbados, Bolivia, Costa Rica (hasta 1997), República Dominicana, Ecuador, El Salvador, Honduras, Jamaica, Nicaragua, Panamá (hasta 1998), Paraguay (hasta 2004, 2013 y 2014), Perú (hasta 2004) y Venezuela dado que los datos no están disponibles.

1. Datos estimados.
2. Se utilizan los datos 2013 en 3000, 4000, 5000 y 6000.
3. Representa un grupo de 22 países de América Latina y el Caribe. Chile y México son también parte del grupo OCDE (34).
4. Representa el promedio no ponderado para los países miembros de la OCDE.

StatLink http://dx.doi.org/10.1787/888933337933

Table 3.3. Tax revenue of main headings as percentage of total taxation, 2014
Cuadro 3.3. Ingresos tributarios en las principales partidas en porcentaje del total de ingresos tributarios, 2014

	1000 Income & profits / Renta & utilidades	2000 Social security / Seguridad social	3000 Payroll / Nómina	4000 Property / Patrimonio	5000 Goods and services / Bienes & servicios	6000 Others / Otros
Argentina	18.9	21.6	0.0	9.1	49.5	0.9
Bahamas	0.0	16.5	0.0	7.0	66.1	10.4
Barbados[1]	26.5	20.1	0.0	4.3	47.9	1.2
Bolivia[1]	14.4	4.7	0.0	0.7	63.9	16.2
Brazil / Brasil	20.7	26.2	2.6	5.8	41.7	3.0
Chile	33.0	7.2	0.0	4.3	55.3	0.2
Colombia	32.7	12.6	1.7	10.4	37.3	5.3
Costa Rica	18.2	34.0	4.5	1.9	40.3	1.1
Dominican Republic / República Dominicana	31.7	0.4	0.0	4.5	63.5	0.0
Ecuador	21.7	24.6	0.0	0.0	53.0	0.7
El Salvador	36.7	10.7	0.0	0.6	52.0	0.0
Guatemala	30.9	14.2	0.0	1.5	52.9	0.6
Honduras	26.8	15.4	0.0	2.6	55.2	0.0
Jamaica[1]	35.9	3.9	0.0	1.6	55.1	3.5
Mexico / México[2]	30.2	15.5	1.7	1.5	49.8	1.3
Nicaragua	28.3	24.3	0.0	0.6	46.6	0.1
Panama / Panamá	25.2	35.2	1.7	4.2	30.0	3.7
Paraguay[1]	15.6	23.9	0.0	1.3	58.6	0.6
Peru / Perú	40.8	11.0	0.0	2.0	44.0	2.2
Trinidad and Tobago / Trinidad y Tobago	71.1	6.1	0.0	1.5	20.8	0.6
Uruguay	21.3	28.0	0.0	6.7	43.8	0.2
Venezuela[1]	32.7	5.0	0.0	0.2	60.7	1.4
Unweighted average / Promedio simple						
LAC / ALC[3]	**27.9**	**16.4**	**0.6**	**3.3**	**49.5**	**2.4**
OECD / OCDE[2,4]	**33.7**	**26.1**	**1.1**	**5.6**	**32.7**	**0.6**

Note: The figures exclude local government revenues for Argentina (but include provincial revenues), Bahamas, Barbados, Bolivia, Costa Rica (up to 1997), Dominican Republic, Ecuador, El Salvador, Honduras, Jamaica, Nicaragua, Panama (up to 1998), Paraguay (up to 2004, 2013 and 2014), Peru (up to 2004) and Venezuela as the data are not available.

1. The data are estimated.
2. The data for 2013 are used.
3. Represents a group of 22 Latin American and Caribbean countries. Chile and Mexico are also part of the OECD (34) group.
4. Represents the unweighted average for OECD member countries.

Nota : Las cifras excluyen los ingresos de gobiernos locales en Argentina (pero incluye ingresos de las provincias), Bahamas, Barbados, Bolivia, Costa Rica (hasta 1997), República Dominicana, Ecuador, El Salvador, Honduras, Jamaica, Nicaragua, Panamá (hasta 1998), Paraguay (hasta 2004, 2013 y 2014), Perú (hasta 2004) y Venezuela dado que los datos no están disponibles.

1. Datos estimados.
2. Se utilizan los datos 2013.
3. Representa un grupo de 22 países de América Latina y el Caribe. Chile y México son también parte del grupo OCDE (34).
4. Representa el promedio no ponderado para los países miembros de la OCDE.

StatLink http://dx.doi.org/10.1787/888933337941

Table 3.4. Taxes on income and profits (1000) as percentage of GDP
Cuadro 3.4. Impuestos sobre la renta y las utilidades (1000) en porcentaje del PIB

	1990	2000	2005	2008	2009	2010	2011	2012	2013	2014
Argentina	0.5	3.3	4.5	4.3	4.0	4.3	4.8	5.1	5.5	6.1
Bahamas	0.0	0.0	0.0	0.0	0.0	0.0	0.0	0.0	0.0	0.0
Barbados	6.2	9.2	8.2	9.0	10.2	8.6	9.0	8.6	7.0	8.1
Bolivia	0.8	1.9	2.7	3.8	3.9	3.9	3.8	4.0	3.9	4.2
Brazil / Brasil	4.6	5.7	6.9	7.5	7.0	6.7	7.2	6.8	7.0	6.9
Chile	3.9	4.4	7.5	8.0	5.4	7.5	8.5	8.4	6.9	6.5
Colombia	2.7	3.4	5.1	5.1	5.6	4.8	5.4	6.6	6.7	6.6
Costa Rica	1.8	2.6	3.4	4.4	4.1	3.9	4.0	3.9	4.1	4.1
Dominican Republic / República Dominicana	2.0	2.6	2.8	3.5	3.1	2.7	2.9	3.9	4.2	4.5
Ecuador	0.9	1.6	2.3	3.8	4.0	3.4	3.8	3.8	4.1	4.1
El Salvador	2.0	3.1	3.7	4.7	4.6	4.6	4.9	5.2	6.1	6.0
Guatemala	1.6	2.5	2.9	3.3	3.2	3.1	3.4	3.4	3.8	3.9
Honduras	3.4	2.8	4.1	5.1	4.6	4.7	5.1	4.9	5.2	5.3
Jamaica	11.7	10.2	10.0	11.5	11.7	10.3	9.9	9.6	9.1	8.7
Mexico / México	4.2	4.5	4.3	5.1	4.9	5.2	5.3	5.1	6.0	5.8
Nicaragua	..	1.8	3.7	4.3	4.6	4.5	5.1	5.3	5.4	5.8
Panama / Panamá	3.6	4.2	3.6	4.8	5.3	5.0	4.3	5.5	5.4	4.6
Paraguay	1.1	1.9	1.7	1.9	2.8	2.2	2.5	2.7	2.5	2.7
Peru / Perú	0.7	2.9	5.0	7.3	6.0	6.6	7.7	7.9	7.3	7.7
Trinidad and Tobago / Trinidad y Tobago	12.0	11.8	19.0	22.2	18.9	18.6	19.4	19.1	18.8	20.1
Uruguay	0.9	2.0	2.8	5.4	5.4	5.5	5.5	5.6	6.1	5.7
Venezuela	15.1	5.9	6.1	5.8	5.5	3.6	3.9	4.3	4.3	6.0
Unweighted average / Promedio simple										
LAC / ALC[1]	**3.8**	**4.0**	**5.0**	**5.9**	**5.7**	**5.4**	**5.7**	**5.9**	**5.9**	**6.1**
OECD / OCDE[2]	**12.2**	**12.2**	**11.9**	**11.9**	**11.0**	**10.9**	**11.1**	**11.4**	**11.5**	**11.7**

Note: The figures exclude local government revenues for Argentina (but include provincial revenues), Bahamas, Barbados, Bolivia, Costa Rica (up to 1997), Dominican Republic, Ecuador, El Salvador, Honduras, Jamaica, Nicaragua, Panama (up to 1998), Paraguay (up to 2004, 2013 and 2014), Peru (up to 2004) and Venezuela as the data are not available.

1. Represents a group of 22 Latin American and Caribbean countries. Chile and Mexico are also part of the OECD (34) group.
2. Represents the unweighted average for OECD member countries. The OECD average for 2014 is estimated by applying the unweighted average percentage change for 2014 in the 31 countries providing data for that year to the OECD average for 2013.

Nota : Las cifras excluyen los ingresos de gobiemos locales en Argentina (pero incluye ingresos de las provincias), Bahamas, Barbados, Bolivia, Costa Rica (hasta 1997), República Dominicana, Ecuador, El Salvador, Honduras, Jamaica, Nicaragua, Panamá (hasta 1998), Paraguay (hasta 2004, 2013 y 2014), Perú (hasta 2004) y Venezuela dado que los datos no están disponibles.

1. Representa un grupo de 22 países de América Latina y el Caribe. Chile y México son también parte del grupo OCDE (34).
2. Representa el promedio no ponderado para los países miembros de la OCDE. El promedio OCDE del 2014 es calculado aplicando el promedio no ponderado en el cambio porcentual para el 2014 en los 31 países con datos disponibles para ese año al promedio OCDE del 2013.

StatLink http://dx.doi.org/10.1787/888933337952

Table 3.5. Taxes on income and profits (1000) as percentage of total taxation
Cuadro 3.5. Impuestos sobre la renta y las utilidades (1000) en porcentaje del total de ingresos tributarios

	1990	2000	2005	2008	2009	2010	2011	2012	2013	2014
Argentina	3.7	18.5	20.4	17.2	15.8	16.2	17.2	17.3	17.8	18.9
Bahamas	0.0	0.0	0.0	0.0	0.0	0.0	0.0	0.0	0.0	0.0
Barbados	27.0	30.5	27.8	29.0	33.2	28.0	27.7	25.9	23.9	26.5
Bolivia	9.8	11.4	12.4	14.9	14.9	16.6	14.6	14.6	13.4	14.4
Brazil / Brasil	18.1	19.4	21.0	22.3	21.7	20.5	21.6	20.5	20.8	20.7
Chile	23.2	23.3	36.3	37.5	31.1	38.4	40.1	39.0	34.8	33.0
Colombia	29.9	23.3	28.2	27.1	29.9	26.7	28.6	33.4	33.5	32.7
Costa Rica	11.1	14.4	16.9	19.3	19.3	18.8	18.7	18.4	18.2	18.2
Dominican Republic / República Dominicana	26.0	22.3	20.1	24.8	24.6	22.0	23.9	29.6	30.5	31.7
Ecuador	12.8	15.9	19.3	27.0	27.0	20.7	22.1	19.5	21.1	21.7
El Salvador	18.9	25.7	26.7	31.0	32.0	30.8	31.7	32.6	35.7	36.7
Guatemala	18.1	19.9	22.2	25.4	25.8	25.1	27.0	26.7	29.2	30.9
Honduras	21.2	18.3	24.1	27.1	26.8	27.0	30.1	27.3	28.4	26.8
Jamaica	50.9	44.8	42.8	45.9	47.1	41.2	40.4	39.2	36.3	35.9
Mexico / México[1]	27.1	27.3	24.1	24.8	28.6	27.8	27.3	26.3	30.2	30.2
Nicaragua	..	13.6	22.9	25.3	27.1	24.8	27.1	27.2	27.1	28.3
Panama / Panamá	24.3	24.0	23.9	27.3	29.5	26.3	23.1	28.5	28.1	25.2
Paraguay	21.1	13.1	12.6	13.4	17.2	13.4	14.7	15.1	15.2	15.6
Peru / Perú	5.7	19.8	30.1	38.3	35.8	36.9	41.5	42.0	39.5	40.8
Trinidad and Tobago / Trinidad y Tobago	51.6	55.1	71.0	75.2	66.5	67.6	72.6	69.6	68.6	71.1
Uruguay	4.8	9.4	11.8	20.7	20.8	21.2	20.8	20.9	22.2	21.3
Venezuela	83.7	43.2	38.4	41.4	38.6	30.6	29.0	30.5	28.8	32.7
Unweighted average / Promedio simple										
LAC / ALC[2]	**23.3**	**22.4**	**25.1**	**27.9**	**27.9**	**26.4**	**27.3**	**27.5**	**27.4**	**27.9**
OECD / OCDE[3]	**37.2**	**35.1**	**34.5**	**35.4**	**33.5**	**33.2**	**33.5**	**33.6**	**33.7**	..

Note: The figures exclude local government revenues for Argentina (but include provincial revenues), Bahamas, Barbados, Bolivia, Costa Rica (up to 1997), Dominican Republic, Ecuador, El Salvador, Honduras, Jamaica, Nicaragua, Panama (up to 1998), Paraguay (up to 2004, 2013 and 2014), Peru (up to 2004) and Venezuela as the data are not available.

1. The data for 2013 are used for 2014.
2. Represents a group of 22 Latin American and Caribbean countries. Chile and Mexico are also part of the OECD (34) group.
3. Represents the unweighted average for OECD member countries.

Nota : Las cifras excluyen los ingresos de gobiernos locales en Argentina (pero incluye ingresos de las provincias), Bahamas, Barbados, Bolivia, Costa Rica (hasta 1997), República Dominicana, Ecuador, El Salvador, Honduras, Jamaica, Nicaragua, Panamá (hasta 1998), Paraguay (hasta 2004, 2013 y 2014), Perú (hasta 2004) y Venezuela dado que los datos no están disponibles.

1. Para el 2014 se utilizan los datos 2013.
2. Representa un grupo de 22 países de América Latina y el Caribe. Chile y México son también parte del grupo OCDE (34).
3. Representa el promedio no ponderado para los países miembros de la OCDE.

StatLink http://dx.doi.org/10.1787/888933337969

Table 3.6. Social security contributions (2000) as percentage of GDP
Cuadro 3.6. Contribuciones a la seguridad social (2000) en porcentaje del PIB

	1990	2000	2005	2008	2009	2010	2011	2012	2013	2014
Argentina	3.1	2.8	2.7	4.1	5.5	5.7	5.9	6.5	6.9	7.0
Bahamas	1.6	1.8	1.8	1.9	2.0	2.1	2.4	2.5	2.7	2.9
Barbados	3.3	4.7	5.2	5.7	5.7	5.9	6.0	6.1	5.9	6.1
Bolivia[1]	0.0	1.3	1.2	1.1	1.2	1.2	1.6	1.5	1.4	1.4
Brazil / Brasil	6.1	6.9	7.7	7.9	8.2	8.1	8.3	8.6	8.6	8.7
Chile	1.5	1.4	1.4	1.4	1.4	1.3	1.3	1.4	1.4	1.4
Colombia	0.7	2.4	2.3	2.0	2.0	2.1	1.7	1.8	2.3	2.5
Costa Rica	4.4	5.1	5.5	5.9	6.2	6.3	6.5	6.5	7.6	7.7
Dominican Republic / República Dominicana	0.1	0.1	0.0	0.1	0.1	0.1	0.1	0.1	0.1	0.1
Ecuador	1.6	1.2	2.7	3.4	3.3	3.7	5.0	5.4	4.8	4.7
El Salvador	1.4	2.0	1.7	1.7	1.7	1.7	1.7	1.7	1.7	1.8
Guatemala	1.4	1.9	2.0	1.9	1.9	1.9	1.9	2.0	2.0	1.8
Honduras	1.4	1.6	2.4	2.8	2.9	2.9	2.1	3.0	3.3	3.0
Jamaica[1]	0.0	0.0	0.7	0.7	0.6	0.8	0.9	0.9	1.0	0.9
Mexico / México	2.1	2.7	2.8	2.6	2.9	2.8	2.8	2.9	3.1	3.2
Nicaragua	..	2.6	3.2	3.7	4.0	4.3	4.3	4.5	4.8	4.9
Panama / Panamá	4.5	6.4	5.4	5.8	5.7	6.2	6.5	6.0	6.6	6.4
Paraguay	0.4	3.7	3.0	3.4	3.9	3.7	3.8	4.5	4.1	4.1
Peru / Perú	0.9	1.8	1.6	1.9	2.0	1.9	1.9	2.0	2.1	2.1
Trinidad and Tobago / Trinidad y Tobago	0.9	1.4	1.2	1.2	2.1	1.9	1.7	1.7	1.7	1.7
Uruguay	6.0	6.4	5.0	5.5	6.0	6.2	6.5	7.0	7.3	7.6
Venezuela[1]	0.9	0.7	0.6	0.8	1.0	1.0	1.0	1.0	1.0	0.9
Unweighted average / Promedio simple										
LAC / ALC[2]	**2.0**	**2.7**	**2.7**	**3.0**	**3.2**	**3.3**	**3.4**	**3.5**	**3.7**	**3.7**
OECD / OCDE[3]	**7.4**	**8.6**	**8.6**	**8.6**	**8.9**	**8.8**	**8.9**	**9.0**	**9.1**	..

Note: The figures exclude local government revenues for Argentina (but include provincial revenues), Bahamas, Barbados, Bolivia, Costa Rica (up to 1997), Dominican Republic, Ecuador, El Salvador, Honduras, Jamaica, Nicaragua, Panama (up to 1998), Paraguay (up to 2004, 2013 and 2014), Peru (up to 2004) and Venezuela as the data are not available.

1. The data are estimated for 2011 to 2014 (Venezuela) and for 2013 and 2014 (Bolivia).
2. Represents a group of 22 Latin American and Caribbean countries. Chile and Mexico are also part of the OECD (34) group.
3. Represents the unweighted average for OECD member countries.

Nota : Las cifras excluyen los ingresos de gobiernos locales en Argentina (pero incluye ingresos de las provincias), Bahamas, Barbados, Bolivia, Costa Rica (hasta 1997), República Dominicana, Ecuador, El Salvador, Honduras, Jamaica, Nicaragua, Panamá (hasta 1998), Paraguay (hasta 2004, 2013 y 2014), Perú (hasta 2004) y Venezuela dado que los datos no están disponibles.

1. Datos estimados del 2011 al 2014 (Venezuela) y por 2013 y 2014 (Bolivia).
2. Representa un grupo de 22 países de América Latina y el Caribe. Chile y México son también parte del grupo OCDE (34).
3. Representa el promedio no ponderado para los países miembros de la OCDE.

StatLink http://dx.doi.org/10.1787/888933337970

Table 3.7. Social security contributions (2000) as percentage of total taxation
Cuadro 3.7. Contribuciones a la seguridad social (2000) en porcentaje del total de ingresos tributarios

	1990	2000	2005	2008	2009	2010	2011	2012	2013	2014
Argentina	25.3	15.8	12.2	16.6	21.4	21.2	21.5	22.2	22.6	21.6
Bahamas	13.2	11.9	12.8	10.9	12.4	13.1	12.8	13.7	15.9	16.5
Barbados	14.2	15.7	17.8	18.4	18.6	19.3	18.6	18.4	19.9	20.1
Bolivia[1]	0.0	7.8	5.6	4.4	4.8	5.1	6.1	5.6	4.9	4.7
Brazil / Brasil	24.0	23.5	23.7	23.5	25.4	25.0	24.9	25.8	25.6	26.2
Chile	9.0	7.3	6.5	6.4	8.3	6.9	6.3	6.5	7.2	7.2
Colombia	7.9	16.4	12.8	10.7	11.0	11.7	8.8	9.0	11.7	12.6
Costa Rica	27.2	28.0	27.6	26.0	29.3	30.3	30.5	30.6	33.7	34.0
Dominican Republic / República Dominicana	0.8	1.0	0.0	0.4	0.5	0.8	0.5	0.4	0.4	0.4
Ecuador	22.5	12.3	22.9	24.2	22.1	22.5	28.9	27.9	25.0	24.6
El Salvador	13.3	16.6	11.9	11.0	12.1	11.4	10.8	10.5	10.3	10.7
Guatemala	15.6	15.5	15.0	14.4	15.4	15.6	15.2	15.6	15.7	14.2
Honduras	8.8	10.6	14.2	14.7	17.2	16.7	12.3	16.9	18.1	15.4
Jamaica[1]	0.0	0.0	3.1	2.8	2.6	3.2	3.8	3.6	4.1	3.9
Mexico / México[2]	13.4	16.5	15.7	12.7	16.7	15.4	14.5	14.9	15.5	15.5
Nicaragua	..	19.9	19.8	21.7	23.6	24.1	22.9	22.9	23.9	24.3
Panama / Panamá	30.4	36.8	35.1	33.1	31.8	32.7	35.0	31.1	34.2	35.2
Paraguay	8.3	25.6	21.4	23.7	24.5	22.7	22.4	25.1	25.2	23.9
Peru / Perú	7.7	12.3	9.9	10.0	11.8	10.7	10.4	10.6	11.3	11.0
Trinidad and Tobago / Trinidad y Tobago	3.6	6.4	4.4	3.9	7.4	6.8	6.2	6.2	6.2	6.1
Uruguay	30.5	29.6	21.1	20.9	23.3	23.7	24.5	26.1	26.8	28.0
Venezuela[1]	4.9	5.4	3.9	5.3	6.7	8.0	7.0	6.7	6.6	5.0
Unweighted average / Promedio simple										
LAC / ALC[3]	**13.4**	**15.2**	**14.4**	**14.4**	**15.8**	**15.8**	**15.6**	**15.9**	**16.6**	**16.4**
OECD / OCDE[4]	**21.9**	**24.5**	**24.9**	**25.2**	**26.4**	**26.4**	**26.1**	**26.1**	**26.1**	..

Note: The figures exclude local government revenues for Argentina (but include provincial revenues), Bahamas, Barbados, Bolivia, Costa Rica (up to 1997), Dominican Republic, Ecuador, El Salvador, Honduras, Jamaica, Nicaragua, Panama (up to 1998), Paraguay (up to 2004, 2013 and 2014), Peru (up to 2004) and Venezuela as the data are not available.

1. The data are estimated for 2011 to 2014 (Venezuela) and for 2013 and 2014 (Bolivia).
2. The data for 2013 are used for 2014.
3. Represents a group of 22 Latin American and Caribbean countries. Chile and Mexico are also part of the OECD (34) group.
4. Represents the unweighted average for OECD member countries.

Nota : Las cifras excluyen los ingresos de gobiernos locales en Argentina (pero incluye ingresos de las provincias), Bahamas, Barbados, Bolivia, Costa Rica (hasta 1997), República Dominicana, Ecuador, El Salvador, Honduras, Jamaica, Nicaragua, Panamá (hasta 1998), Paraguay (hasta 2004, 2013 y 2014), Perú (hasta 2004) y Venezuela dado que los datos no están disponibles.

1. Datos estimados del 2011 al 2014 (Venezuela) y por 2013 y 2014 (Bolivia).
2. Para el 2014 se utilizan los datos 2013.
3. Representa un grupo de 22 países de América Latina y el Caribe. Chile y México son también parte del grupo OCDE (34).
4. Representa el promedio no ponderado para los países miembros de la OCDE.

StatLink http://dx.doi.org/10.1787/888933337981

Table 3.8. Taxes on property (4000) as percentage of GDP
Cuadro 3.8. Impuestos sobre la propiedad (4000) en porcentaje del PIB

	1990	2000	2005	2008	2009	2010	2011	2012	2013	2014
Argentina	1.6	1.1	2.5	2.4	2.4	2.4	2.5	2.6	2.8	2.9
Bahamas	0.5	0.5	0.7	0.9	1.1	1.2	1.2	1.2	1.4	1.2
Barbados	1.0	1.5	1.6	1.3	1.7	1.3	1.3	1.7	1.4	1.3
Bolivia	0.5	0.0	0.8	0.3	0.3	0.3	0.2	0.2	0.2	0.2
Brazil / Brasil	1.6	2.4	2.6	1.9	1.8	1.9	2.0	2.0	1.9	1.9
Chile	1.0	1.3	1.3	1.2	0.8	0.7	0.8	0.9	0.8	0.9
Colombia	0.2	1.0	1.4	1.9	1.6	1.5	2.1	2.0	2.1	2.1
Costa Rica	0.1	0.3	0.3	0.3	0.3	0.3	0.3	0.4	0.4	0.4
Dominican Republic / República Dominicana	0.1	0.1	0.6	0.7	0.6	0.6	0.7	0.8	0.9	0.6
Ecuador	0.0	0.0	0.0	0.0	0.0	0.0	0.0	0.0	0.0	0.0
El Salvador	0.5	0.1	0.1	0.1	0.1	0.1	0.1	0.1	0.1	0.1
Guatemala	0.1	0.1	0.2	0.2	0.2	0.2	0.2	0.2	0.2	0.2
Honduras	0.1	0.2	0.1	0.1	0.1	0.1	0.1	0.3	0.3	0.5
Jamaica[1]	0.2	0.2	0.2	0.2	0.2	0.2	0.2	0.2	0.4	0.4
Mexico / México[1]	0.2	0.2	0.3	0.3	0.3	0.3	0.3	0.3	0.3	0.3
Nicaragua	..	0.0	0.0	0.0	0.0	0.1	0.1	0.1	0.1	0.1
Panama / Panamá	0.7	0.5	0.7	0.7	0.7	0.8	0.7	0.7	0.8	0.8
Paraguay[1]	0.3	0.0	0.0	0.3	0.3	0.3	0.3	0.3	0.2	0.2
Peru / Perú	1.9	0.0	0.5	0.6	0.6	0.5	0.4	0.4	0.4	0.4
Trinidad and Tobago / Trinidad y Tobago	0.7	0.5	0.4	0.3	0.4	0.3	0.3	0.3	0.4	0.4
Uruguay	1.6	2.2	2.8	2.4	2.3	2.1	2.0	2.0	1.9	1.8
Venezuela	0.1	0.5	0.9	0.9	0.0	0.0	0.0	0.0	0.0	0.0
Unweighted average / Promedio simple										
LAC / ALC[2]	**0.6**	**0.6**	**0.8**	**0.8**	**0.7**	**0.7**	**0.7**	**0.8**	**0.8**	**0.8**
OECD / OCDE[3]	**1.8**	**1.8**	**1.8**	**1.7**	**1.7**	**1.7**	**1.8**	**1.8**	**1.9**	**..**

Note: The figures exclude local government revenues for Argentina (but include provincial revenues), Bahamas, Barbados, Bolivia, Costa Rica (up to 1997), Dominican Republic, Ecuador, El Salvador, Honduras, Jamaica, Nicaragua, Panama (up to 1998), Paraguay (up to 2004, 2013 and 2014), Peru (up to 2004) and Venezuela as the data are not available.

1. The data for 2013 are used for 2014.
2. Represents a group of 22 Latin American and Caribbean countries. Chile and Mexico are also part of the OECD (34) group.
3. Represents the unweighted average for OECD member countries.

Nota : Las cifras excluyen los ingresos de gobiernos locales en Argentina (pero incluye ingresos de las provincias), Bahamas, Barbados, Bolivia, Costa Rica (hasta 1997), República Dominicana, Ecuador, El Salvador, Honduras, Jamaica, Nicaragua, Panamá (hasta 1998), Paraguay (hasta 2004, 2013 y 2014), Perú (hasta 2004) y Venezuela dado que los datos no están disponibles.

1. Para el 2014 se utilizan los datos 2013.
2. Representa un grupo de 22 países de América Latina y el Caribe. Chile y México son también parte del grupo OCDE (34).
3. Representa el promedio no ponderado para los países miembros de la OCDE.

StatLink http://dx.doi.org/10.1787/888933337997

Table 3.9. Taxes on property (4000) as percentage of total taxation
Cuadro 3.9. Impuestos sobre la propiedad (4000) en porcentaje del total de ingresos tributarios

	1990	2000	2005	2008	2009	2010	2011	2012	2013	2014
Argentina	12.7	6.4	11.2	9.7	9.2	9.0	9.0	9.0	9.3	9.1
Bahamas	3.8	3.3	5.1	5.1	6.6	7.2	6.2	6.4	8.0	7.0
Barbados	4.2	4.9	5.5	4.2	5.5	4.2	4.0	5.2	4.9	4.3
Bolivia	5.7	0.0	3.8	1.2	1.1	1.1	0.9	0.8	0.7	0.7
Brazil / Brasil	6.5	8.1	7.9	5.5	5.7	5.9	5.9	5.9	5.6	5.8
Chile	6.2	7.0	6.3	5.4	4.8	3.6	4.0	4.3	4.1	4.3
Colombia	2.2	6.6	7.9	9.9	8.8	8.5	11.1	10.4	10.6	10.4
Costa Rica	0.3	1.4	1.3	1.3	1.3	1.6	1.6	1.7	1.8	1.9
Dominican Republic / República Dominicana	0.7	1.0	4.4	4.8	5.0	5.2	5.6	6.0	6.3	4.5
Ecuador	0.0	0.0	0.0	0.0	0.0	0.0	0.0	0.0	0.0	0.0
El Salvador	5.1	0.7	0.7	0.5	0.5	0.5	0.5	0.5	0.5	0.6
Guatemala	1.6	1.0	1.3	1.3	1.5	1.5	1.4	1.5	1.4	1.5
Honduras	0.8	1.2	0.5	0.5	0.5	0.5	0.5	1.8	1.7	2.6
Jamaica[1]	0.9	0.7	0.9	0.9	0.7	1.0	0.8	0.9	1.6	1.6
Mexico / México[1]	1.5	1.4	1.6	1.4	1.7	1.6	1.5	1.5	1.5	1.5
Nicaragua	..	0.0	0.0	0.0	0.2	0.4	0.5	0.5	0.6	0.6
Panama / Panamá	4.9	3.1	4.6	4.0	4.0	4.2	3.9	3.7	4.3	4.2
Paraguay[1]	4.9	0.0	0.0	2.2	2.0	1.7	1.6	1.6	1.5	1.3
Peru / Perú	15.3	0.0	3.3	3.2	3.3	3.0	2.2	2.0	2.1	2.0
Trinidad and Tobago / Trinidad y Tobago	3.0	2.5	1.4	1.1	1.5	1.1	1.1	1.0	1.4	1.5
Uruguay	8.4	10.2	11.9	9.1	9.0	8.1	7.8	7.4	6.9	6.7
Venezuela	0.3	3.7	5.9	6.5	0.2	0.2	0.1	0.1	0.2	0.2
Unweighted average / Promedio simple										
LAC / ALC[2]	**4.2**	**2.9**	**3.9**	**3.5**	**3.3**	**3.2**	**3.2**	**3.3**	**3.4**	**3.3**
OECD / OCDE[3]	**5.7**	**5.5**	**5.6**	**5.4**	**5.6**	**5.5**	**5.5**	**5.5**	**5.6**	..

Note: The figures exclude local government revenues for Argentina (but include provincial revenues), Bahamas, Barbados, Bolivia, Costa Rica (up to 1997), Dominican Republic, Ecuador, El Salvador, Honduras, Jamaica, Nicaragua, Panama (up to 1998), Paraguay (up to 2004, 2013 and 2014), Peru (up to 2004) and Venezuela as the data are not available.

1. The data for 2013 are used for 2014.
2. Represents a group of 22 Latin American and Caribbean countries. Chile and Mexico are also part of the OECD (34) group.
3. Represents the unweighted average for OECD member countries.

Nota : Las cifras excluyen los ingresos de gobiernos locales en Argentina (pero incluye ingresos de las provincias), Bahamas, Barbados, Bolivia, Costa Rica (hasta 1997), República Dominicana, Ecuador, El Salvador, Honduras, Jamaica, Nicaragua, Panamá (hasta 1998), Paraguay (hasta 2004, 2013 y 2014), Perú (hasta 2004) y Venezuela dado que los datos no están disponibles.

1. Para el 2014 se utilizan los datos 2013.
2. Representa un grupo de 22 países de América Latina y el Caribe. Chile y México son también parte del grupo OCDE (34).
3. Representa el promedio no ponderado para los países miembros de la OCDE.

StatLink http://dx.doi.org/10.1787/888933338004

Table 3.10. Taxes on goods and services (5000) as percentage of GDP
Cuadro 3.10. Impuestos sobre bienes y servicios (5000) en porcentaje del PIB

	1990	2000	2005	2008	2009	2010	2011	2012	2013	2014
Argentina	6.9	10.2	12.0	13.6	13.3	14.0	14.1	14.7	15.2	15.9
Bahamas	9.4	11.4	9.5	11.2	10.5	10.0	12.0	12.4	11.3	11.6
Barbados[1]	10.4	14.4	14.1	14.3	12.2	14.0	15.7	16.4	14.8	14.6
Bolivia	5.1	10.0	12.6	16.4	14.1	14.5	16.4	17.0	18.3	18.4
Brazil / Brasil	12.1	13.7	14.6	14.8	13.7	14.0	14.1	14.1	14.3	13.9
Chile	10.7	12.0	10.7	10.8	9.6	10.0	10.5	10.8	10.8	11.0
Colombia	4.8	6.4	7.6	8.2	7.5	7.7	7.9	7.6	7.3	7.6
Costa Rica	7.9	9.3	9.9	11.1	9.5	9.2	9.4	9.3	9.2	9.1
Dominican Republic / República Dominicana	5.4	8.7	10.2	10.0	8.9	8.9	8.6	8.4	8.7	9.0
Ecuador	4.4	7.3	6.8	6.8	7.2	8.8	8.5	10.0	10.2	10.1
El Salvador	5.4	6.9	8.5	8.7	8.0	8.7	8.8	9.0	9.1	8.6
Guatemala	5.5	7.7	7.9	7.5	6.8	7.0	7.0	7.0	6.9	6.7
Honduras	11.2	10.7	10.4	10.9	9.5	9.7	9.6	9.6	9.5	10.9
Jamaica	9.8	11.6	11.2	11.4	11.4	12.9	12.6	13.1	13.6	13.3
Mexico / México[1]	8.6	8.8	10.0	12.3	8.6	9.7	10.5	10.6	9.8	9.8
Nicaragua	..	8.6	9.2	8.9	8.3	9.1	9.3	9.6	9.6	9.5
Panama / Panamá	5.5	4.9	4.5	5.3	5.2	5.7	6.0	5.9	5.6	5.4
Paraguay[1]	2.8	8.4	8.0	8.7	8.9	10.0	10.2	10.2	9.4	10.0
Peru / Perú	7.9	8.9	8.8	8.7	7.7	8.3	8.1	8.0	8.2	8.3
Trinidad and Tobago / Trinidad y Tobago	9.5	7.5	5.9	5.7	6.8	6.6	5.2	6.2	6.4	5.9
Uruguay	11.1	11.2	13.1	12.9	12.1	12.2	12.4	12.2	12.0	11.8
Venezuela	2.0	6.5	8.2	6.6	7.8	7.2	8.0	8.7	9.3	11.1
Unweighted average / Promedio simple										
LAC / ALC[2]	**7.5**	**9.3**	**9.7**	**10.2**	**9.4**	**9.9**	**10.2**	**10.5**	**10.4**	**10.6**
OECD / OCDE[3]	**10.2**	**11.0**	**11.0**	**10.6**	**10.4**	**10.6**	**10.8**	**10.9**	**11.0**	..

Note: The figures exclude local government revenues for Argentina (but include provincial revenues), Bahamas, Barbados, Bolivia, Costa Rica (up to 1997), Dominican Republic, Ecuador, El Salvador, Honduras, Jamaica, Nicaragua, Panama (up to 1998), Paraguay (up to 2004, 2013 and 2014), Peru (up to 2004) and Venezuela as the data are not available.

1. The data for 2013 are used for 2014.
2. Represents a group of 22 Latin American and Caribbean countries. Chile and Mexico are also part of the OECD (34) group.
3. Represents the unweighted average for OECD member countries.

Nota : Las cifras excluyen los ingresos de gobiernos locales en Argentina (pero incluye ingresos de las provincias), Bahamas, Barbados, Bolivia, Costa Rica (hasta 1997), República Dominicana, Ecuador, El Salvador, Honduras, Jamaica, Nicaragua, Panamá (hasta 1998), Paraguay (hasta 2004, 2013 y 2014), Perú (hasta 2004) y Venezuela dado que los datos no están disponibles.

1. Para el 2014 se utilizan los datos 2013.
2. Representa un grupo de 22 países de América Latina y el Caribe. Chile y México son también parte del grupo OCDE (34).
3. Representa el promedio no ponderado para los países miembros de la OCDE.

StatLink http://dx.doi.org/10.1787/888933338015

Table 3.11. Taxes on goods and services (5000) as percentage of total taxation
Cuadro 3.11. Impuestos sobre bienes y servicios (5000) en porcentaje del total de ingresos tributarios

	1990	2000	2005	2008	2009	2010	2011	2012	2013	2014
Argentina	55.7	56.5	54.6	55.2	52.2	52.4	51.2	50.5	49.6	49.5
Bahamas	76.4	74.9	69.4	65.1	63.9	62.3	63.4	68.8	66.1	66.1
Barbados[1]	44.8	47.6	47.9	45.8	40.0	45.7	48.4	49.5	50.2	47.9
Bolivia	62.5	61.3	58.2	65.0	54.3	62.3	62.8	61.5	63.4	63.9
Brazil / Brasil	47.7	46.3	44.7	43.9	42.1	43.0	42.4	42.4	42.5	41.7
Chile	62.9	63.8	51.5	50.6	55.9	51.3	49.3	50.1	54.0	55.3
Colombia	53.8	43.8	42.1	43.4	40.6	42.9	41.7	38.5	36.4	37.3
Costa Rica	49.0	51.1	49.4	48.7	45.1	44.3	44.2	43.8	40.8	40.3
Dominican Republic / República Dominicana	69.9	74.6	74.4	70.0	69.9	72.0	70.0	64.0	62.8	63.5
Ecuador	62.1	71.8	57.8	48.3	48.4	54.2	48.8	51.9	53.2	53.0
El Salvador	51.3	57.0	60.7	57.5	55.5	57.3	57.1	56.3	53.5	52.0
Guatemala	61.0	62.4	60.3	57.9	55.7	56.5	55.1	54.6	52.9	52.9
Honduras	69.1	70.0	61.2	57.6	55.4	55.8	57.1	53.9	51.7	55.2
Jamaica	42.5	50.9	47.8	45.5	46.1	51.6	51.4	53.1	54.5	55.1
Mexico / México[1]	55.3	53.0	56.7	59.2	50.2	52.6	54.1	54.5	49.8	49.8
Nicaragua	..	66.3	57.2	52.9	49.1	50.7	49.5	49.4	48.2	46.6
Panama / Panamá	37.6	28.4	29.4	30.2	29.0	30.2	32.5	30.5	28.8	30.0
Paraguay[1]	51.4	58.0	58.0	59.9	55.5	60.5	60.6	57.5	57.5	58.6
Peru / Perú	65.6	60.9	53.5	46.0	45.8	46.6	43.6	42.5	44.4	44.0
Trinidad and Tobago / Trinidad y Tobago	40.8	35.0	22.3	19.1	24.0	24.1	19.6	22.6	23.3	20.8
Uruguay	56.7	51.8	55.1	49.3	46.9	47.1	46.9	45.6	44.0	43.8
Venezuela	11.1	47.7	51.8	46.8	54.6	61.2	58.9	61.0	63.1	60.7
Unweighted average / Promedio simple										
LAC / ALC[2]	**53.7**	**56.1**	**52.9**	**50.8**	**49.1**	**51.1**	**50.4**	**50.1**	**49.6**	**49.5**
OECD / OCDE[3]	**33.0**	**33.1**	**33.2**	**32.1**	**32.5**	**33.1**	**33.0**	**32.9**	**32.7**	..

Note: The figures exclude local government revenues for Argentina (but include provincial revenues), Bahamas, Barbados, Bolivia, Costa Rica (up to 1997), Dominican Republic, Ecuador, El Salvador, Honduras, Jamaica, Nicaragua, Panama (up to 1998), Paraguay (up to 2004, 2013 and 2014), Peru (up to 2004) and Venezuela as the data are not available.

1. The data for 2013 are used for 2014.
2. Represents a group of 22 Latin American and Caribbean countries. Chile and Mexico are also part of the OECD (34) group.
3. Represents the unweighted average for OECD member countries.

Nota : Las cifras excluyen los ingresos de gobiernos locales en Argentina (pero incluye ingresos de las provincias), Bahamas, Barbados, Bolivia, Costa Rica (hasta 1997), República Dominicana, Ecuador, El Salvador, Honduras, Jamaica, Nicaragua, Panamá (hasta 1998), Paraguay (hasta 2004, 2013 y 2014), Perú (hasta 2004) y Venezuela dado que los datos no están disponibles.

1. Para el 2014 se utilizan los datos 2013.
2. Representa un grupo de 22 países de América Latina y el Caribe. Chile y México son también parte del grupo OCDE (34).
3. Representa el promedio no ponderado para los países miembros de la OCDE.

StatLink http://dx.doi.org/10.1787/888933338023

Table 3.12. Taxes on general consumption (5110) as percentage of GDP
Cuadro 3.12. Impuestos generales sobre el consumo (5110) en porcentaje del PIB

	1990	2000	2005	2008	2009	2010	2011	2012	2013	2014
Argentina	3.0	7.2	7.7	8.6	8.8	9.1	9.5	10.1	11.0	11.4
Bahamas	0.0	0.0	0.0	0.0	0.0	0.0	0.0	0.0	0.0	0.0
Barbados	4.8	8.0	7.8	8.9	7.4	8.5	10.3	10.5	10.0	9.8
Bolivia	3.2	5.1	5.9	7.0	6.3	6.7	7.3	7.6	7.8	8.2
Brazil / Brasil	12.0	12.8	13.5	13.4	12.7	12.8	12.9	13.0	13.2	12.9
Chile	6.3	7.9	7.8	8.4	7.3	7.6	7.9	8.1	8.2	8.2
Colombia	2.3	4.6	5.9	6.5	6.0	6.1	6.4	6.3	5.7	6.0
Costa Rica	3.2	4.5	5.1	6.0	4.9	4.8	4.9	4.9	4.8	4.7
Dominican Republic / República Dominicana	1.2	2.5	3.8	4.5	4.0	4.1	4.0	3.9	4.4	4.7
Ecuador	2.0	4.6	4.8	4.6	4.8	5.6	5.3	6.2	6.4	6.3
El Salvador	2.8	5.4	6.5	6.8	6.1	6.7	6.8	7.0	7.1	6.8
Guatemala	2.4	4.7	5.2	5.5	4.9	5.1	5.2	5.3	5.2	5.1
Honduras	2.7	4.8	5.2	6.3	5.2	5.4	5.7	5.6	5.5	6.8
Jamaica	0.0	3.4	3.9	4.0	3.8	3.9	3.9	3.9	4.0	4.0
Mexico / México[1]	3.2	3.1	3.4	3.7	3.4	3.8	3.7	3.7	3.5	3.5
Nicaragua	..	4.5	5.3	5.5	5.2	5.5	5.9	6.2	6.2	6.3
Panama / Panamá	1.3	0.6	0.9	2.3	2.3	2.9	3.3	3.3	3.1	3.1
Paraguay	0.0	4.7	4.6	5.5	5.6	6.3	6.5	6.5	6.3	6.8
Peru / Perú	1.5	5.4	6.0	7.1	6.3	6.8	6.7	6.7	6.8	7.0
Trinidad and Tobago / Trinidad y Tobago	4.6	3.7	2.9	3.6	4.2	4.3	3.0	3.8	3.9	3.3
Uruguay	5.5	6.5	8.2	9.2	8.6	8.6	8.6	8.5	8.3	8.1
Venezuela	0.0	4.1	6.4	4.6	5.9	5.5	6.2	6.8	7.5	8.6
Unweighted average / Promedio simple										
LAC / ALC[2]	**3.1**	**5.1**	**5.7**	**6.3**	**5.9**	**6.2**	**6.4**	**6.6**	**6.6**	**6.7**
OECD / OCDE[3]	**5.7**	**6.7**	**6.8**	**6.6**	**6.5**	**6.6**	**6.8**	**6.8**	**6.8**	..

Note: The figures exclude local government revenues for Argentina (but include provincial revenues), Bahamas, Barbados, Bolivia, Costa Rica (up to 1997), Dominican Republic, Ecuador, El Salvador, Honduras, Jamaica, Nicaragua, Panama (up to 1998), Paraguay (up to 2004, 2013 and 2014), Peru (up to 2004) and Venezuela as the data are not available.

1. The data for 2013 are used for 2014.
2. Represents a group of 22 Latin American and Caribbean countries. Chile and Mexico are also part of the OECD (34) group.
3. Represents the unweighted average for OECD member countries.

Nota : Las cifras excluyen los ingresos de gobiernos locales en Argentina (pero incluye ingresos de las provincias), Bahamas, Barbados, Bolivia, Costa Rica (hasta 1997), República Dominicana, Ecuador, El Salvador, Honduras, Jamaica, Nicaragua, Panamá (hasta 1998), Paraguay (hasta 2004, 2013 y 2014), Perú (hasta 2004) y Venezuela dado que los datos no están disponibles.

1. Para el 2014 se utilizan los datos 2013.
2. Representa un grupo de 22 países de América Latina y el Caribe. Chile y México son también parte del grupo OCDE (34).
3. Representa el promedio no ponderado para los países miembros de la OCDE.

StatLink http://dx.doi.org/10.1787/888933338033

Table 3.13. Taxes on general consumption (5110) as percentage of total taxation
Cuadro 3.13. Impuestos generales sobre el consumo (5110) en porcentaje del total de ingresos tributarios

	1990	2000	2005	2008	2009	2010	2011	2012	2013	2014
Argentina	23.9	40.2	34.7	34.7	34.5	34.1	34.5	34.6	36.0	35.4
Bahamas	0.0	0.0	0.0	0.0	0.0	0.0	0.0	0.0	0.0	0.0
Barbados	20.9	26.6	26.6	28.6	24.1	27.7	31.8	31.6	33.8	32.2
Bolivia	39.5	31.2	27.5	27.5	24.4	28.9	27.8	27.6	26.9	28.5
Brazil / Brasil	47.4	43.4	41.4	39.5	39.2	39.5	38.7	39.2	39.3	38.6
Chile	37.4	41.8	37.8	39.4	42.5	38.7	37.0	37.7	40.8	41.6
Colombia	26.1	31.4	32.4	34.4	32.1	33.8	34.1	31.9	28.4	29.4
Costa Rica	20.0	24.9	25.3	26.3	23.3	23.1	23.2	23.2	21.2	21.1
Dominican Republic / República Dominicana	15.2	21.1	27.6	31.5	31.7	33.6	32.8	29.7	31.9	33.3
Ecuador	28.1	45.2	40.7	32.6	32.4	34.3	30.6	31.8	33.3	33.2
El Salvador	26.2	45.1	46.3	45.1	42.2	44.3	44.3	43.8	41.8	41.5
Guatemala	27.2	37.9	39.6	42.3	39.9	41.2	41.4	41.5	39.8	40.3
Honduras	16.9	31.5	30.7	33.2	30.5	31.0	33.6	31.4	29.9	34.2
Jamaica	0.1	14.9	16.7	16.1	15.4	15.7	15.7	15.8	16.1	16.6
Mexico / México[1]	20.8	18.7	19.1	18.0	19.7	20.5	19.0	19.0	17.6	17.6
Nicaragua	..	34.8	32.9	32.5	30.7	30.8	31.3	31.5	31.3	31.1
Panama / Panamá	9.0	3.4	5.8	13.1	12.8	15.3	17.9	17.0	16.2	17.0
Paraguay	0.0	32.1	33.3	37.5	34.6	38.3	38.9	37.0	38.4	39.7
Peru / Perú	12.1	36.8	36.3	37.1	37.2	38.4	36.4	35.4	37.0	37.3
Trinidad and Tobago / Trinidad y Tobago	19.5	17.2	11.0	12.3	15.0	15.5	11.3	14.0	14.3	11.6
Uruguay	28.1	30.2	34.2	35.0	33.3	33.0	32.6	31.7	30.6	30.0
Venezuela	0.0	30.2	40.4	32.8	41.2	46.6	45.9	47.9	50.6	47.4
Unweighted average / Promedio simple										
LAC / ALC[2]	**20.9**	**30.4**	**30.5**	**30.9**	**30.3**	**31.6**	**31.4**	**31.1**	**31.2**	**31.3**
OECD / OCDE[3]	**18.1**	**19.7**	**20.2**	**19.8**	**19.9**	**20.3**	**20.3**	**20.2**	**20.2**	..

Note: The figures exclude local government revenues for Argentina (but include provincial revenues), Bahamas, Barbados, Bolivia, Costa Rica (up to 1997), Dominican Republic, Ecuador, El Salvador, Honduras, Jamaica, Nicaragua, Panama (up to 1998), Paraguay (up to 2004, 2013 and 2014), Peru (up to 2004) and Venezuela as the data are not available.

1. The data for 2013 are used for 2014.
2. Represents a group of 22 Latin American and Caribbean countries. Chile and Mexico are also part of the OECD (34) group.
3. Represents the unweighted average for OECD member countries.

Nota : Las cifras excluyen los ingresos de gobiernos locales en Argentina (pero incluye ingresos de las provincias), Bahamas, Barbados, Bolivia, Costa Rica (hasta 1997), República Dominicana, Ecuador, El Salvador, Honduras, Jamaica, Nicaragua, Panamá (hasta 1998), Paraguay (hasta 2004, 2013 y 2014), Perú (hasta 2004) y Venezuela dado que los datos no están disponibles.

1. Para el 2014 se utilizan los datos 2013.
2. Representa un grupo de 22 países de América Latina y el Caribe. Chile y México son también parte del grupo OCDE (34).
3. Representa el promedio no ponderado para los países miembros de la OCDE.

StatLink http://dx.doi.org/10.1787/888933338041

Table 3.14. Taxes on specific goods and services (5120) as percentage of GDP
Cuadro 3.14. Impuestos específicos sobre bienes y servicios (5120) en porcentaje del PIB

	1990	2000	2005	2008	2009	2010	2011	2012	2013	2014
Argentina	3.8	2.7	4.2	4.9	4.3	4.7	4.4	4.4	3.9	4.3
Bahamas	8.7	10.3	8.5	9.9	9.0	8.5	10.1	10.5	9.6	9.1
Barbados	5.5	4.7	4.7	4.1	3.6	3.8	3.9	3.9	3.6	3.1
Bolivia	1.9	4.9	6.6	9.5	7.8	7.8	9.1	9.4	10.5	10.2
Brazil / Brasil	0.0	0.7	0.8	1.2	0.9	1.1	1.2	1.1	1.1	1.0
Chile	3.9	3.5	2.3	1.9	1.7	1.9	2.0	2.0	2.0	2.0
Colombia	2.5	1.8	1.7	1.7	1.6	1.6	1.4	1.3	1.6	1.6
Costa Rica	4.3	4.3	4.4	4.6	4.1	3.9	4.0	3.6	3.6	3.4
Dominican Republic / República Dominicana	4.2	6.1	6.3	5.4	4.7	4.6	4.5	4.4	4.2	4.1
Ecuador	2.4	2.6	1.8	2.0	2.2	3.0	2.9	3.7	3.6	3.5
El Salvador	2.6	1.4	2.0	1.9	1.9	2.0	2.0	2.0	2.0	1.7
Guatemala	2.9	2.9	2.6	1.9	1.8	1.7	1.6	1.4	1.3	1.3
Honduras	8.5	5.9	5.2	4.6	4.3	4.3	4.0	4.0	4.0	4.2
Jamaica	9.6	8.0	7.1	7.2	7.4	8.8	8.6	9.0	9.4	9.1
Mexico / México	5.3	5.5	6.5	8.4	5.1	5.8	6.7	6.8	6.2	6.2
Nicaragua	..	4.1	3.9	3.4	3.1	3.6	3.4	3.5	3.4	3.2
Panama / Panamá	2.3	4.0	3.3	2.7	2.6	2.7	2.6	2.5	2.3	2.2
Paraguay[1]	2.8	3.8	3.4	3.1	3.2	3.4	3.4	3.4	2.9	3.1
Peru / Perú	6.5	3.5	2.8	1.7	1.4	1.5	1.3	1.3	1.4	1.2
Trinidad and Tobago / Trinidad y Tobago	4.4	3.2	2.7	1.8	2.3	2.0	1.9	2.0	2.1	2.2
Uruguay	5.1	3.7	4.3	3.1	3.0	3.2	3.3	3.3	3.2	3.2
Venezuela	2.0	2.4	1.8	2.0	1.9	1.7	1.8	1.9	1.8	2.4
Unweighted average / Promedio simple										
LAC / ALC[2]	**4.2**	**4.1**	**4.0**	**3.9**	**3.5**	**3.7**	**3.8**	**3.9**	**3.8**	**3.7**
OECD / OCDE[3]	**3.9**	**3.7**	**3.6**	**3.4**	**3.3**	**3.4**	**3.5**	**3.5**	**3.5**	..

Note: The figures exclude local government revenues for Argentina (but include provincial revenues), Bahamas, Barbados, Bolivia, Costa Rica (up to 1997), Dominican Republic, Ecuador, El Salvador, Honduras, Jamaica, Nicaragua, Panama (up to 1998), Paraguay (up to 2004, 2013 and 2014), Peru (up to 2004) and Venezuela as the data are not available.

1. The data for 2013 are used for 2014.
2. Represents a group of 22 Latin American and Caribbean countries. Chile and Mexico are also part of the OECD (34) group.
3. Represents the unweighted average for OECD member countries.

Nota : Las cifras excluyen los ingresos de gobiernos locales en Argentina (pero incluye ingresos de las provincias), Bahamas, Barbados, Bolivia, Costa Rica (hasta 1997), República Dominicana, Ecuador, El Salvador, Honduras, Jamaica, Nicaragua, Panamá (hasta 1998), Paraguay (hasta 2004, 2013 y 2014), Perú (hasta 2004) y Venezuela dado que los datos no están disponibles.

1. Para el 2014 se utilizan los datos 2013.
2. Representa un grupo de 22 países de América Latina y el Caribe. Chile y México son también parte del grupo OCDE (34).
3. Representa el promedio no ponderado para los países miembros de la OCDE.

StatLink http://dx.doi.org/10.1787/888933338055

Table 3.15. Taxes on specific goods and services (5120) as percentage of total taxation
Cuadro 3.15. Impuestos específicos sobre bienes y servicios (5120) en porcentaje del total de ingresos tributarios

	1990	2000	2005	2008	2009	2010	2011	2012	2013	2014
Argentina	30.6	15.0	19.0	19.7	16.8	17.6	16.0	15.1	12.7	13.3
Bahamas	70.1	67.8	62.0	57.3	54.6	52.6	53.7	58.7	55.8	51.8
Barbados	23.9	15.5	15.8	13.2	11.7	12.5	12.2	11.8	12.3	10.3
Bolivia	23.0	30.1	30.7	37.5	29.9	33.4	34.9	33.9	36.4	35.5
Brazil / Brasil	0.0	2.4	2.6	3.6	2.9	3.5	3.7	3.2	3.2	3.1
Chile	23.0	18.8	10.9	8.7	10.1	9.8	9.4	9.4	9.9	10.3
Colombia	27.8	12.4	9.7	9.0	8.4	9.1	7.6	6.5	8.0	7.9
Costa Rica	26.8	23.9	22.1	20.3	19.3	18.6	18.9	16.8	15.8	15.3
Dominican Republic / República Dominicana	53.6	51.9	45.6	37.7	37.2	37.5	36.2	33.2	30.0	29.3
Ecuador	33.8	26.1	15.8	14.6	14.7	18.6	17.0	18.9	18.8	18.6
El Salvador	25.0	11.9	14.4	12.4	13.3	13.0	12.7	12.5	11.7	10.5
Guatemala	32.8	23.4	19.6	14.6	14.6	14.0	12.4	11.3	10.3	10.3
Honduras	52.2	38.5	30.4	24.5	24.9	24.9	23.5	22.5	21.8	21.0
Jamaica	41.6	35.1	30.5	28.7	29.9	35.3	35.0	36.5	37.6	37.7
Mexico / México	34.0	33.4	36.6	40.3	29.4	31.2	34.3	34.9	31.6	31.6
Nicaragua	..	31.5	24.3	20.4	18.4	19.9	18.3	17.9	16.9	15.5
Panama / Panamá	15.5	22.9	21.4	15.4	14.6	14.1	13.8	12.7	11.8	12.2
Paraguay[1]	51.4	25.9	24.6	21.1	19.9	20.8	20.4	19.3	18.0	17.9
Peru / Perú	53.5	24.2	17.2	8.9	8.6	8.2	7.2	7.0	7.4	6.6
Trinidad and Tobago / Trinidad y Tobago	18.8	15.2	10.1	6.0	7.9	7.4	7.2	7.3	7.8	7.9
Uruguay	25.9	17.3	17.9	11.7	11.5	12.2	12.6	12.2	11.6	11.9
Venezuela	11.1	17.5	11.4	14.0	13.4	14.6	13.0	13.1	12.5	13.4
Unweighted average / Promedio simple										
LAC / ALC[2]	**32.1**	**25.5**	**22.4**	**20.0**	**18.7**	**19.5**	**19.1**	**18.9**	**18.3**	**17.8**
OECD / OCDE[3]	**13.2**	**11.6**	**11.1**	**10.5**	**10.6**	**10.9**	**10.8**	**10.8**	**10.5**	..

Note: The figures exclude local government revenues for Argentina (but include provincial revenues), Bahamas, Barbados, Bolivia, Costa Rica (up to 1997), Dominican Republic, Ecuador, El Salvador, Honduras, Jamaica, Nicaragua, Panama (up to 1998), Paraguay (up to 2004, 2013 and 2014), Peru (up to 2004) and Venezuela as the data are not available.

1. The data for 2013 are used for 2014.
2. Represents a group of 22 Latin American and Caribbean countries. Chile and Mexico are also part of the OECD (34) group.
3. Represents the unweighted average for OECD member countries.

Nota : Las cifras excluyen los ingresos de gobiernos locales en Argentina (pero incluye ingresos de las provincias), Bahamas, Barbados, Bolivia, Costa Rica (hasta 1997), República Dominicana, Ecuador, El Salvador, Honduras, Jamaica, Nicaragua, Panamá (hasta 1998), Paraguay (hasta 2004, 2013 y 2014), Perú (hasta 2004) y Venezuela dado que los datos no están disponibles.

1. Para el 2014 se utilizan los datos 2013.
2. Representa un grupo de 22 países de América Latina y el Caribe. Chile y México son también parte del grupo OCDE (34).
3. Representa el promedio no ponderado para los países miembros de la OCDE.

StatLink http://dx.doi.org/10.1787/888933338063

Table 3.16. Gross domestic product for tax reporting years at market prices, in billions of national currency units
Cuadro 3.16. Producto interno bruto para los años fiscales a precios de mercado, en millardos de moneda local

	1990	2000	2005	2008	2009	2010	2011	2012	2013	2014
Argentina	82	340	647	1 284	1 412	1 811	2 312	2 766	3 406	4 426
Bahamas	4	6	8	8	8	8	8	8	8	9
Barbados	4	6	8	9	9	9	9	9	9	9
Bolivia	15	52	77	121	122	138	166	187	212	228
Brazil / Brasil	0	1 202	2 172	3 108	3 328	3 887	4 375	4 713	5 158	5 521
Chile	10 482	42 095	68 883	93 848	96 444	110 999	121 319	129 028	137 029	147 185
Colombia	28 651	208 531	340 156	480 087	504 647	544 924	619 894	664 240	710 257	756 152
Costa Rica	664	4 915	9 539	15 702	16 845	19 087	20 852	22 782	24 607	26 675
Dominican Republic / República Dominicana	82	414	1 088	1 657	1 729	1 979	2 218	2 378	2 559	2 786
Ecuador	15	18	42	62	63	70	79	88	95	101
El Salvador	5	13	17	21	21	21	23	24	24	25
Guatemala	31	133	208	296	308	333	371	395	423	455
Honduras	13	107	184	262	276	299	335	361	377	410
Jamaica	34	385	700	997	1 065	1 153	1 239	1 312	1 430	1 545
Mexico / México	825	6 132	9 425	12 257	12 073	13 267	14 527	15 600	16 083	17 125
Nicaragua	0	65	106	164	170	187	219	246	268	306
Panama / Panamá	6	12	15	23	24	27	31	36	40	44
Paraguay	6 474	24 737	53 962	80 735	79 117	94 934	105 203	108 832	124 853	138 260
Peru / Perú	5	178	247	356	365	420	470	508	545	575
Trinidad and Tobago / Trinidad y Tobago	22	51	101	175	121	141	163	165	170	175
Uruguay	12	276	425	636	715	808	926	1 044	1 178	1 336
Venezuela	2	80	304	678	707	1 017	1 357	1 635	2 204	3 150

Source: OECD National Accounts data for Chile and Mexico and official National Accounts data for the other countries. The World Economic Outlook (IMF) was used for Bahamas, Panama (2013 and 2014) and Venezuela (2013 and 2014).

Fuente : Datos de Cuentas Nacionales de la OCDE para Chile y México y estadísticas oficiales de Cuentas Nacionales para el resto de países. Para Bahamas, Panamá (2013 and 2014) y Venezuela (2013 and 2014) se utilizó el World Economic Outlook (FMI).

StatLink http://dx.doi.org/10.1787/888933338078

3.2. Comparative charts / 3.2. Gráficos comparativos

Figure 3.1. **Tax revenue of main headings as percentage of total tax revenue, 2014**
Gráfico 3.1. **Ingresos tributarios de categorías principales como porcentaje del ingreso tributario total, 2014**

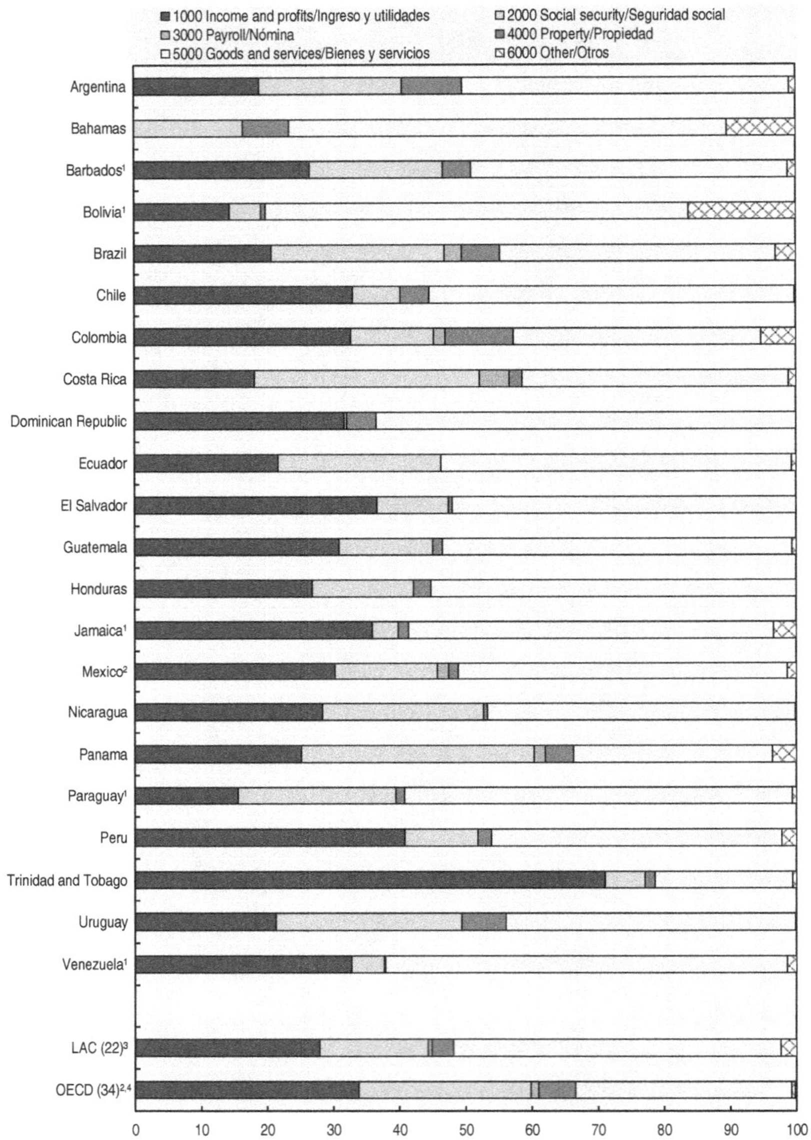

1. The data are estimated.
1. Datos estimados.
2. Data for 2013 is used.
2. Se utilizan datos del 2013.
3. Represents the unweighted average for a group of 22 Latin American and Caribbean countries. Chile and Mexico are also part of the OECD (34) group.
3. Representa el promedio no ponderado para un grupo de 22 países de América Latina y el Caribe. Chile y México son también parte del grupo OCDE(34).
4. Represents the unweighted average for OECD member countries.
4. Representa el promedio no ponderado para los países miembros de la OCDE.

StatLink http://dx.doi.org/10.1787/888933337897

Figure 3.2. **Tax structures in Latin American and Caribbean countries, 1990-2014**

Receipts as percentage of total tax revenues

Gráfico 3.2. **Estructuras impositivas en países de América Latina y el Caribe, 1990-2014**

Ingresos como porcentaje de los ingresos tributarios totales

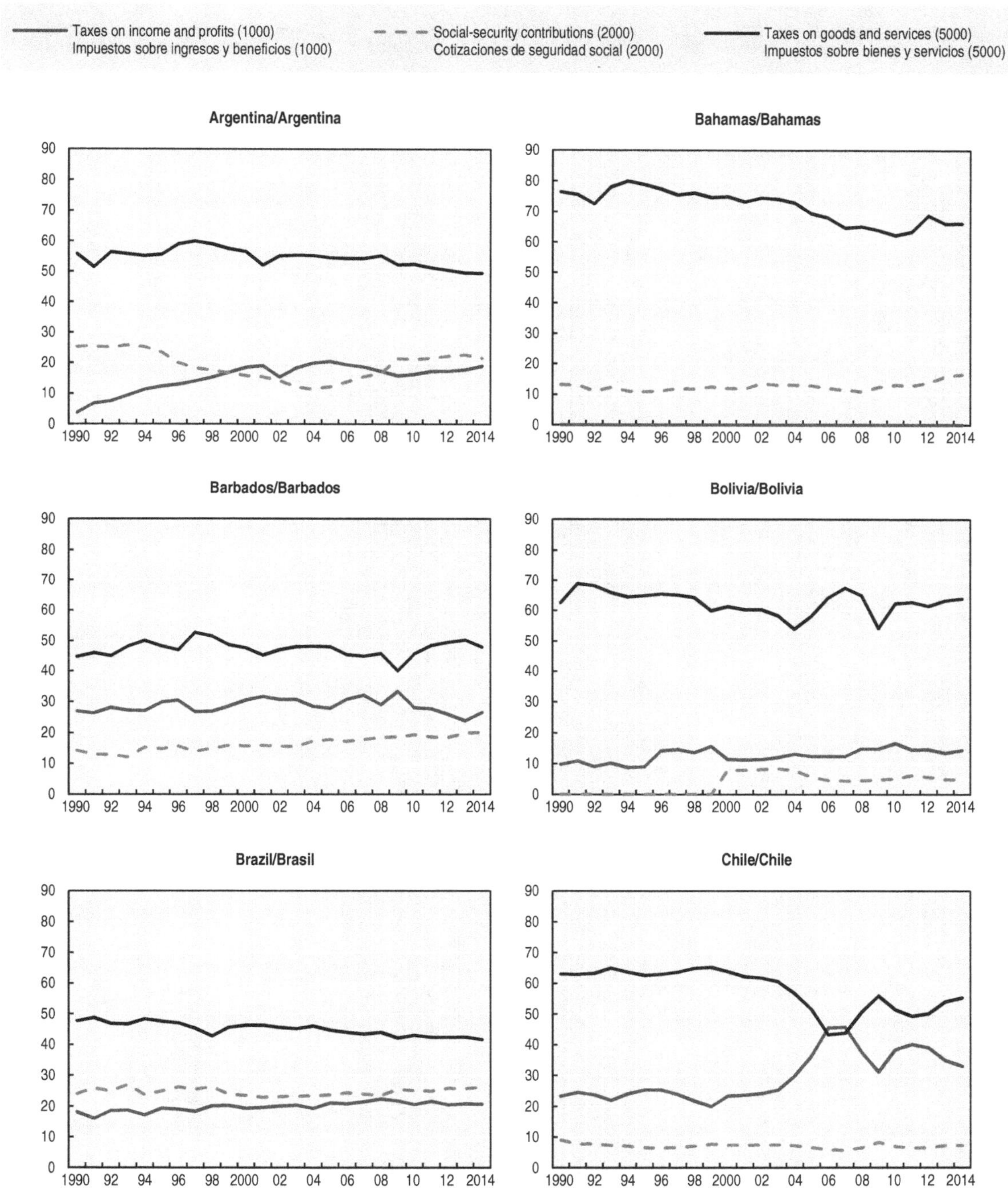

Figure 3.2. **Tax structures in Latin American and Caribbean countries, 1990-2014** *(cont.)*

Receipts as percentage of total tax revenues

Gráfico 3.2. **Estructuras impositivas en países de América Latina y el Caribe, 1990-2014** *(cont.)*

Ingresos como porcentaje de los ingresos tributarios totales

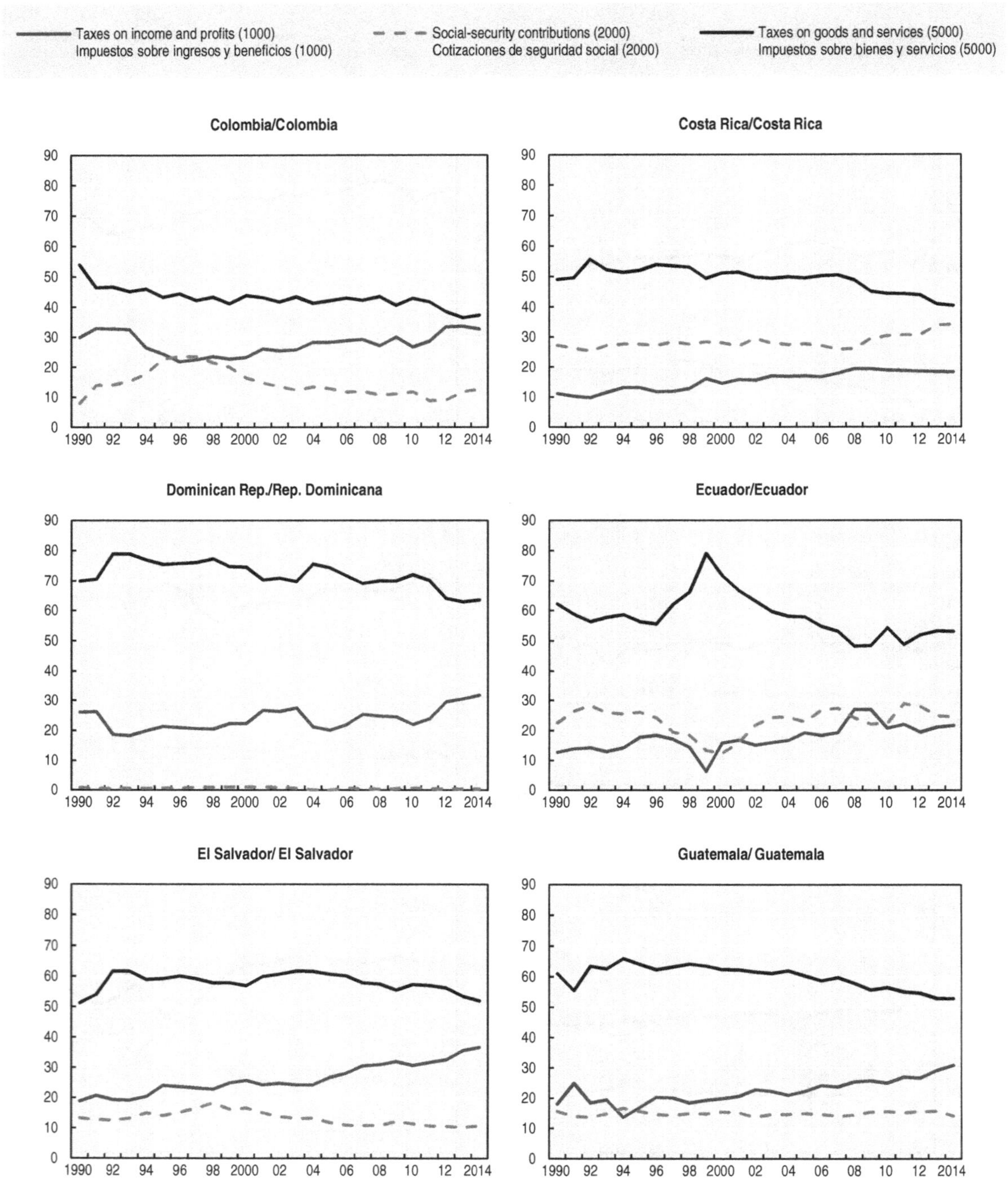

Figure 3.2. **Tax structures in Latin American and Caribbean countries, 1990-2014** *(cont.)*

Receipts as percentage of total tax revenues

Gráfico 3.2. **Estructuras impositivas en países de América Latina y el Caribe, 1990-2014** *(cont.)*

Ingresos como porcentaje de los ingresos tributarios totales

Figure 3.2. **Tax structures in Latin American and Caribbean countries, 1990-2014** *(cont.)*

Receipts as percentage of total tax revenues

Gráfico 3.2. **Estructuras impositivas en países de América Latina y el Caribe, 1990-2014** *(cont.)*

Ingresos como porcentaje de los ingresos tributarios totales

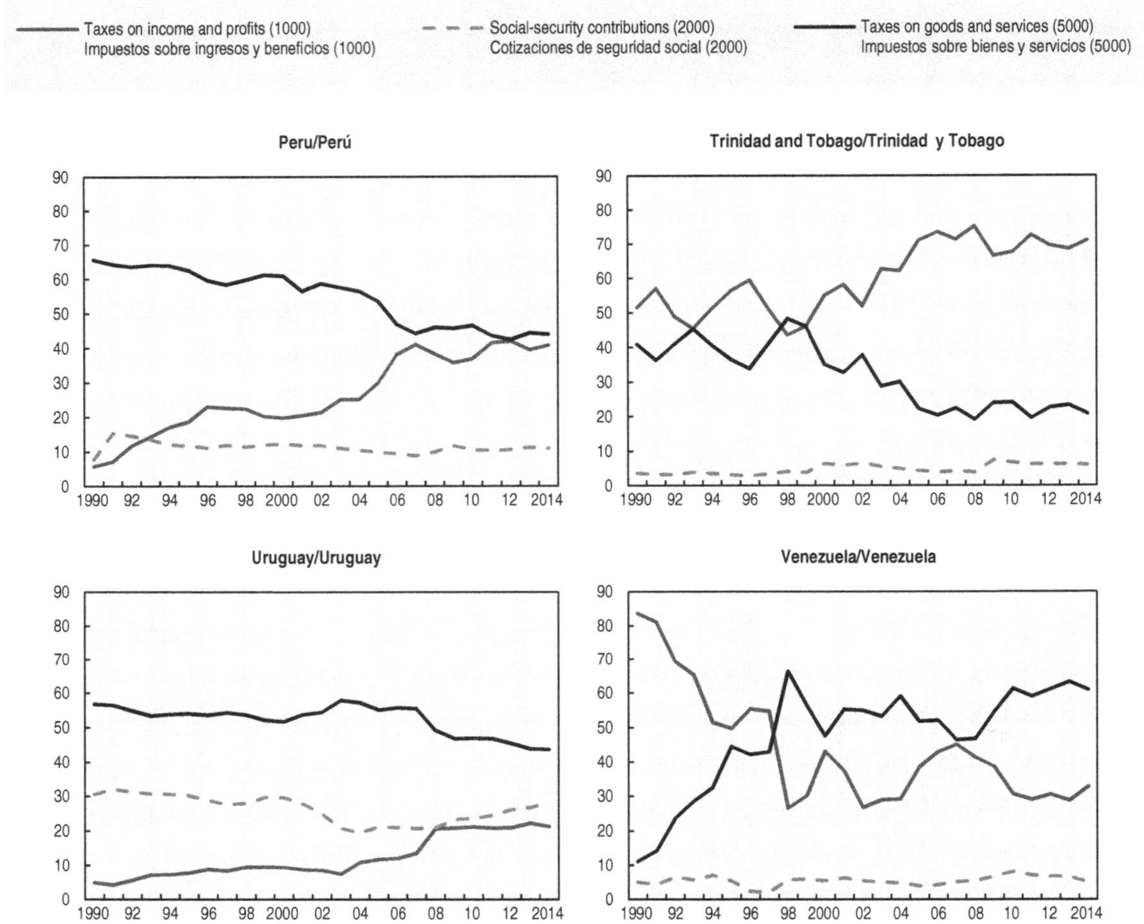

StatLink http://dx.doi.org/10.1787/888933337901

CHAPTER 4

COUNTRY TABLES, 1990-2014 – TAX REVENUES

CAPÍTULO 4

CUADROS PAÍS, 1990-2014 – INGRESOS TRIBUTARIOS

Table 4.1. Argentina / Argentina
Details of tax revenue / Ingresos tributarios detallados

Million ARS

	1990	2000	2005	2008	2009	2010	2011	2012	2013	2014
Total tax revenue	**10 218**	**61 085**	**142 905**	**317 585**	**360 951**	**483 014**	**638 428**	**808 130**	**1 043 967**	**1 424 524**
1000 Taxes on income, profits and capital gains	**382**	**11 304**	**29 202**	**54 722**	**56 887**	**78 427**	**110 119**	**140 108**	**185 688**	**269 808**
1100 Of individuals	12	3 937	8 192	17 614	19 574	23 980	36 870	54 494	79 804	125 502
1110 On income and profits	..	3 855	8 151	17 534	19 460	23 858	36 713	54 279	79 450	125 066
1120 On capital gains	12	82	41	80	114	122	157	215	354	436
1200 Corporate	..	6 575	19 601	34 026	33 921	50 664	68 128	81 938	99 345	132 178
1210 On profits	..	6 575	19 601	34 026	33 921	50 664	68 128	81 938	99 345	132 178
Corporate income taxes	..	5 956	18 494	33 031	32 702	49 012	66 767	80 490	97 614	129 881
Tax on assets	..	19	5	7	6	4	4	5	3	6
Tax on assumed minimum income	..	600	1 102	988	1 213	1 648	1 357	1 443	1 728	2 291
1220 On capital gains	..	..	..	..	..	..	..	..	..	..
1300 Unallocable between 1100 and 1200	371	792	1 409	3 082	3 392	3 783	5 121	3 676	6 539	12 128
Non resident taxpayers	0	792	1 409	3 082	3 392	3 783	5 121	3 676	6 539	12 128
Other	371	0	0	0	0	0	0	0	0	0
2000 Social security contributions	**2 583**	**9 670**	**17 400**	**52 565**	**77 230**	**102 460**	**137 187**	**179 777**	**236 072**	**307 657**
2100 Employees	..	2 486	3 690	12 917	28 871	37 990	51 715	70 087	91 768	121 942
2110 On a payroll basis	..	2 486	3 690	12 917	28 871	37 990	51 715	70 087	91 768	121 942
2120 On an income tax basis	..	0	0	0	0	0	0	0	0	0
2200 Employers	..	6 069	12 557	32 459	40 473	54 713	75 550	100 029	133 290	174 299
2210 On a payroll basis	..	6 069	12 557	32 459	40 473	54 713	75 550	100 029	133 290	174 299
2220 On an income tax basis	..	0	0	0	0	0	0	0	0	0
2300 Self-employed or non-employed	98	1 115	1 153	7 189	7 886	9 757	9 922	9 661	11 014	11 416
2310 On a payroll basis	98	1 115	1 153	7 189	7 886	9 757	9 922	9 661	11 014	11 416
2320 On an income tax basis	0	0	0	0	0	0	0	0	0	0
2400 Unallocable between 2100, 2200 and 2300	2 485	0	0	0	0	0	0	0	0	0
2410 On a payroll basis	2 485	..	..	..	..	..	..	..	..	..
2420 On an income tax basis	0	..	..	..	..	..	..	..	..	..
3000 Taxes on payroll and workforce	**0**	**0**	**0**	**0**	**0**	**0**	**0**	**0**	**0**	**0**
4000 Taxes on property	**1 302**	**3 896**	**15 997**	**30 859**	**33 167**	**43 539**	**57 537**	**72 374**	**96 679**	**129 066**
4100 Recurrent taxes on immovable property	412	1 809	2 836	3 929	4 170	5 035	6 099	9 921	14 097	17 547
4110 Households	0	0	0	0	0	0	0	0	0	0
4120 Others	412	1 809	2 836	3 929	4 170	5 035	6 099	9 921	14 097	17 547
4200 Recurrent taxes on net wealth	235	1 084	1 868	3 446	4 123	5 248	6 018	7 408	10 471	14 576
4210 Individual	232	1 024	1 813	3 375	4 041	5 147	5 892	7 263	10 296	14 356
Personal assets	232	1 024	1 813	3 375	4 041	5 147	5 892	7 263	10 296	14 356
Recurrent taxes on net wealth	0	0	0	0	0	0	0	0	0	0
4220 Corporate	3	60	55	71	82	101	126	145	175	220
4300 Estate, inheritance and gift taxes	0	0	0	0	0	0	0	0	0	0
4310 Estate and inheritance taxes	..	..	..	..	..	..	..	..	..	..
4320 Gift taxes	..	..	..	..	..	..	..	..	..	..
4400 Taxes on financial and capital transactions	656	933	11 272	23 480	24 870	33 253	45 420	55 044	72 111	96 943
Immovable property transfers	0	54	116	439	372	539	775	721	734	912
Movable property transfers	0	0	0	0	0	0	0	0	0	0
Bank accounts' credits and debits	415	0	9 434	19 495	20 561	26 885	36 179	43 931	56 515	76 740
Provincial taxes on financial and capital transactions	160	833	1 722	3 546	3 937	5 829	8 466	10 392	14 862	19 291
Stamp taxes	81	46	0	0	0	0	0	0	0	0
4500 Non-recurrent taxes	0	70	21	4	4	3	0	1	0	0
4510 On net wealth	..	0	0	0	0	0	..	0	..	..
4520 Other non-recurrent taxes	..	70	21	4	4	3	..	1	..	..
4600 Other recurrent taxes on property	0	0	0	0	0	0	0	0	0	0
5000 Taxes on goods and services	**5 692**	**34 510**	**77 960**	**175 234**	**188 345**	**253 092**	**327 059**	**407 714**	**517 591**	**704 678**
5100 Taxes on production, sale, transfer, etc	5 559	33 706	76 671	172 726	185 117	249 494	322 131	401 305	508 532	692 668
5110 General taxes	2 437	24 541	49 581	110 212	124 407	164 478	220 123	279 602	376 236	503 875
5111 Value added taxes	1 591	18 427	34 968	77 335	84 935	113 330	149 547	188 509	243 612	319 988
5112 Sales tax	0	0	0	0	0	0	0	0	0	0
5113 Other	846	6 114	14 613	32 877	39 472	51 148	70 576	91 093	132 624	183 887
5120 Taxes on specific goods and services	3 122	9 165	27 090	62 514	60 710	85 016	102 008	121 703	132 296	188 793
5121 Excises	2 082	5 850	10 611	16 439	19 522	26 207	30 851	40 799	49 680	69 977
Alcoholic beverages	0	36	73	116	169	238	322	422	525	673
Non alcoholic beverages	0	90	189	411	441	501	654	912	1 195	1 586
Beers	0	50	131	228	226	212	210	332	650	879
Tobacco products	0	1 875	3 460	4 686	5 751	6 884	8 620	10 310	12 343	17 432
Liquid fuel and gas	1 068	3 478	6 019	9 701	11 593	15 269	18 131	25 785	31 010	44 490
Electricity	72	205	283	556	559	591	616	610	547	607
Motor vehicles	0	20	0	15	36	27	24	153	185	121
Other	942	96	456	726	747	2 485	2 274	2 275	3 225	4 189
5122 Profits of fiscal monopolies	0	0	0	0	0	0	0	0	0	0

Table 4.1. Argentina / Argentina *(cont.)*
Details of tax revenue / Ingresos tributarios detallados

Million ARS

	1990	2000	2005	2008	2009	2010	2011	2012	2013	2014
5123 Customs and import duties	219	1 976	3 876	8 988	7 700	11 429	14 678	16 640	23 550	30 058
Import duties	166	1 938	3 780	8 803	7 526	11 183	14 373	16 313	23 134	29 482
Import fees	53	38	96	185	174	246	305	327	416	576
5124 Taxes on exports	724	32	12 323	36 055	32 042	45 547	54 163	61 316	55 465	84 088
5125 Taxes on investment goods	0	0	0	0	0	0	0	0	0	0
5126 Taxes on specific services	0	1 233	151	769	1 191	1 429	1 819	2 227	2 677	3 534
Insurance services	..	194	8	13	17	21	27	35	46	65
Financial services	..	855	2	1	0	0	0	0	0	0
Telephone services	..	33	110	480	779	936	1 163	1 391	1 605	1 983
Other specific services	..	151	31	275	395	472	629	801	1 026	1 486
5127 Other taxes on internat. trade and transactions	97	74	129	263	255	404	497	721	924	1 136
5128 Other taxes	0	0	0	0	0	0	0	0	0	0
5130 Unallocable between 5110 and 5120	0	0	0	0	0	0	0	0	0	0
5200 Taxes on use of goods and perform activities	133	804	1 289	2 508	3 228	3 598	4 928	6 409	9 059	12 010
5210 Recurrent taxes	133	804	1 289	2 508	3 228	3 598	4 928	6 409	9 059	12 010
5211 Paid by households: motor vehicles	0	0	0	0	0	0	0	0	0	0
5212 Paid by others: motor vehicles	133	804	1 289	2 508	3 228	3 598	4 928	6 409	9 059	12 010
5213 Paid in respect of other goods	0	0	0	0	0	0	0	0	0	0
5220 Non-recurrent taxes	0	0	0	0	0	0	0	0	0	0
5300 Unallocable between 5100 and 5200	0	0	0	0	0	0	0	0	0	0
6000 Other taxes	**258**	**1 705**	**2 346**	**4 205**	**5 322**	**5 496**	**6 526**	**8 157**	**7 937**	**13 315**
6100 Paid solely by business	0	354	757	1 355	1 550	2 093	2 983	3 825	4 423	4 259
Simplified system for small taxpayers	..	354	757	1 355	1 550	2 093	2 983	3 825	4 423	4 259
6200 Other	258	1 351	1 589	2 850	3 772	3 403	3 543	4 332	3 514	9 056
Tax debt payments	135	24	112	237	1 629	293	710	934	-1 313	1 340
Special payments	80	6	1	0	0	0	0	0	0	0
Other national level	0	12	7	0	0	0	0	0	0	0
Other provincial level	43	1 309	1 469	2 613	2 143	3 110	2 833	3 398	4 827	7 716

Note: Year ending 31st December.
The data are on cash basis.
The figures exclude local government tax revenues as the data are not available.
Heading 5212: In ECLAC data, property tax on motor vehicles is classified in category 4000.

Source: Subsecretaría de Ingresos Públicos, Dirección Nacional de Coordinación Fiscal con las Provincias, Ministry of Economy and Production.

StatLink http://dx.doi.org/10.1787/888933338087

Table 4.2. Bahamas / Bahamas
Details of tax revenue / Ingresos tributarios detallados

Million BSD

	1990	2000	2005	2008	2009	2010	2011	2012	2013	2014
Total tax revenue	**505**	**965**	**1 060**	**1 423**	**1 290**	**1 277**	**1 487**	**1 480**	**1 445**	**1 491**
1000 Taxes on income, profits and capital gains	**0**	**0**	**0**	**0**	**0**	**0**	**0**	**0**	**0**	**0**
1100 Of individuals	..	..	..	..	..	..	..	..	..	..
1110 On income and profits	..	..	..	..	..	..	..	..	..	..
1120 On capital gains	..	..	..	..	..	..	..	..	..	..
1200 Corporate	..	..	..	..	..	..	..	..	..	..
1210 On profits	..	..	..	..	..	..	..	..	..	..
1220 On capital gains	..	..	..	..	..	..	..	..	..	..
1300 Unallocable between 1100 and 1200	..	..	..	..	..	..	..	..	..	..
2000 Social security contributions	**66**	**115**	**136**	**155**	**160**	**167**	**190**	**203**	**229**	**246**
2100 Employees	..	..	..	..	..	..	..	..	..	..
2110 On a payroll basis	..	..	..	..	..	..	..	..	..	..
2120 On an income tax basis	..	..	..	..	..	..	..	..	..	..
2200 Employers	..	..	..	..	..	..	..	..	..	..
2210 On a payroll basis	..	..	..	..	..	..	..	..	..	..
2220 On an income tax basis	..	..	..	..	..	..	..	..	..	..
2300 Self-employed or non-employed	..	..	..	..	..	..	..	..	..	..
2310 On a payroll basis	..	..	..	..	..	..	..	..	..	..
2320 On an income tax basis	..	..	..	..	..	..	..	..	..	..
2400 Unallocable between 2100, 2200 and 2300	66	115	136	155	160	167	190	203	229	246
2410 On a payroll basis	..	..	..	..	..	..	..	..	..	..
2420 On an income tax basis	..	..	..	..	..	..	..	..	..	..
3000 Taxes on payroll and workforce	**0**	**0**	**0**	**0**	**0**	**0**	**0**	**0**	**0**	**0**
4000 Taxes on property	**19**	**32**	**54**	**73**	**85**	**92**	**92**	**95**	**115**	**104**
4100 Recurrent taxes on immovable property	19	32	54	73	85	92	92	95	115	104
4110 Households	0	0	0	0	0	0	0	0	0	0
4120 Others	19	32	54	73	85	92	92	95	115	104
4200 Recurrent taxes on net wealth	0	0	0	0	0	0	0	0	0	0
4210 Individual	..	..	..	..	..	..	..	..	..	..
4220 Corporate	..	..	..	..	..	..	..	..	..	..
4300 Estate, inheritance and gift taxes	0	0	0	0	0	0	0	0	0	0
4310 Estate and inheritance taxes	..	..	..	..	..	..	..	..	..	..
4320 Gift taxes	..	..	..	..	..	..	..	..	..	..
4400 Taxes on financial and capital transactions	0	0	0	0	0	0	0	0	0	0
4500 Non-recurrent taxes	0	0	0	0	0	0	0	0	0	0
4510 On net wealth	..	..	..	..	..	..	..	..	..	..
4520 Other non-recurrent taxes	..	..	..	..	..	..	..	..	..	..
4600 Other recurrent taxes on property	0	0	0	0	0	0	0	0	0	0
5000 Taxes on goods and services	**386**	**723**	**736**	**926**	**824**	**795**	**944**	**1 018**	**955**	**986**
5100 Taxes on production, sale, transfer, etc	354	654	657	815	704	672	799	868	806	772
5110 General taxes	0	0	0	0	0	0	0	0	0	0
5111 Value added taxes	..	..	..	..	..	..	..	..	..	..
5112 Sales tax	..	..	..	..	..	..	..	..	..	..
5113 Other	..	..	..	..	..	..	..	..	..	..
5120 Taxes on specific goods and services	354	654	657	815	704	672	799	868	806	772
5121 Excises	0	0	0	0	187	188	254	331	246	249
5122 Profits of fiscal monopolies	0	0	0	0	0	0	0	0	0	0
5123 Customs and import duties	289	537	525	679	395	364	370	366	350	336
Import tax	289	435	413	530	379	348	354	348	332	336
Stamp tax from imports duties	0	102	112	150	15	15	16	18	18	0
5124 Taxes on exports	6	13	13	15	13	14	13	15	14	10
Export tax	6	13	13	15	13	14	13	15	14	10
Stamp tax from exports	0	0	0	0	0	0	0	0	0	0
5125 Taxes on investment goods	0	0	0	0	0	0	0	0	0	0
5126 Taxes on specific services	59	104	119	120	110	106	162	156	196	178
Departure tax	27	64	69	74	70	70	103	102	144	125
Gaming tax	27	20	25	13	13	10	18	11	10	8
Hotel occupancy tax	5	20	25	33	26	25	41	43	42	45
5127 Other taxes on internat. trade and transactions	0	0	0	0	0	0	0	0	0	0
5128 Other taxes	0	0	0	0	0	0	0	0	0	0
5130 Unallocable between 5110 and 5120	0	0	0	0	0	0	0	0	0	0
5200 Taxes on use of goods and perform activities	32	69	78	112	120	123	145	150	149	214
5210 Recurrent taxes	32	69	78	112	120	123	145	150	149	214
Motor vehicle tax	10	14	18	23	23	21	27	29	28	29
5211 Paid by households: motor vehicles	..	..	..	..	..	..	..	..	..	..
5212 Paid by others: motor vehicles	..	..	..	..	..	..	..	..	..	..

Table 4.2. Bahamas / Bahamas (*cont.*)
Details of tax revenue / Ingresos tributarios detallados

Million BSD

	1990	2000	2005	2008	2009	2010	2011	2012	2013	2014
5213 Paid in respect of other goods	22	55	61	88	97	102	118	121	121	185
Company fees and registration	0	5	5	7	6	5	5	5	5	5
International business companies	0	17	15	22	20	19	17	17	17	17
Others	22	33	40	60	71	78	95	99	99	163
5220 Non-recurrent taxes	0	0	0	0	0	0	0	0	0	0
5300 Unallocable between 5100 and 5200	0	0	0	0	0	0	0	0	0	0
6000 Other taxes	**33**	**95**	**135**	**268**	**221**	**223**	**261**	**163**	**145**	**155**
6100 Paid solely by business	0	0	0	0	0	0	0	0	0	0
6200 Other	33	95	135	268	221	223	261	163	145	155
All other stamp taxes	37	74	135	258	194	162	258	174	160	164
Incentive acts and other refunds	-8	14	-15	-9	5	11	-9	-11	-15	-8
Other taxes	4	7	15	19	22	49	12	0	0	0

Note: Fiscal year ending on 30th June.

The data are on cash basis.

The figures exclude local government tax revenues as the data are not available.

Source: Ministry of Finance and BID-CIAT (2015) *Equivalent Fiscal Pressure for Latin America and the Caribbean.*

StatLink http://dx.doi.org/10.1787/888933338096

Table 4.3. Barbados / Barbados

Details of tax revenue / Ingresos tributarios detallados

Million BAR

	1990	2000	2005	2008	2009	2010	2011	2012	2013	2014
Total tax revenue	**942 335**	**1 884 313**	**2 297 009**	**2 862 355**	**2 810 305**	**2 719 302**	**2 821 723**	**2 869 093**	**2 576 301**	**2 646 853**
1000 Taxes on income, profits and capital gains	**254 016**	**573 920**	**639 432**	**829 428**	**934 345**	**762 340**	**781 866**	**744 289**	**615 036**	**702 017**
1100 Of individuals	128 857	288 692	295 737	335 285	410 348	388 177	419 468	379 969	343 828	428 599
1110 On income and profits	128 857	288 692	295 737	335 285	410 348	388 177	419 468	379 969	343 828	428 599
1120 On capital gains	..	..	..	..	..	..	..	..	..	..
1200 Corporate	111 111	252 291	294 320	419 233	457 825	327 471	298 535	276 296	191 636	208 087
1210 On profits	111 111	252 291	294 320	419 233	457 825	327 471	298 535	276 296	191 636	208 087
1220 On capital gains	..	..	..	..	..	..	..	..	..	..
1300 Unallocable between 1100 and 1200	14 048	32 937	49 375	74 910	66 172	46 692	63 863	88 024	79 572	65 331
2000 Social security contributions	**133 866**	**295 268**	**408 109**	**527 999**	**523 444**	**525 467**	**525 706**	**529 263**	**512 521**	**532 084**
2100 Employees	..	..	..	..	..	..	..	..	..	..
2110 On a payroll basis	..	..	..	..	..	..	..	..	..	..
2120 On an income tax basis	..	..	..	..	..	..	..	..	..	..
2200 Employers	..	..	..	..	..	..	..	..	..	..
2210 On a payroll basis	..	..	..	..	..	..	..	..	..	..
2220 On an income tax basis	..	..	..	..	..	..	..	..	..	..
2300 Self-employed or non-employed	..	..	..	..	..	..	..	..	..	..
2310 On a payroll basis	..	..	..	..	..	..	..	..	..	..
2320 On an income tax basis	..	..	..	..	..	..	..	..	..	..
2400 Unallocable between 2100, 2200 and 2300	133 866	295 268	408 109	527 999	523 444	525 467	525 706	529 263	512 521	532 084
2410 On a payroll basis	..	..	..	..	..	..	..	..	..	..
2420 On an income tax basis	..	..	..	..	..	..	..	..	..	..
3000 Taxes on payroll and workforce	**0**	**0**	**0**	**0**	**0**	**0**	**0**	**0**	**0**	**0**
4000 Taxes on property	**39 117**	**91 928**	**127 362**	**120 295**	**154 772**	**113 533**	**111 726**	**148 176**	**124 972**	**112 998**
4100 Recurrent taxes on immovable property	25 991	60 216	76 247	92 491	137 649	97 595	95 149	133 321	109 436	94 059
Land tax	25 991	60 216	76 247	92 491	137 649	97 595	95 149	133 321	109 436	94 059
4110 Households	..	..	..	..	..	..	..	..	..	..
4120 Others	..	..	..	..	..	..	..	..	..	..
4200 Recurrent taxes on net wealth	0	0	0	0	0	0	0	0	0	0
4210 Individual	..	..	..	..	..	..	..	..	..	..
4220 Corporate	..	..	..	..	..	..	..	..	..	..
4300 Estate, inheritance and gift taxes	0	0	0	0	0	0	0	0	0	0
4310 Estate and inheritance taxes	..	..	..	..	..	..	..	..	..	..
4320 Gift taxes	..	..	..	..	..	..	..	..	..	..
4400 Taxes on financial and capital transactions	0	0	0	0	0	0	0	0	0	0
4500 Non-recurrent taxes	13 126	31 712	51 115	27 804	17 123	15 938	16 577	14 855	15 536	18 939
4510 On net wealth	..	..	..	..	..	..	..	..	..	..
4520 Other non-recurrent taxes	..	..	..	..	..	..	..	..	..	..
4600 Other recurrent taxes on property	0	0	0	0	0	0	0	0	0	0
5000 Taxes on goods and services	**422 259**	**897 092**	**1 101 319**	**1 310 038**	**1 124 028**	**1 242 416**	**1 366 659**	**1 420 525**	**1 292 470**	**1 267 522**
5100 Taxes on production, sale, transfer, etc	422 259	793 469	973 944	1 196 532	1 005 599	1 092 106	1 240 429	1 244 945	1 187 410	1 125 148
5110 General taxes	196 817	501 399	609 915	817 511	677 415	753 003	897 020	907 255	870 692	851 769
5111 Value added taxes	0	500 951	609 915	817 511	677 415	753 003	897 020	907 255	870 692	851 769
5112 Sales tax	196 817	448	0	0	0	0	0	0	0	0
5113 Other	0	0	0	0	0	0	0	0	0	0
5120 Taxes on specific goods and services	225 442	292 069	364 029	379 021	328 184	339 103	343 409	337 690	316 718	273 379
5121 Excises	4 767	158 803	172 377	162 696	144 895	148 191	158 864	137 286	128 730	62 364
5122 Profits of fiscal monopolies	0	0	0	0	0	0	0	0	0	0
5123 Customs and import duties	202 731	132 668	191 652	216 325	183 289	190 912	184 545	200 404	187 988	211 015
Import duties	112 315	132 668	191 652	216 325	183 289	190 912	184 545	200 404	187 988	211 015
Stamp duties	90 416	0	0	0	0	0	0	0	0	0
5124 Taxes on exports	0	0	0	0	0	0	0	0	0	0
5125 Taxes on investment goods	0	0	0	0	0	0	0	0	0	0
5126 Taxes on specific services	17 944	598	0	0	0	0	0	0	0	0
Hotel and restaurant tax	17 944	598	0	0	0	0	0	0	0	0
5127 Other taxes on internat. trade and transactions	0	0	0	0	0	0	0	0	0	0
5128 Other taxes	0	0	0	0	0	0	0	0	0	0
5130 Unallocable between 5110 and 5120	0	0	0	0	0	0	0	0	0	0
5200 Taxes on use of goods and perform activities	0	103 623	127 375	113 506	118 429	150 310	126 230	175 580	105 060	142 374
5210 Recurrent taxes	..	103 623	127 375	113 506	118 429	150 310	126 230	175 580	105 060	142 374
5211 Paid by households: motor vehicles	..	0	0	0	0	0	0	0	0	0
5212 Paid by others: motor vehicles	..	0	0	0	0	0	0	0	0	0
5213 Paid in respect of other goods	..	0	0	0	0	0	0	0	0	0
5220 Non-recurrent taxes	..	0	0	0	0	0	0	0	0	0
5300 Unallocable between 5100 and 5200	0	0	0	0	0	0	0	0	0	0
6000 Other taxes	**93 077**	**26 105**	**20 787**	**74 594**	**73 716**	**75 546**	**35 766**	**26 840**	**31 302**	**32 232**
6100 Paid solely by business	0	0	0	0	0	0	0	0	0	0

Table 4.3. Barbados / Barbados *(cont.)*
Details of tax revenue / Ingresos tributarios detallados

Million BAR

	1990	2000	2005	2008	2009	2010	2011	2012	2013	2014
6200 Other	93 077	26 105	20 787	74 594	73 716	75 546	35 766	26 840	31 302	32 232
Levies	85 937	13 993	0	55 242	60 589	61 015	23 824	15 669	21 027	19 711
Stamp duties	7 140	12 112	20 787	19 352	13 127	14 531	11 942	11 171	10 275	12 521

Note: Year ending 31st December.
The data are on cash basis.
The figures exclude local government tax revenues as the data are not available.
Heading 5210: The data are estimated for 2014.
Source: The Central Bank of Barbados and the Inland Revenue Department.

StatLink http://dx.doi.org/10.1787/888933338106

Table 4.4. Bolivia / Bolivia
Details of tax revenue / Ingresos tributarios detallados

Million BOB

	1990	2000	2005	2008	2009	2010	2011	2012	2013	2014
Total tax revenue	**1 257**	**8 494**	**16 624**	**30 496**	**31 575**	**32 102**	**43 490**	**51 670**	**61 321**	**65 519**
1000 Taxes on income, profits and capital gains	**123**	**967**	**2 058**	**4 540**	**4 700**	**5 326**	**6 331**	**7 556**	**8 246**	**9 463**
1100 Of individuals	62	161	187	232	255	237	260	260	333	401
1110 On income and profits	62	161	187	232	255	237	260	260	333	401
1120 On capital gains	..	..	..	..	..	..	..	..	..	..
1200 Corporate	61	806	1 871	4 308	4 445	5 089	6 072	7 296	7 914	9 062
1210 On profits	61	806	1 871	4 308	4 445	5 089	6 072	7 296	7 914	9 062
Presume profit of enterprises	60	2	0	0	0	0	0	0	0	0
Mining profits	0	0	75	80	61	473	616	322	283	82
Tax regularisation	0	0	0	0	0	0	0	0	0	0
Corporate tax	0	546	1 481	3 657	3 761	3 874	4 724	6 256	6 824	8 026
Corporate tax remittances	0	258	315	571	623	742	732	718	806	954
1220 On capital gains	..	..	..	..	..	..	..	..	..	..
1300 Unallocable between 1100 and 1200	0	0	0	0	0	0	0	0	0	0
2000 Social security contributions	**0**	**666**	**936**	**1 347**	**1 515**	**1 645**	**2 665**	**2 878**	**3 000**	**3 100**
2100 Employees	..	..	..	..	..	..	..	..	..	..
2110 On a payroll basis	..	..	..	..	..	..	..	..	..	..
2120 On an income tax basis	..	..	..	..	..	..	..	..	..	..
2200 Employers	..	..	..	..	..	..	..	..	..	..
2210 On a payroll basis	..	..	..	..	..	..	..	..	..	..
2220 On an income tax basis	..	..	..	..	..	..	..	..	..	..
2300 Self-employed or non-employed	..	..	..	..	..	..	..	..	..	..
2310 On a payroll basis	..	..	..	..	..	..	..	..	..	..
2320 On an income tax basis	..	..	..	..	..	..	..	..	..	..
2400 Unallocable between 2100, 2200 and 2300	..	666	936	1 347	1 515	1 645	2 665	2 878	3 000	3 100
2410 On a payroll basis	..	666	936	1 347	1 515	1 645	2 665	2 878	3 000	3 100
2420 On an income tax basis	..	0	0	0	0	0	0	0	0	0
2430 Unallocable	..	0	0	0	0	0	0	0	0	0
3000 Taxes on payroll and workforce	**0**	**0**	**0**	**0**	**0**	**0**	**0**	**0**	**0**	**0**
4000 Taxes on property	**72**	**3**	**640**	**354**	**357**	**367**	**401**	**401**	**412**	**433**
4100 Recurrent taxes on immovable property	0	0	0	0	0	0	0	0	0	0
4110 Households	..	..	..	..	..	..	..	..	..	..
4120 Others	..	..	..	..	..	..	..	..	..	..
4200 Recurrent taxes on net wealth	0	0	0	0	0	0	0	0	0	0
4210 Individual	..	..	..	..	..	..	..	..	..	..
4220 Corporate	..	..	..	..	..	..	..	..	..	..
4300 Estate, inheritance and gift taxes	1	3	7	14	18	20	22	23	28	32
4310 Estate and inheritance taxes	1	3	7	14	18	20	22	23	28	32
4320 Gift taxes	0	0	0	0	0	0	0	0	0	0
4400 Taxes on financial and capital transactions	0	0	633	340	339	347	380	378	384	401
4500 Non-recurrent taxes	0	0	0	0	0	0	0	0	0	0
4510 On net wealth	..	..	..	..	..	..	..	..	..	..
4520 Other non-recurrent taxes	..	..	..	..	..	..	..	..	..	..
4600 Other recurrent taxes on property	71	0	0	0	0	0	0	0	0	0
5000 Taxes on goods and services	**786**	**5 206**	**9 674**	**19 816**	**17 142**	**20 011**	**27 300**	**31 762**	**38 850**	**41 895**
5100 Taxes on production, sale, transfer, etc	786	5 206	9 674	19 816	17 142	20 011	27 300	31 762	38 850	41 895
5110 General taxes	497	2 649	4 574	8 393	7 705	9 293	12 109	14 245	16 514	18 663
5111 Value added taxes	497	2 649	4 574	8 393	7 705	9 293	12 109	14 245	16 514	18 663
5112 Sales tax	0	0	0	0	0	0	0	0	0	0
5113 Other	0	0	0	0	0	0	0	0	0	0
5120 Taxes on specific goods and services	289	2 557	5 100	11 423	9 437	10 718	15 191	17 517	22 336	23 232
5121 Excises	83	1 930	4 274	9 986	8 220	9 126	13 077	14 992	19 410	20 016
Excises (Internal)	61	244	209	717	739	933	1 204	1 157	1 468	1 365
Excises (Imports)	22	298	208	594	367	379	642	580	719	1 051
Special tax on hydrocarbons and derivatives	0	1 387	1 529	2 031	650	1 070	2 236	1 144	1 681	1 998
Excise tax on hydrocarbons	0	0	2 328	6 644	6 465	6 744	8 996	12 111	15 543	15 602
5122 Profits of fiscal monopolies	0	0	0	0	0	0	0	0	0	0
5123 Customs and import duties	204	612	794	1 406	1 179	1 545	2 049	2 465	2 835	3 104
5124 Taxes on exports	0	0	0	0	0	0	0	0	0	0
5125 Taxes on investment goods	0	0	0	0	0	0	0	0	0	0
5126 Taxes on specific services	2	15	32	31	38	47	65	60	91	112
Air departure tax	2	15	32	31	38	47	52	51	71	82
Tax on gambling	0	0	0	0	0	0	13	9	20	30
5127 Other taxes on internat. trade and transactions	0	0	0	0	0	0	0	0	0	0
5128 Other taxes	0	0	0	0	0	0	0	0	0	0
5130 Unallocable between 5110 and 5120	0	0	0	0	0	0	0	0	0	0
5200 Taxes on use of goods and perform activities	0	0	0	0	0	0	0	0	0	0
5210 Recurrent taxes	..	..	..	..	..	..	..	..	..	..

Table 4.4. Bolivia / Bolivia (*cont.*)
Details of tax revenue / Ingresos tributarios detallados

Million BOB

	1990	2000	2005	2008	2009	2010	2011	2012	2013	2014
5211 Paid by households: motor vehicles	..	..	..	..	..	..	..	..	..	..
5212 Paid by others: motor vehicles	..	..	..	..	..	..	..	..	..	..
5213 Paid in respect of other goods	..	..	..	..	..	..	..	..	..	..
5220 Non-recurrent taxes	..	..	..	..	..	..	..	..	..	..
5300 Unallocable between 5100 and 5200	0	0	0	0	0	0	0	0	0	0
6000 Other taxes	**277**	**1 651**	**3 316**	**4 439**	**7 861**	**4 752**	**6 791**	**9 074**	**10 813**	**10 629**
6100 Paid solely by business	4	6	4	11	12	12	13	14	17	20
Simplified tax regime	3	6	4	11	11	12	13	14	17	20
Integrated tax system	1	0	0	0	0	0	0	0	0	0
6200 Other	273	1 645	3 312	4 428	7 850	4 740	6 779	9 060	10 796	10 608
Rural property tax	2	1	5	9	12	14	17	22	23	23
Fiscal notes	135	701	1 852	2 166	5 834	2 552	3 989	5 836	7 186	6 505
Transactions	136	943	1 455	2 253	2 003	2 174	2 772	3 202	3 587	4 081

Note: Year ending 31st December.

The data are on cash basis.

The figures exclude local government tax revenues as the data are not available.

Heading 1100: In previous publications, the VAT complementary regime was classified under heading 3000. In this publication it has been reclassified under heading 1100 since the taxable base is solely personal income tax.

Heading 2000: The data for social security contributions are available from the year 2000 only and are estimated for 2013 and 2014.

Heading 5121: In ECLAC data the excise tax on hydrocarbons (IDH) is treated as non-tax revenues.

Heading 6200: In previous publications heading 4400 included the general tax on transactions. For this publication, this tax has been reclassified under heading 6200 since the taxable base does not cover property alone.

Source: Ministerio de Economía y Finanzas Públicas, Ministry of Economy and Public Finance.

Unidad de Análisis de Políticas Sociales y Económicas, Social and Economic Policy Analysis Unit.

StatLink http://dx.doi.org/10.1787/888933338119

Table 4.5. Brazil / Brasil
Details of tax revenue / Ingresos tributarios detallados

Million BRL

	1990	2000	2005	2008	2009	2010	2011	2012	2013	2014
Total tax revenue	**3**	**354 760**	**711 145**	**1 049 541**	**1 078 476**	**1 259 796**	**1 457 980**	**1 569 737**	**1 735 438**	**1 842 864**
1000 Taxes on income, profits and capital gains	**1**	**68 667**	**149 309**	**234 380**	**234 400**	**258 738**	**314 298**	**321 461**	**360 568**	**381 862**
1100 Of individuals	0	3 406	6 981	73 639	73 962	87 828	104 335	116 340	126 025	140 438
1110 On income and profits	0	3 406	6 981	73 639	73 962	87 828	104 335	116 340	126 025	140 438
Withholding taxes on income and profits	..	..	..	59 847	60 337	71 580	83 820	93 841	101 837	114 656
1120 On capital gains	..	..	..	..	..	..	..	..	..	..
1200 Corporate	0	25 430	73 071	120 184	120 767	128 255	153 652	148 423	171 003	171 352
1210 On profits	0	25 430	73 071	120 184	120 767	128 255	153 652	148 423	171 003	171 352
Corporate income tax	0	16 680	47 832	78 521	77 343	82 474	94 958	92 589	109 316	109 020
Social contribution on net profits (CSLL)	0	8 750	25 239	41 664	43 424	45 780	58 694	55 834	61 687	62 332
1220 On capital gains	..	..	..	..	..	..	..	..	..	..
1300 Unallocable between 1100 and 1200	0	39 831	69 257	40 556	39 670	42 656	56 311	56 697	63 540	70 072
Withholding taxes	0	39 831	69 257	40 556	39 670	42 656	56 311	56 697	63 540	70 072
2000 Social security contributions	**1**	**83 469**	**168 226**	**246 502**	**273 596**	**314 868**	**362 716**	**404 667**	**444 833**	**482 675**
2100 Employees	..	..	..	..	..	..	..	..	..	..
2110 On a payroll basis	..	..	..	..	..	..	..	..	..	..
2120 On an income tax basis	..	..	..	..	..	..	..	..	..	..
2200 Employers	0	18 709	32 248	50 518	57 183	64 271	74 979	85 813	98 045	108 782
2210 On a payroll basis	0	18 709	32 248	50 518	57 183	64 271	74 979	85 813	98 045	108 782
2220 On an income tax basis	0	0	0	0	0	0	0	0	0	0
2300 Self-employed or non-employed	..	..	..	..	..	..	..	..	..	..
2310 On a payroll basis	..	..	..	..	..	..	..	..	..	..
2320 On an income tax basis	..	..	..	..	..	..	..	..	..	..
2400 Unallocable between 2100, 2200 and 2300	1	64 760	135 978	195 984	216 413	250 597	287 737	318 855	346 789	373 893
2410 On a payroll basis	1	64 760	135 978	195 984	216 413	250 597	287 737	318 855	346 789	373 893
Social security contributions (Federal)	1	59 334	118 869	179 424	200 552	232 838	268 641	296 966	322 516	346 260
Social security contributions (State)	0	4 423	14 682	12 678	11 489	12 635	13 294	15 551	16 499	19 529
Social security contributions (Municipal)	0	1 003	2 427	3 882	4 372	5 124	5 802	6 337	7 774	8 104
2420 On an income tax basis	0	0	0	0	0	0	0	0	0	0
3000 Taxes on payroll and workforce	**0**	**6 749**	**14 468**	**23 318**	**25 246**	**33 052**	**34 204**	**40 169**	**43 391**	**47 724**
PASEP contributions	0	1 312	2 863	4 903	5 137	9 880	6 958	9 398	8 775	9 491
Payroll-based contribution to education	0	2 791	5 906	8 776	9 589	11 049	13 115	14 775	16 561	18 411
"S" System contributions	0	2 646	4 397	7 826	8 524	9 887	11 663	13 519	15 351	16 884
Other	0	0	1 302	1 812	1 996	2 236	2 467	2 477	2 704	2 938
4000 Taxes on property	**0**	**28 818**	**56 274**	**57 925**	**61 202**	**74 373**	**86 692**	**92 092**	**97 927**	**106 834**
4100 Recurrent taxes on immovable property	0	4 753	8 405	13 941	15 608	17 928	20 270	22 154	25 153	28 876
4110 Households	0	0	0	0	0	0	0	0	0	0
4120 Others	0	4 753	8 405	13 941	15 608	17 928	20 270	22 154	25 153	28 876
Tax on rural land property (ITR)	0	234	288	395	421	485	571	614	764	900
Tax on urban land property (IPTU)	0	4 519	8 117	13 546	15 187	17 443	19 699	21 540	24 389	27 976
4200 Recurrent taxes on net wealth	0	0	0	0	0	0	0	0	0	0
4210 Individual	..	..	..	..	..	..	..	..	..	..
4220 Corporate	..	..	..	..	..	..	..	..	..	..
4300 Estate, inheritance and gift taxes	0	329	821	1 489	1 678	2 518	2 768	3 409	4 142	4 698
4310 Estate and inheritance taxes	0	329	821	1 489	1 678	2 518	2 768	3 409	4 142	4 698
4320 Gift taxes	0	0	0	0	0	0	0	0	0	0
4400 Taxes on financial and capital transactions	0	18 442	36 587	25 464	23 809	32 560	39 542	39 500	39 400	40 806
Tax on financial operations (IOF)	0	3 096	5 974	20 168	19 235	26 571	31 999	31 002	29 417	29 756
Real estate property transfers (ITBI)	0	950	1 593	4 324	4 610	6 007	7 464	8 498	9 983	11 050
Other	0	14 396	29 021	971	-36	-18	79	0	0	0
4500 Non-recurrent taxes	0	0	0	0	0	0	0	0	0	0
4510 On net wealth	..	..	..	..	..	..	..	..	..	..
4520 Other non-recurrent taxes	..	..	..	..	..	..	..	..	..	..
4600 Other recurrent taxes on property	0	5 294	10 460	17 031	20 107	21 367	24 112	27 030	29 232	32 453
5000 Taxes on goods and services	**2**	**164 144**	**317 875**	**461 228**	**454 452**	**542 259**	**617 638**	**665 341**	**737 012**	**768 021**
5100 Taxes on production, sale, transfer, etc	2	162 575	312 503	453 039	454 452	542 259	617 638	665 341	737 012	768 021
5110 General taxes	2	154 130	294 251	415 059	423 237	497 896	564 065	614 805	681 333	711 496
5111 Value added taxes	1	100 978	177 589	246 178	247 821	293 489	324 761	358 323	393 742	419 459
Tax on the circulation of goods and services (ICMS)	1	82 279	153 437	221 213	227 830	268 117	297 419	327 369	363 190	384 287
Tax on industrialised products (IPI)	0	18 699	24 153	24 965	19 991	25 372	27 342	30 954	30 552	35 172
5112 Sales tax	0	47 046	105 415	143 864	148 074	171 653	200 926	212 096	239 290	236 646
Contribution to financing social security (COFINS)	0	38 707	86 837	118 431	117 084	140 939	164 982	175 008	197 545	194 696
PIS contribution	0	8 339	18 578	25 433	30 990	30 714	35 944	37 088	41 745	41 950
5113 Other	0	6 106	11 247	25 017	27 341	32 755	38 378	44 386	48 301	55 390
5120 Taxes on specific goods and services	0	8 445	18 252	37 980	31 215	44 363	53 573	50 536	55 679	56 525
5121 Excises	..	0	7 683	17 657	12 652	19 683	22 837	14 585	13 105	14 055
5122 Profits of fiscal monopolies	..	0	0	0	0	0	0	0	0	0
5123 Customs and import duties	..	8 445	8 953	17 101	15 904	21 119	26 763	31 088	36 974	36 774

Table 4.5. Brazil / Brasil (*cont.*)
Details of tax revenue / Ingresos tributarios detallados

Million BRL

	1990	2000	2005	2008	2009	2010	2011	2012	2013	2014
5124 Taxes on exports	..	0	0	0	0	0	0	0	0	0
5125 Taxes on investment goods	..	0	0	0	0	0	0	0	0	0
5126 Taxes on specific services	..	0	983	2 305	1 511	2 350	2 466	2 883	3 367	3 198
5127 Other taxes on internat. trade and transactions	..	0	0	0	0	0	0	0	0	0
5128 Other taxes	..	0	633	917	1 147	1 212	1 507	1 979	2 233	2 499
5130 Unallocable between 5110 and 5120	..	0	0	0	0	0	0	0	0	0
5200 Taxes on use of goods and perform activities	0	1 569	5 372	8 189	0	0	0	0	0	0
5210 Recurrent taxes	0	1 569	5 372	8 189	..	..	..	..	..	..
5211 Paid by households: motor vehicles	0	1 569	5 372	8 189	..	..	..	..	..	..
5212 Paid by others: motor vehicles	0	0	0	0	..	..	..	..	..	..
5213 Paid in respect of other goods	0	0	0	0	..	..	..	..	..	..
5220 Non-recurrent taxes	0	0	0	0	..	..	..	..	..	..
5300 Unallocable between 5100 and 5200	0	0	0	0	0	0	0	0	0	0
6000 Other taxes	**0**	**2 913**	**4 993**	**26 189**	**29 581**	**36 505**	**42 433**	**46 006**	**51 707**	**55 750**
6100 Paid solely by business	0	0	277	186	0	0	0	0	0	0
Revenue service development fund (FUNDAF)	0	0	277	186	0	0	0	0	0	0
6200 Other	0	2 913	4 715	26 003	29 581	36 505	42 433	46 006	51 707	55 750
Other federal taxes	0	941	36	45	44	3 199	4 489	3 407	4 527	5 036
Other social contributions	0	1 273	1 725	5 850	6 752	7 772	8 661	9 491	10 438	11 517
Other state taxes	0	322	1 551	13 190	15 429	17 135	19 825	22 980	25 864	27 352
Other municipal taxes	0	377	1 404	6 919	7 356	8 399	9 458	10 128	10 878	11 844

Note: Year ending 31st December.

The data are on cash basis.

Headings 3000, 5112 and 6200: For years prior to 2000 the PASEP (Program of Formation of the Patrimony of the Public Servants) contributions are combined with PIS (Social Integration Program) contributions in heading 5112.

Headings 5111 and 5121: From 2007 to 2011, a portion of the IPI (Industrial Products Tax) is levied separately as an excise tax on automobiles, beverages, and tobacco products.

Heading 6100: From 2008 FUNDAF (Special Fund for Development and Improvement of Auditing Activities) contributions are included in heading 6200.

Heading 5200: From 2009, taxes paid by households: motor vehicles are included in heading 6200.

Source: Secretaria da Receita Federal (Ministry of Finance) in Carga Tributária no Brasil.

StatLink http://dx.doi.org/10.1787/888933338121

Table 4.6. Chile / Chile
Details of tax revenue / Ingresos tributarios detallados

Million CLP

	1990	2000	2005	2008	2009	2010	2011	2012	2013	2014
Total tax revenue	**1 777 218**	**7 901 998**	**14 265 204**	**20 081 681**	**16 595 349**	**21 678 481**	**25 762 449**	**27 714 772**	**27 381 686**	**29 171 072**
1000 Taxes on income, profits and capital gains	**412 974**	**1 841 630**	**5 171 293**	**7 536 172**	**5 162 043**	**8 329 060**	**10 322 824**	**10 803 031**	**9 520 709**	**9 628 037**
1100 Of individuals	99 154	604 100	738 620	1 146 546	1 252 672	1 492 837	1 690 230	1 893 620	1 964 172	2 114 296
Second category tax	65 552	490 980	700 150	1 110 643	1 239 815	1 449 099	1 663 293	1 917 675	1 981 699	2 140 345
Global complementary tax	33 603	113 120	38 470	35 903	12 857	43 738	26 936	-24 055	-17 527	-26 050
1110 On income and profits	..	..	..	..	..	..	..	..	..	..
1120 On capital gains	..	..	..	..	..	..	..	..	..	..
1200 Corporate	219 586	882 896	3 155 480	4 805 522	4 110 485	4 448 745	6 021 408	7 560 906	6 041 089	6 196 077
First category tax	200 891	815 747	3 040 875	4 252 551	3 729 488	3 913 870	5 254 907	6 770 329	5 473 355	5 182 214
Surtax on state owned enterprises	16 074	47 634	78 267	92 949	44 974	194 203	116 725	80 084	124 220	100 851
Mining tax	0	0	0	417 214	312 473	298 558	598 790	619 150	324 577	801 647
Other	2 621	19 516	36 338	42 808	23 550	42 114	50 987	91 343	118 937	111 365
1210 On profits	..	..	..	..	..	..	..	..	..	..
1220 On capital gains	..	..	..	..	..	..	..	..	..	..
1300 Unallocable between 1100 and 1200	94 233	354 634	1 277 193	1 584 104	-201 113	2 387 478	2 611 186	1 348 506	1 515 449	1 317 664
Adicionel tax	59 082	350 301	799 648	1 363 357	1 023 497	1 414 057	1 187 866	1 178 917	1 337 721	1 454 847
Other	35 151	4 332	477 545	220 747	-1 224 610	973 421	1 423 320	169 589	177 727	-137 183
2000 Social security contributions	**159 559**	**576 758**	**931 717**	**1 289 225**	**1 371 750**	**1 493 987**	**1 623 818**	**1 802 468**	**1 968 973**	**2 110 087**
2100 Employees	154 021	553 937	893 821	1 229 912	1 312 793	1 433 159	1 565 828	1 742 526	1 906 340	2 044 356
2110 On a payroll basis	154 021	553 937	893 821	1 229 912	1 312 793	1 433 159	1 565 828	1 742 526	1 906 340	2 044 356
2120 On an income tax basis	0	0	0	0	0	0	0	0	0	0
2200 Employers	5 538	22 821	37 896	59 313	58 957	60 828	57 990	59 942	62 633	65 731
2210 On a payroll basis	5 538	22 821	37 896	59 313	58 957	60 828	57 990	59 942	62 633	65 731
2220 On an income tax basis	0	0	0	0	0	0	0	0	0	0
2300 Self-employed or non-employed	0	0	0	0	0	0	0	0	0	0
2310 On a payroll basis	..	..	..	..	..	..	..	..	..	..
2320 On an income tax basis	..	..	..	..	..	..	..	..	..	..
2400 Unallocable between 2100, 2200 and 2300	0	0	0	0	0	0	0	0	0	0
2410 On a payroll basis	..	..	..	..	..	..	..	..	..	..
2420 On an income tax basis	..	..	..	..	..	..	..	..	..	..
3000 Taxes on payroll and workforce	**0**	**0**	**0**	**0**	**0**	**0**	**0**	**0**	**0**	**0**
4000 Taxes on property	**109 319**	**554 037**	**901 776**	**1 080 090**	**795 084**	**785 364**	**1 027 627**	**1 180 307**	**1 133 765**	**1 256 000**
4100 Recurrent taxes on immovable property	59 968	302 244	416 565	541 268	532 279	549 125	731 191	788 919	840 842	951 101
4110 Households	..	..	..	..	..	..	..	..	..	..
4120 Others	..	..	..	..	..	..	..	..	..	..
4200 Recurrent taxes on net wealth	0	0	0	0	0	0	0	0	0	0
4210 Individual	..	..	..	..	..	..	..	..	..	..
4220 Corporate	..	..	..	..	..	..	..	..	..	..
4300 Estate, inheritance and gift taxes	3 444	10 906	23 184	35 554	200 203	39 338	30 876	66 719	45 550	31 340
4310 Estate and inheritance taxes	..	..	..	..	..	..	..	..	..	..
4320 Gift taxes	..	..	..	..	..	..	..	..	..	..
4400 Taxes on financial and capital transactions	45 907	240 886	462 027	503 269	62 602	196 901	265 560	324 669	247 373	273 559
4500 Non-recurrent taxes	0	0	0	0	0	0	0	0	0	0
4510 On net wealth	..	..	..	..	..	..	..	..	..	..
4520 Other non-recurrent taxes	..	..	..	..	..	..	..	..	..	..
4600 Other recurrent taxes on property	0	0	0	0	0	0	0	0	0	0
5000 Taxes on goods and services	**1 118 722**	**5 041 769**	**7 346 373**	**10 166 189**	**9 271 910**	**11 131 188**	**12 700 180**	**13 873 611**	**14 779 915**	**16 126 655**
5100 Taxes on production, sale, transfer, etc	1 074 009	4 789 827	6 952 031	9 650 260	8 724 696	10 514 822	11 963 914	13 052 989	13 869 529	15 131 295
5110 General taxes	664 421	3 306 350	5 391 285	7 912 009	7 051 079	8 399 926	9 536 786	10 447 374	11 170 794	12 133 710
5111 Value added taxes	664 421	3 306 350	5 391 285	7 912 009	7 051 079	8 399 926	9 536 786	10 447 374	11 170 794	12 133 710
5112 Sales tax	0	0	0	0	0	0	0	0	0	0
5113 Other	0	0	0	0	0	0	0	0	0	0
5120 Taxes on specific goods and services	409 588	1 483 477	1 560 746	1 738 251	1 673 617	2 114 896	2 427 128	2 605 615	2 698 735	2 997 585
5121 Excises	166 050	816 160	1 107 642	1 190 726	1 248 243	1 561 205	1 750 916	1 892 713	1 987 475	2 224 209
Cigarettes and tobacco	60 604	283 275	382 690	504 480	556 651	647 637	744 302	783 995	815 991	856 595
Gasolene and diesel	105 445	532 885	724 803	661 380	684 698	913 568	1 006 614	1 108 718	1 171 483	1 361 724
Oil stabilisation fund	0	0	149	24 866	6 894	0	0	0	0	0
5122 Profits of fiscal monopolies	0	0	0	0	0	0	0	0	0	0
5123 Customs and import duties	222 486	548 571	286 044	307 265	162 987	267 331	301 828	314 441	303 393	337 839
5124 Taxes on exports	0	0	0	0	0	0	0	0	0	0
5125 Taxes on investment goods	0	0	0	0	0	0	0	0	0	0
5126 Taxes on specific services	21 052	118 746	167 060	240 260	262 387	286 360	374 384	398 461	407 867	435 537
5127 Other taxes on internat. trade and transactions	0	0	0	0	0	0	0	0	0	0
5128 Other taxes	0	0	0	0	0	0	0	0	0	0
5130 Unallocable between 5110 and 5120	0	0	0	0	0	0	0	0	0	0
5200 Taxes on use of goods and perform activities	44 714	251 942	394 343	515 929	547 214	616 366	736 266	820 622	910 386	995 360
5210 Recurrent taxes	44 714	251 942	394 343	515 929	547 214	616 366	736 266	820 622	910 386	995 360
Motor vehicles	24 469	93 880	139 174	177 167	171 141	197 145	267 116	301 895	330 754	364 960

Table 4.6. Chile / Chile *(cont.)*
Details of tax revenue / Ingresos tributarios detallados

Million CLP

	1990	2000	2005	2008	2009	2010	2011	2012	2013	2014
5211 Paid by households: motor vehicles	0	0	0	0	0	0	0	0	0	0
5212 Paid by others: motor vehicles	0	0	0	0	0	0	0	0	0	0
5213 Paid in respect of other goods	20 245	158 062	255 169	338 762	376 073	419 221	469 150	518 727	579 632	630 400
Municipal permits	18 401	136 138	234 460	307 349	342 861	382 245	425 138	468 938	527 955	578 229
Mining patents	3 374	34 730	20 094	30 391	32 690	36 213	42 944	47 899	50 094	50 448
Other	-1 530	-12 806	615	1 022	522	763	1 068	1 890	1 583	1 723
5220 Non-recurrent taxes	0	0	0	0	0	0	0	0	0	0
5300 Unallocable between 5100 and 5200	0	0	0	0	0	0	0	0	0	0
6000 Other taxes	**-23 356**	**-112 195**	**-85 954**	**10 005**	**-5 438**	**-61 117**	**88 000**	**55 355**	**-21 676**	**50 293**
6100 Paid solely by business	0	0	0	0	0	0	0	0	0	0
6200 Other	-23 356	-112 195	-85 954	10 005	-5 438	-61 117	88 000	55 355	-21 676	50 293

Note: Year ending 31st December.

The data are on cash basis.

Heading 5121: In ECLAC data, figures from the Oil Prices Stabilisation Fund (FEPP) are considered as non-tax revenues.

Source: Servicio de Impuestos Internos (Chile's Tax Service).

StatLink http://dx.doi.org/10.1787/888933338137

Table 4.7. Colombia / Colombia
Details of tax revenue / Ingresos tributarios detallados

Million COP

	1990	2000	2005	2008	2009	2010	2011	2012	2013	2014
Total tax revenue	**2 579 426**	**30 512 910**	**61 455 845**	**90 247 603**	**93 898 231**	**98 035 191**	**116 983 509**	**130 708 822**	**142 322 742**	**153 251 499**
1000 Taxes on income, profits and capital gains	**771 694**	**7 103 525**	**17 348 618**	**24 448 371**	**28 116 564**	**26 218 852**	**33 453 048**	**43 671 856**	**47 743 096**	**50 083 349**
1100 Of individuals	47 210	1 499 345	3 594 441	5 030 693	5 229 835	5 192 384	6 407 675	6 841 470	7 955 072	8 827 575
1110 On income and profits	47 210	1 499 345	3 594 441	5 030 693	5 229 835	5 192 384	6 407 675	6 841 470	7 955 072	8 827 575
1120 On capital gains	..	..	..	..	..	..	..	..	..	..
1200 Corporate	359 758	5 119 828	13 044 361	18 489 260	21 954 952	20 405 209	26 110 879	35 669 308	38 531 528	40 125 246
1210 On profits	359 758	5 119 828	13 044 361	18 489 260	21 954 952	20 405 209	26 110 879	35 669 308	38 531 528	40 125 246
Income tax	359 758	5 119 828	13 044 361	18 489 260	21 954 952	20 405 209	26 110 879	35 669 308	35 591 949	27 663 771
Pro Equity Income Tax - CREE	0	0	0	0	0	0	0	0	2 939 579	12 461 475
1220 On capital gains	..	..	..	..	..	..	..	..	..	..
1300 Unallocable between 1100 and 1200	364 726	484 352	709 816	928 417	931 777	621 258	934 494	1 161 078	1 256 496	1 130 528
Income tax	364 726	484 352	709 816	928 417	931 777	621 258	934 494	1 161 078	1 256 496	1 130 528
Pro Equity Income Tax - CREE	0	0	0	0	0	0	0	0	0	0
2000 Social security contributions	**203 596**	**4 989 000**	**7 845 000**	**9 631 000**	**10 335 748**	**11 478 085**	**10 303 830**	**11 815 723**	**16 645 000**	**19 272 000**
2100 Employees	..	..	..	..	..	..	..	..	..	..
2110 On a payroll basis	..	..	..	..	..	..	..	..	..	..
2120 On an income tax basis	..	..	..	..	..	..	..	..	..	..
2200 Employers	..	..	..	..	..	..	..	..	..	..
2210 On a payroll basis	..	..	..	..	..	..	..	..	..	..
2220 On an income tax basis	..	..	..	..	..	..	..	..	..	..
2300 Self-employed or non-employed	..	..	..	..	..	..	..	..	..	..
2310 On a payroll basis	..	..	..	..	..	..	..	..	..	..
2320 On an income tax basis	..	..	..	..	..	..	..	..	..	..
2400 Unallocable between 2100, 2200 and 2300	203 596	4 989 000	7 845 000	9 631 000	10 335 748	11 478 085	10 303 830	11 815 723	16 645 000	19 272 000
2410 On a payroll basis	203 596	4 989 000	7 845 000	9 631 000	10 335 748	11 478 085	10 303 830	11 815 723	16 645 000	19 272 000
2420 On an income tax basis	0	0	0	0	0	0	0	0	0	0
3000 Taxes on payroll and workforce	**0**	**1 286 803**	**2 179 842**	**3 178 259**	**3 587 147**	**4 022 503**	**4 479 886**	**4 775 034**	**3 527 459**	**2 627 958**
4000 Taxes on property	**56 160**	**2 027 654**	**4 838 158**	**8 932 264**	**8 220 499**	**8 359 387**	**13 017 198**	**13 569 680**	**15 130 482**	**15 890 801**
4100 Recurrent taxes on immovable property	56 160	991 070	1 974 213	2 532 996	3 076 434	3 163 084	3 707 079	3 917 577	4 957 894	5 330 636
4110 Households	0	0	0	0	0	0	0	0	0	0
4120 Others	56 160	991 070	1 974 213	2 532 996	3 076 434	3 163 084	3 707 079	3 917 577	4 957 894	5 330 636
4200 Recurrent taxes on net wealth	0	0	462 720	3 199 668	2 022 787	1 970 530	4 240 512	4 183 752	4 274 832	4 118 196
4210 Individual	..	..	462 720	3 199 668	2 022 787	1 970 530	4 240 512	4 183 752	4 274 832	4 118 196
4220 Corporate	..	..	0	0	0	0	0	0	0	0
4300 Estate, inheritance and gift taxes	0	0	0	0	0	0	0	0	0	0
4310 Estate and inheritance taxes	..	..	..	..	..	..	..	..	..	..
4320 Gift taxes	..	..	..	..	..	..	..	..	..	..
4400 Taxes on financial and capital transactions	0	1 036 584	2 401 226	3 199 600	3 121 278	3 225 773	5 069 606	5 468 351	5 897 755	6 441 969
4500 Non-recurrent taxes	0	0	0	0	0	0	0	0	0	0
4510 On net wealth	..	..	..	..	..	..	..	..	..	..
4520 Other non-recurrent taxes	..	..	..	..	..	..	..	..	..	..
4600 Other recurrent taxes on property	0	0	0	0	0	0	0	0	0	0
5000 Taxes on goods and services	**1 388 653**	**13 367 908**	**25 866 553**	**39 194 218**	**38 090 163**	**42 063 441**	**48 790 355**	**50 261 388**	**51 844 491**	**57 219 307**
5100 Taxes on production, sale, transfer, etc	1 388 653	13 367 908	25 866 553	39 194 218	38 090 163	42 063 441	48 790 355	50 261 388	51 844 491	57 219 307
5110 General taxes	672 368	9 585 866	19 934 400	31 074 221	30 185 624	33 118 301	39 941 309	41 731 826	40 473 562	45 117 359
5111 Value added taxes	583 078	8 445 776	17 427 948	27 064 094	25 910 469	28 811 682	35 093 071	36 324 330	34 642 822	38 749 869
5112 Sales tax	89 290	1 140 090	2 506 452	4 010 127	4 275 155	4 306 620	4 848 238	5 407 497	5 830 740	6 367 490
Industry and commerce tax (State)	89 290	1 140 090	2 506 452	4 010 127	4 275 155	4 306 620	4 848 238	5 407 497	5 830 740	6 367 490
5113 Other	0	0	0	0	0	0	0	0	0	0
5120 Taxes on specific goods and services	716 285	3 782 042	5 932 153	8 119 997	7 904 539	8 945 140	8 849 045	8 529 561	11 370 929	12 101 948
5121 Excises	404 699	2 037 944	3 109 633	3 828 119	3 903 697	4 293 141	4 768 330	5 006 241	7 473 746	8 115 224
Oil	141 270	833 004	1 143 308	1 287 969	1 291 493	1 418 766	1 603 227	1 735 062	2 883 410	2 980 883
Restaurant, vehicles sale and mobile telephony	52 898	213 410	287 379	333 170	317 317	391 852	471 441	447 731	472 360	455 964
Tobacco (State)	85 722	471 137	867 569	1 268 054	1 381 248	1 434 560	1 444 067	1 565 738	1 673 211	1 710 008
Beer (State)	124 808	520 393	811 377	938 925	913 640	1 047 963	1 249 595	1 257 711	1 262 767	1 319 901
Liquors (State)	0	0	0	0	0	0	0	0	1 181 998	1 648 467
5122 Profits of fiscal monopolies	0	0	0	0	0	0	0	0	0	0
5123 Customs and import duties	311 586	1 744 097	2 822 520	4 291 878	4 000 842	4 651 999	4 080 716	3 523 320	3 897 184	3 986 724
Custom duties	180 989	1 744 097	2 822 520	4 291 878	4 000 842	4 651 999	4 080 716	3 523 320	3 897 184	3 986 724
Imports surcharge	130 597	0	0	0	0	0	0	0	0	0
5124 Taxes on exports	0	0	0	0	0	0	0	0	0	0
5125 Taxes on investment goods	0	0	0	0	0	0	0	0	0	0
5126 Taxes on specific services	0	0	0	0	0	0	0	0	0	0
5127 Other taxes on internat. trade and transactions	0	0	0	0	0	0	0	0	0	0
5128 Other taxes	0	0	0	0	0	0	0	0	0	0
5130 Unallocable between 5110 and 5120	0	0	0	0	0	0	0	0	0	0
5200 Taxes on use of goods and perform activities	0	0	0	0	0	0	0	0	0	0
5210 Recurrent taxes	..	..	..	..	..	..	..	..	..	..

Table 4.7. Colombia / Colombia (cont.)
Details of tax revenue / Ingresos tributarios detallados

Million COP

	1990	2000	2005	2008	2009	2010	2011	2012	2013	2014
5211 Paid by households: motor vehicles	..	..	..	..	..	..	..	..	..	..
5212 Paid by others: motor vehicles	..	..	..	..	..	..	..	..	..	..
5213 Paid in respect of other goods	..	..	..	..	..	..	..	..	..	..
5220 Non-recurrent taxes	..	..	..	..	..	..	..	..	..	..
5300 Unallocable between 5100 and 5200	0	0	0	0	0	0	0	0	0	0
6000 Other taxes	**159 323**	**1 738 020**	**3 377 674**	**4 863 490**	**5 548 110**	**5 892 923**	**6 939 193**	**6 615 141**	**7 432 215**	**8 158 085**
6100 Paid solely by business	0	0	0	0	0	0	0	0	0	0
6200 Other	159 323	1 738 020	3 377 674	4 863 490	5 548 110	5 892 923	6 939 193	6 615 141	7 432 215	8 158 085
Stamp tax	0	401 497	633 586	768 580	611 832	357 160	123 923	58 973	58 378	72 425
Other	78 306	79 287	48 498	88 432	120 721	126 602	143 770	174 845	200 465	260 721
Other (sub-national)	81 017	1 257 236	2 695 589	4 006 478	4 815 557	5 409 160	6 671 500	6 381 323	7 173 372	7 824 939

Note: Year ending 31st December.

The data are on cash basis.

Includes the reported consolidated revenues of the territorial entities (departments and municipalities).

Before 2013, social security contributions did not include all the contributions entering FOSYGA (Solidarity and Guarantee Fund). Only the portion of the contributions used to finance the subsidised regime (up to 1.5 pp of the 12.5% of the monthly wage paid by employers and employees as an obligatory health contribution) was included. The part of the contributions entering FOSYGA to finance the contributory regime was classified in the social security sector as "other incomes". From 2013 onwards, all of the health contributions entering FOSYGA are classified as Social Security Contributions. The portion of the contributions not entering FOSYGA that is both collected and spent by the health insurers –EPS- is not part of the fiscal accounts).

Headings 1100 and 1200: The data are estimated.

Source: Ministry of Finance and Central Bank of Colombia.

StatLink http://dx.doi.org/10.1787/888933338145

Table 4.8. Costa Rica / Costa Rica
Details of tax revenue / Ingresos tributarios detallados

Million CRC

	1990	2000	2005	2008	2009	2010	2011	2012	2013	2014
Total tax revenue	**106 778**	**893 812**	**1 915 942**	**3 565 410**	**3 564 323**	**3 979 101**	**4 438 852**	**4 846 611**	**5 563 744**	**6 011 761**
1000 Taxes on income, profits and capital gains	**11 820**	**128 805**	**324 224**	**689 225**	**687 420**	**748 093**	**828 691**	**891 669**	**1 014 440**	**1 091 470**
1100 Of individuals	..	..	16 438	104 536	156 936	202 849	233 486	307 489	316 894	349 139
1110 On income and profits	..	..	16 438	104 536	156 936	202 849	233 486	307 489	316 894	349 139
1120 On capital gains	..	..	..	..	..	..	..	..	..	..
1200 Corporate	..	..	288 355	481 736	444 242	450 312	486 001	461 481	545 183	574 137
1210 On profits	..	..	288 355	481 736	444 242	450 312	486 001	461 481	545 183	574 137
1220 On capital gains	..	..	..	..	..	..	..	..	..	..
1300 Unallocable between 1100 and 1200	11 820	128 805	19 430	102 953	86 241	94 932	109 204	122 699	152 363	168 194
2000 Social security contributions	**29 065**	**249 886**	**528 132**	**927 932**	**1 044 617**	**1 204 995**	**1 354 199**	**1 482 847**	**1 874 010**	**2 045 389**
2100 Employees	..	3 405	5 354	7 465	8 777	9 649	11 014	12 936	12 774	22 151
2110 On a payroll basis	..	3 405	5 354	7 465	8 777	9 649	11 014	12 936	12 774	22 151
2120 On an income tax basis	..	0	0	0	0	0	0	0	0	0
2200 Employers	..	0	24 481	38 126	47 925	56 332	63 094	68 092	344 622	370 268
2210 On a payroll basis	..	..	..	..	..	..	..	..	..	..
2220 On an income tax basis	..	..	..	..	..	..	..	..	..	..
2300 Self-employed or non-employed	..	5 858	16 414	24 555	30 656	33 778	36 733	39 462	21 090	22 404
2310 On a payroll basis	..	5 858	16 414	24 555	30 656	33 778	36 733	39 462	21 090	22 404
2320 On an income tax basis	..	0	0	0	0	0	0	0	0	0
2400 Unallocable between 2100, 2200 and 2300	29 065	240 623	481 883	857 787	957 260	1 105 236	1 243 358	1 362 357	1 495 525	1 630 566
2410 On a payroll basis	..	..	..	..	..	..	..	..	..	..
2420 On an income tax basis	..	..	..	..	..	..	..	..	..	..
3000 Taxes on payroll and workforce	**7 054**	**41 918**	**81 290**	**147 785**	**163 991**	**182 529**	**201 667**	**226 575**	**247 775**	**270 834**
4000 Taxes on property	**366**	**12 681**	**25 110**	**46 610**	**48 040**	**63 663**	**70 927**	**81 868**	**99 771**	**115 174**
4100 Recurrent taxes on immovable property	0	5 310	14 245	27 700	34 233	47 607	50 279	60 918	71 526	82 474
Land tax	..	0	0	0	0	0	0	0	0	0
Additional land tax	..	0	0	0	0	0	0	0	0	0
Tax on sumptuary constructions	..	0	0	0	0	0	0	0	0	0
Immovable property tax	..	0	0	0	55	3 527	2 475	2 638	3 998	4 013
Municipal immovable property tax	..	5 310	14 245	27 700	34 178	44 080	47 804	58 280	67 528	78 461
4110 Households	..	..	..	..	..	..	..	..	..	..
4120 Others	..	..	..	..	..	..	..	..	..	..
4200 Recurrent taxes on net wealth	0	4 284	0	0	0	0	0	0	0	0
4210 Individual	..	0	..	..	..	..	..	..	..	..
4220 Corporate	..	4 284	..	..	..	..	..	..	..	..
Tax on corporate assets	..	4 284	..	..	..	..	..	..	..	..
4300 Estate, inheritance and gift taxes	0	0	0	0	0	0	0	0	0	0
4310 Estate and inheritance taxes	..	..	..	..	..	..	..	..	..	..
4320 Gift taxes	..	..	..	..	..	..	..	..	..	..
4400 Taxes on financial and capital transactions	366	3 007	10 846	17 204	12 734	14 743	19 053	20 950	28 245	32 700
4500 Non-recurrent taxes	0	0	0	0	0	0	0	0	0	0
4510 On net wealth	..	..	..	..	..	..	..	..	..	..
4520 Other non-recurrent taxes	..	..	..	..	..	..	..	..	..	..
4600 Other recurrent taxes on property	0	80	19	1 706	1 072	1 313	1 595	0	0	0
5000 Taxes on goods and services	**52 360**	**456 707**	**946 970**	**1 737 642**	**1 606 222**	**1 762 591**	**1 963 833**	**2 122 589**	**2 268 536**	**2 423 583**
5100 Taxes on production, sale, transfer, etc	49 980	437 334	914 200	1 665 700	1 524 363	1 664 652	1 872 449	2 015 909	2 149 169	2 288 435
5110 General taxes	21 326	222 775	485 168	936 721	830 538	920 298	1 029 811	1 122 978	1 176 758	1 266 798
5111 Value added taxes	21 326	222 775	485 168	936 721	830 538	920 298	1 029 811	1 122 978	1 176 758	1 266 798
5112 Sales tax	0	0	0	0	0	0	0	0	0	0
5113 Other	0	0	0	0	0	0	0	0	0	0
5120 Taxes on specific goods and services	28 654	213 499	423 486	722 432	688 697	739 494	837 573	813 013	880 232	916 915
5121 Excises	11 096	157 204	296 222	485 696	481 147	523 617	596 268	629 423	689 528	706 016
Fuels and energy	0	0	172 028	268 070	308 274	320 638	359 425	354 149	404 210	404 901
Alcohol beverages	0	8 229	20 219	29 413	29 639	28 035	32 936	35 620	35 254	36 293
Non alcoholic beverages	0	0	12 491	22 716	24 426	26 566	27 804	30 205	32 519	34 874
Soaps	0	0	573	1 009	1 110	1 317	1 425	1 487	1 989	1 493
Cement	0	0	0	220	253	227	250	247	291	340
Tobacco	0	0	0	0	0	0	0	19 852	38 860	32 277
Abolished specific taxes on production and consumption	0	31 756	0	0	0	0	0	0	0	0
Other specific taxes on consumption	11 096	117 219	90 913	164 268	117 444	146 834	174 428	187 863	176 405	195 838
5122 Profits of fiscal monopolies	0	0	0	0	0	0	0	0	0	0
5123 Customs and import duties	15 053	40 485	82 446	156 816	117 256	126 135	146 511	152 275	154 576	169 120
Import duties	13 977	32 336	66 598	124 550	97 001	103 851	122 355	128 358	130 634	142 226
Custom duties	1 076	8 149	15 848	32 266	20 255	22 284	24 156	23 917	23 942	26 894

Table 4.8. Costa Rica / Costa Rica (*cont.*)
Details of tax revenue / Ingresos tributarios detallados

Million CRC

	1990	2000	2005	2008	2009	2010	2011	2012	2013	2014
5124 Taxes on exports	2 226	2 238	969	4 667	4 677	3 973	3 990	3 823	4 877	4 853
Export duties	2 226	1 835	830	4 508	4 534	3 816	3 827	3 663	4 104	3 067
Export duties Law 133	0	0	0	0	0	0	0	0	0	0
Export duties Law 5519	0	253	0	0	0	0	0	0	0	0
Tax on banana exports	0	150	139	160	143	157	163	160	168	176
Export duties on ground transportation	0	0	0	0	0	0	0	0	605	1 610
5125 Taxes on investment goods	0	0	0	0	0	0	0	0	0	0
5126 Taxes on specific services	280	13 488	43 755	74 376	84 619	84 270	88 744	25 579	28 571	34 081
Casinos and gambling	0	225	519	458	411	445	288	213	1 000	897
Electronic betting business	0	0	0	0	0	0	0	0	19	43
Port cargo movements	0	6	13	0	12	0	0	0	0	0
Overseas departure tax	0	0	19 022	24 939	24 794	24 322	23 902	25 366	27 552	33 141
10% on public shows	0	26	0	0	0	0	0	0	0	0
Pro-national airport's stamp tax	0	6	0	0	0	0	0	0	0	0
Stamp tax on the use of borders and ports	280	2 697	0	0	0	0	0	0	0	0
Municipal licences and permits	0	8 692	19 974	39 841	52 492	52 637	55 606	0	0	0
Municipal tax on construction	0	1 836	4 226	9 137	6 910	6 866	8 948	0	0	0
5127 Other taxes on internat. trade and transactions	0	83	94	877	998	1 499	2 060	1 913	2 680	2 845
5128 Other taxes	0	0	0	0	0	0	0	0	0	0
5130 Unallocable between 5110 and 5120	0	1 061	5 546	6 547	5 128	4 860	5 065	79 918	92 179	104 723
5200 Taxes on use of goods and perform activities	2 380	19 357	32 758	71 871	81 705	97 803	91 266	106 557	119 235	135 005
5210 Recurrent taxes	2 380	19 357	32 758	71 871	81 705	97 803	91 266	106 557	119 235	135 005
5211 Paid by households: motor vehicles	0	0	0	0	0	0	0	0	0	0
5212 Paid by others: motor vehicles	1 425	15 487	30 918	68 299	77 924	94 101	85 152	101 903	113 727	130 000
Property tax on vehicles, aircraft and boats	1 425	15 374	30 918	68 299	77 924	94 101	85 152	101 903	113 727	130 000
Special tax on the use of public roads	0	113	0	0	0	0	0	0	0	0
5213 Paid in respect of other goods	955	3 870	1 841	3 572	3 781	3 702	6 114	4 654	5 508	5 005
Hunting and fishing licences	0	0	0	0	0	0	0	0	0	0
Hunting and fishing licences (Ministry of Natural Resources, Energy and Mines)	0	4	0	0	0	0	0	0	0	0
Spirits license	0	0	0	0	0	0	0	0	0	0
Revenue stamps	955	3 866	1 841	3 572	3 781	3 702	6 114	4 654	5 508	5 005
Sport stamp tax	0	0	0	0	0	0	0	0	0	0
5220 Non-recurrent taxes	0	0	0	0	0	0	0	0	0	0
5300 Unallocable between 5100 and 5200	0	15	12	71	153	136	118	123	132	142
6000 Other taxes	**6 113**	**3 816**	**10 216**	**16 216**	**14 034**	**17 230**	**19 535**	**41 063**	**59 212**	**65 311**
6100 Paid solely by business	0	15	624	1 068	521	459	526	22 724	36 125	39 542
6200 Other	6 113	3 801	9 592	15 148	13 513	16 771	19 009	18 339	23 087	25 769
Transfers of vehicles, aircraft and boat	497	2 530	6 357	10 554	9 612	12 311	13 672	12 947	17 177	19 099

Note: Year ending 31st December.

The data are on cash basis.

The figures for years up to and including 1997 exclude local government tax revenues as the data are not available.

Heading 2000: In ECLAC data, social security contributions include INA (National Institute of Apprenticeship), IMAS (Joint Social Aid Institute), and FODESAF (Social Development and Family Allowances Fund).

Heading 3000: In ECLAC data, social security contributions from decentralised institutions are classified under heading 2000.

Heading 5121: In ECLAC data, the tax on transfers of vehicles is classified as a property tax 4000.

Heading 5212: In ECLAC data, Property tax on vehicles, aircraft and boats is classified in category 4000.

Heading 6000: In ECLAC data, the tax on the transfer of used vehicles Law No. 7088 of 30/11/87 is classified as a property tax (4000).

Source: Secretaría Técnica de la Autoridad Presupuestaria, Ministry of Finance and Contraloría General de la República.

StatLink http://dx.doi.org/10.1787/888933338154

Table 4.9. Dominican Republic / República Dominicana
Details of tax revenue / Ingresos tributarios detallados

Million DOP

	1990	2000	2005	2008	2009	2010	2011	2012	2013	2014
Total tax revenue	**6 416**	**48 310**	**149 636**	**236 147**	**220 373**	**243 943**	**273 132**	**312 064**	**355 314**	**393 157**
1000 Taxes on income, profits and capital gains	**1 670**	**10 782**	**30 041**	**58 516**	**54 127**	**53 643**	**65 205**	**92 274**	**108 248**	**124 518**
1100 Of individuals	..	4 088	7 587	16 563	15 436	17 088	20 673	21 731	24 928	28 996
1110 On income and profits	..	4 070	7 508	16 369	15 199	16 901	20 220	21 432	24 503	28 590
1120 On capital gains	..	18	79	194	237	187	453	299	424	406
1200 Corporate	..	4 679	16 222	26 999	22 546	21 475	25 083	46 624	50 782	72 747
1210 On profits	..	4 605	16 147	26 853	22 414	21 325	24 900	46 411	50 595	72 574
1220 On capital gains	..	74	75	146	132	151	182	213	187	173
Casinos	..	59	73	146	132	151	182	213	187	173
Racetracks	..	15	2	0	0	0	0	0	0	0
1300 Unallocable between 1100 and 1200	1 670	2 015	6 232	14 954	16 145	15 080	19 450	23 919	32 539	22 775
2000 Social security contributions	**53**	**490**	**35**	**860**	**1 009**	**1 845**	**1 328**	**1 250**	**1 552**	**1 515**
2100 Employees	..	..	..	..	..	..	..	..	..	..
2110 On a payroll basis	..	..	..	..	..	..	..	..	..	..
2120 On an income tax basis	..	..	..	..	..	..	..	..	..	..
2200 Employers	..	..	..	..	..	..	..	..	..	..
2210 On a payroll basis	..	..	..	..	..	..	..	..	..	..
2220 On an income tax basis	..	..	..	..	..	..	..	..	..	..
2300 Self-employed or non-employed	..	..	..	..	..	..	..	..	..	..
2310 On a payroll basis	..	..	..	..	..	..	..	..	..	..
2320 On an income tax basis	..	..	..	..	..	..	..	..	..	..
2400 Unallocable between 2100, 2200 and 2300	53	490	35	860	1 009	1 845	1 328	1 250	1 552	1 515
2410 On a payroll basis	53	490	35	860	1 009	1 845	1 328	1 250	1 552	1 515
2420 On an income tax basis	0	0	0	0	0	0	0	0	0	0
3000 Taxes on payroll and workforce	**0**	**0**	**0**	**0**	**0**	**0**	**0**	**0**	**0**	**0**
4000 Taxes on property	**46**	**505**	**6 555**	**11 441**	**11 127**	**12 738**	**15 306**	**18 867**	**22 333**	**17 634**
4100 Recurrent taxes on immovable property	9	115	1 710	2 567	2 702	3 004	5 235	8 351	10 183	5 037
4110 Households	9	115	1 710	552	473	555	629	686	1 518	1 579
4120 Others	0	0	0	2 016	2 230	2 449	4 605	7 665	8 666	3 458
Tax on assets	..	..	..	2 016	2 230	2 449	2 790	3 044	3 337	3 454
Tax on financial assets (Law 139-11)	..	..	..	0	0	0	1 816	4 620	5 329	4
4200 Recurrent taxes on net wealth	0	0	0	0	0	0	0	0	0	0
4210 Individual	..	..	..	..	..	..	..	..	..	..
4220 Corporate	..	..	..	..	..	..	..	..	..	..
4300 Estate, inheritance and gift taxes	11	96	84	221	199	231	237	227	315	325
4310 Estate and inheritance taxes	0	0	0	0	0	0	0	0	0	0
4320 Gift taxes	0	0	0	0	0	0	0	0	0	0
4400 Taxes on financial and capital transactions	22	217	4 546	7 876	7 181	8 125	8 255	8 723	10 404	10 496
Tax on checks	0	0	3 133	4 472	3 919	4 262	4 492	4 852	5 168	5 620
Real estate operations	22	217	1 413	3 404	3 262	3 864	3 763	3 872	5 236	4 876
4500 Non-recurrent taxes	3	32	89	324	282	488	578	609	412	677
4510 On net wealth	3	32	89	324	282	488	578	609	412	677
4520 Other non-recurrent taxes	0	0	0	0	0	0	0	0	0	0
4600 Other recurrent taxes on property	1	45	127	452	763	891	1 002	957	1 019	1 100
5000 Taxes on goods and services	**4 488**	**36 038**	**111 344**	**165 306**	**154 105**	**175 716**	**191 294**	**199 673**	**223 181**	**249 490**
5100 Taxes on production, sale, transfer, etc	4 410	35 281	109 602	163 286	151 840	173 403	188 560	196 473	219 939	246 107
5110 General taxes	973	10 195	41 368	74 319	69 877	81 871	89 610	92 819	113 345	131 017
5111 Value added taxes	973	10 195	41 368	74 319	69 877	81 871	89 610	92 819	113 345	131 017
5112 Sales tax	0	0	0	0	0	0	0	0	0	0
5113 Other	0	0	0	0	0	0	0	0	0	0
5120 Taxes on specific goods and services	3 437	25 086	68 234	88 966	81 964	91 531	98 950	103 654	106 595	115 090
5121 Excises	500	6 474	27 158	57 192	52 445	60 144	67 174	71 033	72 581	77 810
Vehicle registration	0	0	0	4 798	3 163	4 234	4 268	4 505	4 595	5 683
Transfer tax	18	160	170	386	507	533	572	682	805	898
Alcoholic beverages	251	2 451	8 142	13 030	13 343	15 054	16 240	17 089	17 969	19 779
Tobacco products	102	469	2 879	4 180	4 131	4 529	4 241	4 470	4 356	4 382
Petroleum products	105	3 143	14 712	33 905	30 373	34 598	40 303	42 460	42 222	44 335
Other	24	251	1 255	894	927	1 197	1 549	1 827	2 634	2 734
5122 Profits of fiscal monopolies	0	0	0	0	0	0	0	0	0	0
5123 Customs and import duties	1 194	13 469	14 403	21 182	18 293	19 492	18 850	18 920	19 076	21 331
Custom duties	615	13 456	14 293	21 141	18 264	19 455	18 801	18 776	18 916	21 238
Other	579	13	110	41	29	37	49	144	160	92
5124 Taxes on exports	6	4	46	128	132	146	181	264	34	12
5125 Taxes on investment goods	0	0	0	0	0	0	0	0	0	0

Table 4.9. Dominican Republic / República Dominicana *(cont.)*
Details of tax revenue / Ingresos tributarios detallados

Million DOP

	1990	2000	2005	2008	2009	2010	2011	2012	2013	2014
5126 Taxes on specific services	347	1 593	5 620	10 017	10 799	11 407	12 404	13 128	14 501	15 556
Telecommunications	85	0	3 193	4 100	4 592	4 886	4 947	5 124	5 897	6 129
Insurance premiums	33	584	0	2 796	2 978	3 088	3 238	3 437	3 674	3 965
Travel tickets	204	809	2 414	3 073	3 222	3 428	3 632	3 951	4 283	4 839
Hotels	22	191	0	0	0	0	0	0	0	0
Others	4	9	12	48	6	5	588	616	647	623
5127 Other taxes on internat. trade and transactions	1 390	3 546	21 008	447	295	342	340	309	402	381
Exchange commission	857	0	0	0	0	0	0	0	0	0
Consular fees	77	32	271	143	138	132	138	130	143	142
Other	457	3 514	20 737	304	156	210	202	179	260	240
5128 Other taxes	0	0	0	0	0	0	0	0	0	0
5130 Unallocable between 5110 and 5120	0	0	0	0	0	0	0	0	0	0
5200 Taxes on use of goods and perform activities	77	757	1 742	2 020	2 265	2 313	2 733	3 199	3 242	3 383
5210 Recurrent taxes	77	757	1 742	2 020	2 265	2 313	2 733	3 199	3 242	3 383
5211 Paid by households: motor vehicles	45	268	977	1 183	1 225	1 277	1 300	1 271	1 073	1 289
5212 Paid by others: motor vehicles	0	0	0	0	0	0	0	0	0	0
5213 Paid in respect of other goods	33	489	766	837	1 040	1 036	1 433	1 929	2 169	2 094
Licenses to carry firearms	17	237	244	214	346	296	253	194	240	200
Licenses to operate gambling houses	0	114	155	187	199	211	571	1 076	1 229	1 221
Licenses to operate slot machines	4	60	102	385	409	457	528	567	598	576
Other	12	78	264	51	86	72	82	92	102	97
5220 Non-recurrent taxes	0	0	0	0	0	0	0	0	0	0
5300 Unallocable between 5100 and 5200	0	0	0	0	0	0	0	0	0	0
6000 Other taxes	**159**	**495**	**1 661**	**25**	**5**	**0**	**0**	**0**	**0**	**1**
6100 Paid solely by business	0	0	0	0	0	..	..	0	0	0
6200 Other	159	495	1 661	25	5	..	..	0	0	1

Note: Year ending 31st December.

The data are on cash basis.

The figures exclude local government tax revenues as the data are not available.

Heading 1110: Includes non-wage and wage personal income taxes. In previous publications the personal income taxes on wages were classified under heading 3000 (taxes on payroll on workforce). For this publication, they have been reclassified as an income tax since the tax is levied on net income.

Heading 2000: The data exclude social security contributions to general government managed by the private sector.

Heading 5121: In ECLAC data, the tax on transfer of movable goods is classified as a property tax (4000).

Heading 6000: In ECLAC data, the Vehicle transfer tax is classified as a property tax (4000).

Source: Ministerio de Hacienda, Ministry of Finance.

StatLink http://dx.doi.org/10.1787/888933338161

Table 4.10. Ecuador / Ecuador

Details of tax revenue / Ingresos tributarios detallados

Million USD

	1990	2000	2005	2008	2009	2010	2011	2012	2013	2014
Total tax revenue	**1 076**	**1 851**	**4 850**	**8 667**	**9 318**	**11 343**	**13 736**	**17 007**	**18 214**	**19 178**
1000 Taxes on income, profits and capital gains	**138**	**293**	**937**	**2 339**	**2 518**	**2 353**	**3 030**	**3 313**	**3 847**	**4 161**
1100 Of individuals	..	..	..	..	..	..	..	..	..	..
1110 On income and profits	..	..	..	..	..	..	..	..	..	..
1120 On capital gains	..	..	..	..	..	..	..	..	..	..
1200 Corporate	..	..	..	..	..	..	..	..	..	..
1210 On profits	..	..	..	..	..	..	..	..	..	..
1220 On capital gains	..	..	..	..	..	..	..	..	..	..
1300 Unallocable between 1100 and 1200	138	293	937	2 339	2 518	2 353	3 030	3 313	3 847	4 161
2000 Social security contributions	**243**	**228**	**1 109**	**2 097**	**2 061**	**2 549**	**3 971**	**4 752**	**4 547**	**4 718**
2100 Employees	..	..	..	..	..	..	..	..	..	..
2110 On a payroll basis	..	..	..	..	..	..	..	..	..	..
2120 On an income tax basis	..	..	..	..	..	..	..	..	..	..
2200 Employers	..	..	..	..	..	..	..	..	..	..
2210 On a payroll basis	..	..	..	..	..	..	..	..	..	..
2220 On an income tax basis	..	..	..	..	..	..	..	..	..	..
2300 Self-employed or non-employed	..	..	..	..	..	..	..	..	..	..
2310 On a payroll basis	..	..	..	..	..	..	..	..	..	..
2320 On an income tax basis	..	..	..	..	..	..	..	..	..	..
2400 Unallocable between 2100, 2200 and 2300	243	228	1 109	2 097	2 061	2 549	3 971	4 752	4 547	4 718
2410 On a payroll basis	..	..	..	..	..	..	..	..	..	..
2420 On an income tax basis	..	..	..	..	..	..	..	..	..	..
3000 Taxes on payroll and workforce	**0**	**0**	**0**	**0**	**0**	**0**	**0**	**0**	**0**	**0**
4000 Taxes on property	**0**	**0**	**0**	**0**	**0**	**0**	**0**	**0**	**0**	**0**
4100 Recurrent taxes on immovable property	..	..	..	..	..	..	..	..	..	..
4110 Households	..	..	..	..	..	..	..	..	..	..
4120 Others	..	..	..	..	..	..	..	..	..	..
4200 Recurrent taxes on net wealth	..	..	..	..	..	..	..	..	..	..
4210 Individual	..	..	..	..	..	..	..	..	..	..
4220 Corporate	..	..	..	..	..	..	..	..	..	..
4300 Estate, inheritance and gift taxes	..	..	..	..	..	..	..	..	..	..
4310 Estate and inheritance taxes	..	..	..	..	..	..	..	..	..	..
4320 Gift taxes	..	..	..	..	..	..	..	..	..	..
4400 Taxes on financial and capital transactions	..	..	..	..	..	..	..	..	..	..
4500 Non-recurrent taxes	..	..	..	..	..	..	..	..	..	..
4510 On net wealth	..	..	..	..	..	..	..	..	..	..
4520 Other non-recurrent taxes	..	..	..	..	..	..	..	..	..	..
4600 Other recurrent taxes on property	..	..	..	..	..	..	..	..	..	..
5000 Taxes on goods and services	**668**	**1 330**	**2 802**	**4 183**	**4 508**	**6 152**	**6 707**	**8 830**	**9 688**	**10 170**
5100 Taxes on production, sale, transfer, etc	665	1 319	2 742	4 088	4 390	5 997	6 533	8 636	9 474	9 942
5110 General taxes	302	836	1 975	2 825	3 019	3 886	4 200	5 415	6 056	6 376
5111 Value added taxes	302	836	1 975	2 825	3 019	3 886	4 200	5 415	6 056	6 376
5112 Sales tax	0	0	0	0	0	0	0	0	0	0
5113 Other	0	0	0	0	0	0	0	0	0	0
5120 Taxes on specific goods and services	363	483	767	1 263	1 372	2 110	2 332	3 221	3 418	3 566
5121 Excises	90	75	221	474	448	530	618	685	744	803
Alcohol products	..	30	89	..	..	..	..	..	..	..
Soft drinks and mineral water	..	9	15	..	..	..	..	..	..	..
Cigarettes	..	24	71	..	..	..	..	..	..	..
Luxury goods and vehicles	..	11	46	..	..	..	..	..	..	..
5122 Profits of fiscal monopolies	0	0	0	0	0	0	0	0	0	0
5123 Customs and import duties	227	217	547	789	923	1 152	1 156	1 261	1 352	1 357
5124 Taxes on exports	0	0	0	0	0	0	0	0	0	0
5125 Taxes on investment goods	0	0	0	0	0	0	0	0	0	0
5126 Taxes on specific services	7	17	0	0	0	428	558	1 275	1 322	1 406
Exit taxes	7	17	0	0	0	428	558	1 275	1 322	1 406
5127 Other taxes on internat. trade and transactions	40	175	0	0	0	0	0	0	0	0
On capital movements	0	169	..	..	..	..	..	..	..	..
On purchase of foreign exchange	22	4	..	..	..	..	..	..	..	..
On credit operations in national currency	18	2	..	..	..	..	..	..	..	..
5128 Other taxes	0	0	0	0	0	0	0	0	0	0
5130 Unallocable between 5110 and 5120	0	0	0	0	0	0	0	0	0	0
5200 Taxes on use of goods and perform activities	3	11	60	95	118	156	174	194	214	228
5210 Recurrent taxes	3	11	60	95	118	156	174	194	214	228
5211 Paid by households: motor vehicles	0	0	0	0	0	0	0	0	0	0
5212 Paid by others: motor vehicles	3	11	60	95	118	156	174	194	214	228
Annual tax on motor vehicles	3	11	60	95	118	156	174	194	214	228
5213 Paid in respect of other goods	0	0	0	0	0	0	0	0	0	0

Table 4.10. Ecuador / Ecuador (*cont.*)
Details of tax revenue / Ingresos tributarios detallados

Million USD

	1990	2000	2005	2008	2009	2010	2011	2012	2013	2014
5220 Non-recurrent taxes	0	0	0	0	0	0	0	0	0	0
5300 Unallocable between 5100 and 5200	0	0	0	0	0	0	0	0	0	0
6000 Other taxes	**27**	**0**	**2**	**48**	**231**	**289**	**28**	**111**	**132**	**129**
6100 Paid solely by business	0	..	0	0	0	0	0	0	0	0
6200 Other	27	..	2	48	231	289	28	111	132	129

Note: Year ending 31st December.
The data are on cash basis.
The figures exclude local government tax revenues as the data are not available.
Social security data is recorded at the non-financial public sector level.
Heading 5212: In ECLAC data, the annual tax on motor vehicles is classified as a property tax (4000).
Source: Banco Central del Ecuador, Central Bank of Ecuador.

StatLink http://dx.doi.org/10.1787/888933338170

Table 4.11. El Salvador / El Salvador

Details of tax revenue / Ingresos tributarios detallados

Million USD

	1990	2000	2005	2008	2009	2010	2011	2012	2013	2014
Total tax revenue	**506**	**1 585**	**2 382**	**3 240**	**2 966**	**3 235**	**3 552**	**3 828**	**4 139**	**4 148**
1000 Taxes on income, profits and capital gains	**95**	**407**	**637**	**1 004**	**948**	**995**	**1 127**	**1 250**	**1 479**	**1 522**
1100 Of individuals	0	0	312	536	444	571	456	697	578	627
1110 On income and profits	..	..	312	536	444	571	456	697	578	627
1120 On capital gains	..	..	..	..	..	..	..	..	..	..
1200 Corporate	0	0	356	518	559	423	631	555	793	693
1210 On profits	..	..	356	518	559	423	631	555	793	693
1220 On capital gains	..	..	..	..	..	..	..	..	..	..
1300 Unallocable between 1100 and 1200	95	407	-31	-49	-55	0	41	-2	108	201
Withholding income tax	95	429	0	0	0	55	107	66	135	204
Income tax refunds	0	-22	-31	-49	-55	-55	-66	-68	-27	-3
2000 Social security contributions	**67**	**263**	**282**	**356**	**358**	**369**	**382**	**404**	**425**	**445**
2100 Employees	..	75	76	96	96	99	100	106	112	117
2110 On a payroll basis	..	75	76	96	96	99	100	106	112	117
2120 On an income tax basis	..	0	0	0	0	0	0	0	0	0
2200 Employers	..	176	181	230	230	238	245	260	273	286
2210 On a payroll basis	..	176	181	230	230	238	245	260	273	286
2220 On an income tax basis	..	0	0	0	0	0	0	0	0	0
2300 Self-employed or non-employed	..	13	25	29	31	33	36	38	40	42
2310 On a payroll basis	..	13	25	29	31	33	36	38	40	42
2320 On an income tax basis	..	0	0	0	0	0	0	0	0	0
2400 Unallocable between 2100, 2200 and 2300	67	0	0	0	0	0	0	0	0	0
2410 On a payroll basis	67	0	0	0	0	0	0	0	0	0
2420 On an income tax basis	0	0	0	0	0	0	0	0	0	0
3000 Taxes on payroll and workforce	**0**	**0**	**0**	**0**	**0**	**0**	**0**	**0**	**0**	**0**
4000 Taxes on property	**26**	**12**	**16**	**18**	**13**	**16**	**16**	**20**	**21**	**24**
4100 Recurrent taxes on immovable property	0	0	0	0	0	0	0	0	0	0
4110 Households	..	..	..	..	..	..	..	..	..	..
4120 Others	..	..	..	..	..	..	..	..	..	..
4200 Recurrent taxes on net wealth	16	0	0	0	0	0	0	0	0	0
4210 Individual	16	..	..	..	..	..	..	..	..	..
4220 Corporate	0	..	..	..	..	..	..	..	..	..
4300 Estate, inheritance and gift taxes	0	0	0	0	0	0	0	0	0	0
4310 Estate and inheritance taxes	..	..	..	..	..	..	..	..	..	..
4320 Gift taxes	..	..	..	..	..	..	..	..	..	..
4400 Taxes on financial and capital transactions	10	12	16	18	13	16	16	20	21	24
4500 Non-recurrent taxes	0	0	0	0	0	0	0	0	0	0
4510 On net wealth	..	..	..	..	..	..	..	..	..	..
4520 Other non-recurrent taxes	..	..	..	..	..	..	..	..	..	..
4600 Other recurrent taxes on property	0	0	0	0	0	0	0	0	0	0
5000 Taxes on goods and services	**259**	**903**	**1 447**	**1 863**	**1 646**	**1 855**	**2 027**	**2 155**	**2 213**	**2 158**
5100 Taxes on production, sale, transfer, etc	259	903	1 447	1 863	1 646	1 855	2 027	2 155	2 213	2 158
5110 General taxes	133	714	1 104	1 461	1 251	1 433	1 574	1 677	1 731	1 720
5111 Value added taxes	0	714	1 104	1 461	1 251	1 433	1 574	1 677	1 731	1 720
5112 Sales tax	0	0	0	0	0	0	0	0	0	0
5113 Other	133	0	0	0	0	0	0	0	0	0
5120 Taxes on specific goods and services	127	189	344	402	395	422	453	478	483	438
5121 Excises	65	49	162	194	202	218	238	262	249	234
Consumption of products	65	49	0	0	0	0	0	0	0	0
Alcoholic beverages	0	0	39	43	44	44	52	64	60	46
Cigarettes	0	0	23	27	31	31	38	40	27	22
Soft drinks	0	0	33	24	24	31	35	40	42	43
Beer	0	0	1	0	1	1	1	1	1	1
Weapons, ammunition and explosives	0	0	1	1	1	1	1	1	1	1
Special Contribution- Sugar	0	0	0	33	34	35	35	36	36	37
Special Contribution- Public transportation	0	0	66	65	68	69	69	71	72	74
Special Contribution- FOVIAL	0	0	0	0	0	7	8	9	11	11
5122 Profits of fiscal monopolies	0	0	0	0	0	0	0	0	0	0
5123 Customs and import duties	61	141	181	179	138	148	167	180	199	181
5124 Taxes on exports	0	0	0	0	0	0	0	0	0	0
5125 Taxes on investment goods	0	0	0	0	0	0	0	0	0	0
5126 Taxes on specific services	0	0	0	30	55	56	48	36	34	22
5127 Other taxes on internat. trade and transactions	0	0	0	0	0	0	0	0	0	0
5128 Other taxes	0	0	0	0	0	0	0	0	0	0
5130 Unallocable between 5110 and 5120	0	0	0	0	0	0	0	0	0	0
5200 Taxes on use of goods and perform activities	0	0	0	0	0	0	0	0	0	0
5210 Recurrent taxes	..	..	..	..	..	..	..	..	..	..
5211 Paid by households: motor vehicles	..	..	..	..	..	..	..	..	..	..

Table 4.11. El Salvador / El Salvador (cont.)
Details of tax revenue / Ingresos tributarios detallados

Million USD

	1990	2000	2005	2008	2009	2010	2011	2012	2013	2014
5212 Paid by others: motor vehicles	..	..	..	..	..	..	..	..	..	..
5213 Paid in respect of other goods	..	..	..	..	..	..	..	..	..	..
5220 Non-recurrent taxes	..	..	..	..	..	..	..	..	..	..
5300 Unallocable between 5100 and 5200	0	0	0	0	0	0	0	0	0	0
6000 Other taxes	**58**	**0**	**0**	**0**	**0**	**0**	**0**	**0**	**0**	**0**
6100 Paid solely by business	0	0	..	..	..	..	..	..	..	..
6200 Other	58	0	..	..	..	..	..	..	..	..

Note: Year ending 31st December.

The data are on cash basis.

The figures exclude local government tax revenues as the data are not available.

Heading 1000: For 2002 and from 2006 onwards sub-headings 1100 and 1200 are presented on a gross basis i.e. not including income tax refunds. The latter are classified under heading 1300.

Heading 2000: Corresponds to social security contributions paid to the Salvadoran Institute of Social Security and excludes payments to privately managed pension funds (AFPs).

Source: Dirección General de Tesorería, Ministry of Finance (for national taxes). Central Reserve Bank of El Salvador from 1990 to 1996 and Salvadoran Institute of Social Security for subsequent years (for social security contribution figures).

StatLink http://dx.doi.org/10.1787/888933338180

Table 4.12. Guatemala / Guatemala
Details of tax revenue / Ingresos tributarios detallados

Million GTQ

	1990	2000	2005	2008	2009	2010	2011	2012	2013	2014
Total tax revenue	**2 801**	**16 531**	**27 187**	**38 206**	**37 661**	**41 189**	**46 984**	**50 441**	**54 954**	**57 522**
1000 Taxes on income, profits and capital gains	**507**	**3 295**	**6 049**	**9 698**	**9 706**	**10 319**	**12 696**	**13 445**	**16 041**	**17 752**
1100 Of individuals	25	143	645	945	1 060	1 225	1 462	1 477	1 246	1 784
1110 On income and profits	25	143	645	945	1 060	1 225	1 462	1 477	1 246	1 784
Personal income tax	25	137	642	945	1 060	1 225	1 462	1 476	1 246	1 784
Income from financial products	0	6	4	0	0	0	0	1	0	0
1120 On capital gains	..	..	..	..	..	..	..	..	..	..
1200 Corporate	482	3 149	3 756	6 417	6 141	6 520	8 609	9 119	11 532	12 426
1210 On profits	482	3 149	3 756	6 417	6 141	6 520	8 609	9 119	11 532	12 426
Corporate income tax	482	1 610	3 495	6 085	5 768	6 132	8 198	8 656	11 477	12 423
Income from financial products	0	248	235	322	371	386	403	463	52	0
Commercial and agricultural enterprises	0	1 291	26	11	2	2	8	0	3	3
1220 On capital gains	..	..	..	..	..	..	..	..	..	..
1300 Unallocable between 1100 and 1200	0	2	1 647	2 336	2 505	2 574	2 625	2 849	3 263	3 543
Extraordinary and temporary solidarity tax in support of peace agreements	..	0	1 647	2 336	677	44	54	4	21	9
Solidarity tax	..	0	0	0	1 829	2 530	2 571	2 845	3 243	3 534
Extraordinary and temporary solidarity tax	..	2	0	0	0	0	0	0	0	0
2000 Social security contributions	**436**	**2 569**	**4 072**	**5 516**	**5 801**	**6 408**	**7 125**	**7 858**	**8 617**	**8 157**
2100 Employees	..	..	..	..	..	..	..	..	..	..
2110 On a payroll basis	..	..	..	..	..	..	..	..	..	..
2120 On an income tax basis	..	..	..	..	..	..	..	..	..	..
2200 Employers	..	..	..	..	..	..	..	..	..	..
2210 On a payroll basis	..	..	..	..	..	..	..	..	..	..
2220 On an income tax basis	..	..	..	..	..	..	..	..	..	..
2300 Self-employed or non-employed	..	..	..	..	..	..	..	..	..	..
2310 On a payroll basis	..	..	..	..	..	..	..	..	..	..
2320 On an income tax basis	..	..	..	..	..	..	..	..	..	..
2400 Unallocable between 2100, 2200 and 2300	436	2 569	4 072	5 516	5 801	6 408	7 125	7 858	8 617	8 157
2410 On a payroll basis	436	2 569	4 072	5 516	5 801	6 408	7 125	7 858	8 617	8 157
2420 On an income tax basis	0	0	0	0	0	0	0	0	0	0
3000 Taxes on payroll and workforce	**0**	**0**	**0**	**0**	**0**	**0**	**0**	**0**	**0**	**0**
4000 Taxes on property	**45**	**165**	**350**	**496**	**578**	**631**	**648**	**743**	**791**	**843**
4100 Recurrent taxes on immovable property	0	153	341	481	569	621	635	735	780	829
4110 Households	..	0	0	0	0	0	0	0	0	0
4120 Others	..	153	341	481	569	621	635	735	780	829
Property tax	..	6	1	1	1	1	1	1	1	1
Property tax (municipal)	..	147	341	480	568	620	634	734	779	827
4200 Recurrent taxes on net wealth	0	0	0	0	0	0	0	0	0	0
4210 Individual	..	..	..	..	..	..	..	..	..	..
4220 Corporate	..	..	..	..	..	..	..	..	..	..
4300 Estate, inheritance and gift taxes	0	0	0	0	0	0	0	0	0	0
4310 Estate and inheritance taxes	..	..	..	..	..	..	..	..	..	..
4320 Gift taxes	..	..	..	..	..	..	..	..	..	..
4400 Taxes on financial and capital transactions	45	12	8	15	9	10	13	8	10	15
4500 Non-recurrent taxes	0	0	0	0	0	0	0	0	0	0
4510 On net wealth	..	..	..	..	..	..	..	..	..	..
4520 Other non-recurrent taxes	..	..	..	..	..	..	..	..	..	..
4600 Other recurrent taxes on property	0	0	0	0	0	0	0	0	0	0
5000 Taxes on goods and services	**1 709**	**10 317**	**16 402**	**22 118**	**20 980**	**23 259**	**25 876**	**27 518**	**29 075**	**30 411**
5100 Taxes on production, sale, transfer, etc	1 681	10 131	16 083	21 716	20 513	22 754	25 317	26 614	27 545	29 092
5110 General taxes	762	6 259	10 753	16 155	15 015	16 980	19 472	20 913	21 874	23 153
5111 Value added taxes	762	6 259	10 753	16 155	15 015	16 980	19 472	20 913	21 874	23 153
5112 Sales tax	0	0	0	0	0	0	0	0	0	0
5113 Other	0	0	0	0	0	0	0	0	0	0
5120 Taxes on specific goods and services	919	3 872	5 330	5 561	5 497	5 773	5 845	5 701	5 671	5 939
5121 Excises	258	1 797	1 262	2 822	3 058	3 101	3 013	3 072	3 372	3 552
Tobacco and derivatives	76	205	312	342	340	347	259	312	385	405
Beer	0	97	122	147	143	159	176	191	217	243
Alcoholic beverages	0	77	76	91	90	98	101	100	90	56
Soft drinks	0	15	172	196	200	220	245	263	282	300
Other beverages	77	12	2	2	1	2	2	1	1	3
Cement	0	0	93	105	99	99	104	102	100	101
Oil and derivatives	105	1 389	485	1 938	2 184	2 179	2 125	2 103	2 297	2 445
5122 Profits of fiscal monopolies	0	0	0	0	0	0	0	0	0	0
5123 Customs and import duties	506	1 806	3 715	2 427	2 139	2 368	2 533	2 311	1 965	2 044
5124 Taxes on exports	0	0	0	0	0	0	0	0	0	0
5125 Taxes on investment goods	0	0	0	0	0	0	0	0	0	0

Table 4.12. Guatemala / Guatemala *(cont.)*
Details of tax revenue / Ingresos tributarios detallados

Million GTQ

	1990	2000	2005	2008	2009	2010	2011	2012	2013	2014
5126 Taxes on specific services	155	269	354	311	301	304	300	318	334	343
5127 Other taxes on internat. trade and transactions	0	0	0	0	0	0	0	0	0	0
5128 Other taxes	0	0	0	0	0	0	0	0	0	0
5130 Unallocable between 5110 and 5120	0	0	0	0	0	0	0	0	0	0
5200 Taxes on use of goods and perform activities	28	186	319	402	468	505	558	904	1 530	1 320
5210 Recurrent taxes	28	186	319	402	468	505	558	904	1 530	1 320
5211 Paid by households: motor vehicles	0	0	0	0	0	0	0	331	694	747
5212 Paid by others: motor vehicles	28	186	319	402	468	505	558	573	836	572
5213 Paid in respect of other goods	0	0	0	0	0	0	0	0	0	0
5220 Non-recurrent taxes	0	0	0	0	0	0	0	0	0	0
5300 Unallocable between 5100 and 5200	0	0	0	0	0	0	0	0	0	0
6000 Other taxes	**104**	**186**	**315**	**378**	**596**	**572**	**639**	**878**	**430**	**359**
6100 Paid solely by business	0	0	0	0	0	0	0	0	0	0
6200 Other	104	186	315	378	596	572	639	878	430	359
Revenue stamps and stamped paper	104	182	313	376	595	572	638	877	430	359
Other indirect taxes	0	4	1	2	1	1	1	1	1	0

Note: Year ending 31st December.

The data are on cash basis.

The figures exclude some local government tax revenues as the data are not available. Revenues from the municipal property tax (IUSI) are included.

Heading 2000: Corresponds to social security contributions paid to the Guatemalan Social Security Institute (IGSS) and payments by public employees to the government's pension fund.

Headings 4120 and 4400: For years prior to 2000 the property tax under heading 4120 is included in the total under heading 4400.

Heading 5121: Up to 1999 "Other beverages" contains all alcoholic and non-alcoholic beverages.

Source: Superintendencia de Administración Tributaria, Ministry of Finance (for national and local taxes). Guatemalan Social Security Institute. (IGSS) from 1990 to 1994 and Superintendencia de Administración Tributaria for subsequent years (for social security contribution figures).

StatLink http://dx.doi.org/10.1787/888933338194

Table 4.13. Honduras / Honduras
Details of tax revenue / Ingresos tributarios detallados

Million HNL

	1990	2000	2005	2008	2009	2010	2011	2012	2013	2014
Total tax revenue	**2 032**	**16 347**	**31 123**	**49 637**	**47 157**	**51 844**	**56 479**	**64 153**	**69 055**	**81 066**
1000 Taxes on income, profits and capital gains	**431**	**2 985**	**7 498**	**13 443**	**12 658**	**13 972**	**16 979**	**17 531**	**19 597**	**21 722**
1100 Of individuals	157	991	2 312	4 259	4 067	4 528	5 232	5 745	6 478	7 312
1110 On income and profits	157	991	2 312	4 259	4 067	4 528	5 232	5 745	6 478	7 312
1120 On capital gains	..	..	..	..	..	..	..	..	..	..
1200 Corporate	274	1 916	4 725	8 904	8 424	8 705	11 437	11 556	12 875	14 021
1210 On profits	274	1 916	4 725	8 904	8 424	8 705	11 437	11 556	12 875	14 021
Corporate income tax	274	1 916	4 121	7 572	7 230	7 400	9 447	10 088	11 523	12 756
Income tax surcharge	0	0	604	1 332	1 194	1 305	1 990	1 468	1 352	1 265
1220 On capital gains	..	..	..	..	..	..	..	..	..	..
1300 Unallocable between 1100 and 1200	0	78	461	279	167	740	310	230	245	389
Tax on net assets	..	78	144	279	167	359	310	230	245	389
Revaluation of assets	..	0	316	0	0	381	0	0	0	0
2000 Social security contributions	**179**	**1 727**	**4 416**	**7 308**	**8 122**	**8 671**	**6 955**	**10 854**	**12 529**	**12 467**
2100 Employees	..	..	..	..	..	..	..	..	..	..
2110 On a payroll basis	..	..	..	..	..	..	..	..	..	..
2120 On an income tax basis	..	..	..	..	..	..	..	..	..	..
2200 Employers	..	..	..	..	..	..	..	..	..	..
2210 On a payroll basis	..	..	..	..	..	..	..	..	..	..
2220 On an income tax basis	..	..	..	..	..	..	..	..	..	..
2300 Self-employed or non-employed	..	..	..	..	..	..	..	..	..	..
2310 On a payroll basis	..	..	..	..	..	..	..	..	..	..
2320 On an income tax basis	..	..	..	..	..	..	..	..	..	..
2400 Unallocable between 2100, 2200 and 2300	179	1 727	4 416	7 308	8 122	8 671	6 955	10 854	12 529	12 467
2410 On a payroll basis	179	1 727	4 416	7 308	8 122	8 671	6 955	10 854	12 529	12 467
2420 On an income tax basis	0	0	0	0	0	0	0	0	0	0
3000 Taxes on payroll and workforce	**0**	**0**	**0**	**0**	**0**	**0**	**0**	**0**	**0**	**0**
4000 Taxes on property	**16**	**189**	**170**	**265**	**224**	**254**	**290**	**1 148**	**1 201**	**2 121**
4100 Recurrent taxes on immovable property	0	0	0	0	0	0	0	0	0	0
4110 Households	..	..	..	..	..	..	..	..	..	..
4120 Others	..	..	..	..	..	..	..	..	..	..
4200 Recurrent taxes on net wealth	0	0	0	0	0	0	0	0	0	0
4210 Individual	..	..	..	..	..	..	..	..	..	..
4220 Corporate	..	..	..	..	..	..	..	..	..	..
4300 Estate, inheritance and gift taxes	0	0	0	0	0	0	0	0	0	0
4310 Estate and inheritance taxes	..	..	..	..	..	..	..	..	..	..
4320 Gift taxes	..	..	..	..	..	..	..	..	..	..
4400 Taxes on financial and capital transactions	0	0	0	0	0	0	0	821	903	1 846
4500 Non-recurrent taxes	0	0	0	0	0	0	0	0	0	0
4510 On net wealth	..	..	..	..	..	..	..	..	..	..
4520 Other non-recurrent taxes	..	..	..	..	..	..	..	..	..	..
4600 Other recurrent taxes on property	16	189	170	265	224	254	290	327	298	275
5000 Taxes on goods and services	**1 405**	**11 445**	**19 032**	**28 608**	**26 141**	**28 937**	**32 247**	**34 610**	**35 720**	**44 748**
5100 Taxes on production, sale, transfer, etc	1 405	11 445	19 032	28 608	26 141	28 937	32 247	34 610	35 720	44 748
5110 General taxes	344	5 146	9 565	16 464	14 396	16 050	18 967	20 150	20 637	27 734
5111 Value added taxes	344	5 146	9 565	16 464	14 396	16 050	18 967	20 150	20 637	27 734
5112 Sales tax	0	0	0	0	0	0	0	0	0	0
5113 Other	0	0	0	0	0	0	0	0	0	0
5120 Taxes on specific goods and services	1 061	6 299	9 468	12 145	11 746	12 887	13 279	14 460	15 082	17 014
5121 Excises	256	3 600	6 322	7 581	8 022	8 458	8 670	9 490	10 119	11 588
Beer	71	376	338	373	344	376	466	503	503	525
Soft drinks	25	240	268	413	415	514	632	675	725	754
Liquors	32	48	69	79	76	121	164	165	165	188
Petroleum products	43	347	0	0	0	0	0	0	0	0
Cigarettes	57	369	437	568	646	607	660	633	495	610
Fuel tax	0	1 962	4 916	5 570	6 032	6 288	6 177	6 868	7 613	8 874
Other	28	258	295	577	509	551	572	646	618	638
5122 Profits of fiscal monopolies	0	0	0	0	0	0	0	0	0	0
5123 Customs and import duties	498	2 083	2 174	2 975	2 065	2 505	2 626	2 933	2 651	2 974
Petroleum	0	297	0	0	0	0	0	0	0	0
Other	498	1 786	2 174	2 975	2 065	2 505	2 626	2 933	2 651	2 974
5124 Taxes on exports	217	6	0	0	0	0	0	0	0	0
Bananas	39	5	..	..	..	..	..	..	..	..
Coffee	1	0	..	..	..	..	..	..	..	..
Temporary export tax	163	0	..	..	..	..	..	..	..	..
Other	15	1	..	..	..	..	..	..	..	..
5125 Taxes on investment goods	0	0	0	0	0	0	0	0	0	0
5126 Taxes on specific services	0	0	0	0	0	0	0	0	0	0

Table 4.13. Honduras / Honduras (cont.)
Details of tax revenue / Ingresos tributarios detallados

Million HNL

	1990	2000	2005	2008	2009	2010	2011	2012	2013	2014
5127 Other taxes on internat. trade and transactions	0	0	0	0	0	0	0	0	0	0
5128 Other taxes	90	610	971	1 589	1 659	1 924	1 983	2 038	2 312	2 451
5130 Unallocable between 5110 and 5120	0	0	0	0	0	0	0	0	0	0
5200 Taxes on use of goods and perform activities	0	0	0	0	0	0	0	0	0	0
5210 Recurrent taxes	..	..	..	..	..	..	..	..	..	..
5211 Paid by households: motor vehicles	..	..	..	..	..	..	..	..	..	..
5212 Paid by others: motor vehicles	..	..	..	..	..	..	..	..	..	..
5213 Paid in respect of other goods	..	..	..	..	..	..	..	..	..	..
5220 Non-recurrent taxes	..	..	..	..	..	..	..	..	..	..
5300 Unallocable between 5100 and 5200	0	0	0	0	0	0	0	0	0	0
6000 Other taxes	**1**	**2**	**7**	**13**	**12**	**9**	**9**	**10**	**8**	**7**
6100 Paid solely by business	0	0	0	0	0	0	0	0	0	0
6200 Other	1	2	7	13	12	9	9	10	8	7

Note: Year ending 31st December.
The data are on cash basis.
The figures exclude local government tax revenues as the data are not available.
Heading 1300: In ECLAC data, the tax on net assets is classified as a property tax (4000).
Source: Secretaria de Finanzas, Ministry of Finance.

StatLink http://dx.doi.org/10.1787/888933338205

Table 4.14. Jamaica / Jamaica
Details of tax revenue / Ingresos tributarios detallados

Million JAM

	1990	2000	2005	2008	2009	2010	2011	2012	2013	2014
Total tax revenue	**7 748**	**87 713**	**163 359**	**249 330**	**264 389**	**288 380**	**303 947**	**322 948**	**357 979**	**379 339**
1000 Taxes on income, profits and capital gains	**3 944**	**39 277**	**69 894**	**114 481**	**124 475**	**118 708**	**122 752**	**126 441**	**129 951**	**134 083**
1100 Of individuals	1 687	17 441	36 043	59 802	62 043	54 798	62 792	64 315	66 282	70 867
1110 On income and profits	1 687	17 441	36 043	59 802	62 043	54 798	62 792	64 315	66 282	70 867
PAYE	1 489	16 515	34 223	55 572	58 577	50 828	58 851	60 637	62 172	66 645
Other individuals	198	926	1 820	4 230	3 466	3 969	3 940	3 678	4 111	4 223
1120 On capital gains	..	..	..	..	..	..	..	..	..	..
1200 Corporate	1 280	7 627	13 134	24 510	25 463	33 091	31 858	32 706	34 539	31 991
1210 On profits	1 280	7 627	13 134	24 510	25 463	33 091	31 858	32 706	34 539	31 991
Bauxite/alumina	134	430	446	10	19	866	0	1	0	0
Other companies	1 146	7 197	12 688	24 500	25 443	32 224	31 857	32 705	34 539	31 991
1220 On capital gains	..	..	..	..	..	..	..	..	..	..
1300 Unallocable between 1100 and 1200	977	14 209	20 718	30 169	36 969	30 820	28 103	29 419	29 130	31 224
Tax on dividends	68	854	248	214	230	1 059	1 028	1 080	1 175	1 904
Tax on interests	605	9 535	13 277	18 476	24 552	16 970	12 376	13 437	10 706	10 103
Education tax	305	3 821	7 193	11 479	12 187	12 792	14 699	14 903	17 249	19 217
2000 Social security contributions	**0**	**0**	**5 110**	**7 014**	**6 820**	**9 248**	**11 628**	**11 689**	**14 559**	**14 600**
2100 Employees	..	..	..	..	..	..	..	..	..	..
2110 On a payroll basis	..	..	..	..	..	..	..	..	..	..
2120 On an income tax basis	..	..	..	..	..	..	..	..	..	..
2200 Employers	..	..	..	..	..	..	..	..	..	..
2210 On a payroll basis	..	..	..	..	..	..	..	..	..	..
2220 On an income tax basis	..	..	..	..	..	..	..	..	..	..
2300 Self-employed or non-employed	..	..	..	..	..	..	..	..	..	..
2310 On a payroll basis	..	..	..	..	..	..	..	..	..	..
2320 On an income tax basis	..	..	..	..	..	..	..	..	..	..
2400 Unallocable between 2100, 2200 and 2300	..	..	5 110	7 014	6 820	9 248	11 628	11 689	14 559	14 600
National Insurance Scheme (NIS) contributions	..	..	5 110	7 014	6 820	9 248	11 628	11 689	14 559	14 600
2410 On a payroll basis	..	..	..	..	..	..	..	..	..	..
2420 On an income tax basis	..	..	..	..	..	..	..	..	..	..
3000 Taxes on payroll and workforce	**0**	**0**	**0**	**0**	**0**	**0**	**0**	**0**	**0**	**0**
4000 Taxes on property	**67**	**639**	**1 474**	**2 286**	**1 831**	**2 792**	**2 531**	**2 805**	**5 842**	**5 800**
4100 Recurrent taxes on immovable property	67	639	1 474	2 286	1 831	2 792	2 531	2 805	5 842	5 800
4110 Households	67	639	1 474	2 286	1 831	2 792	2 531	2 805	5 842	5 800
Property tax	67	0	0	0	0	0	0	0	0	0
Property tax (municipal)	0	639	1 474	2 286	1 831	2 792	2 531	2 805	5 842	5 800
4120 Others	0	0	0	0	0	0	0	0	0	0
4200 Recurrent taxes on net wealth	0	0	0	0	0	0	0	0	0	0
4210 Individual	..	..	..	..	..	..	..	..	..	..
4220 Corporate	..	..	..	..	..	..	..	..	..	..
4300 Estate, inheritance and gift taxes	0	0	0	0	0	0	0	0	0	0
4310 Estate and inheritance taxes	..	..	..	..	..	..	..	..	..	..
4320 Gift taxes	..	..	..	..	..	..	..	..	..	..
4400 Taxes on financial and capital transactions	0	0	0	0	0	0	0	0	0	0
4500 Non-recurrent taxes	0	0	0	0	0	0	0	0	0	0
4510 On net wealth	..	..	..	..	..	..	..	..	..	..
4520 Other non-recurrent taxes	..	..	..	..	..	..	..	..	..	..
4600 Other recurrent taxes on property	0	0	0	0	0	0	0	0	0	0
5000 Taxes on goods and services	**3 294**	**44 638**	**78 147**	**113 423**	**121 928**	**148 894**	**156 308**	**171 332**	**194 929**	**211 819**
5100 Taxes on production, sale, transfer, etc	3 230	43 838	77 036	111 569	119 749	146 850	154 208	168 940	192 166	208 885
5110 General taxes	4	13 059	27 274	40 111	40 825	45 152	47 788	50 963	57 474	62 023
5111 Value added taxes	0	13 059	27 274	40 111	40 825	45 152	47 788	50 963	57 474	62 023
5112 Sales tax	4	0	0	0	0	0	0	0	0	0
Sales tax on used cars	4	..	..	..	..	..	..	..	..	..
5113 Other	0	0	0	0	0	0	0	0	0	0
5120 Taxes on specific goods and services	3 226	30 779	49 762	71 458	78 925	101 698	106 419	117 977	134 692	146 862
5121 Excises	1 158	5 344	3 536	3 626	5 272	9 168	9 403	11 216	12 149	10 991
Excise duty	44	0	0	0	0	0	0	0	0	0
Special consumption tax	1 115	5 344	3 536	3 626	5 272	9 168	9 403	11 216	12 149	10 991
5122 Profits of fiscal monopolies	0	0	0	0	0	0	0	0	0	0
5123 Customs and import duties	1 545	22 932	43 260	64 650	70 608	87 510	90 180	97 497	103 747	115 279
Custom duty	782	8 498	14 999	20 535	20 048	19 959	20 638	22 905	25 938	26 281
Stamp duty	470	731	1 083	1 268	1 284	1 352	1 444	1 635	1 945	1 910
General consumption tax (imports)	293	9 297	18 328	30 194	27 533	37 255	40 932	44 069	50 186	56 733
Special consumption tax (imports)	0	4 407	8 851	12 653	21 744	28 944	27 167	28 889	25 678	30 356
5124 Taxes on exports	0	0	0	0	0	0	0	0	0	0
5125 Taxes on investment goods	0	0	0	0	0	0	0	0	0	0

Table 4.14. Jamaica / Jamaica *(cont.)*
Details of tax revenue / Ingresos tributarios detallados

Million JAM

	1990	2000	2005	2008	2009	2010	2011	2012	2013	2014
5126 Taxes on specific services	523	2 503	2 966	3 183	3 044	5 020	6 837	9 264	18 796	20 592
Bank and trust	204	0	0	0	0	0	0	0	0	0
Entertainment tax	11	0	0	0	0	0	0	0	0	0
Betting, gaming and lottery	50	504	1 052	1 370	1 390	1 508	1 586	1 893	2 225	2 661
Accommodation tax	87	0	0	0	0	0	0	265	1 636	1 900
Telephone call tax	86	0	0	0	0	0	0	2 342	6 405	6 687
Travel tax	86	1 999	1 914	1 812	1 654	3 512	5 251	4 763	8 531	9 344
5127 Other taxes on internat. trade and transactions	0	0	0	0	0	0	0	0	0	0
5128 Other taxes	0	0	0	0	0	0	0	0	0	0
5130 Unallocable between 5110 and 5120	0	0	0	0	0	0	0	0	0	0
5200 Taxes on use of goods and perform activities	64	800	1 111	1 854	2 179	2 045	2 100	2 393	2 763	2 934
5210 Recurrent taxes	64	800	1 111	1 854	2 179	2 045	2 100	2 393	2 763	2 934
5211 Paid by households: motor vehicles	47	751	935	1 486	1 734	1 775	1 748	2 043	2 493	2 666
5212 Paid by others: motor vehicles	0	0	0	0	0	0	0	0	0	0
5213 Paid in respect of other goods	17	49	176	368	445	270	352	350	270	268
5220 Non-recurrent taxes	0	0	0	0	0	0	0	0	0	0
5300 Unallocable between 5100 and 5200	0	0	0	0	0	0	0	0	0	0
6000 Other taxes	**444**	**3 159**	**8 733**	**12 127**	**9 336**	**8 738**	**10 729**	**10 680**	**12 606**	**13 037**
6100 Paid solely by business	0	0	0	0	0	0	0	0	0	0
6200 Other	444	3 159	8 733	12 127	9 336	8 738	10 729	10 680	12 606	13 037
Environmental levy	0	0	0	2 405	2 147	2 002	2 217	2 103	2 159	2 200
Contractors levy	16	266	475	735	812	748	1 139	1 198	1 091	909
Stamp duty (domestic)	428	2 893	8 259	8 988	6 378	5 987	7 372	7 380	9 356	9 928

Note: Data collected by fiscal year (1 April - 31 March) for 1990-2003, then by calendar year (year ending 31st December).
The data are on cash basis.
The figures exclude local government tax revenues as the data are not available.
Heading 2000: The data for social security contributions are available from 2003 to 2013 only. The data are estimated for 2014.
Heading 4110: The data for property tax (municipal) are estimated for 2014.
Heading 6200: The data for the environmental levy under heading 6200 are estimated for 2014.
Source: Ministry of Finance and Planning.

StatLink http://dx.doi.org/10.1787/888933338211

Table 4.15. Mexico / México
Details of tax revenue / Ingresos tributarios detallados

Million MXN

	1990	2000	2005	2008	2009	2010	2011	2012	2013	2014
Total tax revenue	**127 959**	**1 014 625**	**1 667 424**	**2 539 615**	**2 071 854**	**2 458 249**	**2 830 477**	**3 048 561**	**3 165 976**	**3 171 938**
1000 Taxes on income, profits and capital gains	**34 673**	**276 548**	**402 036**	**629 135**	**591 942**	**683 604**	**772 704**	**803 071**	**957 213**	**979 251**
1100 Of individuals	..	..	195 869	285 270	280 230	313 473	352 386	397 701	425 621	514 208
Tax on income of individuals	..	..	195 869	285 270	280 230	313 473	352 386	397 701	425 621	514 208
1110 On income and profits	..	..	..	..	..	..	..	..	..	..
1120 On capital gains	..	..	..	..	..	..	..	..	..	..
1200 Corporate	..	..	135 840	214 611	191 685	246 745	303 176	288 360	392 199	441 317
Tax on income of corporations	..	..	135 840	214 611	191 685	246 745	303 176	288 360	392 199	441 317
1210 On profits	..	..	..	..	..	..	..	..	..	..
1220 On capital gains	..	..	..	..	..	..	..	..	..	..
1300 Unallocable between 1100 and 1200	34 673	276 548	70 327	129 254	120 027	123 386	117 143	117 010	139 393	23 726
Tax on income of other individuals and corporations	..	244 841	40 780	61 208	64 816	66 937	66 004	74 042	89 028	31 076
Tax on asset	..	13 913	12 033	1 134	-2 540	-624	-1 120	-1 192	-1 325	-735
Credit on salary	..	17 794	17 514	15 886	12 113	9 708	2 076	1 387	1 274	2 423
Oil yields tax	..	0	0	4 441	921	2 296	3 019	573	3 210	4 669
IETU	..	0	0	46 586	44 718	45 069	47 165	42 199	47 205	-13 707
2000 Social security contributions	**17 165**	**167 292**	**261 673**	**321 843**	**346 031**	**378 006**	**411 289**	**454 778**	**490 918**	**538 213**
2100 Employees	..	..	..	..	..	..	..	..	..	..
2110 On a payroll basis	..	..	..	..	..	..	..	..	..	..
2120 On an income tax basis	..	..	..	..	..	..	..	..	..	..
2200 Employers	..	..	..	..	..	..	..	..	..	..
2210 On a payroll basis	..	..	..	..	..	..	..	..	..	..
2220 On an income tax basis	..	..	..	..	..	..	..	..	..	..
2300 Self-employed or non-employed	..	..	..	..	..	..	..	..	..	..
2310 On a payroll basis	..	..	..	..	..	..	..	..	..	..
2320 On an income tax basis	..	..	..	..	..	..	..	..	..	..
2400 Unallocable between 2100, 2200 and 2300	17 165	167 292	261 673	321 843	346 031	378 006	411 289	454 778	490 918	538 213
2410 On a payroll basis	..	167 292	261 673	321 843	346 031	378 006	411 289	454 778	490 918	538 213
2420 On an income tax basis	..	0	0	0	0	0	0	0	0	0
3000 Taxes on payroll and workforce	**1 797**	**11 217**	**20 461**	**31 123**	**31 965**	**36 911**	**41 980**	**48 033**	**53 042**	**0**
Substitute tax on salary	..	0	0	0	0	0	0	0	0	0
Payroll tax	..	11 101	15 746	22 919	23 530	27 813	31 817	35 480	41 184	0
Tax on remuneration to the personal work	..	65	4 562	7 992	8 180	8 841	9 990	12 333	11 645	0
Tax on professions and fees	..	36	53	72	70	71	58	48	50	0
Tax on operations by contract	..	15	100	140	186	186	116	173	163	0
4000 Taxes on property	**1 914**	**13 964**	**26 796**	**35 847**	**35 484**	**38 955**	**41 186**	**45 186**	**46 238**	**0**
4100 Recurrent taxes on immovable property	1 036	9 948	16 641	21 394	22 862	25 724	28 728	31 544	31 338	..
4110 Households	0	0	0	0	0	0	0	0	0	..
4120 Others	1 036	9 948	16 641	21 394	22 862	25 724	28 728	31 544	31 338	..
Property tax	..	9 948	16 641	21 394	22 862	25 724	28 728	31 544	31 338	..
4200 Recurrent taxes on net wealth	0	0	0	0	0	0	0	0	0	..
4210 Individual	..	..	..	..	..	..	..	..	..	..
4220 Corporate	..	..	..	..	..	..	..	..	..	..
4300 Estate, inheritance and gift taxes	8	0	0	0	0	0	0	0	0	..
4310 Estate and inheritance taxes	8	..	..	..	..	..	..	..	..	..
4320 Gift taxes	0	..	..	..	..	..	..	..	..	..
4400 Taxes on financial and capital transactions	870	4 017	10 155	14 452	12 622	13 231	12 458	13 642	14 900	..
Alienation of immovable property	..	1 763	984	1 310	1 163	1 122	1 379	1 341	1 271	..
Transfer of ownership of real estate	..	2 236	5 528	5 825	5 005	5 027	3 923	4 575	4 518	..
Purchasing property	..	18	3 643	7 318	6 454	7 082	7 157	7 725	9 110	..
4500 Non-recurrent taxes	0	0	0	0	0	0	0	0	0	..
4510 On net wealth	..	..	..	..	..	..	..	..	..	..
4520 Other non-recurrent taxes	..	..	..	..	..	..	..	..	..	..
4600 Other recurrent taxes on property	0	0	0	0	0	0	0	0	0	..
5000 Taxes on goods and services	**70 791**	**537 953**	**944 766**	**1 502 941**	**1 039 344**	**1 293 373**	**1 530 906**	**1 660 413**	**1 576 887**	**1 630 254**
5100 Taxes on production, sale, transfer, etc	70 125	528 666	928 979	1 480 972	1 017 627	1 271 581	1 508 269	1 643 337	1 557 226	1 629 822
5110 General taxes	26 635	189 606	318 432	457 248	407 795	504 509	537 143	579 988	556 794	667 085
5111 Value added taxes	26 635	189 606	318 432	457 248	407 795	504 509	537 143	579 988	556 794	667 085
5112 Sales tax	0	0	0	0	0	0	0	0	0	0
5113 Other	0	0	0	0	0	0	0	0	0	0
5120 Taxes on specific goods and services	43 473	339 060	610 547	1 023 723	609 832	767 072	971 126	1 063 349	1 000 432	962 737
5121 Excises	10 072	86 163	55 286	60 462	69 770	86 098	94 623	98 490	104 111	155 764
Special tax on production and services	..	81 544	49 627	55 391	65 708	81 427	89 544	92 620	97 860	149 337
Tax on new automobiles	..	4 619	5 659	5 071	4 063	4 671	5 079	5 870	6 252	6 427
Tax on luxury goods and services	..	0	0	0	0	0	0	0	0	0
5122 Profits of fiscal monopolies	0	0	0	0	0	0	0	0	0	0

Table 4.15. Mexico / México (cont.)

Details of tax revenue / Ingresos tributarios detallados

Million MXN

	1990	2000	2005	2008	2009	2010	2011	2012	2013	2014
5123 Customs and import duties	6 998	33 285	27 512	37 831	31 732	26 602	29 946	31 161	32 324	36 841
Step customs officer	..	423	692	2 048	1 535	2 071	3 065	3 255	3 065	2 913
Import taxes	..	32 861	26 820	35 783	30 196	24 531	26 881	27 906	29 260	33 928
5124 Taxes on exports	75	4	0	1	1	0	2	1	1	1
Taxes on exports	..	4	0	1	1	0	2	1	1	1
5125 Taxes on investment goods	0	0	0	0	0	0	0	0	0	0
5126 Taxes on specific services	132	1 042	1 578	20 097	18 461	10 958	-5 610	7 169	-1 441	-12 322
IDE	132	0	0	17 700	15 888	8 022	-8 442	2 786	-5 988	-12 322
Tax on lodging	0	504	798	1 178	1 147	1 384	1 375	1 702	1 890	0
Public entertainment tax	0	240	349	383	486	462	360	625	566	0
Tax on lotteries, raffles and gambling	0	267	417	717	789	923	952	1 329	1 213	0
Tax on commercials	0	4	15	118	150	166	145	16	203	0
Various indirect taxes	0	28	0	0	0	1	0	711	674	0
5127 Other taxes on internat. trade and transactions	0	0	0	0	0	0	0	0	0	0
5128 Other taxes	26 196	218 567	526 171	905 332	489 869	643 414	852 166	926 528	865 438	782 454
Ordinary fee on oil production	..	125 329	334 784	0	0	0	0	0	0	0
Extraordinary fee on oil production	..	68 235	129 967	0	0	0	0	0	0	0
Additional fee on oil production	..	2 576	6 772	3 715	149	0	0	0	0	0
Tax on oil yields	..	22 201	54 298	0	0	0	0	0	0	0
Mining fees	..	226	350	68	1 782	1 956	2 858	3 243	3 886	2 040
Ordinary	..	0	0	794 030	410 437	543 895	721 209	769 489	721 790	653 619
Stabilization Fund	..	0	0	71 536	63 839	77 071	81 247	106 151	106 401	103 941
Extraordinary on crude petroleum export	..	0	0	33 640	-556	6 644	24 152	19 594	10 313	5 746
Scientific research and technologica Fund in the matter of energy	..	0	0	1 583	2 046	3 616	5 635	8 441	8 422	8 001
For oil control	..	0	0	37	23	29	35	42	39	37
Rights on the extraction of mineral oils	..	0	0	158	2 663	3 533	5 601	7 185	6 178	4 595
Special rights on mineral oils for fields in the "Paleoncanal icontepec"	..	0	0	565	7 676	2 494	6 117	7 521	5 450	3 386
Special rights on hydrocarbons	..	0	0	0	1 813	4 032	1 308	0	0	0
Special right on hydrocarbons in deep water fields	..	0	0	0	0	143	4 003	4 493	2 574	0
Right to register for exploration and exploitation of hydrocarbons	..	0	0	0	0	0	0	370	385	357
5130 Unallocable between 5110 and 5120	17	0	0	0	0	0	0	0	0	0
5200 Taxes on use of goods and perform activities	666	9 287	15 787	21 970	21 717	21 792	22 637	17 076	19 660	431
5210 Recurrent taxes	666	9 287	15 787	21 970	21 717	21 792	22 637	17 076	19 660	431
5211 Paid by households: motor vehicles	567	8 878	15 237	21 492	21 301	21 319	22 186	16 464	19 174	0
Tax on motor vehicules	..	8 878	15 237	21 492	21 301	21 319	22 186	16 464	19 174	0
5212 Paid by others: motor vehicles	0	301	357	311	270	281	296	370	357	367
Tax on federal auto transport	..	301	357	311	270	281	296	370	357	367
5213 Paid in respect of other goods	99	108	193	166	147	193	155	242	129	65
Sport fishing	..	40	80	85	68	59	50	55	50	65
Sport hunting	..	3	0	1	0	0	0	0	0	0
Tax on commercial activities	..	63	113	33	42	50	66	42	26	0
Trade in books and magazines	..	0	0	0	0	0	0	0	3	0
Tax on industrial activities	..	2	0	47	35	82	38	145	49	0
5220 Non-recurrent taxes	0	0	0	0	0	0	0	0	0	0
5300 Unallocable between 5100 and 5200	0	0	0	0	0	0	0	0	0	0
6000 Other taxes	**1 619**	**7 651**	**11 693**	**18 726**	**27 087**	**27 399**	**32 412**	**37 080**	**41 679**	**24 221**
6100 Paid solely by business	0	0	0	0	0	0	0	0	0	0
6200 Other	1 619	7 651	11 693	18 726	27 087	27 399	32 412	37 080	41 679	24 221
Accessories	..	5 504	9 543	13 744	21 710	22 206	24 059	24 077	25 301	23 717
Unallocable between 1000 and 5000 caused in exercices fiscal previous liquidation slopes or of payment	..	374	-927	58	7	30	-118	2 260	1 618	504
Additional state and local taxes	..	1 773	3 077	4 924	5 361	5 162	8 471	10 743	14 760	0
Total tax revenue	**127 959**	**1 014 625**	**1 667 424**	**2 539 615**	**2 071 854**	**2 458 249**	**2 830 477**	**3 048 561**	**3 165 976**	**3 171 938**
Fees levied on hydrocarbon production	**-26 196**	**-218 567**	**-526 171**	**-905 332**	**-489 869**	**-643 414**	**-852 166**	**-926 528**	**-865 438**	**-782 454**
Total tax revenue (net of fees on hydrocarbons)	**101 763**	**796 059**	**1 141 254**	**1 634 282**	**1 581 985**	**1 814 835**	**1 978 312**	**2 122 033**	**2 300 538**	**2 389 484**

Note: Year ending 31st December.

The data are on cash basis.

The 2014 data for tax revenues of the State and Local levels of government are not available. They comprise revenues in categories 3000, 4000, 5000 and 6000.

Heading 1000: In ECLAC data, income taxes are presented net of credit on salary figures.

Heading 2000: In ECLAC data, social security contributions are presented net of transfers from the Federal government for the payment of IMSS (Mexican Social Security Institute) pensions.

Heading 5128: In ECLAC and CIAT data, fees levied on hydrocarbon production are treated as non-tax revenues. As a result they publish tax revenues net of these fees. The final three rows of the table display the impact of this.

Source: Ministry of Finance, Economic Department.

StatLink http://dx.doi.org/10.1787/888933338220

Table 4.16. Nicaragua / Nicaragua
Details of tax revenue / Ingresos tributarios detallados

Million NIO

	1990	2000	2005	2008	2009	2010	2011	2012	2013	2014
Total tax revenue	..	**8 418**	**17 009**	**27 697**	**28 863**	**33 620**	**41 185**	**48 131**	**53 486**	**62 330**
1000 Taxes on income, profits and capital gains	..	**1 144**	**3 902**	**7 002**	**7 818**	**8 351**	**11 144**	**13 107**	**14 521**	**17 658**
1100 Of individuals	..	..	..	..	..	..	..	..	..	..
1110 On income and profits	..	..	..	..	..	..	..	..	..	..
1120 On capital gains	..	..	..	..	..	..	..	..	..	..
1200 Corporate	..	..	..	..	..	..	..	..	..	..
1210 On profits	..	..	..	..	..	..	..	..	..	..
1220 On capital gains	..	..	..	..	..	..	..	..	..	..
1300 Unallocable between 1100 and 1200	..	1 144	3 902	7 002	7 818	8 351	11 144	13 107	14 521	17 658
Income tax	..	1 144	3 902	7 002	7 818	8 351	11 144	13 107	14 521	17 658
2000 Social security contributions	..	**1 678**	**3 363**	**6 023**	**6 804**	**8 090**	**9 433**	**11 007**	**12 805**	**15 161**
2100 Employees	..	..	..	..	..	..	..	..	..	..
2110 On a payroll basis	..	..	..	..	..	..	..	..	..	..
2120 On an income tax basis	..	..	..	..	..	..	..	..	..	..
2200 Employers	..	..	..	..	..	..	..	..	..	..
2210 On a payroll basis	..	..	..	..	..	..	..	..	..	..
2220 On an income tax basis	..	..	..	..	..	..	..	..	..	..
2300 Self-employed or non-employed	..	..	..	..	..	..	..	..	..	..
2310 On a payroll basis	..	..	..	..	..	..	..	..	..	..
2320 On an income tax basis	..	..	..	..	..	..	..	..	..	..
2400 Unallocable between 2100, 2200 and 2300	..	1 678	3 363	6 023	6 804	8 090	9 433	11 007	12 805	15 161
2410 On a payroll basis	..	1 678	3 363	6 023	6 804	8 090	9 433	11 007	12 805	15 161
2420 On an income tax basis	..	0	0	0	0	0	0	0	0	0
3000 Taxes on payroll and workforce	..	**0**	**0**	**0**	**0**	**0**	**0**	**0**	**0**	**0**
4000 Taxes on property	..	**0**	**2**	**0**	**48**	**130**	**191**	**239**	**311**	**374**
4100 Recurrent taxes on immovable property	..	..	0	0	0	0	0	0	0	0
4110 Households	..	..	..	..	..	..	..	..	..	..
4120 Others	..	..	..	..	..	..	..	..	..	..
4200 Recurrent taxes on net wealth	..	..	2	0	48	130	191	239	311	374
4210 Individual	..	..	2	0	48	130	191	239	311	374
4220 Corporate	..	..	0	0	0	0	0	0	0	0
4300 Estate, inheritance and gift taxes	..	..	0	0	0	0	0	0	0	0
4310 Estate and inheritance taxes	..	..	..	..	..	..	..	..	..	..
4320 Gift taxes	..	..	..	..	..	..	..	..	..	..
4400 Taxes on financial and capital transactions	..	..	0	0	0	0	0	0	0	0
4500 Non-recurrent taxes	..	..	0	0	0	0	0	0	0	0
4510 On net wealth	..	..	..	..	..	..	..	..	..	..
4520 Other non-recurrent taxes	..	..	0	0	0	0	0	0	0	0
4600 Other recurrent taxes on property	..	..	0	0	0	0	0	0	0	0
5000 Taxes on goods and services	..	**5 584**	**9 725**	**14 650**	**14 170**	**17 029**	**20 395**	**23 754**	**25 771**	**29 050**
5100 Taxes on production, sale, transfer, etc	..	5 584	9 725	14 650	14 170	17 029	20 395	23 754	25 771	29 050
5110 General taxes	..	2 931	5 599	9 009	8 871	10 353	12 876	15 151	16 736	19 385
5111 Value added taxes	..	2 931	5 599	9 009	8 871	10 353	12 876	15 151	16 736	19 385
5112 Sales tax	..	0	0	0	0	0	0	0	0	0
5113 Other	..	0	0	0	0	0	0	0	0	0
5120 Taxes on specific goods and services	..	2 653	4 126	5 641	5 299	6 676	7 519	8 603	9 035	9 665
5121 Excises	..	2 034	3 227	4 518	4 392	5 541	6 070	6 884	7 254	7 761
Liquor	..	84	102	189	147	198	240	214	253	230
Beer	..	203	340	561	556	645	781	915	1 047	1 184
Cigarettes	..	70	143	177	171	45	0	0	174	1
Soft drinks	..	123	128	194	188	248	292	351	389	423
Petroleum products	..	1 359	1 756	2 162	2 277	2 699	2 700	3 045	3 418	3 938
Excise taxes on imports	..	196	734	1 180	975	1 559	1 901	2 233	1 924	1 908
Other specific excises on consumption	..	-1	25	55	77	148	156	126	49	78
5122 Profits of fiscal monopolies	..	0	0	0	0	0	0	0	0	0
5123 Customs and import duties	..	619	856	1 123	908	1 135	1 449	1 719	1 782	1 904
Custom duties	..	452	837	1 093	870	1 094	1 400	1 661	1 717	1 828
Temporary protection duty	..	96	0	0	0	0	0	0	0	0
On products originating in Colombia or Honduras	..	72	18	29	38	41	49	58	64	76
5124 Taxes on exports	..	0	0	0	0	0	0	0	0	0
5125 Taxes on investment goods	..	0	0	0	0	0	0	0	0	0
5126 Taxes on specific services	..	0	0	0	0	0	0	0	0	0
5127 Other taxes on internat. trade and transactions	..	0	43	0	0	0	0	0	0	0
5128 Other taxes	..	0	0	0	0	0	0	0	0	0
5130 Unallocable between 5110 and 5120	..	0	0	0	0	0	0	0	0	0
5200 Taxes on use of goods and perform activities	..	0	0	0	0	0	0	0	0	0
5210 Recurrent taxes	..	..	..	..	..	..	..	..	..	..
5211 Paid by households: motor vehicles	..	..	..	..	..	..	..	..	..	..

Table 4.16. Nicaragua / Nicaragua *(cont.)*
Details of tax revenue / Ingresos tributarios detallados

Million NIO

	1990	2000	2005	2008	2009	2010	2011	2012	2013	2014
5212 Paid by others: motor vehicles	..	..	..	..	..	..	..	..	..	..
5213 Paid in respect of other goods	..	..	..	..	..	..	..	..	..	..
5220 Non-recurrent taxes	..	..	..	..	..	..	..	..	..	..
5300 Unallocable between 5100 and 5200	..	0	0	0	0	0	0	0	0	0
6000 Other taxes	**..**	**11**	**17**	**21**	**24**	**20**	**22**	**24**	**77**	**87**
6100 Paid solely by business	..	0	0	0	0	0	0	0	0	0
6200 Other	..	11	17	21	24	20	22	24	77	87
Stamp tax	..	11	17	21	24	20	22	24	77	87

Note: Year ending 31st December.
The data are on cash basis.
Comparable statistics for 1990 cannot be shown due to the devaluation of the Nicaraguan cordoba.
Source: Banco Central de Nicaragua, Central Bank of Nicaragua. Ministerio de Hacienda y Crédito Público, Ministry of Finance.

StatLink http://dx.doi.org/10.1787/888933338239

Table 4.17. Panama / Panamá
Details of tax revenue / Ingresos tributarios detallados

Million PAB

	1990	2000	2005	2008	2009	2010	2011	2012	2013	2014
Total tax revenue	**892 837**	**2 018 072**	**2 354 542**	**4 013 074**	**4 351 502**	**5 012 449**	**5 832 848**	**6 971 352**	**7 822 406**	**7 939 051**
1000 Taxes on income, profits and capital gains	**216 950**	**484 872**	**562 852**	**1 097 062**	**1 285 649**	**1 317 028**	**1 349 792**	**1 985 220**	**2 199 534**	**1 997 822**
1100 Of individuals	14 155	20 343	24 395	30 098	38 811	35 456	28 458	37 825	51 598	57 690
1110 On income and profits	14 155	20 343	24 395	30 098	38 811	35 456	28 458	37 825	51 598	57 690
1120 On capital gains	..	..	..	..	..	..	..	..	..	..
1200 Corporate	72 413	186 351	255 073	544 752	731 493	749 818	701 364	1 257 178	1 182 374	1 095 127
1210 On profits	72 413	186 351	255 073	544 752	731 493	749 818	701 364	1 257 178	1 182 374	1 095 127
1220 On capital gains	..	..	..	..	..	..	..	..	..	..
1300 Unallocable between 1100 and 1200	130 382	278 178	283 384	522 212	515 345	531 754	619 970	690 217	965 562	845 006
Payroll	115 138	222 025	226 563	370 755	394 854	352 550	420 411	455 553	568 026	602 339
Panama Canal commissio	10 225	52 774	52 325	62 899	62 109	52 398	65 377	60 246	59 325	61 936
Colón Free Zone	5 019	3 379	4 496	21 323	17 855	19 666	24 074	50 735	38 903	43 266
Other	0	0	0	67 235	40 527	107 140	110 108	123 682	299 308	137 465
2000 Social security contributions	**271 300**	**742 000**	**827 300**	**1 330 200**	**1 383 300**	**1 637 100**	**2 041 500**	**2 168 500**	**2 676 700**	**2 794 000**
2100 Employees	..	..	..	..	..	..	..	..	..	..
2110 On a payroll basis	..	..	..	..	..	..	..	..	..	..
2120 On an income tax basis	..	..	..	..	..	..	..	..	..	..
2200 Employers	..	..	..	..	..	..	..	..	..	..
2210 On a payroll basis	..	..	..	..	..	..	..	..	..	..
2220 On an income tax basis	..	..	..	..	..	..	..	..	..	..
2300 Self-employed or non-employed	..	..	..	..	..	..	..	..	..	..
2310 On a payroll basis	..	..	..	..	..	..	..	..	..	..
2320 On an income tax basis	..	..	..	..	..	..	..	..	..	..
2400 Unallocable between 2100, 2200 and 2300	271 300	742 000	827 300	1 330 200	1 383 300	1 637 100	2 041 500	2 168 500	2 676 700	2 794 000
2410 On a payroll basis	..	..	..	..	..	..	..	..	..	..
2420 On an income tax basis	..	..	..	..	..	..	..	..	..	..
3000 Taxes on payroll and workforce	**0**	**36 400**	**36 243**	**45 248**	**50 962**	**58 844**	**65 200**	**70 400**	**82 400**	**134 100**
Education insurance	0	36 400	36 243	45 248	50 962	58 844	65 200	70 400	82 400	134 100
4000 Taxes on property	**43 443**	**62 090**	**109 086**	**160 530**	**175 370**	**212 194**	**229 398**	**261 033**	**337 721**	**336 903**
4100 Recurrent taxes on immovable property	28 330	33 898	56 424	80 919	104 522	107 791	109 986	119 964	180 621	175 627
4110 Households	28 330	33 898	56 424	80 919	104 522	107 791	109 986	119 964	180 621	175 627
4120 Others	0	0	0	0	0	0	0	0	0	0
4200 Recurrent taxes on net wealth	0	0	0	0	0	0	0	0	0	0
4210 Individual	..	..	..	..	..	..	..	..	..	..
4220 Corporate	..	..	..	..	..	..	..	..	..	..
4300 Estate, inheritance and gift taxes	154	0	0	0	0	0	0	0	0	0
4310 Estate and inheritance taxes	..	..	..	..	..	..	..	..	..	..
4320 Gift taxes	..	..	..	..	..	..	..	..	..	..
4400 Taxes on financial and capital transactions	3 419	9 343	21 049	40 528	24 456	29 810	36 195	40 998	49 391	44 800
4500 Non-recurrent taxes	0	0	0	0	0	0	0	0	0	0
4510 On net wealth	..	..	..	..	..	..	..	..	..	..
4520 Other non-recurrent taxes	..	..	..	..	..	..	..	..	..	..
4600 Other recurrent taxes on property	11 540	18 849	31 613	39 083	46 392	74 593	83 218	100 071	107 709	116 476
Commercial licences	11 540	18 849	31 613	39 083	46 392	74 593	83 218	100 071	107 709	116 476
5000 Taxes on goods and services	**335 470**	**573 374**	**692 339**	**1 212 812**	**1 261 432**	**1 513 066**	**1 893 533**	**2 124 349**	**2 253 273**	**2 384 195**
5100 Taxes on production, sale, transfer, etc	331 758	530 329	641 713	1 143 757	1 191 097	1 472 515	1 845 207	2 067 189	2 193 455	2 318 577
5110 General taxes	80 303	69 013	137 585	526 710	557 166	766 154	1 042 213	1 183 878	1 269 055	1 351 246
5111 Value added taxes	80 303	69 013	137 585	526 710	557 166	766 154	1 042 213	1 183 878	1 269 055	1 351 246
5112 Sales tax	0	0	0	0	0	0	0	0	0	0
5113 Other	0	0	0	0	0	0	0	0	0	0
5120 Taxes on specific goods and services	138 623	461 316	504 128	617 047	633 931	706 360	802 993	883 311	924 401	967 331
5121 Excises	0	141 348	106 469	158 821	188 411	238 728	310 441	355 717	397 055	452 292
Gasoline products	..	108 783	69 400	85 824	111 404	96 518	90 136	100 903	117 377	133 266
Beer	..	18 249	22 317	28 459	30 635	31 025	32 715	34 572	35 641	41 882
Wine and liquor	..	11 971	10 741	12 279	11 071	10 775	10 769	10 486	15 751	22 689
Soft drinks	..	2 292	2 935	4 404	4 951	5 646	6 207	6 622	6 773	6 736
Various products	..	0	821	27 760	30 302	94 726	170 595	45 285	53 248	47 960
Automobiles	..	0	0	0	0	0	0	132 880	141 220	175 560
Other	..	53	255	95	48	38	19	24 969	27 045	24 200
5122 Profits of fiscal monopolies	0	0	0	0	0	0	0	0	0	0
5123 Customs and import duties	124 914	298 323	363 687	411 586	390 129	390 024	393 668	420 448	408 901	381 382
5124 Taxes on exports	12 621	158	0	283	104	104	0	0	0	0
5125 Taxes on investment goods	0	0	0	0	0	0	0	0	0	0
5126 Taxes on specific services	0	16 637	26 554	37 492	45 323	65 110	80 484	86 146	96 144	109 158
Insurance premiums	0	16 637	19 482	26 929	34 514	47 056	51 664	54 188	60 483	62 840
Cable and telecommunications	0	0	5 987	9 645	9 870	17 015	27 827	30 507	33 729	44 805
Gambling	0	0	1 085	918	939	1 039	993	1 451	1 932	1 512

Table 4.17. Panama / Panamá (*cont.*)
Details of tax revenue / Ingresos tributarios detallados

Million PAB

	1990	2000	2005	2008	2009	2010	2011	2012	2013	2014
5127 Other taxes on internat. trade and transactions	1 088	4 850	7 418	8 865	9 964	12 395	18 400	21 000	22 300	24 500
Banks, financial institutions, and currency exchange	0	2 005	7 418	8 865	9 964	12 395	18 400	21 000	22 300	24 500
Other	1 088	2 845	0	0	0	0	0	0	0	0
5128 Other taxes	0	0	0	0	0	0	0	0	0	0
5130 Unallocable between 5110 and 5120	112 832	0	0	0	0	0	0	0	0	0
5200 Taxes on use of goods and perform activities	3 712	43 045	50 626	69 055	70 335	40 551	48 327	57 160	59 817	65 618
5210 Recurrent taxes	0	38 758	43 177	53 373	55 807	40 551	48 327	57 160	59 817	65 618
5211 Paid by households: motor vehicles	0	7 042	8 423	10 863	11 332	0	0	0	0	0
5212 Paid by others: motor vehicles	0	4 682	4 387	4 924	5 173	0	0	0	0	0
5213 Paid in respect of other goods	0	27 033	30 367	37 586	39 302	40 551	48 327	57 160	59 817	65 618
On commercial activities	0	25 405	28 685	35 547	37 184	38 367	45 723	54 382	56 739	62 485
On industrial activities	0	1 628	1 682	2 039	2 118	2 184	2 604	2 778	3 078	3 132
5220 Non-recurrent taxes	3 712	4 287	7 449	15 682	14 528	0	0	0	0	0
Building and construction	..	..	..	..	..	..	..	..	..	..
Ship registration	..	..	..	..	..	..	..	..	..	..
5300 Unallocable between 5100 and 5200	0	0	0	0	0	0	0	0	0	0
6000 Other taxes	**25 674**	**119 336**	**126 722**	**167 222**	**194 790**	**274 217**	**253 424**	**361 851**	**272 778**	**292 031**
6100 Paid solely by business	0	11	0	27	0	0	0	0	0	0
Fiscal documents	..	..	..	..	..	..	..	..	..	..
Others	..	..	..	..	..	..	..	..	..	..
6200 Other	25 674	119 325	126 722	167 195	194 790	274 217	253 424	361 851	272 778	292 031
Legal services	16 691	42 330	27 684	37 912	36 278	41 064	47 000	44 900	46 200	41 450

Note: Year ending 31st December.

The data are on cash basis.

Heading 3000: In ECLAC data, Education insurance is classified as "Other taxes" (6000).

Heading 5127: In CIAT and ECLAC data, the tax on banks, financial institutions, and currency exchange is classified as a property tax.

Heading 6200: Includes for this publication revenue from fiscal documents.

Source: Contraloría General de la República, General Controller of the Republic of Panama.

StatLink http://dx.doi.org/10.1787/888933338242

Table 4.18. Paraguay / Paraguay
Details of tax revenue / Ingresos tributarios detallados

Million PYG

	1990	2000	2005	2008	2009	2010	2011	2012	2013	2014
Total tax revenue	**348 889**	**3 587 451**	**7 434 024**	**11 749 612**	**12 725 017**	**15 637 675**	**17 724 559**	**19 261 951**	**20 451 372**	**23 585 312**
1000 Taxes on income, profits and capital gains	**73 726**	**470 388**	**938 886**	**1 571 467**	**2 187 607**	**2 096 498**	**2 607 282**	**2 902 725**	**3 100 223**	**3 678 392**
1100 Of individuals	..	..	..	318	574	1 150	154	507	13 375	83 921
1110 On income and profits	..	..	..	318	574	1 150	154	507	13 375	83 921
1120 On capital gains	..	..	..	..	..	..	..	..	..	..
1200 Corporate	..	4 238	6 091	11 535	11 315	13 405	8 855	10 651	12 532	18 918
1210 On profits	..	4 238	6 091	11 535	11 315	13 405	8 855	10 651	12 532	18 918
Income tax on small businesses	..	0	0	9 128	8 838	9 380	5 129	5 764	7 831	9 063
Simplified tax on small businesses	..	4 238	5 802	1 181	644	715	544	317	32	72
Simplified tax on maquiladoras	..	0	289	1 226	1 833	3 310	3 182	4 570	4 669	9 783
1220 On capital gains	..	..	..	..	..	..	..	..	..	..
1300 Unallocable between 1100 and 1200	73 726	466 150	932 795	1 559 614	2 175 718	2 081 943	2 598 273	2 891 567	3 074 316	3 575 553
Income tax on agricultural activities	0	15 042	22 477	16 227	22 651	30 113	59 788	66 108	71 813	277 157
Tax on industrial, commercial, and service activities	0	451 108	910 318	1 543 387	2 153 067	2 051 830	2 538 485	2 825 459	3 002 503	3 298 396
Other	73 726	0	0	0	0	0	0	0	0	0
2000 Social security contributions	**28 882**	**919 533**	**1 591 980**	**2 784 731**	**3 118 645**	**3 552 640**	**3 976 795**	**4 844 111**	**5 158 072**	**5 630 392**
2100 Employees	..	..	..	..	..	..	..	..	..	..
2110 On a payroll basis	..	..	..	..	..	..	..	..	..	..
2120 On an income tax basis	..	..	..	..	..	..	..	..	..	..
2200 Employers	..	..	..	..	..	..	..	..	..	..
2210 On a payroll basis	..	..	..	..	..	..	..	..	..	..
2220 On an income tax basis	..	..	..	..	..	..	..	..	..	..
2300 Self-employed or non-employed	..	..	..	..	..	..	..	..	..	..
2310 On a payroll basis	..	..	..	..	..	..	..	..	..	..
2320 On an income tax basis	..	..	..	..	..	..	..	..	..	..
2400 Unallocable between 2100, 2200 and 2300	28 882	919 533	1 591 980	2 784 731	3 118 645	3 552 640	3 976 795	4 844 111	5 158 072	5 630 392
2410 On a payroll basis	28 882	919 533	1 591 980	2 784 731	3 118 645	3 552 640	3 976 795	4 844 111	5 158 072	5 630 392
2420 On an income tax basis	0	0	0	0	0	0	0	0	0	0
3000 Taxes on payroll and workforce	**0**	**0**	**0**	**0**	**0**	**0**	**0**	**0**	**0**	**0**
4000 Taxes on property	**17 162**	**0**	**0**	**255 333**	**253 821**	**272 385**	**289 456**	**310 237**	**310 000**	**310 000**
4100 Recurrent taxes on immovable property	17 162	..	..	239 680	240 217	254 306	266 371	289 493	..	..
4110 Households	17 162	..	..	239 680	240 217	254 306	266 371	289 493	..	..
Real estate tax	0	..	..	230 570	233 423	249 697	261 051	285 034	..	..
Tax on vacant lots	0	..	..	3 855	2 953	2 925	3 212	3 472	..	..
Other	17 162	..	..	5 256	3 841	1 684	2 109	987	..	..
4120 Others	0	..	..	0	0	0	0	0	..	..
4200 Recurrent taxes on net wealth	0	..	..	0	0	0	0	0	..	..
4210 Individual	..	..	..	..	..	..	..	..	..	..
4220 Corporate	..	..	..	..	..	..	..	..	..	..
4300 Estate, inheritance and gift taxes	0	..	..	0	0	0	0	0	..	..
4310 Estate and inheritance taxes	..	..	..	..	..	..	..	..	..	..
4320 Gift taxes	..	..	..	..	..	..	..	..	..	..
4400 Taxes on financial and capital transactions	0	..	..	15 170	13 391	16 316	22 406	20 061	..	..
Real estate transfer tax	..	..	..	11 275	9 675	11 766	16 362	14 704	..	..
Other	..	..	..	3 895	3 716	4 551	6 044	5 357	..	..
4500 Non-recurrent taxes	0	..	..	0	0	0	0	0	..	..
4510 On net wealth	..	..	..	..	..	..	..	..	..	..
4520 Other non-recurrent taxes	..	..	..	..	..	..	..	..	..	..
4600 Other recurrent taxes on property	0	..	..	482	213	1 762	679	682	..	..
5000 Taxes on goods and services	**179 312**	**2 080 878**	**4 309 832**	**7 039 349**	**7 068 556**	**9 460 962**	**10 749 735**	**11 081 105**	**11 759 523**	**13 818 267**
5100 Taxes on production, sale, transfer, etc	179 312	2 080 878	4 309 832	6 887 675	6 928 055	9 249 698	10 501 464	10 849 519	11 524 523	13 583 267
5110 General taxes	0	1 150 496	2 478 998	4 409 140	4 399 503	5 991 694	6 887 685	7 126 623	7 843 002	9 363 648
5111 Value added taxes	..	1 150 496	2 478 998	4 409 140	4 399 503	5 991 694	6 887 685	7 126 623	7 843 002	9 363 648
5112 Sales tax	..	0	0	0	0	0	0	0	0	0
5113 Other	..	0	0	0	0	0	0	0	0	0
5120 Taxes on specific goods and services	179 312	930 382	1 830 834	2 478 535	2 528 552	3 258 004	3 613 779	3 722 896	3 681 521	4 219 619
5121 Excises	41 087	456 561	949 962	1 411 846	1 532 365	1 710 531	1 892 587	2 063 020	2 048 143	2 442 895
Fuels	41 087	316 694	688 773	1 027 042	1 093 058	1 126 143	1 328 213	1 455 820	1 427 769	1 787 112
Other excises	0	136 194	249 239	347 467	399 940	537 887	564 374	607 200	620 374	655 783
Animal health and quality service	0	3 673	11 950	37 337	39 367	46 501	0	0	0	0
Livestock trade	0	0	0	0	0	0	0	0	0	0
5122 Profits of fiscal monopolies	0	0	0	0	0	0	0	0	0	0
5123 Customs and import duties	138 225	473 821	880 872	1 045 788	975 487	1 524 252	1 696 945	1 637 588	1 633 378	1 776 724
5124 Taxes on exports	0	0	0	0	0	0	0	0	0	0
5125 Taxes on investment goods	0	0	0	0	0	0	0	0	0	0

Table 4.18. Paraguay / Paraguay *(cont.)*
Details of tax revenue / Ingresos tributarios detallados

Million PYG

	1990	2000	2005	2008	2009	2010	2011	2012	2013	2014
5126 Taxes on specific services	0	0	0	20 900	20 700	23 221	24 247	22 288	..	..
Advertising	..	..	..	5 109	4 555	5 249	6 047	6 560	..	..
Public transport	..	..	..	4 508	4 245	4 363	4 649	4 121	..	..
Other	..	..	..	11 284	11 900	13 609	13 551	11 607	..	..
5127 Other taxes on internat. trade and transactions	0	0	0	0	0	0	0	0	0	0
5128 Other taxes	0	0	0	0	0	0	0	0	0	0
5130 Unallocable between 5110 and 5120	0	0	0	0	0	0	0	0	0	0
5200 Taxes on use of goods and perform activities	0	0	0	151 211	140 466	211 027	208 542	230 890	235 000	235 000
5210 Recurrent taxes	0	0	0	151 211	140 466	211 027	208 542	230 890	235 000	235 000
5211 Paid by households: motor vehicles	..	..	..	0	0	0	0	0	..	..
5212 Paid by others: motor vehicles	..	..	..	27 174	41 701	52 365	64 667	67 399	..	..
Motor vehicle licences	..	..	..	27 174	41 701	52 365	64 667	67 399	..	..
5213 Paid in respect of other goods	..	..	..	124 037	98 765	158 662	143 875	163 491	..	..
Tax on construction	..	..	..	20 362	24 476	31 696	38 891	50 337	..	..
Licencing fees	..	..	..	103 675	74 289	126 965	104 983	113 153	..	..
5220 Non-recurrent taxes	..	..	..	0	0	0	0	0	..	..
5300 Unallocable between 5100 and 5200	0	0	0	463	35	237	39 730	696	..	..
6000 Other taxes	**49 807**	**116 652**	**593 326**	**98 733**	**96 388**	**255 190**	**101 291**	**123 774**	**123 554**	**148 260**
6100 Paid solely by business	0	0	0	0	0	0	0	0	0	0
6200 Other	49 807	116 652	593 326	98 733	96 388	255 190	101 291	123 774	123 554	148 260
Registration and stamp duties	0	71 777	192 393	6 825	319	332	159	168	179	106
Luxury automobile tax	0	0	3 897	839	118	91	129	153	218	57
Other	49 807	44 875	397 036	91 069	95 951	254 767	101 003	123 453	123 157	148 098

Note: Year ending 31st December.

The data are on cash basis.

The figures for years up to and including 2004, as well as for 2014, exclude local government tax revenues as the data are not available. This affects data in categories 4000, 5000 and 6000.

Heading 2000: Data on social security contributions collected by decentralised institutions are not available for 2011 to 2014, with the exception of the contributions made to the Instituto de Previsión Social (Social Security Institute).

Heading 4000: The data are estimated for 2013 and 2014.

Heading 5000: The data are estimated for 2013 and 2014.

Heading 5121: Data for animal health and quality service are not available for 2011, 2012 and 2013.

Heading 5210: The data are estimated for 2013 and 2014.

Source: Ministry of Finance.

StatLink http://dx.doi.org/10.1787/888933338257

Table 4.19. Peru / Perú
Details of tax revenue / Ingresos tributarios detallados

Million PEN

	1990	2000	2005	2008	2009	2010	2011	2012	2013	2014
Total tax revenue	**645**	**25 890**	**40 739**	**67 640**	**61 648**	**74 685**	**86 723**	**95 655**	**100 335**	**107 970**
1000 Taxes on income, profits and capital gains	**37**	**5 130**	**12 260**	**25 907**	**22 068**	**27 589**	**35 979**	**40 159**	**39 626**	**44 043**
1100 Of individuals	3	2 117	3 327	5 584	5 861	6 518	8 208	9 462	10 570	11 423
First category	..	167	181	241	145	160	196	253	310	374
Second category	..	7	250	712	661	869	1 291	1 136	1 275	1 214
Fourth category	..	234	395	437	473	521	567	637	744	834
Fifth category	..	1 641	2 369	3 966	4 329	4 735	5 877	7 054	7 820	8 473
Tax debt payments	..	68	130	228	254	233	277	382	421	529
1110 On income and profits	..	0	0	0	0	0	0	0	0	0
1120 On capital gains	..	..	..	..	..	..	..	..	..	..
1200 Corporate	32	3 012	8 933	20 322	16 207	21 071	27 712	30 255	28 718	32 247
1210 On profits	32	3 012	8 933	20 322	16 207	21 071	27 712	30 255	28 718	32 247
Third category	..	2 023	5 316	14 921	10 691	14 652	19 321	20 744	19 633	18 536
Income tax on non-residents	..	487	542	1 204	1 391	1 511	1 735	2 244	2 848	6 027
Income tax special regime	..	47	55	79	89	118	153	202	246	275
Other incomes corporate	..	18	41	110	98	148	224	229	187	193
Tax debt payments	..	438	1 908	2 248	2 216	2 856	3 987	4 397	3 029	3 703
Temporary tax on net assets	..	0	1 073	1 761	1 722	1 788	2 293	2 439	2 776	3 513
1220 On capital gains	..	..	..	..	..	..	..	..	..	..
1300 Unallocable between 1100 and 1200	1	0	0	0	0	0	59	442	337	372
2000 Social security contributions	**50**	**3 184**	**4 023**	**6 768**	**7 244**	**7 957**	**8 979**	**10 185**	**11 303**	**11 893**
2100 Employees	..	541	667	1 765	1 978	2 385	2 657	2 879	3 143	3 139
2110 On a payroll basis	..	541	644	1 209	1 401	1 618	1 997	2 389	2 786	3 027
2120 On an income tax basis	..	0	23	557	577	768	661	491	357	112
Solidarity contribution for pension plan	..	0	23	557	577	768	661	491	357	112
2200 Employers	..	2 447	3 207	4 774	5 015	5 283	6 099	7 075	7 928	8 524
2210 On a payroll basis	..	2 447	3 207	4 774	5 015	5 283	6 099	7 075	7 928	8 524
2220 On an income tax basis	..	0	0	0	0	0	0	0	0	0
2300 Self-employed or non-employed	..	95	36	38	38	42	46	51	55	58
2310 On a payroll basis	..	95	36	38	38	42	46	51	55	58
2320 On an income tax basis	..	0	0	0	0	0	0	0	0	0
2400 Unallocable between 2100, 2200 and 2300	50	102	113	190	213	246	177	179	177	172
2410 On a payroll basis	50	102	113	190	213	246	177	179	177	172
2420 On an income tax basis	0	0	0	0	0	0	0	0	0	0
3000 Taxes on payroll and workforce	**0**	**1 038**	**27**	**7**	**6**	**3**	**1**	**2**	**1**	**3**
4000 Taxes on property	**99**	**0**	**1 340**	**2 174**	**2 042**	**2 236**	**1 876**	**1 897**	**2 130**	**2 159**
4100 Recurrent taxes on immovable property	0	0	460	615	676	731	856	958	1 126	1 234
4110 Households	..	..	..	..	..	..	..	..	..	..
4120 Others	..	..	..	..	..	..	..	..	..	..
4200 Recurrent taxes on net wealth	61	0	0	0	0	0	0	0	0	0
4210 Individual	60	0	0	..	..	..	..	..	..	..
4220 Corporate	1	0	0	..	..	..	..	..	..	..
Revaluation of fixed assets	1	..	..	..	..	..	..	..	..	..
4300 Estate, inheritance and gift taxes	0	0	0	0	0	0	0	0	0	0
4310 Estate and inheritance taxes	..	..	..	..	..	..	..	..	..	..
4320 Gift taxes	..	..	..	..	..	..	..	..	..	..
4400 Taxes on financial and capital transactions	38	0	803	1 559	1 366	1 505	1 020	939	1 004	925
Financial transactions tax	0	..	706	1 138	968	944	395	126	134	153
Real estate transfer tax	0	..	97	421	398	561	625	813	870	772
Tax Law Decree 519	38	..	0	0	0	0	0	0	0	0
4500 Non-recurrent taxes	0	0	0	0	0	0	0	0	0	0
4510 On net wealth	..	..	..	..	..	..	..	..	..	..
4520 Other non-recurrent taxes	..	..	..	..	..	..	..	..	..	..
4600 Other recurrent taxes on property	0	0	76	0	0	0	0	0	0	0
5000 Taxes on goods and services	**423**	**15 777**	**21 804**	**31 120**	**28 210**	**34 785**	**37 832**	**40 612**	**44 584**	**47 468**
5100 Taxes on production, sale, transfer, etc	423	15 777	21 804	31 120	28 210	34 785	37 832	40 612	44 584	47 468
5110 General taxes	78	9 519	14 779	25 109	22 918	28 691	31 556	33 897	37 142	40 320
5111 Value added taxes	78	9 472	14 732	25 109	22 918	28 691	31 556	33 897	37 142	40 320
5112 Sales tax	0	0	0	0	0	0	0	0	0	0
5113 Other	0	47	47	0	0	0	0	0	0	0
5120 Taxes on specific goods and services	345	6 258	7 025	6 011	5 291	6 094	6 276	6 715	7 442	7 148
5121 Excises	232	3 521	4 205	3 682	4 288	4 879	5 001	5 243	5 814	5 514
Fuels	151	2 120	2 607	1 457	2 255	2 410	2 231	2 149	2 502	2 041
Gasoline sales tax	3	97	140	222	143	210	282	325	335	380
Other	78	1 304	1 459	2 003	1 890	2 258	2 487	2 769	2 978	3 094
5122 Profits of fiscal monopolies	0	0	0	0	0	0	0	0	0	0
5123 Customs and import duties	64	2 737	2 646	1 945	613	787	815	976	1 043	1 020
5124 Taxes on exports	2	0	0	0	0	0	0	0	0	0

Table 4.19. Peru / Perú (cont.)
Details of tax revenue / Ingresos tributarios detallados

Million PEN

	1990	2000	2005	2008	2009	2010	2011	2012	2013	2014
5125 Taxes on investment goods	0	0	0	0	0	0	0	0	0	0
5126 Taxes on specific services	0	0	173	385	390	428	460	496	585	614
Casinos and slot machines	..	..	49	170	163	187	195	219	269	279
Tourism tax	..	..	74	93	104	105	116	115	118	127
Municipal taxes on services	..	..	50	122	123	136	149	162	198	208
5127 Other taxes on internat. trade and transactions	48	0	0	0	0	0	0	0	0	0
5128 Other taxes	0	0	0	0	0	0	0	0	0	0
5130 Unallocable between 5110 and 5120	0	0	0	0	0	0	0	0	0	0
5200 Taxes on use of goods and perform activities	0	0	0	0	0	0	0	0	0	0
5210 Recurrent taxes	..	..	..	..	..	..	..	..	..	..
5211 Paid by households: motor vehicles	..	..	..	..	..	..	..	..	..	..
5212 Paid by others: motor vehicles	..	..	..	..	..	..	..	..	..	..
5213 Paid in respect of other goods	..	..	..	..	..	..	..	..	..	..
5220 Non-recurrent taxes	..	..	..	..	..	..	..	..	..	..
5300 Unallocable between 5100 and 5200	0	0	0	0	0	0	0	0	0	0
6000 Other taxes	**36**	**761**	**1 286**	**1 664**	**2 078**	**2 115**	**2 055**	**2 800**	**2 691**	**2 404**
6100 Paid solely by business	0	84	73	91	98	108	118	133	147	158
Single simplified regime	..	84	73	91	98	108	118	133	147	158
University Development Fund	..	0	0	0	0	0	0	0	0	0
6200 Other	36	678	1 213	1 573	1 980	2 007	1 938	2 667	2 544	2 246
Tax debt payments	9	543	397	515	735	714	709	857	893	814
Penalties	0	114	159	268	287	330	453	937	1 001	831
Municipal fees	0	0	450	608	643	672	704	798	568	527
Other national level	28	20	171	146	234	238	0	0	0	0
Other local level	0	0	36	36	80	54	72	76	82	74

Note: Year ending 31st December.
The data are on cash basis.
The figures for years up to and including 2004 exclude local government tax revenues as the data are not available.
Heading 2120: The solidarity contribution for pension plan has been reclassified under heading 2120. In previous publications, this tax was classified under heading 1100 (Personal income tax).

Source: Banco Central de Reserva del Perú, Reserve Bank of Peru. Superintendencia Nacional de Aduanas y de Administración Tributaria, National Superintendency of Tax Administration.

StatLink http://dx.doi.org/10.1787/888933338269

Table 4.20. Trinidad and Tobago / Trinidad y Tobago
Details of tax revenue / Ingresos tributarios detallados

Million TTD

	1990	2000	2005	2008	2009	2010	2011	2012	2013	2014
Total tax revenue	**5 031**	**11 009**	**26 900**	**51 794**	**34 424**	**38 818**	**43 595**	**45 254**	**46 641**	**49 439**
1000 Taxes on income, profits and capital gains	**2 595**	**6 067**	**19 105**	**38 927**	**22 903**	**26 224**	**31 660**	**31 499**	**31 976**	**35 131**
1100 Of individuals	669	2 325	4 452	4 505	4 475	4 674	5 198	5 649	6 458	6 859
1110 On income and profits	571	2 169	4 250	4 291	4 267	4 467	4 961	5 435	6 207	6 620
Health surcharge	92	149	187	196	186	185	216	187	218	210
Insurance surrender tax	6	7	15	19	22	22	21	27	33	29
1120 On capital gains	0	0	0	0	0	0	0	0	0	0
1200 Corporate	1 856	3 547	14 118	33 534	17 250	20 670	25 265	24 767	24 633	27 330
1210 On profits	1 856	3 547	14 118	33 534	17 250	20 670	25 265	24 767	24 633	27 330
Oil companies	1 439	2 441	10 806	25 657	11 881	13 834	16 023	15 827	14 772	16 970
Other companies	383	1 041	3 166	7 644	5 170	6 630	9 034	8 647	9 675	10 151
Business levy	0	65	146	233	199	206	209	294	187	210
National recovery impost	34	0	0	0	0	0	0	0	0	0
1220 On capital gains	0	0	0	0	0	0	0	0	0	0
1300 Unallocable between 1100 and 1200	70	195	536	887	1 178	881	1 197	1 084	885	942
2000 Social security contributions	**183**	**702**	**1 173**	**2 042**	**2 549**	**2 645**	**2 723**	**2 822**	**2 900**	**3 000**
2100 Employees	..	..	..	..	..	..	..	..	..	..
2110 On a payroll basis	..	..	..	..	..	..	..	..	..	..
2120 On an income tax basis	..	..	..	..	..	..	..	..	..	..
2200 Employers	..	..	..	..	..	..	..	..	..	..
2210 On a payroll basis	..	..	..	..	..	..	..	..	..	..
2220 On an income tax basis	..	..	..	..	..	..	..	..	..	..
2300 Self-employed or non-employed	..	..	..	..	..	..	..	..	..	..
2310 On a payroll basis	..	..	..	..	..	..	..	..	..	..
2320 On an income tax basis	..	..	..	..	..	..	..	..	..	..
2400 Unallocable between 2100, 2200 and 2300	183	702	1 173	2 042	2 549	2 645	2 723	2 822	2 900	3 000
2410 On a payroll basis	..	..	..	..	..	..	..	..	..	..
2420 On an income tax basis	..	..	..	..	..	..	..	..	..	..
3000 Taxes on payroll and workforce	**0**	**0**	**0**	**0**	**0**	**0**	**0**	**0**	**0**	**0**
4000 Taxes on property	**148**	**277**	**389**	**567**	**525**	**435**	**471**	**473**	**636**	**743**
4100 Recurrent taxes on immovable property	147	277	389	566	523	433	470	472	635	742
Lands and building taxes	39	64	63	84	71	22	11	5	4	3
House rate tax	108	213	326	482	452	411	459	468	631	738
4110 Households	..	..	..	..	..	..	..	..	..	..
4120 Others	..	..	..	..	..	..	..	..	..	..
4200 Recurrent taxes on net wealth	0	0	0	0	0	0	0	0	0	0
4210 Individual	..	..	..	..	..	..	..	..	..	..
4220 Corporate	..	..	..	..	..	..	..	..	..	..
4300 Estate, inheritance and gift taxes	1	0	0	0	0	0	0	0	0	0
4310 Estate and inheritance taxes	1	..	..	..	..	..	..	..	..	..
4320 Gift taxes	0	..	..	..	..	..	..	..	..	..
4400 Taxes on financial and capital transactions	0	0	0	0	0	0	0	0	0	0
4500 Non-recurrent taxes	0	0	0	1	1	2	2	1	1	1
4510 On net wealth	..	..	..	..	..	..	..	..	..	..
4520 Other non-recurrent taxes	..	..	..	..	..	..	..	..	..	..
4600 Other recurrent taxes on property	0	0	0	0	0	0	0	0	0	0
5000 Taxes on goods and services	**2 055**	**3 852**	**5 988**	**9 908**	**8 258**	**9 342**	**8 556**	**10 245**	**10 883**	**10 280**
5100 Taxes on production, sale, transfer, etc	1 928	3 559	5 690	9 476	7 880	8 924	8 077	9 663	10 273	9 648
5110 General taxes	980	1 890	2 963	6 389	5 147	6 032	4 917	6 337	6 658	5 745
5111 Value added taxes	927	1 890	2 963	6 389	5 147	6 032	4 917	6 337	6 657	5 745
5112 Sales tax	54	0	0	0	0	0	0	0	0	0
5113 Other	0	0	0	0	0	0	0	0	0	0
5120 Taxes on specific goods and services	948	1 669	2 727	3 086	2 733	2 891	3 160	3 326	3 616	3 903
5121 Excises	481	801	1 072	651	629	708	708	729	707	714
Excise duties	473	801	1 071	650	627	705	705	725	704	676
Alcohol and tobacco taxes	9	0	1	1	2	2	3	3	3	38
5122 Profits of fiscal monopolies	0	0	0	0	0	0	0	0	0	0
5123 Customs and import duties	260	748	1 473	2 169	1 828	1 905	2 168	2 319	2 588	2 861
5124 Taxes on exports	0	0	0	0	0	0	0	0	0	0
5125 Taxes on investment goods	0	0	0	0	0	0	0	0	0	0
5126 Taxes on specific services	4	120	182	266	275	278	284	278	322	328
Insurance premium tax	0	56	98	141	146	167	172	174	194	197
Transaction tax on financial services	0	23	33	57	53	53	55	57	64	75
Hotel room tax	0	23	42	54	52	46	43	46	50	56
Betting and entertainment taxes	4	17	9	14	24	12	14	0	13	0
5127 Other taxes on internat. trade and transactions	202	0	0	0	0	1	0	0	0	0
5128 Other taxes	0	0	0	0	0	0	0	0	0	0
5130 Unallocable between 5110 and 5120	0	0	0	0	0	0	0	0	0	0

Table 4.20. Trinidad and Tobago / Trinidad y Tobago *(cont.)*
Details of tax revenue / Ingresos tributarios detallados

Million TTD

	1990	2000	2005	2008	2009	2010	2011	2012	2013	2014
5200 Taxes on use of goods and perform activities	127	293	299	433	378	418	479	582	610	632
5210 Recurrent taxes	127	293	299	433	378	418	479	582	610	632
Motor vehicle taxes and duties	76	239	217	370	327	375	429	524	552	569
5211 Paid by households: motor vehicles	0	0	0	0	0	0	0	0	0	0
5212 Paid by others: motor vehicles	0	0	0	0	0	0	0	0	0	0
5213 Paid in respect of other goods	51	53	82	63	50	43	50	57	58	63
Liquor and miscellaneous business license fees	5	10	10	10	10	10	11	10	11	11
Other taxes on the use of goods	45	44	72	53	40	33	39	47	47	52
5220 Non-recurrent taxes	0	0	0	0	0	0	0	0	0	0
5300 Unallocable between 5100 and 5200	0	0	0	0	0	0	0	0	0	0
6000 Other taxes	**49**	**111**	**245**	**350**	**190**	**172**	**185**	**214**	**246**	**285**
6100 Paid solely by business	0	0	0	0	0	0	0	0	0	0
6200 Other	49	111	245	350	190	172	185	214	246	285
Stamp duties	49	111	245	350	190	172	185	214	246	285

Note: Fiscal year ending on 30th September.
The data are on cash basis.
The figures exclude local government tax revenues as the data are not available.
Source: Ministry of Finance and BID-CIAT (2015) *Equivalent Fiscal Pressure for Latin America and the Caribbean.*

StatLink http://dx.doi.org/10.1787/888933338278

Table 4.21. Uruguay / Uruguay
Details of tax revenue / Ingresos tributarios detallados

Million UYU

	1990	2000	2005	2008	2009	2010	2011	2012	2013	2014
Total tax revenue	**2 352**	**59 656**	**101 306**	**166 284**	**184 547**	**210 191**	**244 433**	**278 304**	**320 895**	**360 417**
1000 Taxes on income, profits and capital gains	**114**	**5 620**	**11 969**	**34 366**	**38 457**	**44 573**	**50 957**	**58 291**	**71 365**	**76 786**
1100 Of individuals	0	0	44	14 823	16 431	19 654	24 429	30 071	34 611	41 851
1110 On income and profits	..	..	44	2 441	3 990	5 011	6 007	7 537	8 564	10 486
First category	..	..	0	1 781	1 921	2 358	2 946	3 764	4 278	4 967
Social security assistance	..	..	0	660	2 066	2 651	3 061	3 773	4 285	5 518
1120 On capital gains	..	..	..	12 381	12 441	14 643	18 422	22 534	26 048	31 365
Second category	..	..	..	12 381	12 441	14 643	18 422	22 534	26 048	31 365
1200 Corporate	114	5 620	11 925	18 518	20 240	23 257	23 940	26 166	34 075	31 698
1210 On profits	114	5 620	11 925	18 518	20 240	23 257	23 940	26 166	34 075	31 698
Corporate income tax (IRAE)	0	0	0	11 724	16 512	21 280	21 719	23 937	31 812	29 152
Corporate income tax (IRIC)	97	5 096	10 516	5 313	2 355	491	469	414	387	396
Small firms (minimum VAT)	0	296	457	573	596	586	600	631	686	741
Other	17	228	952	907	777	900	1 151	1 185	1 190	1 408
1220 On capital gains	..	..	..	..	..	..	..	..	..	..
1300 Unallocable between 1100 and 1200	0	0	0	1 025	1 785	1 662	2 588	2 053	2 679	3 237
Non resident taxpayers	..	..	..	1 025	1 785	1 662	2 588	2 053	2 679	3 237
2000 Social security contributions	**717**	**17 679**	**21 425**	**34 778**	**42 922**	**49 742**	**59 930**	**72 601**	**86 012**	**100 993**
2100 Employees	..	..	..	..	..	..	..	..	..	..
2110 On a payroll basis	..	..	..	..	..	..	..	..	..	..
2120 On an income tax basis	..	..	..	..	..	..	..	..	..	..
2200 Employers	..	..	..	..	..	..	..	..	..	..
2210 On a payroll basis	..	..	..	..	..	..	..	..	..	..
2220 On an income tax basis	..	..	..	..	..	..	..	..	..	..
2300 Self-employed or non-employed	..	..	..	..	..	..	..	..	..	..
2310 On a payroll basis	..	..	..	..	..	..	..	..	..	..
2320 On an income tax basis	..	..	..	..	..	..	..	..	..	..
2400 Unallocable between 2100, 2200 and 2300	717	17 679	21 425	34 778	42 922	49 742	59 930	72 601	86 012	100 993
2410 On a payroll basis	717	17 679	21 425	34 778	42 922	49 742	59 930	72 601	86 012	100 993
2420 On an income tax basis	0	0	0	0	0	0	0	0	0	0
3000 Taxes on payroll and workforce	**0**	**0**	**0**	**0**	**0**	**0**	**0**	**0**	**0**	**0**
4000 Taxes on property	**197**	**6 077**	**12 039**	**15 213**	**16 581**	**16 935**	**18 960**	**20 569**	**22 195**	**24 307**
4100 Recurrent taxes on immovable property	72	2 521	4 639	6 780	6 622	6 308	6 941	7 622	8 307	8 948
4110 Households	..	..	..	..	..	..	..	..	..	..
4120 Others	..	..	..	..	..	..	..	..	..	..
4200 Recurrent taxes on net wealth	94	2 076	4 943	6 939	8 634	8 948	10 030	11 067	11 892	13 714
4210 Individual	64	108	336	325	371	382	422	445	491	629
4220 Corporate	30	1 968	4 607	6 614	8 263	8 567	9 607	10 622	11 401	13 085
Corporate wealth	28	1 661	4 383	6 380	8 056	8 354	9 413	10 609	11 390	13 079
Other	1	307	224	234	207	213	194	13	11	6
4300 Estate, inheritance and gift taxes	0	0	0	0	0	0	0	0	0	0
4310 Estate and inheritance taxes	..	..	..	..	..	..	..	..	..	..
4320 Gift taxes	..	..	..	..	..	..	..	..	..	..
4400 Taxes on financial and capital transactions	0	372	933	1 206	1 027	1 350	1 545	1 414	1 516	1 442
Capital transfers	..	372	886	1 202	1 027	1 347	1 545	1 413	1 516	1 442
Capital transfers (additional)	..	0	0	0	0	0	0	0	0	0
4500 Non-recurrent taxes	0	0	0	0	0	0	0	0	0	0
4510 On net wealth	..	..	..	..	..	..	..	..	..	..
4520 Other non-recurrent taxes	..	..	..	..	..	..	..	..	..	..
4600 Other recurrent taxes on property	31	1 107	1 524	288	299	328	445	466	480	203
5000 Taxes on goods and services	**1 334**	**30 877**	**55 798**	**81 919**	**86 505**	**98 942**	**114 586**	**126 844**	**141 108**	**157 790**
5100 Taxes on production, sale, transfer, etc	1 270	28 301	52 727	77 784	82 657	94 990	110 473	122 310	135 349	151 001
5110 General taxes	660	18 009	34 641	58 277	61 469	69 365	79 672	88 338	98 071	108 260
5111 Value added taxes	660	17 995	34 601	58 277	61 469	69 365	79 672	88 338	98 071	108 260
5112 Sales tax	1	14	40	0	0	0	0	0	0	0
5113 Other	0	0	0	0	0	0	0	0	0	0
5120 Taxes on specific goods and services	610	10 291	18 086	19 507	21 188	25 625	30 801	33 972	37 278	42 741
5121 Excises	393	7 673	10 524	11 560	13 312	16 401	19 401	21 417	23 365	26 362
Fuels	203	4 067	4 900	4 437	5 462	6 551	8 447	9 147	10 269	11 816
Tobacco products	80	1 741	2 705	2 948	3 248	4 236	4 925	4 768	4 755	4 913
Alcoholic beverages	24	229	375	533	657	602	622	800	840	918
Beer	8	205	308	402	480	602	895	895	1 024	1 035
Non-alcoholic beverages	19	464	532	990	1 240	1 172	1 451	1 518	1 718	1 926
Motor vehicles	20	656	977	1 616	1 662	2 289	2 710	3 025	3 388	3 924
Sales of agricultural goods (MEVIR and INIA)	4	76	260	417	414	451	538	648	681	736
Other	35	235	468	217	148	497	-188	616	689	1 094
5122 Profits of fiscal monopolies	0	0	0	0	0	0	0	0	0	0
5123 Customs and import duties	214	1 967	5 195	7 103	7 042	8 478	10 543	11 670	13 020	15 167

Table 4.21. Uruguay / Uruguay (cont.)
Details of tax revenue / Ingresos tributarios detallados

Million UYU

	1990	2000	2005	2008	2009	2010	2011	2012	2013	2014
5124 Taxes on exports	1	92	287	371	349	371	446	432	422	520
5125 Taxes on investment goods	0	0	0	0	0	0	0	0	0	0
5126 Taxes on specific services	3	293	1 590	472	484	376	411	454	470	691
5127 Other taxes on internat. trade and transactions	0	265	489	0	0	0	0	0	0	0
5128 Other taxes	0	0	0	0	0	0	0	0	0	0
5130 Unallocable between 5110 and 5120	0	0	0	0	0	0	0	0	0	0
5200 Taxes on use of goods and perform activities	64	2 576	3 071	4 135	3 848	3 952	4 113	4 534	5 759	6 789
5210 Recurrent taxes	64	2 576	3 071	4 135	3 848	3 952	4 113	4 534	5 759	6 789
5211 Paid by households: motor vehicles	0	0	0	0	0	0	0	0	0	0
5212 Paid by others: motor vehicles	64	2 576	3 071	4 135	3 848	3 952	4 113	4 534	5 759	6 789
5213 Paid in respect of other goods	0	0	0	0	0	0	0	0	0	0
5220 Non-recurrent taxes	0	0	0	0	0	0	0	0	0	0
5300 Unallocable between 5100 and 5200	0	0	0	0	0	0	0	0	0	0
6000 Other taxes	**-10**	**-596**	**76**	**8**	**82**	**0**	**0**	**0**	**214**	**541**
6100 Paid solely by business	-10	-596	76	8	82	0	0	0	214	541
6200 Other	0	0	0	0	0	0	0	0	0	0

Note: Year ending 31st December.

The data are on cash basis.

Heading 2000: Figures for 1990-1998 are reconstructed estimates, as the current methodology used to calculate social security contributions was not employed until 1999.

Headings 4000 and 5000: In ECLAC data, the tax on sales in public auctions is classified in category 4000.

Heading 5112: In ECLAC data, the tax on the sale of goods by public auctions is classified in category 4000.

Source: Dirección General Impositiva, Ministry of Economy and Finance. Banco de Previsión Social, Social Welfare Bank. Insituto Nacional de Estadística, National Institute of Statistics.

StatLink http://dx.doi.org/10.1787/888933338286

Table 4.22. Venezuela / Venezuela
Details of tax revenue / Ingresos tributarios detallados

Million VEF

	1990	2000	2005	2008	2009	2010	2011	2012	2013	2014
Total tax revenue	**412**	**10 849**	**48 285**	**95 791**	**101 014**	**120 455**	**183 748**	**232 106**	**325 472**	**574 426**
1000 Taxes on income, profits and capital gains	**344**	**4 686**	**18 529**	**39 632**	**38 966**	**36 836**	**53 280**	**70 739**	**93 694**	**187 884**
1100 Of individuals	..	..	..	..	..	..	..	..	..	..
1110 On income and profits	..	..	..	..	..	..	..	..	..	..
1120 On capital gains	..	..	..	..	..	..	..	..	..	..
1200 Corporate	315	3 368	11 184	17 834	12 944	8 700	16 510	22 879	25 270	67 601
1210 On profits	315	3 368	11 184	17 834	12 944	8 700	16 510	22 879	25 270	67 601
Oil	315	3 368	11 184	17 834	12 944	8 700	16 510	22 879	25 270	67 601
1220 On capital gains	..	..	..	..	..	..	..	..	..	..
1300 Unallocable between 1100 and 1200	30	1 317	7 345	21 798	26 022	28 137	36 770	47 859	68 424	120 283
2000 Social security contributions	**20**	**591**	**1 890**	**5 085**	**6 740**	**9 690**	**12 936**	**15 585**	**21 422**	**28 600**
2100 Employees	..	..	..	..	..	..	..	..	..	..
2110 On a payroll basis	..	..	..	..	..	..	..	..	..	..
2120 On an income tax basis	..	..	..	..	..	..	..	..	..	..
2200 Employers	..	..	..	..	..	..	..	..	..	..
2210 On a payroll basis	..	..	..	..	..	..	..	..	..	..
2220 On an income tax basis	..	..	..	..	..	..	..	..	..	..
2300 Self-employed or non-employed	..	..	..	..	..	..	..	..	..	..
2310 On a payroll basis	..	..	..	..	..	..	..	..	..	..
2320 On an income tax basis	..	..	..	..	..	..	..	..	..	..
2400 Unallocable between 2100, 2200 and 2300	20	591	1 890	5 085	6 740	9 690	12 936	15 585	21 422	28 600
2410 On a payroll basis	..	..	..	..	..	..	..	..	..	..
2420 On an income tax basis	..	..	..	..	..	..	..	..	..	..
3000 Taxes on payroll and workforce	**0**	**0**	**0**	**0**	**0**	**0**	**0**	**0**	**0**	**0**
4000 Taxes on property	**1**	**400**	**2 834**	**6 250**	**175**	**222**	**273**	**346**	**530**	**1 044**
4100 Recurrent taxes on immovable property	0	0	0	0	0	0	0	0	0	0
4110 Households	..	..	..	..	..	..	..	..	..	..
4120 Others	..	..	..	..	..	..	..	..	..	..
4200 Recurrent taxes on net wealth	0	0	0	0	0	0	0	0	0	0
4210 Individual	..	..	..	..	..	..	..	..	..	..
4220 Corporate	..	..	..	..	..	..	..	..	..	..
4300 Estate, inheritance and gift taxes	1	19	55	119	175	222	273	346	530	1 044
4310 Estate and inheritance taxes	..	..	..	..	..	..	..	..	..	..
4320 Gift taxes	..	..	..	..	..	..	..	..	..	..
4400 Taxes on financial and capital transactions	0	381	2 779	6 132	0	0	0	0	0	0
Bank debits	0	292	2 743	6 132	..	..	..	..	..	..
Registration of immovable property rights	0	89	36	0	..	..	..	..	..	..
4500 Non-recurrent taxes	0	0	0	0	..	..	..	..	..	..
4510 On net wealth	..	..	..	..	..	..	..	..	..	..
4520 Other non-recurrent taxes	..	..	..	..	..	..	..	..	..	..
4600 Other recurrent taxes on property	0	0	0	0	0	0	0	0	0	0
5000 Taxes on goods and services	**46**	**5 173**	**25 032**	**44 824**	**55 134**	**73 707**	**108 268**	**141 505**	**205 423**	**348 872**
5100 Taxes on production, sale, transfer, etc	46	5 173	25 032	44 824	55 134	73 707	108 268	141 505	205 423	348 872
5110 General taxes	0	3 272	19 513	31 396	41 611	56 101	84 348	111 102	164 737	272 187
5111 Value added taxes	..	3 272	19 513	31 396	41 611	56 101	84 348	111 102	164 737	272 187
5112 Sales tax	..	0	0	0	0	0	0	0	0	0
5113 Other	..	0	0	0	0	0	0	0	0	0
5120 Taxes on specific goods and services	46	1 901	5 519	13 428	13 523	17 606	23 920	30 403	40 686	76 685
5121 Excises	16	774	1 604	5 744	6 727	8 872	8 774	11 247	16 371	30 525
Oil	6	468	472	1 174	756	1 280	0	0	0	0
Alcoholic beverages	6	85	427	1 323	1 765	2 192	2 762	3 542	5 975	10 888
Tobacco	4	220	704	3 246	4 205	5 401	6 011	7 706	10 397	19 636
Matches	0	1	1	1	2	0	0	0	0	0
5122 Profits of fiscal monopolies	0	0	0	0	0	0	0	0	0	0
5123 Customs and import duties	30	972	3 652	7 267	6 409	8 504	15 017	19 052	24 185	45 998
5124 Taxes on exports	0	0	0	0	0	0	0	0	0	0
5125 Taxes on investment goods	0	0	0	0	0	0	0	0	0	0
5126 Taxes on specific services	0	155	263	417	386	230	129	104	130	162
Telecommunications	0	151	237	247	183	0	0	0	0	0
Casinos, bingo and slot machines	0	5	26	171	203	230	129	104	130	162
5127 Other taxes on internat. trade and transactions	0	0	0	0	0	0	0	0	0	0
5128 Other taxes	0	0	0	0	0	0	0	0	0	0
5130 Unallocable between 5110 and 5120	0	0	0	0	0	0	0	0	0	0
5200 Taxes on use of goods and perform activities	0	0	0	0	0	0	0	0	0	0
5210 Recurrent taxes	..	..	..	..	..	..	..	..	..	..
5211 Paid by households: motor vehicles	..	..	..	..	..	..	..	..	..	..
5212 Paid by others: motor vehicles	..	..	..	..	..	..	..	..	..	..
5213 Paid in respect of other goods	..	..	..	..	..	..	..	..	..	..

Table 4.22. Venezuela / Venezuela *(cont.)*

Details of tax revenue / Ingresos tributarios detallados

Million VEF

	1990	2000	2005	2008	2009	2010	2011	2012	2013	2014
5220 Non-recurrent taxes	..	..	..	..	..	..	..	..	..	..
5300 Unallocable between 5100 and 5200	0	0	0	0	0	0	0	0	0	0
6000 Other taxes	**0**	**0**	**0**	**0**	**0**	**0**	**8 991**	**3 931**	**4 403**	**8 026**
6100 Paid solely by business	..	..	..	..	..	..	0	0	0	0
6200 Other	..	..	..	..	..	..	8 991	3 931	4 403	8 026

Note: Year ending 31st December.

The data are on cash basis.

The figures exclude state and local government tax revenues as the data are not available.

Heading 2000: The data on social security contributions are estimated for 2011 to 2014.

Heading 5121: Data oil excises are not available from 2011.

Source: Servicio Nacional Integrado de Administración Aduanera y Tributaria, Ministry of Finance.

StatLink http://dx.doi.org/10.1787/888933338298

CHAPTER 5

TAX REVENUES BY SUB-SECTORS OF GENERAL GOVERNMENT

Revenues of both the Latin American and the OECD countries have been attributed to the different levels of government according to the revised guidelines set out in to the final version of the 2008 System of National Accounts (SNA). Under this, revenues are generally attributed to the level of government that exercises the authority to impose the tax or has the final discretion to set and vary the tax rate.

CAPÍTULO 5

INGRESOS TRIBUTARIOS POR SUB-SECTORES DE GOBIERNO GENERAL

Los ingresos de los países latinoamericanos y de los países de la OCDE se han atribuido a los diferentes niveles de gobierno de acuerdo con lo recogido en la versión final 2008 del Sistema de Cuentas Nacionales (SCN), según el cual, los ingresos se atribuyen por lo general al nivel de gobierno que ejerce la facultad de aplicar el impuesto o que puede a su discreción establecer y modificar la tasa del impuesto.

Table 5.1. Attribution of tax revenues to sub-sectors of general government as percentage of total tax revenue[1]

Cuadro 5.1. Atribución de los ingresos tributarios en los sub-sectores del gobierno general como porcentaje del ingreso tributario total[1]

	Central government			State or regional government			Local government			Social security funds			
	1995	2000	2013	1995	2000	2013	1995	2000	2013	1995	2000	2013	
Federal countries													**Países federales**
Argentina	59.0	66.4	60.6	17.5	17.8	16.8				23.4	15.8	22.6	Argentina
Brazil	44.7	47.8	42.6	26.8	25.3	25.8	3.7	3.4	5.9	24.8	23.5	25.6	Brasil
Mexico	80.1	80.7	80.1	2.1	2.0	3.1	1.1	0.8	1.2	16.6	16.5	15.5	México
Venezuela	94.6	94.6	93.4							5.4	5.4	6.6	Venezuela
OECD[2,3]	53.2	56.5	54.2	15.9	15.3	16.5	7.7	6.9	7.5	22.9	21.1	21.3	OCDE[2,3]
Regional countries													**Países regionales**
Colombia[4]	63.2	68.6	73.3	5.5	5.6	4.2	8.6	9.4	10.8	22.7	16.4	11.7	Colombia[4]
OECD[5]	50.4	49.0	22.3	4.8	7.6	13.7	8.5	9.1	9.9	35.8	33.8	34.0	OCDE[5]
Unitary countries													**Países unitarios**
Bahamas	89.1	88.1	84.1							10.9	11.9	15.9	Bahamas
Barbados	85.3	84.3	80.1							14.7	15.7	19.9	Barbados
Bolivia	100.0	92.2	95.1							0.0	7.8	4.9	Bolivia
Chile	89.9	87.8	87.0				6.5	7.9	7.3	3.6	4.4	5.7	Chile
Costa Rica	66.2	65.3	58.8					2.1	3.0	33.8	32.6	38.1	Costa Rica
Dominican Republic	99.3	99.0	99.6							0.7	1.0	0.4	República Dominicana
Ecuador	73.9	87.7	75.0							26.1	12.3	25.0	Ecuador
El Salvador	86.3	84.8	89.7							14.1	16.6	10.3	El Salvador
Guatemala	83.8	83.6	82.9				0.6	0.9	1.4	15.6	15.5	15.7	Guatemala
Honduras	90.1	89.4	81.9							9.9	10.6	18.1	Honduras
Jamaica	100.0	99.3	94.3				0.0	0.7	1.6	0.0	0.0	4.1	Jamaica
Nicaragua	84.1	80.1	76.1							15.9	19.9	23.9	Nicaragua
Panama	62.0	61.1	64.3				0.0	2.1	1.5	38.0	36.8	34.2	Panamá
Paraguay	100.0	82.7	80.0				0.0	0.0	2.7	0.0	17.3	17.4	Paraguay[6]
Peru	88.2	87.7	85.7				0.0	0.0	3.1	11.8	12.3	11.3	Perú
Trinidad and Tobago	94.5	91.7	92.4				2.4	1.9	1.4	3.1	6.4	6.2	Trinidad y Tobago
Uruguay	62.0	62.5	69.3				7.8	7.9	3.9	30.1	29.6	26.8	Uruguay
OECD[2,6]	65.8	66.4	63.2				10.8	11.0	12.0	23.1	22.3	24.6	OCDE[2,6]

1. The figures exclude local government revenues for Argentina (but include provincial revenues), Bahamas, Barbados, Bolivia, Costa Rica (up to 1997), Dominican Republic, Ecuador, El Salvador, Honduras, Jamaica, Nicaragua, Panama (up to 1998), Paraguay, Peru (up to 2004) and Venezuela as the data are not available.
1. Las cifras excluyen los ingresos de gobiernos locales en Argentina (pero incluye ingresos de las provincias), Bahamas, Barbados, Bolivia, Costa Rica (hasta 1997), República Dominicana, Ecuador, El Salvador, Honduras, Jamaica, Nicaragua, Panamá (hasta 1998), Paraguay, Perú (hasta 2004) y Venezuela dado que los datos no están disponibles.
2. Chile and Mexico are also part of the OECD group.
2. Chile y México son también parte del grupo OCDE.
3. Represents the unweighted average for OECD federal member countries.
3. Representa el promedio no ponderado para los países federales miembros de la OCDE.
4. Colombia is constitutionally a unitary country with high autonomy of its territorial entities.
4. Colombia es constitucionalmente un país unitario con una estructura política descentralizada.
5. Represents Spain, which is constitutionally a non-federal country with a highly decentralised political structure.
5. Representa a España, que es constitucionalmente un país no federal con una estructura política altamente descentralizada.
6. Represents the unweighted average for OECD unitary countries.
6. Representa el promedio no ponderado para los países unitarios miembros de la OCDE.

StatLink http://dx.doi.org/10.1787/888933338308

Table 5.2. Argentina, tax revenues by sub-sectors of government

Million ARS

	Federal government					State/Regional				
	1990	2000	2005	2010	2014	1990	2000	2005	2010	2014
1000 Taxes on income, profits and capital gains	**382**	**11 304**	**29 202**	**78 427**	**269 808**	**0**	**0**	**0**	**0**	**0**
1100 Of individuals	12	3 937	8 192	23 980	125 502	..	..	..	..	..
1200 Corporate	..	6 575	19 601	50 664	132 178	..	..	..	..	..
1300 Unallocable between 1100 and 1200	371	792	1 409	3 783	12 128	..	..	..	..	..
2000 Social security contributions	**0**	**0**	**0**	**0**	**0**	**0**	**0**	**0**	**0**	**0**
2100 Employees	..	..	..	..	..	..	..	..	..	..
2200 Employers	..	..	..	..	..	..	..	..	..	..
2300 Self-employed or non-employed	..	..	..	..	..	..	..	..	..	..
2400 Unallocable between 2100, 2200 and 2300	..	..	..	..	..	..	..	..	..	..
3000 Taxes on payroll and workforce	**0**	**0**	**0**	**0**	**0**	**0**	**0**	**0**	**0**	**0**
4000 Taxes on property	**730**	**1 254**	**11 439**	**32 675**	**92 228**	**572**	**2 642**	**4 558**	**10 864**	**36 838**
4100 Recurrent taxes on immovable property	0	0	0	0	0	412	1 809	2 836	5 035	17 547
4200 Recurrent taxes on net wealth	235	1 084	1 868	5 248	14 576	0	0	0	0	0
4300 Estate, inheritance and gift taxes	0	0	0	0	0	0	0	0	0	0
4400 Taxes on financial and capital transactions	496	100	9 550	27 424	77 652	160	833	1 722	5 829	19 291
4500 Non-recurrent taxes	0	70	21	3	0	0	0	0	0	0
4600 Other recurrent taxes on property	0	0	0	0	0	0	0	0	0	0
5000 Taxes on goods and services	**4 713**	**27 592**	**62 058**	**198 346**	**508 781**	**979**	**6 918**	**15 902**	**54 746**	**195 897**
5100 Taxes on production, sale, transfer, etc	4 713	27 592	62 058	198 346	508 781	846	6 114	14 613	51 148	183 887
5110 General taxes	1 591	18 427	34 968	113 330	319 988	846	6 114	14 613	51 148	183 887
5120 Taxes on specific goods and services	3 122	9 165	27 090	85 016	188 793	0	0	0	0	0
5130 Unallocable between 5110 and 5120	0	0	0	0	0	0	0	0	0	0
5200 Taxes on use of goods and perform activities[1]	0	0	0	0	0	133	804	1 289	3 598	12 010
5300 Unallocable between 5100 and 5200	0	0	0	0	0	0	0	0	0	0
6000 Other taxes	**215**	**396**	**877**	**2 386**	**5 599**	**43**	**1 309**	**1 469**	**3 110**	**7 716**
6100 Paid solely by business	0	354	757	2 093	4 259	0	0	0	0	0
6200 Other	215	42	120	293	1 340	43	1 309	1 469	3 110	7 716
Total tax revenue	**6 041**	**40 546**	**103 576**	**311 834**	**876 416**	**1 594**	**10 869**	**21 929**	**68 720**	**240 451**

Million ARS

	Local government[2]					Social Security Funds				
	1990	2000	2005	2010	2014	1990	2000	2005	2010	2014
1000 Taxes on income, profits and capital gains	..	..	..	..	..	**0**	**0**	**0**	**0**	**0**
1100 Of individuals	..	..	..	..	..	..	..	..	..	..
1200 Corporate	..	..	..	..	..	..	..	..	..	..
1300 Unallocable between 1100 and 1200	..	..	..	..	..	..	..	..	..	..
2000 Social security contributions	..	..	..	..	..	**2 583**	**9 670**	**17 400**	**102 460**	**307 657**
2100 Employees	..	..	..	..	..	..	2 486	3 690	37 990	121 942
2200 Employers	..	..	..	..	..	..	6 069	12 557	54 713	174 299
2300 Self-employed or non-employed	..	..	..	..	..	98	1 115	1 153	9 757	11 416
2400 Unallocable between 2100, 2200 and 2300	..	..	..	..	..	2 485	0	0	0	0
3000 Taxes on payroll and workforce	..	..	..	..	..	**0**	**0**	**0**	**0**	**0**
4000 Taxes on property	..	..	..	..	..	**0**	**0**	**0**	**0**	**0**
4100 Recurrent taxes on immovable property	..	..	..	..	..	..	..	..	..	..
4200 Recurrent taxes on net wealth	..	..	..	..	..	..	..	..	..	..
4300 Estate, inheritance and gift taxes	..	..	..	..	..	..	..	..	..	..
4400 Taxes on financial and capital transactions	..	..	..	..	..	..	..	..	..	..
4500 Non-recurrent taxes	..	..	..	..	..	..	..	..	..	..
4600 Other recurrent taxes on property	..	..	..	..	..	..	..	..	..	..
5000 Taxes on goods and services	..	..	..	..	..	**0**	**0**	**0**	**0**	**0**
5100 Taxes on production, sale, transfer, etc	..	..	..	..	..	..	..	..	..	..
5110 General taxes	..	..	..	..	..	..	..	..	..	..
5120 Taxes on specific goods and services	..	..	..	..	..	..	..	..	..	..
5130 Unallocable between 5110 and 5120	..	..	..	..	..	..	..	..	..	..
5200 Taxes on use of goods and perform activities[1]	..	..	..	..	..	..	..	..	..	..
5300 Unallocable between 5100 and 5200	..	..	..	..	..	..	..	..	..	..
6000 Other taxes	..	..	..	..	..	**0**	**0**	**0**	**0**	**0**
6100 Paid solely by business	..	..	..	..	..	..	..	..	..	..
6200 Other	..	..	..	..	..	..	..	..	..	..
Total tax revenue	..	..	..	..	..	**2 583**	**9 670**	**17 400**	**102 460**	**307 657**

1. In ECLAC data, property tax on motor vehicles is classified in category 4000.
2. The figures exclude local government tax revenues as the data are not available.

StatLink http://dx.doi.org/10.1787/888933338316

Table 5.3. Bahamas, tax revenues by sub-sectors of government

Million BSD

	Federal government					State/Regional				
	1990	2000	2005	2010	2014	1990	2000	2005	2010	2014
1000 Taxes on income, profits and capital gains	**0**	**0**	**0**	**0**	**0**	..	..	..	..	..
1100 Of individuals	..	..	..	..	..	..	..	..	..	..
1200 Corporate	..	..	..	..	..	..	..	..	..	..
1300 Unallocable between 1100 and 1200	..	..	..	..	..	..	..	..	..	..
2000 Social security contributions	**0**	**0**	**0**	**0**	**0**	..	..	..	..	..
2100 Employees	..	..	..	..	..	..	..	..	..	..
2200 Employers	..	..	..	..	..	..	..	..	..	..
2300 Self-employed or non-employed	..	..	..	..	..	..	..	..	..	..
2400 Unallocable between 2100, 2200 and 2300	..	..	..	..	..	..	..	..	..	..
3000 Taxes on payroll and workforce	**0**	**0**	**0**	**0**	**0**	..	..	..	..	..
4000 Taxes on property	**19**	**32**	**54**	**92**	**104**	..	..	..	..	..
4100 Recurrent taxes on immovable property	19	32	54	92	104	..	..	..	..	..
4200 Recurrent taxes on net wealth	0	0	0	0	0	..	..	..	..	..
4300 Estate, inheritance and gift taxes	0	0	0	0	0	..	..	..	..	..
4400 Taxes on financial and capital transactions	0	0	0	0	0	..	..	..	..	..
4500 Non-recurrent taxes	0	0	0	0	0	..	..	..	..	..
4600 Other recurrent taxes on property	0	0	0	0	0	..	..	..	..	..
5000 Taxes on goods and services	**386**	**723**	**736**	**795**	**986**	..	..	..	..	..
5100 Taxes on production, sale, transfer, etc	354	654	657	672	772	..	..	..	..	..
5110 General taxes	0	0	0	0	0	..	..	..	..	..
5120 Taxes on specific goods and services	354	654	657	672	772	..	..	..	..	..
5130 Unallocable between 5110 and 5120	0	0	0	0	0	..	..	..	..	..
5200 Taxes on use of goods and perform activities	32	69	78	123	214	..	..	..	..	..
5300 Unallocable between 5100 and 5200	0	0	0	0	0	..	..	..	..	..
6000 Other taxes	**33**	**95**	**135**	**223**	**155**	..	..	..	..	..
6100 Paid solely by business	0	0	0	0	0	..	..	..	..	..
6200 Other	33	95	135	223	155	..	..	..	..	..
Total tax revenue	**438**	**849**	**924**	**1 109**	**1 246**	..	..	..	..	..

Million BSD

	Local government[1]					Social Security Funds				
	1990	2000	2005	2010	2014	1990	2000	2005	2010	2014
1000 Taxes on income, profits and capital gains	..	..	..	..	..	**0**	**0**	**0**	**0**	**0**
1100 Of individuals	..	..	..	..	..	..	..	..	..	..
1200 Corporate	..	..	..	..	..	..	..	..	..	..
1300 Unallocable between 1100 and 1200	..	..	..	..	..	..	..	..	..	..
2000 Social security contributions	..	..	..	..	..	**66**	**115**	**136**	**167**	**246**
2100 Employees	..	..	..	..	..	..	..	..	..	..
2200 Employers	..	..	..	..	..	..	..	..	..	..
2300 Self-employed or non-employed	..	..	..	..	..	..	..	..	..	..
2400 Unallocable between 2100, 2200 and 2300	..	..	..	..	..	66	115	136	167	246
3000 Taxes on payroll and workforce	..	..	..	..	..	**0**	**0**	**0**	**0**	**0**
4000 Taxes on property	..	..	..	..	..	**0**	**0**	**0**	**0**	**0**
4100 Recurrent taxes on immovable property	..	..	..	..	..	..	..	..	..	..
4200 Recurrent taxes on net wealth	..	..	..	..	..	..	..	..	..	..
4300 Estate, inheritance and gift taxes	..	..	..	..	..	..	..	..	..	..
4400 Taxes on financial and capital transactions	..	..	..	..	..	..	..	..	..	..
4500 Non-recurrent taxes	..	..	..	..	..	..	..	..	..	..
4600 Other recurrent taxes on property	..	..	..	..	..	..	..	..	..	..
5000 Taxes on goods and services	..	..	..	..	..	**0**	**0**	**0**	**0**	**0**
5100 Taxes on production, sale, transfer, etc	..	..	..	..	..	..	..	..	..	..
5110 General taxes	..	..	..	..	..	..	..	..	..	..
5120 Taxes on specific goods and services	..	..	..	..	..	..	..	..	..	..
5130 Unallocable between 5110 and 5120	..	..	..	..	..	..	..	..	..	..
5200 Taxes on use of goods and perform activities	..	..	..	..	..	..	..	..	..	..
5300 Unallocable between 5100 and 5200	..	..	..	..	..	..	..	..	..	..
6000 Other taxes	..	..	..	..	..	**0**	**0**	**0**	**0**	**0**
6100 Paid solely by business	..	..	..	..	..	..	..	..	..	..
6200 Other	..	..	..	..	..	..	..	..	..	..
Total tax revenue	..	..	..	..	..	**66**	**115**	**136**	**167**	**246**

1. The figures exclude local government tax revenues as the data are not available.

StatLink http://dx.doi.org/10.1787/888933338320

Table 5.4. Barbados, tax revenues by sub-sectors of government

Million BAR

	Federal government[1]					State/Regional				
	1990	2000	2005	2010	2014	1990	2000	2005	2010	2014
1000 Taxes on income, profits and capital gains	**254 016**	**573 920**	**639 432**	**762 340**	**702 017**	..	..	..	..	..
1100 Of individuals	128 857	288 692	295 737	388 177	428 599	..	..	..	..	..
1200 Corporate	111 111	252 291	294 320	327 471	208 087	..	..	..	..	..
1300 Unallocable between 1100 and 1200	14 048	32 937	49 375	46 692	65 331	..	..	..	..	..
2000 Social security contributions	**0**	**0**	**0**	**0**	**0**	..	..	..	..	..
2100 Employees	..	..	..	..	..	..	..	..	..	..
2200 Employers	..	..	..	..	..	..	..	..	..	..
2300 Self-employed or non-employed	..	..	..	..	..	..	..	..	..	..
2400 Unallocable between 2100, 2200 and 2300	..	..	..	..	..	..	..	..	..	..
3000 Taxes on payroll and workforce	**0**	**0**	**0**	**0**	**0**	..	..	..	..	..
4000 Taxes on property	**39 117**	**91 928**	**127 362**	**113 533**	**112 998**	..	..	..	..	..
4100 Recurrent taxes on immovable property	25 991	60 216	76 247	97 595	94 059	..	..	..	..	..
4200 Recurrent taxes on net wealth	0	0	0	0	0	..	..	..	..	..
4300 Estate, inheritance and gift taxes	0	0	0	0	0	..	..	..	..	..
4400 Taxes on financial and capital transactions	0	0	0	0	0	..	..	..	..	..
4500 Non-recurrent taxes	13 126	31 712	51 115	15 938	18 939	..	..	..	..	..
4600 Other recurrent taxes on property	0	0	0	0	0	..	..	..	..	..
5000 Taxes on goods and services	**422 259**	**897 092**	**1 101 319**	**1 242 416**	**1 267 522**	..	..	..	..	..
5100 Taxes on production, sale, transfer, etc	422 259	793 469	973 944	1 092 106	1 125 148	..	..	..	..	..
5110 General taxes	196 817	501 399	609 915	753 003	851 769	..	..	..	..	..
5120 Taxes on specific goods and services	225 442	292 069	364 029	339 103	273 379	..	..	..	..	..
5130 Unallocable between 5110 and 5120	0	0	0	0	0	..	..	..	..	..
5200 Taxes on use of goods and perform activities	0	103 623	127 375	150 310	142 374	..	..	..	..	..
5300 Unallocable between 5100 and 5200	0	0	0	0	0	..	..	..	..	..
6000 Other taxes	**93 077**	**26 105**	**20 787**	**75 546**	**32 232**	..	..	..	..	..
6100 Paid solely by business	0	0	0	0	0	..	..	..	..	..
6200 Other	93 077	26 105	20 787	75 546	32 232	..	..	..	..	..
Total tax revenue	**808 469**	**1 589 045**	**1 888 901**	**2 193 835**	**2 114 769**	..	..	..	..	..

Million BAR

	Local government[2]					Social Security Funds				
	1990	2000	2005	2010	2014	1990	2000	2005	2010	2014
1000 Taxes on income, profits and capital gains	..	..	..	..	..	**0**	**0**	**0**	**0**	**0**
1100 Of individuals	..	..	..	..	..	..	..	..	..	..
1200 Corporate	..	..	..	..	..	..	..	..	..	..
1300 Unallocable between 1100 and 1200	..	..	..	..	..	..	..	..	..	..
2000 Social security contributions	..	..	..	..	..	**133 866**	**295 268**	**408 109**	**525 467**	**532 084**
2100 Employees	..	..	..	..	..	..	..	..	..	..
2200 Employers	..	..	..	..	..	..	..	..	..	..
2300 Self-employed or non-employed	..	..	..	..	..	..	..	..	..	..
2400 Unallocable between 2100, 2200 and 2300	..	..	..	..	..	133 866	295 268	408 109	525 467	532 084
3000 Taxes on payroll and workforce	..	..	..	..	..	**0**	**0**	**0**	**0**	**0**
4000 Taxes on property	..	..	..	..	..	**0**	**0**	**0**	**0**	**0**
4100 Recurrent taxes on immovable property	..	..	..	..	..	..	..	..	..	..
4200 Recurrent taxes on net wealth	..	..	..	..	..	..	..	..	..	..
4300 Estate, inheritance and gift taxes	..	..	..	..	..	..	..	..	..	..
4400 Taxes on financial and capital transactions	..	..	..	..	..	..	..	..	..	..
4500 Non-recurrent taxes	..	..	..	..	..	..	..	..	..	..
4600 Other recurrent taxes on property	..	..	..	..	..	..	..	..	..	..
5000 Taxes on goods and services	..	..	..	..	..	**0**	**0**	**0**	**0**	**0**
5100 Taxes on production, sale, transfer, etc	..	..	..	..	..	..	..	..	..	..
5110 General taxes	..	..	..	..	..	..	..	..	..	..
5120 Taxes on specific goods and services	..	..	..	..	..	..	..	..	..	..
5130 Unallocable between 5110 and 5120	..	..	..	..	..	..	..	..	..	..
5200 Taxes on use of goods and perform activities	..	..	..	..	..	..	..	..	..	..
5300 Unallocable between 5100 and 5200	..	..	..	..	..	..	..	..	..	..
6000 Other taxes	..	..	..	..	..	**0**	**0**	**0**	**0**	**0**
6100 Paid solely by business	..	..	..	..	..	..	..	..	..	..
6200 Other	..	..	..	..	..	..	..	..	..	..
Total tax revenue	..	..	..	..	..	**133 866**	**295 268**	**408 109**	**525 467**	**532 084**

1. For 2014 the data are estimated in category 5200.
2. The figures exclude local government tax revenues as the data are not available.

StatLink http://dx.doi.org/10.1787/888933338334

Table 5.5. Bolivia, tax revenues by sub-sectors of government

Million BOB

	Federal government					State/Regional				
	1990	2000	2005	2010	2014	1990	2000	2005	2010	2014
1000 Taxes on income, profits and capital gains	**123**	**967**	**2 058**	**5 326**	**9 463**	..	..	..	..	..
1100 Of individuals	62	161	187	237	401	..	..	..	..	..
1200 Corporate	61	806	1 871	5 089	9 062	..	..	..	..	..
1300 Unallocable between 1100 and 1200	0	0	0	0	0	..	..	..	..	..
2000 Social security contributions[1]	**0**	**0**	**0**	**0**	**0**	..	..	..	..	..
2100 Employees	..	..	..	..	..	..	..	..	..	..
2200 Employers	..	..	..	..	..	..	..	..	..	..
2300 Self-employed or non-employed	..	..	..	..	..	..	..	..	..	..
2400 Unallocable between 2100, 2200 and 2300	..	..	..	..	..	..	..	..	..	..
3000 Taxes on payroll and workforce	**0**	**0**	**0**	**0**	**0**	..	..	..	..	..
4000 Taxes on property	**72**	**3**	**640**	**367**	**433**	..	..	..	..	..
4100 Recurrent taxes on immovable property	0	0	0	0	0	..	..	..	..	..
4200 Recurrent taxes on net wealth	0	0	0	0	0	..	..	..	..	..
4300 Estate, inheritance and gift taxes	1	3	7	20	32	..	..	..	..	..
4400 Taxes on financial and capital transactions	0	0	633	347	401	..	..	..	..	..
4500 Non-recurrent taxes	0	0	0	0	0	..	..	..	..	..
4600 Other recurrent taxes on property	71	0	0	0	0	..	..	..	..	..
5000 Taxes on goods and services	**786**	**5 206**	**9 674**	**20 011**	**41 895**	..	..	..	..	..
5100 Taxes on production, sale, transfer, etc	786	5 206	9 674	20 011	41 895	..	..	..	..	..
5110 General taxes	497	2 649	4 574	9 293	18 663	..	..	..	..	..
5120 Taxes on specific goods and services	289	2 557	5 100	10 718	23 232	..	..	..	..	..
5130 Unallocable between 5110 and 5120	0	0	0	0	0	..	..	..	..	..
5200 Taxes on use of goods and perform activities	0	0	0	0	0	..	..	..	..	..
5300 Unallocable between 5100 and 5200	0	0	0	0	0	..	..	..	..	..
6000 Other taxes	**277**	**1 651**	**3 316**	**4 752**	**10 629**	..	..	..	..	..
6100 Paid solely by business	4	6	4	12	20	..	..	..	..	..
6200 Other	273	1 645	3 312	4 740	10 608	..	..	..	..	..
Total tax revenue	**1 257**	**7 827**	**15 687**	**30 457**	**62 419**	..	..	..	..	..

Million BOB

	Local government[2]					Social Security Funds				
	1990	2000	2005	2010	2014	1990	2000	2005	2010	2014
1000 Taxes on income, profits and capital gains	..	..	..	..	..	..	**0**	**0**	**0**	**0**
1100 Of individuals	..	..	..	..	..	..	..	..	..	..
1200 Corporate	..	..	..	..	..	..	..	..	..	..
1300 Unallocable between 1100 and 1200	..	..	..	..	..	..	..	..	..	..
2000 Social security contributions[1]	..	..	..	..	..	..	**666**	**936**	**1 645**	**3 100**
2100 Employees	..	..	..	..	..	..	..	..	..	..
2200 Employers	..	..	..	..	..	..	..	..	..	..
2300 Self-employed or non-employed	..	..	..	..	..	..	..	..	..	..
2400 Unallocable between 2100, 2200 and 2300	..	..	..	..	..	..	666	936	1 645	3 100
3000 Taxes on payroll and workforce	..	..	..	..	..	..	**0**	**0**	**0**	**0**
4000 Taxes on property	..	..	..	..	..	..	**0**	**0**	**0**	**0**
4100 Recurrent taxes on immovable property	..	..	..	..	..	..	..	..	..	..
4200 Recurrent taxes on net wealth	..	..	..	..	..	..	..	..	..	..
4300 Estate, inheritance and gift taxes	..	..	..	..	..	..	..	..	..	..
4400 Taxes on financial and capital transactions	..	..	..	..	..	..	..	..	..	..
4500 Non-recurrent taxes	..	..	..	..	..	..	..	..	..	..
4600 Other recurrent taxes on property	..	..	..	..	..	..	..	..	..	..
5000 Taxes on goods and services	..	..	..	..	..	..	**0**	**0**	**0**	**0**
5100 Taxes on production, sale, transfer, etc	..	..	..	..	..	..	..	..	..	..
5110 General taxes	..	..	..	..	..	..	..	..	..	..
5120 Taxes on specific goods and services	..	..	..	..	..	..	..	..	..	..
5130 Unallocable between 5110 and 5120	..	..	..	..	..	..	..	..	..	..
5200 Taxes on use of goods and perform activities	..	..	..	..	..	..	..	..	..	..
5300 Unallocable between 5100 and 5200	..	..	..	..	..	..	..	..	..	..
6000 Other taxes	..	..	..	..	..	..	**0**	**0**	**0**	**0**
6100 Paid solely by business	..	..	..	..	..	..	..	..	..	..
6200 Other	..	..	..	..	..	..	..	..	..	..
Total tax revenue	..	..	..	..	..	..	**666**	**936**	**1 645**	**3 100**

1. The data for social security contributions are available from the year 2000 only and are estimated for 2013 and 2014.
2. The figures exclude local government tax revenues as the data are not available.

StatLink http://dx.doi.org/10.1787/888933338346

Table 5.6. Brazil, tax revenues by sub-sectors of government

Million BRL

	Federal government					State/Regional				
	1990	2000	2005	2010	2014	1990	2000	2005	2010	2014
1000 Taxes on income, profits and capital gains	**1**	**68 667**	**149 309**	**236 631**	**341 567**	**0**	**0**	**0**	**16 499**	**29 021**
1100 Of individuals	0	3 406	6 981	65 721	100 143	..	..	..	16 499	29 021
1200 Corporate	0	25 430	73 071	128 255	171 352	..	..	..	0	0
1300 Unallocable between 1100 and 1200	0	39 831	69 257	42 656	70 072	..	..	..	0	0
2000 Social security contributions	**0**	**0**	**0**	**0**	**0**	**0**	**0**	**0**	**0**	**0**
2100 Employees	..	..	..	..	..	..	..	..	..	..
2200 Employers	..	..	..	..	..	..	..	..	..	..
2300 Self-employed or non-employed	..	..	..	..	..	..	..	..	..	..
2400 Unallocable between 2100, 2200 and 2300	..	..	..	..	..	..	..	..	..	..
3000 Taxes on payroll and workforce[1]	**0**	**6 749**	**14 468**	**33 052**	**47 724**	**0**	**0**	**0**	**0**	**0**
4000 Taxes on property	**0**	**17 726**	**35 282**	**27 038**	**30 656**	**0**	**5 623**	**11 282**	**23 885**	**37 151**
4100 Recurrent taxes on immovable property	0	234	288	485	900	0	0	0	0	0
4200 Recurrent taxes on net wealth	0	0	0	0	0	0	0	0	0	0
4300 Estate, inheritance and gift taxes	0	0	0	0	0	0	329	821	2 518	4 698
4400 Taxes on financial and capital transactions	0	17 492	34 994	26 553	29 756	0	0	0	0	0
4500 Non-recurrent taxes	0	0	0	0	0	0	0	0	0	0
4600 Other recurrent taxes on property	0	0	0	0	0	0	5 294	10 460	21 367	32 453
5000 Taxes on goods and services	**1**	**74 190**	**147 819**	**241 388**	**328 344**	**1**	**83 848**	**158 809**	**268 117**	**384 287**
5100 Taxes on production, sale, transfer, etc	1	74 190	147 819	241 388	328 344	1	82 279	153 437	268 117	384 287
5110 General taxes[1]	1	65 745	129 567	197 025	271 818	1	82 279	153 437	268 117	384 287
5120 Taxes on specific goods and services	0	8 445	18 252	44 363	56 525	0	0	0	0	0
5130 Unallocable between 5110 and 5120	..	0	0	0	0	0	0	0	0	0
5200 Taxes on use of goods and perform activities	0	0	0	0	0	0	1 569	5 372	0	0
5300 Unallocable between 5100 and 5200	0	0	0	0	0	0	0	0	0	0
6000 Other taxes[2]	**0**	**2 214**	**2 039**	**10 971**	**16 553**	**0**	**322**	**1 551**	**17 135**	**27 352**
6100 Paid solely by business	0	0	277	0	0	0	0	0	0	0
6200 Other[1]	0	2 214	1 761	10 971	16 553	0	322	1 551	17 135	27 352
Total tax revenue	**1**	**169 546**	**348 917**	**549 080**	**764 845**	**1**	**89 793**	**171 641**	**325 636**	**477 811**

Million BRL

	Local government					Social Security Funds				
	1990	2000	2005	2010	2014	1990	2000	2005	2010	2014
1000 Taxes on income, profits and capital gains	**0**	**0**	**0**	**5 608**	**11 274**	**0**	**0**	**0**	**0**	**0**
1100 Of individuals	..	..	..	5 608	11 274	..	..	..	..	..
1200 Corporate	..	..	..	0	0	..	..	..	..	..
1300 Unallocable between 1100 and 1200	..	..	..	0	0	..	..	..	..	..
2000 Social security contributions	**0**	**0**	**0**	**0**	**0**	**1**	**83 469**	**168 226**	**314 868**	**482 675**
2100 Employees	..	..	..	..	..	..	..	..	..	..
2200 Employers	..	..	..	..	..	0	18 709	32 248	64 271	108 782
2300 Self-employed or non-employed	..	..	..	..	..	..	..	..	..	..
2400 Unallocable between 2100, 2200 and 2300	..	..	..	..	..	1	64 760	135 978	250 597	373 893
3000 Taxes on payroll and workforce[1]	**0**	**0**	**0**	**0**	**0**	**0**	**0**	**0**	**0**	**0**
4000 Taxes on property	**0**	**5 469**	**9 710**	**23 450**	**39 026**	**0**	**0**	**0**	**0**	**0**
4100 Recurrent taxes on immovable property	0	4 519	8 117	17 443	27 976	..	..	..	..	..
4200 Recurrent taxes on net wealth	0	0	0	0	0	..	..	..	..	..
4300 Estate, inheritance and gift taxes	0	0	0	0	0	..	..	..	..	..
4400 Taxes on financial and capital transactions	0	950	1 593	6 007	11 050	..	..	..	..	..
4500 Non-recurrent taxes	0	0	0	0	0	..	..	..	..	..
4600 Other recurrent taxes on property	0	0	0	0	0	..	..	..	..	..
5000 Taxes on goods and services	**0**	**6 106**	**11 247**	**32 755**	**55 390**	**0**	**0**	**0**	**0**	**0**
5100 Taxes on production, sale, transfer, etc	0	6 106	11 247	32 755	55 390	..	..	..	..	..
5110 General taxes[1]	0	6 106	11 247	32 755	55 390	..	..	..	..	..
5120 Taxes on specific goods and services	0	0	0	0	0	..	..	..	..	..
5130 Unallocable between 5110 and 5120	0	0	0	0	0	..	..	..	..	..
5200 Taxes on use of goods and perform activities	0	0	0	0	0	..	..	..	..	..
5300 Unallocable between 5100 and 5200	0	0	0	0	0	..	..	..	..	..
6000 Other taxes[2]	**0**	**377**	**1 404**	**8 399**	**11 844**	**0**	**0**	**0**	**0**	**0**
6100 Paid solely by business	0	0	0	0	0	..	..	..	..	..
6200 Other[1]	0	377	1 404	8 399	11 844	..	..	..	..	..
Total tax revenue	**0**	**11 952**	**22 360**	**70 211**	**117 534**	**1**	**83 469**	**168 226**	**314 868**	**482 675**

1. For years prior to 2000 the PASEP (Program of Formation of the Patrimony of the Public Servants) contributions are combined with PIS (Social Integration Program) contributions in heading 5110.
2. From 2008 FUNDAF (Special Fund for Development and Improvement of Auditing Activities) contributions are included in heading 6200.

StatLink http://dx.doi.org/10.1787/888933338353

Table 5.7. Chile, tax revenues by sub-sectors of government

Million CLP

	Federal government					State/Regional				
	1990	2000	2005	2010	2014	1990	2000	2005	2010	2014
1000 Taxes on income, profits and capital gains	**412 974**	**1 841 630**	**5 171 293**	**8 329 060**	**9 628 037**	**..**	**..**	**..**	**..**	**..**
1100 Of individuals	99 154	604 100	738 620	1 492 837	2 114 296	..	..	..	..	..
1200 Corporate	219 586	882 896	3 155 480	4 448 745	6 196 077	..	..	..	..	..
1300 Unallocable between 1100 and 1200	94 233	354 634	1 277 193	2 387 478	1 317 664	..	..	..	..	..
2000 Social security contributions	**66 738**	**232 728**	**287 422**	**371 386**	**430 968**	**..**	**..**	**..**	**..**	**..**
2100 Employees	61 200	209 907	249 526	310 558	365 237	..	..	..	..	..
2200 Employers	5 538	22 821	37 896	60 828	65 731	..	..	..	..	..
2300 Self-employed or non-employed	0	0	0	0	0	..	..	..	..	..
2400 Unallocable between 2100, 2200 and 2300	0	0	0	0	0	..	..	..	..	..
3000 Taxes on payroll and workforce	**0**	**0**	**0**	**0**	**0**	**..**	**..**	**..**	**..**	**..**
4000 Taxes on property	**59 682**	**255 371**	**490 120**	**245 044**	**318 726**	**..**	**..**	**..**	**..**	**..**
4100 Recurrent taxes on immovable property	10 331	3 578	4 909	8 805	13 827	..	..	..	..	..
4200 Recurrent taxes on net wealth	0	0	0	0	0	..	..	..	..	..
4300 Estate, inheritance and gift taxes	3 444	10 906	23 184	39 338	31 340	..	..	..	..	..
4400 Taxes on financial and capital transactions	45 907	240 886	462 027	196 901	273 559	..	..	..	..	..
4500 Non-recurrent taxes	0	0	0	0	0	..	..	..	..	..
4600 Other recurrent taxes on property	0	0	0	0	0	..	..	..	..	..
5000 Taxes on goods and services	**1 063 677**	**4 719 255**	**6 831 421**	**10 330 378**	**14 835 858**	**..**	**..**	**..**	**..**	**..**
5100 Taxes on production, sale, transfer, etc	1 060 304	4 684 525	6 811 328	10 294 165	14 785 410	..	..	..	..	..
5110 General taxes	664 421	3 306 350	5 391 285	8 399 926	12 133 710	..	..	..	..	..
5120 Taxes on specific goods and services[1]	395 883	1 378 175	1 420 043	1 894 239	2 651 700	..	..	..	..	..
5130 Unallocable between 5110 and 5120	0	0	0	0	0	..	..	..	..	..
5200 Taxes on use of goods and perform activities	3 374	34 730	20 094	36 213	50 448	..	..	..	..	..
5300 Unallocable between 5100 and 5200	0	0	0	0	0	..	..	..	..	..
6000 Other taxes	**-23 356**	**-112 195**	**-85 954**	**-61 117**	**50 293**	**..**	**..**	**..**	**..**	**..**
6100 Paid solely by business	0	0	0	0	0	..	..	..	..	..
6200 Other	-23 356	-112 195	-85 954	-61 117	50 293	..	..	..	..	..
Total tax revenue	**1 579 715**	**6 936 788**	**12 694 301**	**19 214 751**	**25 263 882**	**..**	**..**	**..**	**..**	**..**

Million CLP

	Local government					Social Security Funds				
	1990	2000	2005	2010	2014	1990	2000	2005	2010	2014
1000 Taxes on income, profits and capital gains	**0**	**0**	**0**	**0**	**0**	**0**	**0**	**0**	**0**	**0**
1100 Of individuals	0	0	0	0	0	0	0	0	0	0
1200 Corporate	0	0	0	0	0	0	0	0	0	0
1300 Unallocable between 1100 and 1200	0	0	0	0	0	0	0	0	0	0
2000 Social security contributions	**0**	**0**	**0**	**0**	**0**	**92 821**	**344 030**	**644 295**	**1 122 601**	**1 679 119**
2100 Employees	..	..	..	..	..	92 821	344 030	644 295	1 122 601	1 679 119
2200 Employers	..	..	..	..	..	0	0	0	0	0
2300 Self-employed or non-employed	..	..	..	..	..	0	0	0	0	0
2400 Unallocable between 2100, 2200 and 2300	..	..	..	..	..	0	0	0	0	0
3000 Taxes on payroll and workforce	**0**	**0**	**0**	**0**	**0**	**0**	**0**	**0**	**0**	**0**
4000 Taxes on property	**49 637**	**298 666**	**411 656**	**540 320**	**937 274**	**0**	**0**	**0**	**0**	**0**
4100 Recurrent taxes on immovable property	49 637	298 666	411 656	540 320	937 274	..	..	..	..	..
4200 Recurrent taxes on net wealth	0	0	0	0	0	..	..	..	..	..
4300 Estate, inheritance and gift taxes	0	0	0	0	0	..	..	..	..	..
4400 Taxes on financial and capital transactions	0	0	0	0	0	..	..	..	..	..
4500 Non-recurrent taxes	0	0	0	0	0	..	..	..	..	..
4600 Other recurrent taxes on property	0	0	0	0	0	..	..	..	..	..
5000 Taxes on goods and services	**55 045**	**322 514**	**514 952**	**800 810**	**1 290 797**	**0**	**0**	**0**	**0**	**0**
5100 Taxes on production, sale, transfer, etc	13 705	105 302	140 703	220 657	345 885	..	..	..	..	..
5110 General taxes	0	0	0	0	0	..	..	..	..	..
5120 Taxes on specific goods and services[1]	13 705	105 302	140 703	220 657	345 885	..	..	..	..	..
5130 Unallocable between 5110 and 5120	0	0	0	0	0	..	..	..	..	..
5200 Taxes on use of goods and perform activities	41 340	217 212	374 249	580 153	944 912	..	..	..	..	..
5300 Unallocable between 5100 and 5200	0	0	0	0	0	..	..	..	..	..
6000 Other taxes	**0**	**0**	**0**	**0**	**0**	**0**	**0**	**0**	**0**	**0**
6100 Paid solely by business	..	..	..	..	..	..	..	..	..	..
6200 Other	..	..	..	..	..	..	..	..	..	..
Total tax revenue	**104 682**	**621 180**	**926 608**	**1 341 129**	**2 228 071**	**92 821**	**344 030**	**644 295**	**1 122 601**	**1 679 119**

1. ECLAC classifies Oil Prices Stabilisation Fund (FEPP) revenues as non-tax revenues.

StatLink http://dx.doi.org/10.1787/888933338362

Table 5.8. Colombia, tax revenues by sub-sectors of government

Million COP

	Federal government					State/Regional[1]				
	1990	2000	2005	2010	2014	1990	2000	2005	2010	2014
1000 Taxes on income, profits and capital gains	**771 694**	**7 103 525**	**17 348 618**	**26 218 852**	**50 083 349**	**0**	**0**	**0**	**0**	**0**
1100 Of individuals	47 210	1 499 345	3 594 441	5 192 384	8 827 575	..	..	..	..	..
1200 Corporate	359 758	5 119 828	13 044 361	20 405 209	40 125 246	..	..	..	..	..
1300 Unallocable between 1100 and 1200	364 726	484 352	709 816	621 258	1 130 528	..	..	..	..	..
2000 Social security contributions	**0**	**0**	**0**	**0**	**0**	**0**	**0**	**0**	**0**	**0**
2100 Employees	..	..	..	..	..	..	..	..	..	..
2200 Employers	..	..	..	..	..	..	..	..	..	..
2300 Self-employed or non-employed	..	..	..	..	..	..	..	..	..	..
2400 Unallocable between 2100, 2200 and 2300	..	..	..	..	..	..	..	..	..	..
3000 Taxes on payroll and workforce	**0**	**1 286 803**	**2 179 842**	**4 022 503**	**2 627 958**	**0**	**0**	**0**	**0**	**0**
4000 Taxes on property	**0**	**1 036 584**	**2 863 946**	**5 196 303**	**10 560 165**	**0**	**0**	**0**	**0**	**0**
4100 Recurrent taxes on immovable property	..	0	0	0	0	..	..	..	..	..
4200 Recurrent taxes on net wealth	..	0	462 720	1 970 530	4 118 196	..	..	..	..	..
4300 Estate, inheritance and gift taxes	..	0	0	0	0	..	..	..	..	..
4400 Taxes on financial and capital transactions	..	1 036 584	2 401 226	3 225 773	6 441 969	..	..	..	..	..
4500 Non-recurrent taxes	..	0	0	0	0	..	..	..	..	..
4600 Other recurrent taxes on property	..	0	0	0	0	..	..	..	..	..
5000 Taxes on goods and services	**1 035 934**	**11 022 878**	**21 393 776**	**34 882 447**	**47 365 944**	**263 429**	**1 204 940**	**1 966 325**	**2 874 375**	**3 485 874**
5100 Taxes on production, sale, transfer, etc	1 035 934	11 022 878	21 393 776	34 882 447	47 365 944	263 429	1 204 940	1 966 325	2 874 375	3 485 874
5110 General taxes	583 078	8 445 776	17 427 948	28 811 682	38 749 869	0	0	0	0	0
5120 Taxes on specific goods and services	452 856	2 577 102	3 965 828	6 070 765	8 616 074	263 429	1 204 940	1 966 325	2 874 375	3 485 874
5130 Unallocable between 5110 and 5120	0	0	0	0	0	0	0	0	0	0
5200 Taxes on use of goods and perform activities	0	0	0	0	0	0	0	0	0	0
5300 Unallocable between 5100 and 5200	0	0	0	0	0	0	0	0	0	0
6000 Other taxes	**78 306**	**480 784**	**682 084**	**483 762**	**333 146**	**0**	**518 253**	**1 117 016**	**2 005 277**	**2 911 983**
6100 Paid solely by business	0	0	0	0	0	..	0	0	0	0
6200 Other	78 306	480 784	682 084	483 762	333 146	..	518 253	1 117 016	2 005 277	2 911 983
Total tax revenue	**1 885 934**	**20 930 574**	**44 468 266**	**70 803 867**	**110 970 561**	**263 429**	**1 723 193**	**3 083 341**	**4 879 652**	**6 397 857**

Million COP

	Local government[1]					Social Security Funds[2]				
	1990	2000	2005	2010	2014	1990	2000	2005	2010	2014
1000 Taxes on income, profits and capital gains	**0**	**0**	**0**	**0**	**0**	**0**	**0**	**0**	**0**	**0**
1100 Of individuals	..	..	..	..	..	..	..	..	..	..
1200 Corporate	..	..	..	..	..	..	..	..	..	..
1300 Unallocable between 1100 and 1200	..	..	..	..	..	..	..	..	..	..
2000 Social security contributions	**0**	**0**	**0**	**0**	**0**	**203 596**	**4 989 000**	**7 845 000**	**11 478 085**	**19 272 000**
2100 Employees	..	..	..	..	..	..	..	..	..	..
2200 Employers	..	..	..	..	..	..	..	..	..	..
2300 Self-employed or non-employed	..	..	..	..	..	..	..	..	..	..
2400 Unallocable between 2100, 2200 and 2300	..	..	..	..	..	203 596	4 989 000	7 845 000	11 478 085	19 272 000
3000 Taxes on payroll and workforce	**0**	**0**	**0**	**0**	**0**	**0**	**0**	**0**	**0**	**0**
4000 Taxes on property	**56 160**	**991 070**	**1 974 213**	**3 163 084**	**5 330 636**	**0**	**0**	**0**	**0**	**0**
4100 Recurrent taxes on immovable property	56 160	991 070	1 974 213	3 163 084	5 330 636	..	..	..	..	..
4200 Recurrent taxes on net wealth	0	0	0	0	0	..	..	..	..	..
4300 Estate, inheritance and gift taxes	0	0	0	0	0	..	..	..	..	..
4400 Taxes on financial and capital transactions	0	0	0	0	0	..	..	..	..	..
4500 Non-recurrent taxes	0	0	0	0	0	..	..	..	..	..
4600 Other recurrent taxes on property	0	0	0	0	0	..	..	..	..	..
5000 Taxes on goods and services	**89 290**	**1 140 090**	**2 506 452**	**4 306 620**	**6 367 490**	**0**	**0**	**0**	**0**	**0**
5100 Taxes on production, sale, transfer, etc	89 290	1 140 090	2 506 452	4 306 620	6 367 490	..	..	..	..	..
5110 General taxes	89 290	1 140 090	2 506 452	4 306 620	6 367 490	..	..	..	..	..
5120 Taxes on specific goods and services	0	0	0	0	0	..	..	..	..	..
5130 Unallocable between 5110 and 5120	0	0	0	0	0	..	..	..	..	..
5200 Taxes on use of goods and perform activities	0	0	0	0	0	..	..	..	..	..
5300 Unallocable between 5100 and 5200	0	0	0	0	0	..	..	..	..	..
6000 Other taxes	**81 017**	**738 983**	**1 578 573**	**3 403 883**	**4 912 956**	**0**	**0**	**0**	**0**	**0**
6100 Paid solely by business	0	0	0	0	0	..	..	..	..	..
6200 Other	81 017	738 983	1 578 573	3 403 883	4 912 956	..	..	..	..	..
Total tax revenue	**226 467**	**2 870 144**	**6 059 238**	**10 873 586**	**16 611 082**	**203 596**	**4 989 000**	**7 845 000**	**11 478 085**	**19 272 000**

1. Corresponds to the reported consolidated revenues of the territorial entities (departments and municipalities).
2. From 2013, all of the health contributions entering FOSYGA (Solidarity and Guarantee Fund) are classified as social security contributions. Previously only the portion of the contributions used to finance the subsidised regime was included and the part to finance the contributory regime was classified in the social security sector as "other incomes". A more detailed explanation is shown in table 4.7 in the country tables.

StatLink http://dx.doi.org/10.1787/888933338374

Table 5.9. Costa Rica, tax revenues by sub-sectors of government

Million CRC

	Federal government					State/Regional				
	1990	2000	2005	2010	2014	1990	2000	2005	2010	2014
1000 Taxes on income, profits and capital gains	**11 820**	**128 805**	**324 224**	**748 093**	**1 091 470**	..	..	..	..	..
1100 Of individuals	..	..	16 438	202 849	349 139	..	..	..	..	..
1200 Corporate	..	..	288 355	450 312	574 137	..	..	..	..	..
1300 Unallocable between 1100 and 1200	11 820	128 805	19 430	94 932	168 194	..	..	..	..	..
2000 Social security contributions[1]	**0**	**0**	**0**	**0**	**0**	..	..	..	..	..
2100 Employees	..	..	..	..	..	..	..	..	..	..
2200 Employers	..	..	..	..	..	..	..	..	..	..
2300 Self-employed or non-employed	..	..	..	..	..	..	..	..	..	..
2400 Unallocable between 2100, 2200 and 2300	..	..	..	..	..	..	..	..	..	..
3000 Taxes on payroll and workforce	**0**	**0**	**0**	**0**	**0**	..	..	..	..	..
4000 Taxes on property	**366**	**7 291**	**10 846**	**18 270**	**36 713**	..	..	..	..	..
4100 Recurrent taxes on immovable property	0	0	0	3 527	4 013	..	..	..	..	..
4200 Recurrent taxes on net wealth	0	4 284	0	0	0	..	..	..	..	..
4300 Estate, inheritance and gift taxes	0	0	0	0	0	..	..	..	..	..
4400 Taxes on financial and capital transactions	366	3 007	10 846	14 743	32 700	..	..	..	..	..
4500 Non-recurrent taxes	0	0	0	0	0	..	..	..	..	..
4600 Other recurrent taxes on property	0	0	0	0	0	..	..	..	..	..
5000 Taxes on goods and services	**52 360**	**444 726**	**920 160**	**1 696 729**	**2 316 015**	..	..	..	..	..
5100 Taxes on production, sale, transfer, etc	49 980	425 353	887 390	1 598 790	2 180 867	..	..	..	..	..
5110 General taxes	21 326	222 775	485 168	920 298	1 266 798	..	..	..	..	..
5120 Taxes on specific goods and services[2]	28 654	202 887	399 192	678 492	914 070	..	..	..	..	..
5130 Unallocable between 5110 and 5120	0	-308	3 031	0	0	..	..	..	..	..
5200 Taxes on use of goods and perform activities	2 380	19 357	32 758	97 803	135 005	..	..	..	..	..
5300 Unallocable between 5100 and 5200	0	15	12	136	142	..	..	..	..	..
6000 Other taxes[3]	**6 113**	**2 573**	**7 009**	**12 864**	**58 826**	..	..	..	..	..
6100 Paid solely by business	0	15	624	459	39 542	..	..	..	..	..
6200 Other	6 113	2 558	6 385	12 405	19 284	..	..	..	..	..
Total tax revenue	**70 660**	**583 395**	**1 262 240**	**2 475 956**	**3 503 023**	..	..	..	..	..

Million CRC

	Local government[4]					Social Security Funds				
	1990	2000	2005	2010	2014	1990	2000	2005	2010	2014
1000 Taxes on income, profits and capital gains	..	**0**	**0**	**0**	**0**	**0**	**0**	**0**	**0**	**0**
1100 Of individuals	..	..	..	..	..	..	..	..	..	..
1200 Corporate	..	..	..	..	..	..	..	..	..	..
1300 Unallocable between 1100 and 1200	..	..	..	..	..	..	..	..	..	..
2000 Social security contributions[1]	..	**0**	**0**	**0**	**0**	**29 065**	**249 886**	**528 132**	**1 204 995**	**2 045 389**
2100 Employees	..	..	..	..	..	..	3 405	5 354	9 649	22 151
2200 Employers	..	..	..	..	..	..	..	24 481	56 332	370 268
2300 Self-employed or non-employed	..	..	..	..	..	..	5 858	16 414	33 778	22 404
2400 Unallocable between 2100, 2200 and 2300	..	..	..	..	..	29 065	240 623	481 883	1 105 236	1 630 566
3000 Taxes on payroll and workforce	..	**0**	**0**	**0**	**0**	**7 054**	**41 918**	**81 290**	**182 529**	**270 834**
4000 Taxes on property	..	**5 390**	**14 264**	**45 393**	**78 461**	**0**	**0**	**0**	**0**	**0**
4100 Recurrent taxes on immovable property	..	5 310	14 245	44 080	78 461	..	..	..	..	..
4200 Recurrent taxes on net wealth	..	0	0	0	0	..	..	..	..	..
4300 Estate, inheritance and gift taxes	..	0	0	0	0	..	..	..	..	..
4400 Taxes on financial and capital transactions	..	0	0	0	0	..	..	..	..	..
4500 Non-recurrent taxes	..	0	0	0	0	..	..	..	..	..
4600 Other recurrent taxes on property	..	80	19	1 313	0	..	..	..	..	..
5000 Taxes on goods and services	..	**11 981**	**26 810**	**65 862**	**107 568**	**0**	**0**	**0**	**0**	**0**
5100 Taxes on production, sale, transfer, etc	..	11 981	26 810	65 862	107 568	..	..	..	..	..
5110 General taxes	..	0	0	0	0	..	..	..	..	..
5120 Taxes on specific goods and services[2]	..	10 612	24 294	61 002	2 845	..	..	..	..	..
5130 Unallocable between 5110 and 5120	..	1 369	2 515	4 860	104 723	..	..	..	..	..
5200 Taxes on use of goods and perform activities	..	0	0	0	0	..	..	..	..	..
5300 Unallocable between 5100 and 5200	..	0	0	0	0	..	..	..	..	..
6000 Other taxes[3]	..	**1 242**	**3 207**	**4 366**	**6 485**	**0**	**0**	**0**	**0**	**0**
6100 Paid solely by business	..	0	0	0	0	..	..	..	..	..
6200 Other	..	1 242	3 207	4 366	6 485	..	..	..	..	..
Total tax revenue	..	**18 613**	**44 280**	**115 621**	**192 514**	**36 119**	**291 804**	**609 422**	**1 387 524**	**2 316 223**

1. In ECLAC data, social security contributions include INA (National Institute of Apprenticeship), IMAS (Joint Social Aid Institute), and FODESAF (Social Development and Family Allowances Fund).
2. In ECLAC data, the property tax on vehicles, aircraft and boats is classified in category 4000.
3. In ECLAC data, the tax on the transfer of used vehicles Law No. 7088 of 30/11/87 is classified as a property tax (4000).
4. The figures for years up to and including 1997 exclude local government tax revenues as the data are not available.

StatLink http://dx.doi.org/10.1787/888933338384

Table 5.10. Dominican Republic, tax revenues by sub-sectors of government

Million DOP

	Federal government					State/Regional				
	1990	2000	2005	2010	2014	1990	2000	2005	2010	2014
1000 Taxes on income, profits and capital gains	**1 670**	**10 782**	**30 041**	**53 643**	**124 518**	..	..	..	..	..
1100 Of individuals	..	4 088	7 587	17 088	28 996	..	..	..	..	..
1200 Corporate	..	4 679	16 222	21 475	72 747	..	..	..	..	..
1300 Unallocable between 1100 and 1200	1 670	2 015	6 232	15 080	22 775	..	..	..	..	..
2000 Social security contributions	**0**	**0**	**0**	**0**	**0**	..	..	..	..	..
2100 Employees	..	..	..	..	..	..	..	..	..	..
2200 Employers	..	..	..	..	..	..	..	..	..	..
2300 Self-employed or non-employed	..	..	..	..	..	..	..	..	..	..
2400 Unallocable between 2100, 2200 and 2300	..	..	..	..	..	..	..	..	..	..
3000 Taxes on payroll and workforce	**0**	**0**	**0**	**0**	**0**	..	..	..	..	..
4000 Taxes on property	**46**	**505**	**6 555**	**12 738**	**17 634**	..	..	..	..	..
4100 Recurrent taxes on immovable property	9	115	1 710	3 004	5 037	..	..	..	..	..
4200 Recurrent taxes on net wealth	0	0	0	0	0	..	..	..	..	..
4300 Estate, inheritance and gift taxes	11	96	84	231	325	..	..	..	..	..
4400 Taxes on financial and capital transactions	22	217	4 546	8 125	10 496	..	..	..	..	..
4500 Non-recurrent taxes	3	32	89	488	677	..	..	..	..	..
4600 Other recurrent taxes on property	1	45	127	891	1 100	..	..	..	..	..
5000 Taxes on goods and services	**4 488**	**36 038**	**111 344**	**175 716**	**249 490**	..	..	..	..	..
5100 Taxes on production, sale, transfer, etc	4 410	35 281	109 602	173 403	246 107	..	..	..	..	..
5110 General taxes	973	10 195	41 368	81 871	131 017	..	..	..	..	..
5120 Taxes on specific goods and services[1]	3 437	25 086	68 234	91 531	115 090	..	..	..	..	..
5130 Unallocable between 5110 and 5120	0	0	0	0	0	..	..	..	..	..
5200 Taxes on use of goods and perform activities	77	757	1 742	2 313	3 383	..	..	..	..	..
5300 Unallocable between 5100 and 5200	0	0	0	0	0	..	..	..	..	..
6000 Other taxes[2]	**159**	**495**	**1 661**	**0**	**1**	..	..	..	..	..
6100 Paid solely by business	0	0	0	..	0	..	..	..	..	..
6200 Other	159	495	1 661	..	1	..	..	..	..	..
Total tax revenue	**6 362**	**47 820**	**149 601**	**242 097**	**391 642**	..	..	..	..	..

Million DOP

	Local government[3]					Social Security Funds[4]				
	1990	2000	2005	2010	2014	1990	2000	2005	2010	2014
1000 Taxes on income, profits and capital gains	..	..	..	..	..	**0**	**0**	**0**	**0**	**0**
1100 Of individuals	..	..	..	..	..	..	..	..	..	..
1200 Corporate	..	..	..	..	..	..	..	..	..	..
1300 Unallocable between 1100 and 1200	..	..	..	..	..	..	..	..	..	..
2000 Social security contributions	..	..	..	..	..	**53**	**490**	**35**	**1 845**	**1 515**
2100 Employees	..	..	..	..	..	..	..	..	..	..
2200 Employers	..	..	..	..	..	..	..	..	..	..
2300 Self-employed or non-employed	..	..	..	..	..	..	..	..	..	..
2400 Unallocable between 2100, 2200 and 2300	..	..	..	..	..	53	490	35	1 845	1 515
3000 Taxes on payroll and workforce	..	..	..	..	..	**0**	**0**	**0**	**0**	**0**
4000 Taxes on property	..	..	..	..	..	**0**	**0**	**0**	**0**	**0**
4100 Recurrent taxes on immovable property	..	..	..	..	..	..	..	..	..	..
4200 Recurrent taxes on net wealth	..	..	..	..	..	..	..	..	..	..
4300 Estate, inheritance and gift taxes	..	..	..	..	..	..	..	..	..	..
4400 Taxes on financial and capital transactions	..	..	..	..	..	..	..	..	..	..
4500 Non-recurrent taxes	..	..	..	..	..	..	..	..	..	..
4600 Other recurrent taxes on property	..	..	..	..	..	..	..	..	..	..
5000 Taxes on goods and services	..	..	..	..	..	**0**	**0**	**0**	**0**	**0**
5100 Taxes on production, sale, transfer, etc	..	..	..	..	..	..	..	..	..	..
5110 General taxes	..	..	..	..	..	..	..	..	..	..
5120 Taxes on specific goods and services[1]	..	..	..	..	..	..	..	..	..	..
5130 Unallocable between 5110 and 5120	..	..	..	..	..	..	..	..	..	..
5200 Taxes on use of goods and perform activities	..	..	..	..	..	..	..	..	..	..
5300 Unallocable between 5100 and 5200	..	..	..	..	..	..	..	..	..	..
6000 Other taxes[2]	..	..	..	..	..	**0**	**0**	**0**	**0**	**0**
6100 Paid solely by business	..	..	..	..	..	..	..	..	..	..
6200 Other	..	..	..	..	..	..	..	..	..	..
Total tax revenue	..	..	..	..	..	**53**	**490**	**35**	**1 845**	**1 515**

1. In ECLAC data, the tax on transfer of movable goods is classified as a property tax (4000).
2. In ECLAC data, the Vehicle transfer tax is classified as a property tax (4000).
3. The figures exclude local government tax revenues as the data are not available.
4. The figures exclude social security contributions to general government managed by the private sector.

StatLink http://dx.doi.org/10.1787/888933338399

Table 5.11. Ecuador, tax revenues by sub-sectors of government

Million USD

	Federal government					State/Regional				
	1990	2000	2005	2010	2014	1990	2000	2005	2010	2014
1000 Taxes on income, profits and capital gains	**138**	**293**	**937**	**2 353**	**4 161**	..	..	..	..	..
1100 Of individuals	..	..	..	..	..	..	..	..	..	..
1200 Corporate	..	..	..	..	..	..	..	..	..	..
1300 Unallocable between 1100 and 1200	138	293	937	2 353	4 161	..	..	..	..	..
2000 Social security contributions	**0**	**0**	**0**	**0**	**0**	..	..	..	..	..
2100 Employees	..	..	..	..	..	..	..	..	..	..
2200 Employers	..	..	..	..	..	..	..	..	..	..
2300 Self-employed or non-employed	..	..	..	..	..	..	..	..	..	..
2400 Unallocable between 2100, 2200 and 2300	..	..	..	..	..	..	..	..	..	..
3000 Taxes on payroll and workforce	**0**	**0**	**0**	**0**	**0**	..	..	..	..	..
4000 Taxes on property	**0**	**0**	**0**	**0**	**0**	..	..	..	..	..
4100 Recurrent taxes on immovable property	..	..	..	..	..	..	..	..	..	..
4200 Recurrent taxes on net wealth	..	..	..	..	..	..	..	..	..	..
4300 Estate, inheritance and gift taxes	..	..	..	..	..	..	..	..	..	..
4400 Taxes on financial and capital transactions	..	..	..	..	..	..	..	..	..	..
4500 Non-recurrent taxes	..	..	..	..	..	..	..	..	..	..
4600 Other recurrent taxes on property	..	..	..	..	..	..	..	..	..	..
5000 Taxes on goods and services	**668**	**1 330**	**2 802**	**6 152**	**10 170**	..	..	..	..	..
5100 Taxes on production, sale, transfer, etc	665	1 319	2 742	5 997	9 942	..	..	..	..	..
5110 General taxes	302	836	1 975	3 886	6 376	..	..	..	..	..
5120 Taxes on specific goods and services	363	483	767	2 110	3 566	..	..	..	..	..
5130 Unallocable between 5110 and 5120	0	0	0	0	0	..	..	..	..	..
5200 Taxes on use of goods and perform activities[1]	3	11	60	156	228	..	..	..	..	..
5300 Unallocable between 5100 and 5200	0	0	0	0	0	..	..	..	..	..
6000 Other taxes	**27**	**0**	**2**	**289**	**129**	..	..	..	..	..
6100 Paid solely by business	0	..	0	0	0	..	..	..	..	..
6200 Other	27	..	2	289	129	..	..	..	..	..
Total tax revenue	**833**	**1 623**	**3 741**	**8 794**	**14 460**	..	..	..	..	..

Million USD

	Local government[2]					Social Security Funds[3]				
	1990	2000	2005	2010	2014	1990	2000	2005	2010	2014
1000 Taxes on income, profits and capital gains	..	..	..	..	..	**0**	**0**	**0**	**0**	**0**
1100 Of individuals	..	..	..	..	..	..	..	..	..	..
1200 Corporate	..	..	..	..	..	..	..	..	..	..
1300 Unallocable between 1100 and 1200	..	..	..	..	..	..	..	..	..	..
2000 Social security contributions	..	..	..	..	..	**243**	**228**	**1 109**	**2 549**	**4 718**
2100 Employees	..	..	..	..	..	..	..	..	..	..
2200 Employers	..	..	..	..	..	..	..	..	..	..
2300 Self-employed or non-employed	..	..	..	..	..	..	..	..	..	..
2400 Unallocable between 2100, 2200 and 2300	..	..	..	..	..	243	228	1 109	2 549	4 718
3000 Taxes on payroll and workforce	..	..	..	..	..	**0**	**0**	**0**	**0**	**0**
4000 Taxes on property	..	..	..	..	..	**0**	**0**	**0**	**0**	**0**
4100 Recurrent taxes on immovable property	..	..	..	..	..	..	..	..	..	..
4200 Recurrent taxes on net wealth	..	..	..	..	..	..	..	..	..	..
4300 Estate, inheritance and gift taxes	..	..	..	..	..	..	..	..	..	..
4400 Taxes on financial and capital transactions	..	..	..	..	..	..	..	..	..	..
4500 Non-recurrent taxes	..	..	..	..	..	..	..	..	..	..
4600 Other recurrent taxes on property	..	..	..	..	..	..	..	..	..	..
5000 Taxes on goods and services	..	..	..	..	..	**0**	**0**	**0**	**0**	**0**
5100 Taxes on production, sale, transfer, etc	..	..	..	..	..	..	..	..	..	..
5110 General taxes	..	..	..	..	..	..	..	..	..	..
5120 Taxes on specific goods and services	..	..	..	..	..	..	..	..	..	..
5130 Unallocable between 5110 and 5120	..	..	..	..	..	..	..	..	..	..
5200 Taxes on use of goods and perform activities[1]	..	..	..	..	..	..	..	..	..	..
5300 Unallocable between 5100 and 5200	..	..	..	..	..	..	..	..	..	..
6000 Other taxes	..	..	..	..	..	**0**	**0**	**0**	**0**	**0**
6100 Paid solely by business	..	..	..	..	..	..	..	..	..	..
6200 Other	..	..	..	..	..	..	..	..	..	..
Total tax revenue	..	..	..	..	..	**243**	**228**	**1 109**	**2 549**	**4 718**

1. In ECLAC data, the annual tax on motor vehicles is classified as a property tax (4000).
2. The figures exclude local government tax revenues as the data are not available.
3. Social security data is recorded at the non-financial public sector level.

StatLink http://dx.doi.org/10.1787/888933338402

Table 5.12. El Salvador, tax revenues by sub-sectors of government

Million USD

	Federal government					State/Regional				
	1990	2000	2005	2010	2014	1990	2000	2005	2010	2014
1000 Taxes on income, profits and capital gains	**95**	**429**	**668**	**995**	**1 522**	..	..	..	..	..
1100 Of individuals	..	..	312	571	627	..	..	..	..	..
1200 Corporate	..	..	356	423	693	..	..	..	..	..
1300 Unallocable between 1100 and 1200	95	407	-31	0	201	..	..	..	..	..
2000 Social security contributions	**0**	**0**	**0**	**0**	**0**	..	..	..	..	..
2100 Employees	..	..	..	..	..	..	..	..	..	..
2200 Employers	..	..	..	..	..	..	..	..	..	..
2300 Self-employed or non-employed	..	..	..	..	..	..	..	..	..	..
2400 Unallocable between 2100, 2200 and 2300	..	..	..	..	..	..	..	..	..	..
3000 Taxes on payroll and workforce	**0**	**0**	**0**	**0**	**0**	..	..	..	..	..
4000 Taxes on property	**26**	**12**	**16**	**16**	**24**	..	..	..	..	..
4100 Recurrent taxes on immovable property	0	0	0	0	0	..	..	..	..	..
4200 Recurrent taxes on net wealth	16	0	0	0	0	..	..	..	..	..
4300 Estate, inheritance and gift taxes	0	0	0	0	0	..	..	..	..	..
4400 Taxes on financial and capital transactions	10	12	16	16	24	..	..	..	..	..
4500 Non-recurrent taxes	0	0	0	0	0	..	..	..	..	..
4600 Other recurrent taxes on property	0	0	0	0	0	..	..	..	..	..
5000 Taxes on goods and services	**259**	**903**	**1 447**	**1 855**	**2 158**	..	..	..	..	..
5100 Taxes on production, sale, transfer, etc	259	903	1 447	1 855	2 158	..	..	..	..	..
5110 General taxes	133	714	1 104	1 433	1 720	..	..	..	..	..
5120 Taxes on specific goods and services	127	189	344	422	438	..	..	..	..	..
5130 Unallocable between 5110 and 5120	0	0	0	0	0	..	..	..	..	..
5200 Taxes on use of goods and perform activities	0	0	0	0	0	..	..	..	..	..
5300 Unallocable between 5100 and 5200	0	0	0	0	0	..	..	..	..	..
6000 Other taxes	**58**	**0**	**0**	**0**	**0**	..	..	..	..	..
6100 Paid solely by business	0	0	..	..	..	..	..	..	..	..
6200 Other	58	0	..	..	..	..	..	..	..	..
Total tax revenue	**438**	**1 344**	**2 131**	**2 865**	**3 704**	..	..	..	..	..

Million USD

	Local government[1]					Social Security Funds[2,3]				
	1990	2000	2005	2010	2014	1990	2000	2005	2010	2014
1000 Taxes on income, profits and capital gains	..	..	..	..	..	**0**	**0**	**0**	**0**	**0**
1100 Of individuals	..	..	..	..	..	..	..	..	..	..
1200 Corporate	..	..	..	..	..	..	..	..	..	..
1300 Unallocable between 1100 and 1200	..	..	..	..	..	..	..	..	..	..
2000 Social security contributions	..	..	..	..	..	**67**	**263**	**282**	**369**	**445**
2100 Employees	..	..	..	..	..	..	75	76	99	117
2200 Employers	..	..	..	..	..	..	176	181	238	286
2300 Self-employed or non-employed	..	..	..	..	..	..	13	25	33	42
2400 Unallocable between 2100, 2200 and 2300	..	..	..	..	..	67	0	0	0	0
3000 Taxes on payroll and workforce	..	..	..	..	..	**0**	**0**	**0**	**0**	**0**
4000 Taxes on property	..	..	..	..	..	**0**	**0**	**0**	**0**	**0**
4100 Recurrent taxes on immovable property	..	..	..	..	..	..	..	..	..	..
4200 Recurrent taxes on net wealth	..	..	..	..	..	..	..	..	..	..
4300 Estate, inheritance and gift taxes	..	..	..	..	..	..	..	..	..	..
4400 Taxes on financial and capital transactions	..	..	..	..	..	..	..	..	..	..
4500 Non-recurrent taxes	..	..	..	..	..	..	..	..	..	..
4600 Other recurrent taxes on property	..	..	..	..	..	..	..	..	..	..
5000 Taxes on goods and services	..	..	..	..	..	**0**	**0**	**0**	**0**	**0**
5100 Taxes on production, sale, transfer, etc	..	..	..	..	..	..	..	..	..	..
5110 General taxes	..	..	..	..	..	..	..	..	..	..
5120 Taxes on specific goods and services	..	..	..	..	..	..	..	..	..	..
5130 Unallocable between 5110 and 5120	..	..	..	..	..	..	..	..	..	..
5200 Taxes on use of goods and perform activities	..	..	..	..	..	..	..	..	..	..
5300 Unallocable between 5100 and 5200	..	..	..	..	..	..	..	..	..	..
6000 Other taxes	..	..	..	..	..	**0**	**0**	**0**	**0**	**0**
6100 Paid solely by business	..	..	..	..	..	..	..	..	..	..
6200 Other	..	..	..	..	..	..	..	..	..	..
Total tax revenue	..	..	..	..	..	**67**	**263**	**282**	**369**	**445**

1. The figures exclude local government tax revenues as the data are not available.
2. Corresponds to social security contributions paid to the Salvadoran Institute of Social Security.
3. Data on public pension contributions are not available from 2011 to 2014.

StatLink http://dx.doi.org/10.1787/888933338412

Table 5.13. Guatemala, tax revenues by sub-sectors of government

Million GTQ

	Federal government					State/Regional				
	1990	2000	2005	2010	2014	1990	2000	2005	2010	2014
1000 Taxes on income, profits and capital gains	**507**	**3 295**	**6 049**	**10 319**	**17 752**	..	..	..	..	..
1100 Of individuals	25	143	645	1 225	1 784	..	..	..	..	..
1200 Corporate	482	3 149	3 756	6 520	12 426	..	..	..	..	..
1300 Unallocable between 1100 and 1200	0	2	1 647	2 574	3 543	..	..	..	..	..
2000 Social security contributions	**0**	**0**	**0**	**0**	**0**	..	..	..	..	..
2100 Employees	..	..	..	..	..	..	..	..	..	..
2200 Employers	..	..	..	..	..	..	..	..	..	..
2300 Self-employed or non-employed	..	..	..	..	..	..	..	..	..	..
2400 Unallocable between 2100, 2200 and 2300	..	..	..	..	..	..	..	..	..	..
3000 Taxes on payroll and workforce	**0**	**0**	**0**	**0**	**0**	..	..	..	..	..
4000 Taxes on property	**45**	**17**	**9**	**11**	**16**	..	..	..	..	..
4100 Recurrent taxes on immovable property	0	6	1	1	1	..	..	..	..	..
4200 Recurrent taxes on net wealth	0	0	0	0	0	..	..	..	..	..
4300 Estate, inheritance and gift taxes	0	0	0	0	0	..	..	..	..	..
4400 Taxes on financial and capital transactions	45	12	8	10	15	..	..	..	..	..
4500 Non-recurrent taxes	0	0	0	0	0	..	..	..	..	..
4600 Other recurrent taxes on property	0	0	0	0	0	..	..	..	..	..
5000 Taxes on goods and services	**1 709**	**10 317**	**16 402**	**23 259**	**30 411**	..	..	..	..	..
5100 Taxes on production, sale, transfer, etc	1 681	10 131	16 083	22 754	29 092	..	..	..	..	..
5110 General taxes	762	6 259	10 753	16 980	23 153	..	..	..	..	..
5120 Taxes on specific goods and services	919	3 872	5 330	5 773	5 939	..	..	..	..	..
5130 Unallocable between 5110 and 5120	0	0	0	0	0	..	..	..	..	..
5200 Taxes on use of goods and perform activities	28	186	319	505	1 320	..	..	..	..	..
5300 Unallocable between 5100 and 5200	0	0	0	0	0	..	..	..	..	..
6000 Other taxes	**104**	**186**	**315**	**572**	**359**	..	..	..	..	..
6100 Paid solely by business	0	0	0	0	0	..	..	..	..	..
6200 Other	104	186	315	572	359	..	..	..	..	..
Total tax revenue	**2 365**	**13 816**	**22 775**	**34 161**	**48 538**	..	..	..	..	..

Million GTQ

	Local government[1]					Social Security Funds[2]				
	1990	2000	2005	2010	2014	1990	2000	2005	2010	2014
1000 Taxes on income, profits and capital gains	..	**0**	**0**	**0**	**0**	**0**	**0**	**0**	**0**	**0**
1100 Of individuals	..	..	..	..	..	..	..	..	..	..
1200 Corporate	..	..	..	..	..	..	..	..	..	..
1300 Unallocable between 1100 and 1200	..	..	..	..	..	..	..	..	..	..
2000 Social security contributions	..	**0**	**0**	**0**	**0**	**436**	**2 569**	**4 072**	**6 408**	**8 157**
2100 Employees	..	..	..	..	..	..	..	..	..	..
2200 Employers	..	..	..	..	..	..	..	..	..	..
2300 Self-employed or non-employed	..	..	..	..	..	..	..	..	..	..
2400 Unallocable between 2100, 2200 and 2300	..	..	..	..	..	436	2 569	4 072	6 408	8 157
3000 Taxes on payroll and workforce	..	**0**	**0**	**0**	**0**	**0**	**0**	**0**	**0**	**0**
4000 Taxes on property	..	**147**	**341**	**620**	**827**	**0**	**0**	**0**	**0**	**0**
4100 Recurrent taxes on immovable property	..	147	341	620	827	..	..	..	..	..
4200 Recurrent taxes on net wealth	..	0	0	0	0	..	..	..	..	..
4300 Estate, inheritance and gift taxes	..	0	0	0	0	..	..	..	..	..
4400 Taxes on financial and capital transactions	..	0	0	0	0	..	..	..	..	..
4500 Non-recurrent taxes	..	0	0	0	0	..	..	..	..	..
4600 Other recurrent taxes on property	..	0	0	0	0	..	..	..	..	..
5000 Taxes on goods and services	..	**0**	**0**	**0**	**0**	**0**	**0**	**0**	**0**	**0**
5100 Taxes on production, sale, transfer, etc	..	..	..	..	..	..	..	..	..	..
5110 General taxes	..	..	..	..	..	..	..	..	..	..
5120 Taxes on specific goods and services	..	..	..	..	..	..	..	..	..	..
5130 Unallocable between 5110 and 5120	..	..	..	..	..	..	..	..	..	..
5200 Taxes on use of goods and perform activities	..	..	..	..	..	..	..	..	..	..
5300 Unallocable between 5100 and 5200	..	..	..	..	..	..	..	..	..	..
6000 Other taxes	..	**0**	**0**	**0**	**0**	**0**	**0**	**0**	**0**	**0**
6100 Paid solely by business	..	..	..	..	..	..	..	..	..	..
6200 Other	..	..	..	..	..	..	..	..	..	..
Total tax revenue	..	**147**	**341**	**620**	**827**	**436**	**2 569**	**4 072**	**6 408**	**8 157**

1. The figures exclude some local government tax revenues as the data are not available. Revenues from the municipal property tax (IUSI) are included.
2. Corresponds to social security contributions to the Guatemalan Social Security Institute (IGSS) and payments by public employees to the government's pension fund.

StatLink http://dx.doi.org/10.1787/888933338426

Table 5.14. Honduras, tax revenues by sub-sectors of government

Million HNL

	Federal government					State/Regional				
	1990	2000	2005	2010	2014	1990	2000	2005	2010	2014
1000 Taxes on income, profits and capital gains	**431**	**2 985**	**7 498**	**13 972**	**21 722**	..	..	..	..	..
1100 Of individuals	157	991	2 312	4 528	7 312	..	..	..	..	..
1200 Corporate	274	1 916	4 725	8 705	14 021	..	..	..	..	..
1300 Unallocable between 1100 and 1200	0	78	461	740	389	..	..	..	..	..
2000 Social security contributions	**0**	**0**	**0**	**0**	**0**	..	..	..	..	..
2100 Employees	..	..	..	..	..	..	..	..	..	..
2200 Employers	..	..	..	..	..	..	..	..	..	..
2300 Self-employed or non-employed	..	..	..	..	..	..	..	..	..	..
2400 Unallocable between 2100, 2200 and 2300	..	..	..	..	..	..	..	..	..	..
3000 Taxes on payroll and workforce	**0**	**0**	**0**	**0**	**0**	..	..	..	..	..
4000 Taxes on property	**16**	**189**	**170**	**254**	**2 121**	..	..	..	..	..
4100 Recurrent taxes on immovable property	0	0	0	0	0	..	..	..	..	..
4200 Recurrent taxes on net wealth	0	0	0	0	0	..	..	..	..	..
4300 Estate, inheritance and gift taxes	0	0	0	0	0	..	..	..	..	..
4400 Taxes on financial and capital transactions	0	0	0	0	1 846	..	..	..	..	..
4500 Non-recurrent taxes	0	0	0	0	0	..	..	..	..	..
4600 Other recurrent taxes on property	16	189	170	254	275	..	..	..	..	..
5000 Taxes on goods and services	**1 405**	**11 445**	**19 032**	**28 937**	**44 748**	..	..	..	..	..
5100 Taxes on production, sale, transfer, etc	1 405	11 445	19 032	28 937	44 748	..	..	..	..	..
5110 General taxes	344	5 146	9 565	16 050	27 734	..	..	..	..	..
5120 Taxes on specific goods and services	1 061	6 299	9 468	12 887	17 014	..	..	..	..	..
5130 Unallocable between 5110 and 5120	0	0	0	0	0	..	..	..	..	..
5200 Taxes on use of goods and perform activities	0	0	0	0	0	..	..	..	..	..
5300 Unallocable between 5100 and 5200	0	0	0	0	0	..	..	..	..	..
6000 Other taxes	**1**	**2**	**7**	**9**	**7**	..	..	..	..	..
6100 Paid solely by business	0	0	0	0	0	..	..	..	..	..
6200 Other	1	2	7	9	7	..	..	..	..	..
Total tax revenue	**1 853**	**14 620**	**26 708**	**43 173**	**68 598**	..	..	..	..	..

Million HNL

	Local government[1]					Social Security Funds				
	1990	2000	2005	2010	2014	1990	2000	2005	2010	2014
1000 Taxes on income, profits and capital gains	..	..	..	..	..	**0**	**0**	**0**	**0**	**0**
1100 Of individuals	..	..	..	..	..	..	..	..	..	..
1200 Corporate	..	..	..	..	..	..	..	..	..	..
1300 Unallocable between 1100 and 1200	..	..	..	..	..	..	..	..	..	..
2000 Social security contributions	..	..	..	..	..	**179**	**1 727**	**4 416**	**8 671**	**12 467**
2100 Employees	..	..	..	..	..	..	..	..	..	..
2200 Employers	..	..	..	..	..	..	..	..	..	..
2300 Self-employed or non-employed	..	..	..	..	..	..	..	..	..	..
2400 Unallocable between 2100, 2200 and 2300	..	..	..	..	..	179	1 727	4 416	8 671	12 467
3000 Taxes on payroll and workforce	..	..	..	..	..	**0**	**0**	**0**	**0**	**0**
4000 Taxes on property	..	..	..	..	..	**0**	**0**	**0**	**0**	**0**
4100 Recurrent taxes on immovable property	..	..	..	..	..	..	..	..	..	..
4200 Recurrent taxes on net wealth	..	..	..	..	..	..	..	..	..	..
4300 Estate, inheritance and gift taxes	..	..	..	..	..	..	..	..	..	..
4400 Taxes on financial and capital transactions	..	..	..	..	..	..	..	..	..	..
4500 Non-recurrent taxes	..	..	..	..	..	..	..	..	..	..
4600 Other recurrent taxes on property	..	..	..	..	..	..	..	..	..	..
5000 Taxes on goods and services	..	..	..	..	..	**0**	**0**	**0**	**0**	**0**
5100 Taxes on production, sale, transfer, etc	..	..	..	..	..	..	..	..	..	..
5110 General taxes	..	..	..	..	..	..	..	..	..	..
5120 Taxes on specific goods and services	..	..	..	..	..	..	..	..	..	..
5130 Unallocable between 5110 and 5120	..	..	..	..	..	..	..	..	..	..
5200 Taxes on use of goods and perform activities	..	..	..	..	..	..	..	..	..	..
5300 Unallocable between 5100 and 5200	..	..	..	..	..	..	..	..	..	..
6000 Other taxes	..	..	..	..	..	**0**	**0**	**0**	**0**	**0**
6100 Paid solely by business	..	..	..	..	..	..	..	..	..	..
6200 Other	..	..	..	..	..	..	..	..	..	..
Total tax revenue	..	..	..	..	..	**179**	**1 727**	**4 416**	**8 671**	**12 467**

1. The figures exclude local government tax revenues as the data are not available.

StatLink http://dx.doi.org/10.1787/888933338431

Table 5.15. Jamaica, tax revenues by sub-sectors of government

Million JAM

	Federal government					State/Regional[2]				
	1990	2000	2005	2010	2014	1990	2000	2005	2010	2014
1000 Taxes on income, profits and capital gains	**3 944**	**39 277**	**69 894**	**118 708**	**134 083**	..	..	..	..	..
1100 Of individuals	1 687	17 441	36 043	54 798	70 867	..	..	..	..	..
1200 Corporate	1 280	7 627	13 134	33 091	31 991	..	..	..	..	..
1300 Unallocable between 1100 and 1200	977	14 209	20 718	30 820	31 224	..	..	..	..	..
2000 Social security contributions[1]	**0**	**0**	**0**	**0**	**0**	..	..	..	..	..
2100 Employees	..	..	..	..	..	..	..	..	..	..
2200 Employers	..	..	..	..	..	..	..	..	..	..
2300 Self-employed or non-employed	..	..	..	..	..	..	..	..	..	..
2400 Unallocable between 2100, 2200 and 2300	..	..	..	..	..	..	..	..	..	..
3000 Taxes on payroll and workforce	**0**	**0**	**0**	**0**	**0**	..	..	..	..	..
4000 Taxes on property	**67**	**0**	**0**	**0**	**0**	..	..	..	..	..
4100 Recurrent taxes on immovable property[1]	67	..	..	..	..	..	..	..	..	..
4200 Recurrent taxes on net wealth	0	..	..	..	..	..	..	..	..	..
4300 Estate, inheritance and gift taxes	0	..	..	..	..	..	..	..	..	..
4400 Taxes on financial and capital transactions	0	..	..	..	..	..	..	..	..	..
4500 Non-recurrent taxes	0	..	..	..	..	..	..	..	..	..
4600 Other recurrent taxes on property	0	..	..	..	..	..	..	..	..	..
5000 Taxes on goods and services	**3 294**	**44 638**	**78 147**	**148 894**	**205 696**	..	..	..	..	..
5100 Taxes on production, sale, transfer, etc	3 230	43 838	77 036	146 850	202 762	..	..	..	..	..
5110 General taxes	4	13 059	27 274	45 152	62 023	..	..	..	..	..
5120 Taxes on specific goods and services	3 226	30 779	49 762	101 698	140 740	..	..	..	..	..
5130 Unallocable between 5110 and 5120	0	0	0	0	0	..	..	..	..	..
5200 Taxes on use of goods and perform activities	64	800	1 111	2 045	2 934	..	..	..	..	..
5300 Unallocable between 5100 and 5200	0	0	0	0	0	..	..	..	..	..
6000 Other taxes	**444**	**3 159**	**8 733**	**8 738**	**13 037**	..	..	..	..	..
6100 Paid solely by business	0	0	0	0	0	..	..	..	..	..
6200 Other[1]	444	3 159	8 733	8 738	13 037	..	..	..	..	..
Total tax revenue	**7 748**	**87 074**	**156 775**	**276 340**	**352 817**	..	..	..	..	..

Million JAM

	Local government					Social Security Funds				
	1990	2000	2005	2010	2014	1990	2000	2005	2010	2014
1000 Taxes on income, profits and capital gains	**0**	**0**	**0**	**0**	**0**	**0**	**0**	**0**	**0**	..
1100 Of individuals	..	..	..	..	..	..	..	..	..	..
1200 Corporate	..	..	..	..	..	..	..	..	..	..
1300 Unallocable between 1100 and 1200	..	..	..	..	..	..	..	..	..	..
2000 Social security contributions[1]	**0**	**0**	**0**	**0**	**0**	**0**	**0**	**5 110**	**9 248**	**14 600**
2100 Employees	..	..	..	..	..	..	..	..	..	..
2200 Employers	..	..	..	..	..	..	..	..	..	..
2300 Self-employed or non-employed	..	..	..	..	..	..	..	..	..	..
2400 Unallocable between 2100, 2200 and 2300	..	..	..	..	..	..	..	5 110	9 248	14 600
3000 Taxes on payroll and workforce	**0**	**0**	**0**	**0**	**0**	**0**	**0**	**0**	**0**	**0**
4000 Taxes on property	**0**	**639**	**1 474**	**2 792**	**5 800**	**0**	**0**	**0**	**0**	**0**
4100 Recurrent taxes on immovable property[1]	..	639	1 474	2 792	5 800	..	..	..	..	..
4200 Recurrent taxes on net wealth	..	0	0	0	0	..	..	..	..	..
4300 Estate, inheritance and gift taxes	..	0	0	0	0	..	..	..	..	..
4400 Taxes on financial and capital transactions	..	0	0	0	0	..	..	..	..	..
4500 Non-recurrent taxes	..	0	0	0	0	..	..	..	..	..
4600 Other recurrent taxes on property	..	0	0	0	0	..	..	..	..	..
5000 Taxes on goods and services	**0**	**0**	**0**	**0**	**0**	**0**	**0**	**0**	**0**	**0**
5100 Taxes on production, sale, transfer, etc	..	..	..	..	..	..	..	..	..	..
5110 General taxes	..	..	..	..	..	..	..	..	..	..
5120 Taxes on specific goods and services	..	..	..	..	..	..	..	..	..	..
5130 Unallocable between 5110 and 5120	..	..	..	..	..	..	..	..	..	..
5200 Taxes on use of goods and perform activities	..	..	..	..	..	..	..	..	..	..
5300 Unallocable between 5100 and 5200	..	..	..	..	..	..	..	..	..	..
6000 Other taxes	**0**	**0**	**0**	**0**	**0**	**0**	**0**	**0**	**0**	**0**
6100 Paid solely by business	..	..	..	..	..	..	..	..	..	..
6200 Other[1]	..	..	..	..	..	..	..	..	..	..
Total tax revenue	**0**	**639**	**1 474**	**2 792**	**5 800**	**0**	**0**	**5 110**	**9 248**	**14 600**

1. Data are estimated for 2014.
2. The figures exclude state/regional government tax revenues as the data are not available.

StatLink http://dx.doi.org/10.1787/888933338444

Table 5.16. Mexico, tax revenues by sub-sectors of government

Million MXN

	Federal government					State/Regional				
	1990	2000	2005	2010	2014	1990	2000	2005	2010	2014
1000 Taxes on income, profits and capital gains[1]	**34 668**	**276 548**	**402 036**	**683 604**	**979 251**	**3**	**0**	**0**	**0**	**0**
1100 Of individuals	..	..	195 869	313 473	514 208	..	..	..	..	..
1200 Corporate	..	..	135 840	246 745	441 317	..	..	..	..	..
1300 Unallocable between 1100 and 1200	34 668	276 548	70 327	123 386	23 726	3	..	..	..	..
2000 Social security contributions[2]	**0**	**0**	**0**	**0**	**0**	**0**	**0**	**0**	**0**	**0**
2100 Employees	..	..	..	..	..	..	..	..	..	..
2200 Employers	..	..	..	..	..	..	..	..	..	..
2300 Self-employed or non-employed	..	..	..	..	..	..	..	..	..	..
2400 Unallocable between 2100, 2200 and 2300	..	..	..	..	..	..	..	..	..	..
3000 Taxes on payroll and workforce	**818**	**0**	**0**	**0**	**0**	**972**	**11 215**	**20 429**	**36 818**	**0**
4000 Taxes on property	**3**	**0**	**0**	**0**	**0**	**894**	**7 018**	**10 905**	**13 137**	**0**
4100 Recurrent taxes on immovable property	0	..	..	..	..	482	5 238	6 544	8 522	..
4200 Recurrent taxes on net wealth	0	..	..	..	..	0	0	0	0	..
4300 Estate, inheritance and gift taxes	0	..	..	..	..	7	0	0	0	..
4400 Taxes on financial and capital transactions	3	..	..	..	..	405	1 781	4 361	4 615	..
4500 Non-recurrent taxes	0	..	..	..	..	0	0	0	0	..
4600 Other recurrent taxes on property	0	..	..	..	..	0	0	0	0	..
5000 Taxes on goods and services	**70 559**	**536 406**	**942 354**	**1 287 081**	**1 630 254**	**118**	**1 346**	**2 124**	**5 805**	**0**
5100 Taxes on production, sale, transfer, etc	69 983	527 624	927 401	1 268 645	1 629 822	45	910	1 364	2 470	..
5110 General taxes	26 635	189 606	318 432	504 509	667 085	0	0	0	0	..
5120 Taxes on specific goods and services[3]	43 348	338 018	608 969	764 136	962 737	30	910	1 364	2 470	..
5130 Unallocable between 5110 and 5120	0	0	0	0	0	15	0	0	0	..
5200 Taxes on use of goods and perform activities	576	8 782	14 953	18 436	431	73	436	760	3 335	..
5300 Unallocable between 5100 and 5200	0	0	0	0	0	0	0	0	0	..
6000 Other taxes	**1 340**	**5 878**	**8 616**	**22 236**	**24 221**	**165**	**907**	**1 537**	**2 547**	**0**
6100 Paid solely by business	0	0	0	0	0	0	0	0	0	..
6200 Other	1 340	5 878	8 616	22 236	24 221	165	907	1 537	2 547	..
Total tax revenue	**107 388**	**818 832**	**1 353 007**	**1 992 921**	**2 633 725**	**2 152**	**20 485**	**34 995**	**58 307**	**0**

Million MXN

	Local government					Social Security Funds				
	1990	2000	2005	2010	2014	1990	2000	2005	2010	2014
1000 Taxes on income, profits and capital gains[1]	**2**	**0**	**0**	**0**	**0**	**0**	**0**	**0**	**0**	**0**
1100 Of individuals	..	..	..	..	..	..	..	..	..	..
1200 Corporate	..	..	..	..	..	..	..	..	..	..
1300 Unallocable between 1100 and 1200	2	..	..	..	..	..	..	..	..	..
2000 Social security contributions[2]	**0**	**0**	**0**	**0**	**0**	**17 165**	**167 292**	**261 673**	**378 006**	**538 213**
2100 Employees	..	..	..	..	..	..	..	..	..	..
2200 Employers	..	..	..	..	..	..	..	..	..	..
2300 Self-employed or non-employed	..	..	..	..	..	..	..	..	..	..
2400 Unallocable between 2100, 2200 and 2300	..	..	..	..	..	17 165	167 292	261 673	378 006	538 213
3000 Taxes on payroll and workforce	**7**	**2**	**32**	**93**	**0**	**0**	**0**	**0**	**0**	**0**
4000 Taxes on property	**1 017**	**6 946**	**15 891**	**25 818**	**0**	**0**	**0**	**0**	**0**	**0**
4100 Recurrent taxes on immovable property	554	4 710	10 098	17 202	..	..	..	..	..	..
4200 Recurrent taxes on net wealth	0	0	0	0	..	..	..	..	..	..
4300 Estate, inheritance and gift taxes	1	0	0	0	..	..	..	..	..	..
4400 Taxes on financial and capital transactions	462	2 236	5 793	8 616	..	..	..	..	..	..
4500 Non-recurrent taxes	0	0	0	0	..	..	..	..	..	..
4600 Other recurrent taxes on property	0	0	0	0	..	..	..	..	..	..
5000 Taxes on goods and services	**114**	**202**	**288**	**487**	**0**	**0**	**0**	**0**	**0**	**0**
5100 Taxes on production, sale, transfer, etc	97	133	214	466	..	..	..	..	..	..
5110 General taxes	0	0	0	0	..	..	..	..	..	..
5120 Taxes on specific goods and services	95	133	214	466	..	..	..	..	..	..
5130 Unallocable between 5110 and 5120	2	0	0	0	..	..	..	..	..	..
5200 Taxes on use of goods and perform activities	17	69	74	21	..	..	..	..	..	..
5300 Unallocable between 5100 and 5200	0	0	0	0	..	..	..	..	..	..
6000 Other taxes	**114**	**866**	**1 539**	**2 616**	**0**	**0**	**0**	**0**	**0**	**0**
6100 Paid solely by business	0	0	0	0	..	..	..	..	..	..
6200 Other	114	866	1 539	2 616	..	..	..	..	..	..
Total tax revenue	**1 254**	**8 016**	**17 750**	**29 014**	**0**	**17 165**	**167 292**	**261 673**	**378 006**	**538 213**

Note: The 2014 data for tax revenues of the State and Local levels of government are not available. They comprise revenues in categories 3000, 4000, 5000 and 6000.

1. In ECLAC data, income taxes are presented net of credit on salary figures.
2. In ECLAC data, social security contributions are presented net of transfers from the Federal government for the payment of IMSS (Mexican Social Security Institute) pensions.
3. In ECLAC and CIAT data, fees levied on hydro-carbon production are treated as non-tax revenues. As a result they publish figures for Federal Government tax revenues that are net of these fees. See Table 4.15 of this report.

StatLink http://dx.doi.org/10.1787/888933338455

Table 5.17. Nicaragua, tax revenues by sub-sectors of government

Million NIO

	Federal government					State/Regional				
	1990	2000	2005	2010	2014	1990	2000	2005	2010	2014
1000 Taxes on income, profits and capital gains	..	**1 144**	**3 902**	**8 351**	**17 658**	..	..	..	..	..
1100 Of individuals	..	..	..	..	..	..	..	..	..	..
1200 Corporate	..	..	..	..	..	..	..	..	..	..
1300 Unallocable between 1100 and 1200	..	1 144	3 902	8 351	17 658	..	..	..	..	..
2000 Social security contributions	..	**0**	**0**	**0**	**0**	..	..	..	..	..
2100 Employees	..	..	..	..	..	..	..	..	..	..
2200 Employers	..	..	..	..	..	..	..	..	..	..
2300 Self-employed or non-employed	..	..	..	..	..	..	..	..	..	..
2400 Unallocable between 2100, 2200 and 2300	..	..	..	..	..	..	..	..	..	..
3000 Taxes on payroll and workforce	..	**0**	**0**	**0**	**0**	..	..	..	..	..
4000 Taxes on property	..	**0**	**2**	**130**	**374**	..	..	..	..	..
4100 Recurrent taxes on immovable property	..	..	0	0	0	..	..	..	..	..
4200 Recurrent taxes on net wealth	..	..	2	130	374	..	..	..	..	..
4300 Estate, inheritance and gift taxes	..	..	0	0	0	..	..	..	..	..
4400 Taxes on financial and capital transactions	..	..	0	0	0	..	..	..	..	..
4500 Non-recurrent taxes	..	..	0	0	0	..	..	..	..	..
4600 Other recurrent taxes on property	..	..	0	0	0	..	..	..	..	..
5000 Taxes on goods and services	..	**5 584**	**9 725**	**17 029**	**29 050**	..	..	..	..	..
5100 Taxes on production, sale, transfer, etc	..	5 584	9 725	17 029	29 050	..	..	..	..	..
5110 General taxes	..	2 931	5 599	10 353	19 385	..	..	..	..	..
5120 Taxes on specific goods and services	..	2 653	4 126	6 676	9 665	..	..	..	..	..
5130 Unallocable between 5110 and 5120	..	0	0	0	0	..	..	..	..	..
5200 Taxes on use of goods and perform activities	..	0	0	0	0	..	..	..	..	..
5300 Unallocable between 5100 and 5200	..	0	0	0	0	..	..	..	..	..
6000 Other taxes	..	**11**	**17**	**20**	**87**	..	..	..	..	..
6100 Paid solely by business	..	0	0	0	0	..	..	..	..	..
6200 Other	..	11	17	20	87	..	..	..	..	..
Total tax revenue	..	**6 739**	**13 646**	**25 530**	**47 169**	..	..	..	..	..

Million NIO

	Local government[1]					Social Security Funds				
	1990	2000	2005	2010	2014	1990	2000	2005	2010	2014
1000 Taxes on income, profits and capital gains	..	..	..	..	..	..	**0**	**0**	**0**	**0**
1100 Of individuals	..	..	..	..	..	..	..	..	..	..
1200 Corporate	..	..	..	..	..	..	..	..	..	..
1300 Unallocable between 1100 and 1200	..	..	..	..	..	..	..	..	..	..
2000 Social security contributions	..	..	..	..	..	..	**1 678**	**3 363**	**8 090**	**15 161**
2100 Employees	..	..	..	..	..	..	..	..	..	..
2200 Employers	..	..	..	..	..	..	..	..	..	..
2300 Self-employed or non-employed	..	..	..	..	..	..	..	..	..	..
2400 Unallocable between 2100, 2200 and 2300	..	..	..	..	..	..	1 678	3 363	8 090	15 161
3000 Taxes on payroll and workforce	..	..	..	..	..	..	**0**	**0**	**0**	**0**
4000 Taxes on property	..	..	..	..	..	..	**0**	**0**	**0**	**0**
4100 Recurrent taxes on immovable property	..	..	..	..	..	..	..	..	..	..
4200 Recurrent taxes on net wealth	..	..	..	..	..	..	..	..	..	..
4300 Estate, inheritance and gift taxes	..	..	..	..	..	..	..	..	..	..
4400 Taxes on financial and capital transactions	..	..	..	..	..	..	..	..	..	..
4500 Non-recurrent taxes	..	..	..	..	..	..	..	..	..	..
4600 Other recurrent taxes on property	..	..	..	..	..	..	..	..	..	..
5000 Taxes on goods and services	..	..	..	..	..	..	**0**	**0**	**0**	**0**
5100 Taxes on production, sale, transfer, etc	..	..	..	..	..	..	..	..	..	..
5110 General taxes	..	..	..	..	..	..	..	..	..	..
5120 Taxes on specific goods and services	..	..	..	..	..	..	..	..	..	..
5130 Unallocable between 5110 and 5120	..	..	..	..	..	..	..	..	..	..
5200 Taxes on use of goods and perform activities	..	..	..	..	..	..	..	..	..	..
5300 Unallocable between 5100 and 5200	..	..	..	..	..	..	..	..	..	..
6000 Other taxes	..	..	..	..	..	..	**0**	**0**	**0**	**0**
6100 Paid solely by business	..	..	..	..	..	..	..	..	..	..
6200 Other	..	..	..	..	..	..	..	..	..	..
Total tax revenue	..	..	..	..	..	..	**1 678**	**3 363**	**8 090**	**15 161**

Note: Comparable statistics for 1990 cannot be shown due to the devaluation of the Nicaraguan cordoba.

1. The figures exclude local government tax revenues as the data are not available.

StatLink http://dx.doi.org/10.1787/888933338462

Table 5.18. Panama, tax revenues by sub-sectors of government

Million PAB

	Federal government					State/Regional				
	1990	2000	2005	2010	2014	1990	2000	2005	2010	2014
1000 Taxes on income, profits and capital gains	**216 950**	**484 872**	**562 852**	**1 317 028**	**1 997 822**	..	..	..	..	..
1100 Of individuals	14 155	20 343	24 395	35 456	57 690	..	..	..	..	..
1200 Corporate	72 413	186 351	255 073	749 818	1 095 127	..	..	..	..	..
1300 Unallocable between 1100 and 1200	130 382	278 178	283 384	531 754	845 006	..	..	..	..	..
2000 Social security contributions	**0**	**0**	**0**	**0**	**0**	..	..	..	..	..
2100 Employees	..	..	..	..	..	..	..	..	..	..
2200 Employers	..	..	..	..	..	..	..	..	..	..
2300 Self-employed or non-employed	..	..	..	..	..	..	..	..	..	..
2400 Unallocable between 2100, 2200 and 2300	..	..	..	..	..	..	..	..	..	..
3000 Taxes on payroll and workforce[1]	**0**	**36 400**	**36 243**	**58 844**	**134 100**	..	..	..	..	..
4000 Taxes on property	**43 443**	**62 090**	**109 086**	**212 194**	**336 903**	..	..	..	..	..
4100 Recurrent taxes on immovable property	28 330	33 898	56 424	107 791	175 627	..	..	..	..	..
4200 Recurrent taxes on net wealth	0	0	0	0	0	..	..	..	..	..
4300 Estate, inheritance and gift taxes	154	0	0	0	0	..	..	..	..	..
4400 Taxes on financial and capital transactions	3 419	9 343	21 049	29 810	44 800	..	..	..	..	..
4500 Non-recurrent taxes	0	0	0	0	0	..	..	..	..	..
4600 Other recurrent taxes on property	11 540	18 849	31 613	74 593	116 476	..	..	..	..	..
5000 Taxes on goods and services	**335 470**	**530 276**	**641 708**	**1 472 515**	**2 318 577**	..	..	..	..	..
5100 Taxes on production, sale, transfer, etc	331 758	530 276	641 708	1 472 515	2 318 577	..	..	..	..	..
5110 General taxes	80 303	69 013	137 585	766 154	1 351 246	..	..	..	..	..
5120 Taxes on specific goods and services[2]	138 623	461 263	504 123	706 360	967 331	..	..	..	..	..
5130 Unallocable between 5110 and 5120	112 832	0	0	0	0	..	..	..	..	..
5200 Taxes on use of goods and perform activities	3 712	0	0	0	0	..	..	..	..	..
5300 Unallocable between 5100 and 5200	0	0	0	0	0	..	..	..	..	..
6000 Other taxes[3]	**25 674**	**119 325**	**126 722**	**238 684**	**240 120**	..	..	..	..	..
6100 Paid solely by business	0	0	0	0	0	..	..	..	..	..
6200 Other	25 674	119 325	126 722	238 684	240 120	..	..	..	..	..
Total tax revenue	**621 537**	**1 232 963**	**1 476 611**	**3 299 265**	**5 027 522**	..	..	..	..	..

Million PAB

	Local government[3]					Social Security Funds				
	1990	2000	2005	2010	2014	1990	2000	2005	2010	2014
1000 Taxes on income, profits and capital gains	**0**	**0**	**0**	**0**	**0**	**0**	**0**	**0**	**0**	**0**
1100 Of individuals	..	..	..	..	..	..	..	..	..	..
1200 Corporate	..	..	..	..	..	..	..	..	..	..
1300 Unallocable between 1100 and 1200	..	..	..	..	..	..	..	..	..	..
2000 Social security contributions	**0**	**0**	**0**	**0**	**0**	**271 300**	**742 000**	**827 300**	**1 637 100**	**2 794 000**
2100 Employees	..	..	..	..	..	..	..	..	..	..
2200 Employers	..	..	..	..	..	..	..	..	..	..
2300 Self-employed or non-employed	..	..	..	..	..	..	..	..	..	..
2400 Unallocable between 2100, 2200 and 2300	..	..	..	..	..	271 300	742 000	827 300	1 637 100	2 794 000
3000 Taxes on payroll and workforce[1]	**0**	**0**	**0**	**0**	**0**	**0**	**0**	**0**	**0**	**0**
4000 Taxes on property	**0**	**0**	**0**	**0**	**0**	**0**	**0**	**0**	**0**	**0**
4100 Recurrent taxes on immovable property	..	0	0	..	..	..	..	..	..	..
4200 Recurrent taxes on net wealth	..	0	0	..	..	..	..	..	..	..
4300 Estate, inheritance and gift taxes	..	0	0	..	..	..	..	..	..	..
4400 Taxes on financial and capital transactions	..	0	0	..	..	..	..	..	..	..
4500 Non-recurrent taxes	..	0	0	..	..	..	..	..	..	..
4600 Other recurrent taxes on property	..	0	0	..	..	..	..	..	..	..
5000 Taxes on goods and services	**0**	**43 098**	**50 631**	**40 551**	**65 618**	**0**	**0**	**0**	**0**	**0**
5100 Taxes on production, sale, transfer, etc	..	53	5	0	0	..	..	..	..	..
5110 General taxes	..	0	0	0	0	..	..	..	..	..
5120 Taxes on specific goods and services[2]	..	53	5	0	0	..	..	..	..	..
5130 Unallocable between 5110 and 5120	..	0	0	0	0	..	..	..	..	..
5200 Taxes on use of goods and perform activities	..	43 045	50 626	40 551	65 618	..	..	..	..	..
5300 Unallocable between 5100 and 5200	..	0	0	0	0	..	..	..	..	..
6000 Other taxes[3]	**0**	**11**	**0**	**35 533**	**51 911**	**0**	**0**	**0**	**0**	**0**
6100 Paid solely by business	..	0	0	0	0	..	..	..	..	..
6200 Other	..	11	0	35 533	51 911	..	..	..	..	..
Total tax revenue	**0**	**43 109**	**50 631**	**76 085**	**117 529**	**271 300**	**742 000**	**827 300**	**1 637 100**	**2 794 000**

1. In ECLAC data, Education insurance is classified as "Other taxes" (6000).
2. In CIAT and ECLAC data, the tax on banks, financial institutions, and currency exchange is classified as a property tax.
3. From 2011, figures for local government taxes have been estimated as shown under heading 6000. It includes some revenues that would otherwise be shown under 4000 and 5000.

StatLink http://dx.doi.org/10.1787/888933338472

Table 5.19. Paraguay, tax revenues by sub-sectors of government

Million PYG

	Federal government					State/Regional				
	1990	2000	2005	2010	2014	1990	2000	2005	2010	2014
1000 Taxes on income, profits and capital gains	**73 726**	**470 388**	**938 886**	**2 096 498**	**3 678 392**	..	..	..	..	..
1100 Of individuals	..	..	..	1 150	83 921	..	..	..	..	..
1200 Corporate	..	4 238	6 091	13 405	18 918	..	..	..	..	..
1300 Unallocable between 1100 and 1200	73 726	466 150	932 795	2 081 943	3 575 553	..	..	..	..	..
2000 Social security contributions[1]	**28 882**	**300 451**	**541 310**	**1 140 654**	**1 607 000**	..	..	..	..	..
2100 Employees	..	..	..	..	..	..	..	..	..	..
2200 Employers	..	..	..	..	..	..	..	..	..	..
2300 Self-employed or non-employed	..	..	..	..	..	..	..	..	..	..
2400 Unallocable between 2100, 2200 and 2300	28 882	300 451	541 310	1 140 654	1 607 000	..	..	..	..	..
3000 Taxes on payroll and workforce	**0**	**0**	**0**	**0**	**0**	..	..	..	..	..
4000 Taxes on property	**17 162**	**0**	**0**	**0**	**0**	..	..	..	..	..
4100 Recurrent taxes on immovable property	17 162	..	..	..	..	..	..	..	..	..
4200 Recurrent taxes on net wealth	0	..	..	..	..	..	..	..	..	..
4300 Estate, inheritance and gift taxes	0	..	..	..	..	..	..	..	..	..
4400 Taxes on financial and capital transactions	0	..	..	..	..	..	..	..	..	..
4500 Non-recurrent taxes	0	..	..	..	..	..	..	..	..	..
4600 Other recurrent taxes on property	0	..	..	..	..	..	..	..	..	..
5000 Taxes on goods and services	**179 312**	**2 080 878**	**4 309 832**	**9 226 477**	**13 583 267**	..	..	..	..	..
5100 Taxes on production, sale, transfer, etc	179 312	2 080 878	4 309 832	9 226 477	13 583 267	..	..	..	..	..
5110 General taxes	0	1 150 496	2 478 998	5 991 694	9 363 648	..	..	..	..	..
5120 Taxes on specific goods and services	179 312	930 382	1 830 834	3 234 783	4 219 619	..	..	..	..	..
5130 Unallocable between 5110 and 5120	0	0	0	0	0	..	..	..	..	..
5200 Taxes on use of goods and perform activities	0	0	0	0	0	..	..	..	..	..
5300 Unallocable between 5100 and 5200	0	0	0	0	0	..	..	..	..	..
6000 Other taxes	**49 807**	**116 652**	**238 134**	**109 424**	**148 260**	..	..	..	..	..
6100 Paid solely by business	0	0	0	0	0	..	..	..	..	..
6200 Other	49 807	116 652	238 134	109 424	148 260	..	..	..	..	..
Total tax revenue	**348 889**	**2 968 370**	**6 028 162**	**12 573 052**	**19 016 920**	..	..	..	..	..

Million PYG

	Local government[2]					Social Security Funds[3]				
	1990	2000	2005	2010	2014	1990	2000	2005	2010	2014
1000 Taxes on income, profits and capital gains	..	..	**0**	**0**	**0**	..	**0**	**0**	**0**	**0**
1100 Of individuals	..	..	..	..	..	..	..	..	..	..
1200 Corporate	..	..	..	..	..	..	..	..	..	..
1300 Unallocable between 1100 and 1200	..	..	..	..	..	..	..	..	..	..
2000 Social security contributions[1]	..	..	**0**	**0**	**0**	..	**619 082**	**1 050 670**	**2 411 987**	**4 023 392**
2100 Employees	..	..	..	..	..	..	..	..	..	..
2200 Employers	..	..	..	..	..	..	..	..	..	..
2300 Self-employed or non-employed	..	..	..	..	..	..	..	..	..	..
2400 Unallocable between 2100, 2200 and 2300	..	..	..	..	..	..	619 082	1 050 670	2 411 987	4 023 392
3000 Taxes on payroll and workforce	..	..	**0**	**0**	..	..	**0**	**0**	**0**	**0**
4000 Taxes on property	..	..	**0**	**272 385**	**310 000**	..	**0**	**0**	**0**	**0**
4100 Recurrent taxes on immovable property	..	..	..	254 306	..	..	..	..	..	..
4200 Recurrent taxes on net wealth	..	..	..	0	..	..	..	..	..	..
4300 Estate, inheritance and gift taxes	..	..	..	0	..	..	..	..	..	..
4400 Taxes on financial and capital transactions	..	..	..	16 316	..	..	..	..	..	..
4500 Non-recurrent taxes	..	..	..	0	..	..	..	..	..	..
4600 Other recurrent taxes on property	..	..	..	1 762	..	..	..	..	..	..
5000 Taxes on goods and services	..	..	..	**234 485**	**235 000**	..	**0**	**0**	**0**	**0**
5100 Taxes on production, sale, transfer, etc	..	..	..	23 221	..	..	..	..	..	..
5110 General taxes	..	..	..	0	..	..	..	..	..	..
5120 Taxes on specific goods and services	..	..	..	23 221	..	..	..	..	..	..
5130 Unallocable between 5110 and 5120	..	..	..	0	..	..	..	..	..	..
5200 Taxes on use of goods and perform activities	..	..	..	211 027	235 000	..	..	..	..	..
5300 Unallocable between 5100 and 5200	..	..	..	237	..	..	..	..	..	..
6000 Other taxes	..	..	**355 192**	**145 766**	..	..	**0**	**0**	**0**	**0**
6100 Paid solely by business	..	..	0	0	..	..	..	..	..	..
6200 Other	..	..	355 192	145 766	..	..	..	..	..	..
Total tax revenue	..	..	**355 192**	**652 636**	**545 000**	..	**619 082**	**1 050 670**	**2 411 987**	**4 023 392**

1. Data on social security contributions collected by decentralised institutions are not available from 2011, with the exception of the contributions made to the Instituto de Previsión Social (Social Security Institute).
2. The figures for years up to and including 2004, as well as for 2013 and 2014, exclude local government tax revenues as the data are not available.
3. The figures for years up to and including 1998, exclude decentralised institutions as the data are not available. Data are estimated for 2013 and 2014 for the categories 4000,5000 and 5200.

StatLink http://dx.doi.org/10.1787/888933338486

Table 5.20. Peru, tax revenues by sub-sectors of government

Million PEN

	Federal government					State/Regional				
	1990	2000	2005	2010	2014	1990	2000	2005	2010	2014
1000 Taxes on income, profits and capital gains	**37**	**5 130**	**12 260**	**27 589**	**44 043**	..	..	..	..	..
1100 Of individuals	3	2 117	3 327	6 518	11 423	..	..	..	..	..
1200 Corporate	32	3 012	8 933	21 071	32 247	..	..	..	..	..
1300 Unallocable between 1100 and 1200	1	0	0	0	372	..	..	..	..	..
2000 Social security contributions	**0**	**0**	**0**	**0**	**0**	..	..	..	..	..
2100 Employees	..	..	..	..	..	..	..	..	..	..
2200 Employers	..	..	..	..	..	..	..	..	..	..
2300 Self-employed or non-employed	..	..	..	..	..	..	..	..	..	..
2400 Unallocable between 2100, 2200 and 2300	..	..	..	..	..	..	..	..	..	..
3000 Taxes on payroll and workforce	**0**	**1 038**	**27**	**3**	**3**	..	..	..	..	..
4000 Taxes on property	**99**	**0**	**783**	**944**	**153**	..	..	..	..	..
4100 Recurrent taxes on immovable property	0	0	0	0	0	..	..	..	..	..
4200 Recurrent taxes on net wealth	61	0	0	0	0	..	..	..	..	..
4300 Estate, inheritance and gift taxes	0	0	0	0	0	..	..	..	..	..
4400 Taxes on financial and capital transactions	38	0	706	944	153	..	..	..	..	..
4500 Non-recurrent taxes	0	0	0	0	0	..	..	..	..	..
4600 Other recurrent taxes on property	0	0	76	0	0	..	..	..	..	..
5000 Taxes on goods and services	**423**	**15 777**	**21 699**	**34 495**	**46 996**	..	..	..	..	..
5100 Taxes on production, sale, transfer, etc	423	15 777	21 699	34 495	46 996	..	..	..	..	..
5110 General taxes	78	9 519	14 779	28 691	40 320	..	..	..	..	..
5120 Taxes on specific goods and services	345	6 258	6 919	5 803	6 675	..	..	..	..	..
5130 Unallocable between 5110 and 5120	0	0	0	0	0	..	..	..	..	..
5200 Taxes on use of goods and perform activities	0	0	0	0	0	..	..	..	..	..
5300 Unallocable between 5100 and 5200	0	0	0	0	0	..	..	..	..	..
6000 Other taxes	**36**	**761**	**800**	**1 389**	**1 803**	..	..	..	..	..
6100 Paid solely by business	0	84	73	108	158	..	..	..	..	..
6200 Other	36	678	727	1 281	1 645	..	..	..	..	..
Total tax revenue	**595**	**22 706**	**35 568**	**64 420**	**92 998**	..	..	..	..	..

Million PEN

	Local government[1]					Social Security Funds				
	1990	2000	2005	2010	2014	1990	2000	2005	2010	2014
1000 Taxes on income, profits and capital gains	..	..	**0**	**0**	**0**	**0**	**0**	**0**	**0**	**0**
1100 Of individuals	..	..	..	..	..	..	..	..	..	..
1200 Corporate	..	..	..	..	..	..	..	..	..	..
1300 Unallocable between 1100 and 1200	..	..	..	..	..	..	..	..	..	..
2000 Social security contributions	..	..	**0**	**0**	**0**	**50**	**3 184**	**4 023**	**7 957**	**11 893**
2100 Employees	..	..	..	..	..	..	541	667	2 385	3 139
2200 Employers	..	..	..	..	..	..	2 447	3 207	5 283	8 524
2300 Self-employed or non-employed	..	..	..	..	..	..	95	36	42	58
2400 Unallocable between 2100, 2200 and 2300	..	..	..	..	..	50	102	113	246	172
3000 Taxes on payroll and workforce	..	..	**0**	**0**	**0**	**0**	**0**	**0**	**0**	**0**
4000 Taxes on property	..	..	**557**	**1 292**	**2 006**	**0**	**0**	**0**	**0**	**0**
4100 Recurrent taxes on immovable property	..	..	460	731	1 234	..	..	..	..	..
4200 Recurrent taxes on net wealth	..	..	0	0	0	..	..	..	..	..
4300 Estate, inheritance and gift taxes	..	..	0	0	0	..	..	..	..	..
4400 Taxes on financial and capital transactions	..	..	97	561	772	..	..	..	..	..
4500 Non-recurrent taxes	..	..	0	0	0	..	..	..	..	..
4600 Other recurrent taxes on property	..	..	0	0	0	..	..	..	..	..
5000 Taxes on goods and services	..	..	**105**	**290**	**472**	**0**	**0**	**0**	**0**	**0**
5100 Taxes on production, sale, transfer, etc	..	..	105	290	472	..	..	..	..	..
5110 General taxes	..	..	0	0	0	..	..	..	..	..
5120 Taxes on specific goods and services	..	..	105	290	472	..	..	..	..	..
5130 Unallocable between 5110 and 5120	..	..	0	0	0	..	..	..	..	..
5200 Taxes on use of goods and perform activities	..	..	0	0	0	..	..	..	..	..
5300 Unallocable between 5100 and 5200	..	..	0	0	0	..	..	..	..	..
6000 Other taxes	..	..	**486**	**726**	**601**	**0**	**0**	**0**	**0**	**0**
6100 Paid solely by business	..	..	0	0	0	..	..	..	..	..
6200 Other	..	..	486	726	601	..	..	..	..	..
Total tax revenue	..	..	**1 148**	**2 308**	**3 079**	**50**	**3 184**	**4 023**	**7 957**	**11 893**

1. The figures for years up to and including 2004 exclude local government tax revenues as the data are not available.

StatLink http://dx.doi.org/10.1787/888933338497

Table 5.21. Trinidad and Tobago, tax revenues by sub-sectors of government

Million TTD

	Federal government					State/Regional				
	1990	2000	2005	2010	2014	1990	2000	2005	2010	2014
1000 Taxes on income, profits and capital gains	**2 595**	**6 067**	**19 105**	**26 224**	**35 131**	..	..	..	..	..
1100 Of individuals	669	2 325	4 452	4 674	6 859	..	..	..	..	..
1200 Corporate	1 856	3 547	14 118	20 670	27 330	..	..	..	..	..
1300 Unallocable between 1100 and 1200	70	195	536	881	942	..	..	..	..	..
2000 Social security contributions	**0**	**0**	**0**	**0**	**0**	..	..	..	..	..
2100 Employees	..	..	..	..	..	..	..	..	..	..
2200 Employers	..	..	..	..	..	..	..	..	..	..
2300 Self-employed or non-employed	..	..	..	..	..	..	..	..	..	..
2400 Unallocable between 2100, 2200 and 2300	..	..	..	..	..	..	..	..	..	..
3000 Taxes on payroll and workforce	**0**	**0**	**0**	**0**	**0**	..	..	..	..	..
4000 Taxes on property	**41**	**64**	**63**	**24**	**5**	..	..	..	..	..
4100 Recurrent taxes on immovable property	39	64	63	22	3	..	..	..	..	..
4200 Recurrent taxes on net wealth	0	0	0	0	0	..	..	..	..	..
4300 Estate, inheritance and gift taxes	1	0	0	0	0	..	..	..	..	..
4400 Taxes on financial and capital transactions	0	0	0	0	0	..	..	..	..	..
4500 Non-recurrent taxes	0	0	0	2	1	..	..	..	..	..
4600 Other recurrent taxes on property	0	0	0	0	0	..	..	..	..	..
5000 Taxes on goods and services	**2 055**	**3 852**	**5 988**	**9 342**	**10 280**	..	..	..	..	..
5100 Taxes on production, sale, transfer, etc	1 928	3 559	5 690	8 924	9 648	..	..	..	..	..
5110 General taxes	980	1 890	2 963	6 032	5 745	..	..	..	..	..
5120 Taxes on specific goods and services	948	1 669	2 727	2 891	3 903	..	..	..	..	..
5130 Unallocable between 5110 and 5120	0	0	0	0	0	..	..	..	..	..
5200 Taxes on use of goods and perform activities	127	293	299	418	632	..	..	..	..	..
5300 Unallocable between 5100 and 5200	0	0	0	0	0	..	..	..	..	..
6000 Other taxes	**49**	**111**	**245**	**172**	**285**	..	..	..	..	..
6100 Paid solely by business	0	0	0	0	0	..	..	..	..	..
6200 Other	49	111	245	172	285	..	..	..	..	..
Total tax revenue	**4 740**	**10 094**	**25 401**	**35 762**	**45 701**	..	..	..	..	..

Million TTD

	Local government					Social Security Funds				
	1990	2000	2005	2010	2014	1990	2000	2005	2010	2014
1000 Taxes on income, profits and capital gains	**0**	**0**	**0**	**0**	**0**	**0**	**0**	**0**	**0**	**0**
1100 Of individuals	..	..	..	..	..	..	..	..	..	..
1200 Corporate	..	..	..	..	..	..	..	..	..	..
1300 Unallocable between 1100 and 1200	..	..	..	..	..	..	..	..	..	..
2000 Social security contributions	**0**	**0**	**0**	**0**	**0**	**183**	**702**	**1 173**	**2 645**	**3 000**
2100 Employees	..	..	..	..	..	..	..	..	..	..
2200 Employers	..	..	..	..	..	..	..	..	..	..
2300 Self-employed or non-employed	..	..	..	..	..	..	..	..	..	..
2400 Unallocable between 2100, 2200 and 2300	..	..	..	..	..	183	702	1 173	2 645	3 000
3000 Taxes on payroll and workforce	**0**	**0**	**0**	**0**	**0**	**0**	**0**	**0**	**0**	**0**
4000 Taxes on property	**108**	**213**	**326**	**411**	**738**	**0**	**0**	**0**	**0**	**0**
4100 Recurrent taxes on immovable property	108	213	326	411	738	..	..	..	..	..
4200 Recurrent taxes on net wealth	0	0	0	0	0	..	..	..	..	..
4300 Estate, inheritance and gift taxes	0	0	0	0	0	..	..	..	..	..
4400 Taxes on financial and capital transactions	0	0	0	0	0	..	..	..	..	..
4500 Non-recurrent taxes	0	0	0	0	0	..	..	..	..	..
4600 Other recurrent taxes on property	0	0	0	0	0	..	..	..	..	..
5000 Taxes on goods and services	**0**	**0**	**0**	**0**	**0**	**0**	**0**	**0**	**0**	**0**
5100 Taxes on production, sale, transfer, etc	..	..	..	..	..	..	..	..	..	..
5110 General taxes	..	..	..	..	..	..	..	..	..	..
5120 Taxes on specific goods and services	..	..	..	..	..	..	..	..	..	..
5130 Unallocable between 5110 and 5120	..	..	..	..	..	..	..	..	..	..
5200 Taxes on use of goods and perform activities	..	..	..	..	..	..	..	..	..	..
5300 Unallocable between 5100 and 5200	..	..	..	..	..	..	..	..	..	..
6000 Other taxes	**0**	**0**	**0**	**0**	**0**	**0**	**0**	**0**	**0**	**0**
6100 Paid solely by business	..	..	..	..	..	..	..	..	..	..
6200 Other	..	..	..	..	..	..	..	..	..	..
Total tax revenue	**108**	**213**	**326**	**411**	**738**	**183**	**702**	**1 173**	**2 645**	**3 000**

StatLink http://dx.doi.org/10.1787/888933338509

Table 5.22. Uruguay, tax revenues by sub-sectors of government

Million UYU

	Federal government					State/Regional				
	1990	2000	2005	2010	2014	1990	2000	2005	2010	2014
1000 Taxes on income, profits and capital gains	**114**	**5 620**	**11 969**	**44 573**	**76 786**	..	..	..	..	..
1100 Of individuals	0	0	44	19 654	41 851	..	..	..	..	..
1200 Corporate	114	5 620	11 925	23 257	31 698	..	..	..	..	..
1300 Unallocable between 1100 and 1200	0	0	0	1 662	3 237	..	..	..	..	..
2000 Social security contributions[1]	**0**	**0**	**0**	**0**	**0**	..	..	..	..	..
2100 Employees	..	..	..	..	..	..	..	..	..	..
2200 Employers	..	..	..	..	..	..	..	..	..	..
2300 Self-employed or non-employed	..	..	..	..	..	..	..	..	..	..
2400 Unallocable between 2100, 2200 and 2300	..	..	..	..	..	..	..	..	..	..
3000 Taxes on payroll and workforce	**0**	**0**	**0**	**0**	**0**	..	..	..	..	..
4000 Taxes on property[2]	**125**	**3 935**	**8 252**	**11 690**	**16 971**	..	..	..	..	..
4100 Recurrent taxes on immovable property	0	378	852	1 064	1 612	..	..	..	..	..
4200 Recurrent taxes on net wealth	94	2 076	4 943	8 948	13 714	..	..	..	..	..
4300 Estate, inheritance and gift taxes	0	0	0	0	0	..	..	..	..	..
4400 Taxes on financial and capital transactions	0	372	933	1 350	1 442	..	..	..	..	..
4500 Non-recurrent taxes	0	0	0	0	0	..	..	..	..	..
4600 Other recurrent taxes on property	31	1 107	1 524	328	203	..	..	..	..	..
5000 Taxes on goods and services[2]	**1 270**	**28 301**	**52 727**	**94 990**	**151 001**	..	..	..	..	..
5100 Taxes on production, sale, transfer, etc	1 270	28 301	52 727	94 990	151 001	..	..	..	..	..
5110 General taxes[2]	660	18 009	34 641	69 365	108 260	..	..	..	..	..
5120 Taxes on specific goods and services	610	10 291	18 086	25 625	42 741	..	..	..	..	..
5130 Unallocable between 5110 and 5120	0	0	0	0	0	..	..	..	..	..
5200 Taxes on use of goods and perform activities	0	0	0	0	0	..	..	..	..	..
5300 Unallocable between 5100 and 5200	0	0	0	0	0	..	..	..	..	..
6000 Other taxes	**-10**	**-596**	**76**	**0**	**541**	..	..	..	..	..
6100 Paid solely by business	-10	-596	76	0	541	..	..	..	..	..
6200 Other	0	0	0	0	0	..	..	..	..	..
Total tax revenue	**1 500**	**37 259**	**73 023**	**151 253**	**245 299**	..	..	..	..	..

Million UYU

	Local government					Social Security Funds				
	1990	2000	2005	2010	2014	1990	2000	2005	2010	2014
1000 Taxes on income, profits and capital gains	**0**	**0**	**0**	**0**	**0**	**0**	**0**	**0**	**0**	**0**
1100 Of individuals	..	..	..	..	..	..	..	..	..	..
1200 Corporate	..	..	..	..	..	..	..	..	..	..
1300 Unallocable between 1100 and 1200	..	..	..	..	..	..	..	..	..	..
2000 Social security contributions[1]	**0**	**0**	**0**	**0**	**0**	**717**	**17 679**	**21 425**	**49 742**	**100 993**
2100 Employees	..	..	..	..	..	..	..	..	..	..
2200 Employers	..	..	..	..	..	..	..	..	..	..
2300 Self-employed or non-employed	..	..	..	..	..	..	..	..	..	..
2400 Unallocable between 2100, 2200 and 2300	..	..	..	..	..	717	17 679	21 425	49 742	100 993
3000 Taxes on payroll and workforce	**0**	**0**	**0**	**0**	**0**	**0**	**0**	**0**	**0**	**0**
4000 Taxes on property[2]	**72**	**2 142**	**3 787**	**5 245**	**7 336**	**0**	**0**	**0**	**0**	**0**
4100 Recurrent taxes on immovable property	72	2 142	3 787	5 245	7 336	..	..	..	..	..
4200 Recurrent taxes on net wealth	0	0	0	0	0	..	..	..	..	..
4300 Estate, inheritance and gift taxes	0	0	0	0	0	..	..	..	..	..
4400 Taxes on financial and capital transactions	0	0	0	0	0	..	..	..	..	..
4500 Non-recurrent taxes	0	0	0	0	0	..	..	..	..	..
4600 Other recurrent taxes on property	0	0	0	0	0	..	..	..	..	..
5000 Taxes on goods and services[2]	**64**	**2 576**	**3 071**	**3 952**	**6 789**	**0**	**0**	**0**	**0**	**0**
5100 Taxes on production, sale, transfer, etc	0	0	0	0	0	..	..	..	..	..
5110 General taxes[2]	..	..	..	..	..	..	..	..	..	..
5120 Taxes on specific goods and services	..	..	..	..	..	..	..	..	..	..
5130 Unallocable between 5110 and 5120	..	..	..	..	..	..	..	..	..	..
5200 Taxes on use of goods and perform activities	64	2 576	3 071	3 952	6 789	..	..	..	..	..
5300 Unallocable between 5100 and 5200	0	0	0	0	0	..	..	..	..	..
6000 Other taxes	**0**	**0**	**0**	**0**	**0**	**0**	**0**	**0**	**0**	**0**
6100 Paid solely by business	..	..	..	..	..	..	..	..	..	..
6200 Other	..	..	..	..	..	..	..	..	..	..
Total tax revenue	**136**	**4 718**	**6 858**	**9 196**	**14 125**	**717**	**17 679**	**21 425**	**49 742**	**100 993**

1. Figures for 1990-98 are reconstructed estimates, as the current methodology used to calculate social security contributions was not employed until 1999.
2. In ECLAC data, the tax on the sale of goods by public auction is classified in category 4000.

StatLink http://dx.doi.org/10.1787/888933338514

Table 5.23. Venezuela, tax revenues by sub-sectors of government

Million VEF

	Federal government					State/Regional[2]				
	1990	2000	2005	2010	2014	1990	2000	2005	2010	2014
1000 Taxes on income, profits and capital gains	**344**	**4 686**	**18 529**	**36 836**	**187 884**	..	..	..	..	..
1100 Of individuals	..	..	..	..	..	..	..	..	..	..
1200 Corporate	315	3 368	11 184	8 700	67 601	..	..	..	..	..
1300 Unallocable between 1100 and 1200	30	1 317	7 345	28 137	120 283	..	..	..	..	..
2000 Social security contributions[1]	**0**	**0**	**0**	**0**	**0**	..	..	..	..	..
2100 Employees	..	..	..	..	..	..	..	..	..	..
2200 Employers	..	..	..	..	..	..	..	..	..	..
2300 Self-employed or non-employed	..	..	..	..	..	..	..	..	..	..
2400 Unallocable between 2100, 2200 and 2300	..	..	..	..	..	..	..	..	..	..
3000 Taxes on payroll and workforce	**0**	**0**	**0**	**0**	**0**	..	..	..	..	..
4000 Taxes on property	**1**	**400**	**2 834**	**222**	**1 044**	..	..	..	..	..
4100 Recurrent taxes on immovable property	0	0	0	0	0	..	..	..	..	..
4200 Recurrent taxes on net wealth	0	0	0	0	0	..	..	..	..	..
4300 Estate, inheritance and gift taxes	1	19	55	222	1 044	..	..	..	..	..
4400 Taxes on financial and capital transactions	0	381	2 779	0	0	..	..	..	..	..
4500 Non-recurrent taxes	0	0	0	0	0	..	..	..	..	..
4600 Other recurrent taxes on property	0	0	0	0	0	..	..	..	..	..
5000 Taxes on goods and services	**46**	**5 173**	**25 032**	**73 707**	**348 872**	..	..	..	..	..
5100 Taxes on production, sale, transfer, etc	46	5 173	25 032	73 707	348 872	..	..	..	..	..
5110 General taxes	0	3 272	19 513	56 101	272 187	..	..	..	..	..
5120 Taxes on specific goods and services	46	1 901	5 519	17 606	76 685	..	..	..	..	..
5130 Unallocable between 5110 and 5120	0	0	0	0	0	..	..	..	..	..
5200 Taxes on use of goods and perform activities	0	0	0	0	0	..	..	..	..	..
5300 Unallocable between 5100 and 5200	0	0	0	0	0	..	..	..	..	..
6000 Other taxes	**0**	**0**	**0**	**0**	**8 026**	..	..	..	..	..
6100 Paid solely by business	..	..	..	..	0	..	..	..	..	..
6200 Other	..	..	..	..	8 026	..	..	..	..	..
Total tax revenue	**391**	**10 258**	**46 395**	**110 765**	**545 826**	..	..	..	..	..

Million VEF

	Local government[2]					Social Security Funds				
	1990	2000	2005	2010	2014	1990	2000	2005	2010	2014
1000 Taxes on income, profits and capital gains	..	..	..	..	..	**0**	**0**	**0**	**0**	**0**
1100 Of individuals	..	..	..	..	..	..	..	..	..	..
1200 Corporate	..	..	..	..	..	..	..	..	..	..
1300 Unallocable between 1100 and 1200	..	..	..	..	..	..	..	..	..	..
2000 Social security contributions[1]	..	..	..	..	..	**20**	**591**	**1 890**	**9 690**	**28 600**
2100 Employees	..	..	..	..	..	..	..	..	..	..
2200 Employers	..	..	..	..	..	..	..	..	..	..
2300 Self-employed or non-employed	..	..	..	..	..	..	..	..	..	..
2400 Unallocable between 2100, 2200 and 2300	..	..	..	..	..	20	591	1 890	9 690	28 600
3000 Taxes on payroll and workforce	..	..	..	..	..	**0**	**0**	**0**	**0**	**0**
4000 Taxes on property	..	..	..	..	..	**0**	**0**	**0**	**0**	**0**
4100 Recurrent taxes on immovable property	..	..	..	..	..	..	..	..	..	..
4200 Recurrent taxes on net wealth	..	..	..	..	..	..	..	..	..	..
4300 Estate, inheritance and gift taxes	..	..	..	..	..	..	..	..	..	..
4400 Taxes on financial and capital transactions	..	..	..	..	..	..	..	..	..	..
4500 Non-recurrent taxes	..	..	..	..	..	..	..	..	..	..
4600 Other recurrent taxes on property	..	..	..	..	..	..	..	..	..	..
5000 Taxes on goods and services	..	..	..	..	..	**0**	**0**	**0**	**0**	**0**
5100 Taxes on production, sale, transfer, etc	..	..	..	..	..	..	..	..	..	..
5110 General taxes	..	..	..	..	..	..	..	..	..	..
5120 Taxes on specific goods and services	..	..	..	..	..	..	..	..	..	..
5130 Unallocable between 5110 and 5120	..	..	..	..	..	..	..	..	..	..
5200 Taxes on use of goods and perform activities	..	..	..	..	..	..	..	..	..	..
5300 Unallocable between 5100 and 5200	..	..	..	..	..	..	..	..	..	..
6000 Other taxes	..	..	..	..	..	**0**	**0**	**0**	**0**	**0**
6100 Paid solely by business	..	..	..	..	..	..	..	..	..	..
6200 Other	..	..	..	..	..	..	..	..	..	..
Total tax revenue	..	..	..	..	..	**20**	**591**	**1 890**	**9 690**	**28 600**

1. The data on social security contributions are estimated from 2011 to 2014.
2. The figures exclude state and local government tax revenues as the data are not available.

StatLink http://dx.doi.org/10.1787/888933338520

Figure 5.1. **Attribution of tax revenues to sub-sectors of general government, 2013**

Receipts as percentage of total tax revenue

Gráfico 5.1. **Atribución de los ingresos tributarios en los sub-sectores del gobierno general, 2013**

Ingresos como porcentaje de los ingresos tributarios totales

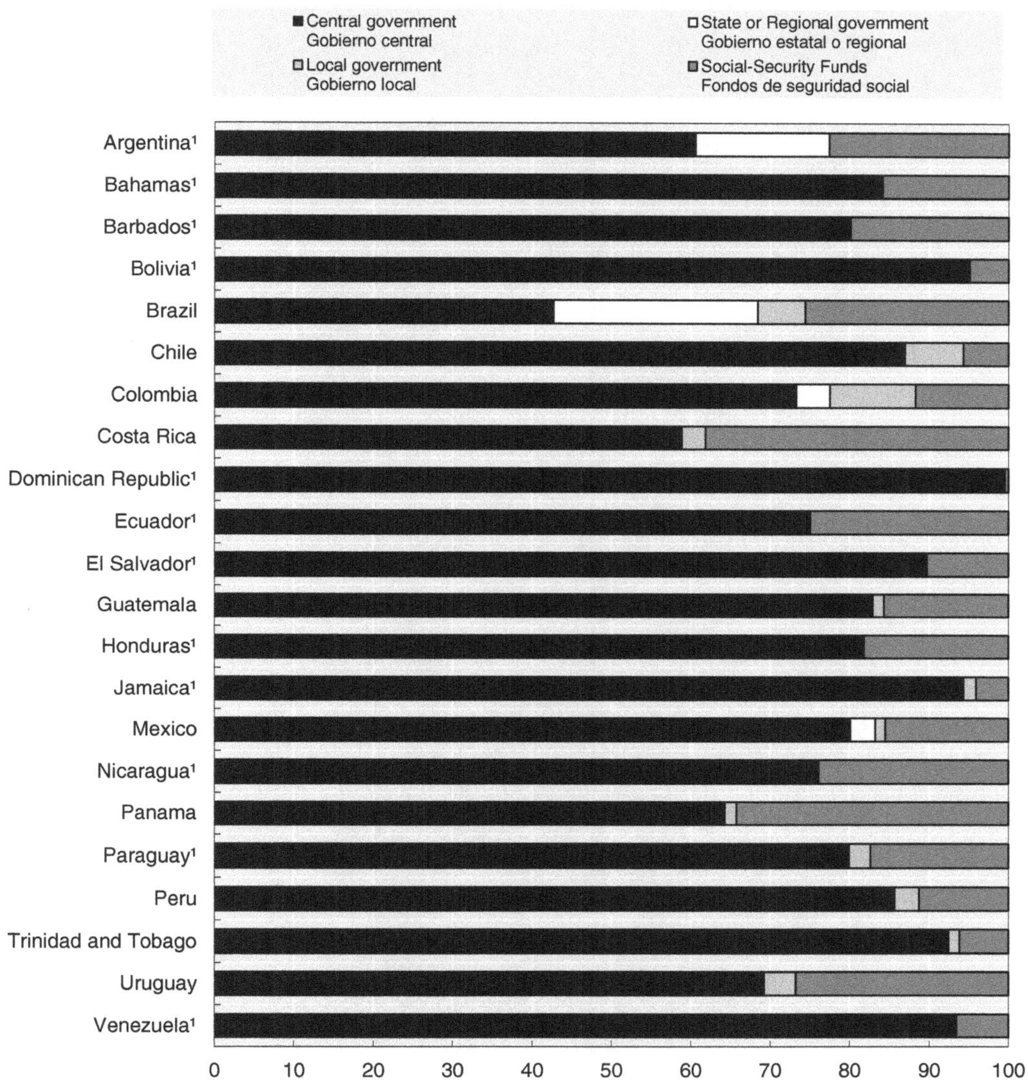

1. The figures exclude local government revenues for Argentina, Bahamas, Barbados, Bolivia, Dominican Republic, Ecuador, El Salvador, Honduras, Jamaica, Nicaragua, Paraguay and Venezuela as the data are not available.

1. Las cifras excluyen los ingresos de gobiernos locales en Argentina, Bahamas, Barbados, Bolivia, Ecuador, El Salvador, Honduras, Jamaica, Nicaragua, Paraguay, República Dominicana y Venezuela dado que los datos no están disponibles.

Source: Table 5.1 in Chapter 5/Cuadro 5.1 en Capítulo 5.

StatLink http://dx.doi.org/10.1787/888933337910

ANNEX A

The OECD Interpretative Guide

Table of contents

A.1. The OECD classification of taxes

1000 *Taxes on income, profits and capital gains*

- 1100 Individuals
  - 1110 Income and profits
  - 1120 Capital gains
- 1200 Corporates
  - 1210 Income and profits
  - 1220 Capital gains
- 1300 Unallocable as between 1100 and 1200

2000 *Social security contributions*

- 2100 Employees
  - 2110 On a payroll basis
  - 2120 On an income tax bas
- 2200 Employers
  - 2210 On a payroll basis
  - 2220 On an income tax basis
- 2300 Self-employed, non-employed
  - 2310 On a payroll basis
  - 2320 On an income tax basis
- 2400 Unallocable as between 2100, 2200 and 2300
  - 2410 On a payroll basis
  - 2420 On an income tax basis

3000 *Taxes on payroll and workforce*

4000 *Taxes on property*

- 4100 Recurrent taxes on immovable property
  - 4110 Households
  - 4120 Other
- 4200 Recurrent net wealth taxes
  - 4210 Individuals
  - 4220 Corporates
- 4300 Estate, inheritance and gift taxes
  - 4310 Estate and inheritance taxes
  - 4320 Gift taxes
- 4400 Taxes on financial and capital transactions

4500 Other non-recurrent taxes on property

4510 On net wealth

4520 Other non-recurrent taxes

4600 Other recurrent taxes on property

5000 *Taxes on goods and services*

5100 Taxes on production, sale and transfer of goods and services

5110 General sales taxes

5111 Value-added taxes

5112 Sales taxes

5113 Other general taxes

5120 Taxes on specific goods and services

5121 Excises

5122 Profits of fiscal monopolies

5123 Customs and import duties

5124 On exports

5125 On investment goods

5126 On specific services

5127 Other taxes on international trade and transactions

5128 Other taxes on specific goods and services

5130 Unallocable as between 5110 and 5120

5200 Taxes on use of goods, or on permission to use goods or perform activities

5210 Recurrent taxes

5211 Motor vehicles taxes households

5212 Motor vehicles taxes others

5213 Other recurrent taxes

5220 Non-recurrent taxes

5300 Unallocable as between 5100 and 5200

6000 *Other taxes*

6100 Paid solely by business

6200 Paid by other than business, or unidentifiable

The OECD Interpretative Guide[1]

A.2. Coverage

General criteria

1. In the OECD classification the term "taxes" is confined to compulsory unrequited payments to general government. Taxes are unrequited in the sense that benefits provided by government to taxpayers are not normally in proportion to their payments.

2. The term 'tax' does not include fines unrelated to tax offences and compulsory loans paid to government. Borderline cases between tax and non-tax revenues in relation to certain fees and charges are discussed in §9–13.

3. General government consists of the central administration, agencies whose operations are under its effective control, state and local governments and their administrations, certain social security schemes and autonomous governmental entities, excluding public enterprises. This definition of government follows that of the 2008 System of National Accounts (SNA).[2] In that publication, the general government sector and its sub-sectors are defined in chapter 4, section F, pages 80-84.

4. Compulsory payments to supra-national bodies and their agencies are no longer included as taxes as from 1998, with some exceptions. However, custom duties collected by EU member states on behalf of the European Union are still identified as memorandum items and included in overall tax revenue amounts in the country tables (Part III) of the country in which they are collected. (See §95). In countries where the church forms part of general government church taxes are included, provided they meet the criteria set out in §1 above. As the data refer to receipts of general government, levies paid to non-government bodies, welfare agencies or social insurance schemes outside general government, trade unions or trade associations, even where such levies are compulsory, are excluded. Compulsory payments to general government earmarked for such bodies are, however, included, provided that the government is not simply acting in an agency capacity.[3] Profits from fiscal monopolies are distinguished from those of other public enterprises and are treated as taxes because they reflect the exercise of the taxing power of the state by the use of monopoly powers (see §62–64), as are profits received by the government from the purchase and sale of foreign exchange at different rates (see §70).

5. Taxes paid by governments (e.g. social security contributions and payroll taxes paid by governments in their capacity as an employer, consumption taxes on their purchases or taxes on their property) are not excluded from the data provided. However, where it is possible to identify the amounts of revenue involved,[4] they are shown in section III.C of this Report.

6. The relationship between this classification and that of the System of National Accounts (SNA) is set out in Sections A.9 and A.11 below. Because of the differences between the two classifications, the data shown in national accounts are sometimes calculated or classified differently from the practice set out in this guide. These and other differences are mentioned where appropriate (e.g. in §13 and §26 below) but it is not possible to refer to all of them. There may also be some differences between this classification and that employed domestically by certain national administrations (e.g. see §10 below), so that OECD and national statistics data may not always be consistent: any such differences, however, are likely to be very slight in terms of amounts of revenues involved.

Social security contributions

7. Compulsory social security contributions, as defined in §35 below, paid to general government, are treated here as tax revenues. Being compulsory payments to general government they clearly resemble taxes. They may, however, differ from other taxes in that the receipt of social security benefits depends, in most countries, upon appropriate contributions having been made, although the size of the benefits is not necessarily related to the amount of the contributions. Better comparability between countries is obtained by treating social security contributions as taxes, but they are listed under a separate heading so that they can be distinguished in any analysis.

8. Social security contributions which are either voluntary or not payable to general government (see §1) are not treated as taxes, though in some countries, as indicated in the country footnotes, there are difficulties in eliminating voluntary contributions and certain compulsory payments to the private sector.

Fees, user charges and licence fees

9. Apart from vehicle licence fees, which are universally regarded as taxes, it is not easy to distinguish between those fees and user charges which are to be treated as taxes and those which are not, since, whilst a fee or charge is levied in connection with a specific service or activity, the strength of the link between the fee and the service provided may vary considerably, as may the relation between the amount of the fee and the cost of providing the service. Where the recipient of a service pays a fee clearly related to the cost of providing the service, the levy may be regarded as requited and under the definition of §1 would not be considered as a tax. In the following cases, however, a levy could be considered as 'unrequited':

a) where the charge greatly exceeds the cost of providing the service;

b) where the payer of the levy is not the receiver of the benefit (e.g. a fee collected from slaughterhouses to finance a service which is provided to farmers);

c) where government is not providing a specific service in return for the levy which it receives even though a licence may be issued to the payer (e.g. where the government grants a hunting, fishing or shooting licence which is not accompanied by the right to use a specific area of government land);

d) where benefits are received only by those paying the levy but the benefits received by each individual are not necessarily in proportion to his payments (e.g. a milk marketing levy paid by dairy farmers and used to promote the consumption of milk).

10. In marginal cases, however, the application of the criteria set out in §1 can be particularly difficult. The solution adopted – given the desirability of international uniformity and the relatively small amounts of revenue usually involved – is to follow the predominant practice among tax administrations rather than to allow each country to adopt its own view as to whether such levies are regarded as taxes or as non-tax revenue.[5]

11. A list of the main fees and charges in question and their normal[6] treatment in this publication is as follows:

Non-tax revenues:	court fees; driving licence fees; harbour fees; passport fees; radio and television licence fees where public authorities provide the service.
Taxes within heading 5200:	permission to perform such activities as distributing films; hunting, fishing and shooting; providing entertainment or gambling facilities; selling alcohol or tobacco; permission to own dogs or to use or own motor vehicles or guns; severance taxes.

12. In practice it may not always be possible to isolate tax receipts from non-tax revenue receipts when they are recorded together. If it is estimated that the bulk of the receipts derive from non-tax revenues, the whole amount involved is treated as a non-tax revenue; otherwise, such government receipts are included and classified according to the rules provided in §28 below.

13. Two differences between the OECD classification and SNA regarding the borderline between tax and non-tax revenues are:

a) SNA classifies a number of levies as indirect taxes if paid by enterprises, but as non-tax revenues if paid by households, a distinction which is regarded as irrelevant in this classification for distinguishing between tax and non-tax revenues.[7]

b) Predominant practice among most OECD tax administrations, which is occasionally used in this classification for distinguishing between tax and non-tax revenues, is not a relevant criterion for SNA purposes.

Royalties

14. Royalty payments for the right to extract oil and gas or to exploit other mineral resources are normally regarded as non-tax revenues since they are property income from government-owned land or resources.

Fines and penalties

15. Receipts from fines and penalties paid for infringement of regulations identified as relating to a particular tax and interest on payments overdue in respect of a particular tax are recorded together with receipts from that tax. Other kinds of fines identifiable as relating to tax offences are classified in the residual heading 6000. Fines not relating to tax offences (e.g. for parking offences), or not identifiable as relating to tax offences, are not treated as taxes.

A.3. Basis of reporting

Accrual reporting

16. The data reported in this publication for recent years are predominantly recorded on an accrual basis, i.e. recorded at the time that the tax liability was created. Further information is provided in the footnotes to the country table in Part III of the Report.

17. However, data for earlier years are still predominantly recorded on a cash basis, i.e. at the time at which the payment was received by government. Thus, for example, taxes withheld by employers in one year but paid to the government in the following year and taxes due in one year but actually paid in the following year are both included in the receipts of the second year. Corrective transactions, such as refunds, repayments and drawbacks, are deducted from gross revenues of the period in which they are made.

18. Data on tax revenues are recorded without offsets for the administrative expenses connected with tax collection. Similarly, where the proceeds of tax are used to subsidise particular members of the community, the subsidy is not deducted from the yield of the tax, though the tax may be shown net of subsidies in the national records of some countries.

19. As regards fiscal monopolies (heading 5122), only the amount actually transferred to the government is included in government revenues. However, if any expenditures of fiscal monopolies are considered to be government expenditures (e.g. social expenditures undertaken by fiscal monopolies at the direction of the government) they are added back for the purpose of arriving at tax revenue figures (see §62 below).

The distinction between tax and expenditure provisions[8]

20. Because this publication is concerned only with the revenue side of government operations, no account being taken of the expenditure side, a distinction has to be made between tax and expenditure provisions. Normally there is no difficulty in making this distinction as expenditures are made outside the tax system and the tax accounts and under legislation separate from the tax legislation. In borderline cases, cash flow is used to distinguish between tax provisions and expenditure provisions. Insofar as a provision affects the flow of tax payments from the taxpayer to the government, it is regarded as a tax provision and is taken into account in the data shown in this publication. A provision which does not affect this flow is seen as an expenditure provision and is disregarded in the data recorded in this publication.

21. Tax allowances, exemptions and deductions against the tax base clearly affect the amount of tax paid to the government and are therefore considered as tax provisions. At the other extreme, those subsidies which cannot be offset against tax liability and which are clearly not connected with the assessment process, do not reduce tax revenues as recorded in this publication. Tax credits are amounts deductible from tax payable (as distinct from deductions from the tax base). Two types of tax credits are distinguished, those (referred to here as wastable tax credits) which are limited to the amount of the tax liability and therefore cannot give rise to a payment by the authorities to the taxpayer, and those (referred to as non-wastable tax credits) which are not so limited, so that the excess of the credit over the tax liability can be paid to the taxpayer.[9] A wastable tax credit, like a tax allowance, clearly affects the amount of tax paid to the government, and is therefore considered as a tax provision. The practice followed for non-wastable tax credits[10] is to distinguish between the "tax expenditure component",[11] which is that portion of the credit that is used to reduce or eliminate a taxpayer's liability, and the 'transfer component', which is the portion that exceeds the taxpayer's liability and is paid to that taxpayer. Reported tax revenues should be reduced by the amount of the tax expenditure component but not by the amount of the transfer component. In addition, the amounts of the tax expenditure and transfer components should be reported as memorandum items in the country tables. Countries that are unable to distinguish between the tax expenditure and transfer components should indicate whether or not the tax revenues have been reduced by the total of these components, and provide any available estimates of the amounts of the two components. Further information is given in section C of Part I of the Report, which illustrates the effect of alternative treatments of non-wastable tax credits on Tax to GDP.

Calendar and fiscal years

22. National authorities whose fiscal years do not correspond to the calendar year show data, where possible, on a calendar year basis to permit maximum comparability with the data of other countries. There remain a few countries where data refer to fiscal years. For these the GDP data used in the comparative tables also correspond to the fiscal years.

A.4. General classification criteria

The main classification criteria

23. The classification of receipts among the main headings (1000, 2000, 3000, 4000, 5000 and 6000) is generally governed by the base on which the tax is levied: 1000 income, profits and capital gains; 2000 and 3000 earnings, payroll or number of employees; 4000 property; 5000 goods and services; 6000 multiple bases, other bases or unidentifiable bases. Where a tax is calculated on more than one base, the receipts are, where possible, split among the various headings (see §28 and §78). The headings 4000 and 5000 cover

not only taxes where the tax base is the property, goods or services themselves but also certain related taxes. Thus, taxes on the transfer of property are included in 4400[12] and taxes on the use of goods or on permission to perform activities in 5200. In headings 4000 and 5000 a distinction is made in certain sub-headings between recurrent and non-recurrent taxes: recurrent taxes are defined as those levied at regular intervals (usually annually) and non-recurrent taxes are levied once and for all (see also §43 to §46, §49, §50 and §76 for particular applications of this distinction).

24. Earmarking of a tax for specific purposes does not affect the classification of tax receipts. However, as explained in §35 on the classification of social security contributions, the conferment of an entitlement to social benefits is crucial to the definition of the 2000 main heading.

25. The way that a tax is levied or collected (e.g. by use of stamps) does not affect classification.

Classification of taxpayers

26. In certain sub-headings distinctions are made between different categories of taxpayers. These distinctions vary from tax to tax:

a) Between individuals and corporations in relation to income and net wealth taxes

The basic distinction is that corporation income taxes, as distinct from individual income taxes, are levied on the corporation as an entity, not on the individuals who own it, and without regard to the personal circumstances of these individuals. The same distinction applies to net wealth taxes on corporations and those on individuals. Taxes paid on the profits of partnerships and the income of institutions, such as life insurance or pension funds, are classified according to the same rule. They are classified as corporate taxes (1200) if they are charged on the partnership or institution as an entity without regard to the personal circumstances of the owners. Otherwise, they are treated as individual taxes (1100). Usually, there is different legislation for the corporation taxes and for the individual taxes.[13] The distinction made here between individuals and corporations does not follow the sector classification between households, enterprises, and so on of the System of National Accounts for income and outlay accounts. The SNA classification requires certain unincorporated businesses[14] to be excluded from the household sector and included with non-financial enterprises and financial institutions. The tax on the profits of these businesses, however, cannot always be separated from the tax on the other income of their owners, or can be separated only on an arbitrary basis. No attempt at this separation is made here and the whole of the individual income tax is shown together without regard to the nature of the income chargeable.

b) Between households and others in relation to taxes on immovable property

Here the distinction is that adopted by the SNA for the production and consumption expenditure accounts. The distinction is between households as consumers (i.e. excluding non-incorporated business) on the one hand and producers on the other hand. However, taxes on dwellings occupied by households, whether paid by owner-occupiers, tenants or landlords, are classified under households. This follows the common distinction made between taxes on domestic property versus taxes on business property. Some countries are not, however, in a position to make this distinction.

c) Between households and others in relation to motor vehicle licences

Here the distinction is between households as consumers on the one hand and producers on the other, as in the production and consumption expenditure accounts of the SNA.

d) Between business and others in relation to the residual taxes (6000)

The distinction is the same as in c) above between producers on the one hand and households as consumers on the other hand. Taxes which are included under the heading 6000 because they involve more than one tax base or because the tax base does not fall within any of the previous categories but which are identifiable as levyable only on producers and not on households are included under "business". The rest of the taxes which are included under the heading 6000 are shown as "other" or non-identified.

Surcharges

27. Receipts from surcharges in respect of particular taxes are usually classified with the receipts from the relevant tax whether or not the surcharge is temporary. If, however, the surcharge has a characteristic which would render it classifiable in a different heading of the OECD list, receipts from the surcharge are classified under that heading separately from the relevant tax.

Unidentifiable tax receipts and residual sub-headings

28. A number of cases arise where taxes cannot be identified as belonging entirely to a heading or sub-heading of the OECD classification and the following practices are applied in such cases:

a) The heading is known, but it is not known how receipts should be allocated between sub-headings: receipts are classified in the appropriate residual sub-heading (1300, 2400, 4520, 4600, 5130, 5300 or 6200).

b) It is known that the bulk of receipts from a group of taxes (usually local taxes) is derived from taxes within a particular heading or sub-heading, but some of the taxes in the group whose amount cannot be precisely ascertained may be classifiable in other headings or sub-headings: receipts are shown in the heading or sub-heading under which most of the receipts fall.

c) Neither the heading nor sub-heading of a tax (usually local) can be identified: the tax is classified in 6200 unless it is known that it is a tax on business in which case it is classified in 6100.

A.5. Commentaries on items of the list

1000 – *Taxes on income, profits and capital gains*

29. This heading covers taxes levied on the net income or profits (i.e. gross income minus allowable tax reliefs) of individuals and enterprises. Also covered are taxes levied on the capital gains of individuals and enterprises, and gains from gambling.

30. Included in the heading are:

a) taxes levied predominantly on income or profits, though partially on other bases. Taxes on various bases which are not predominantly income or profits are classified according to the principles laid down in §28 and §78;

b) taxes on property, which are levied on a presumed or estimated income as part of an income tax (see also §43(a), (c) and (d));

c) compulsory payments to social security fund contributions that are levied on income but do not confer an entitlement to social benefits. When such contributions do confer an entitlement to social benefits, they are included in heading 2000 (see §35);

d) receipts from integrated scheduler income tax systems are classified as a whole in this heading, even though certain of the scheduler taxes may be based upon gross income and may not take into account the personal circumstances of the taxpayer.

31. The main subdivision of this heading is between levies on individuals (1100) and those on corporate enterprises (1200). Under each subdivision a distinction is made between taxes on income and profits (1110 and 1210), and taxes on capital gains (1120 and 1220). If certain receipts cannot be identified as appropriate to either 1100 or 1200, or if in practice this distinction cannot be made (e.g., because there are no reliable data on the recipients of payments from which withholding taxes are deducted) they are classified in 1300 as not-allocable.

Treatment of credits under imputation systems

32. Under imputation systems of corporate income tax, a company's shareholders are wholly or partly relieved of their liability to income tax on dividends paid by the company out of income or profits liable to corporate income tax. In countries with such systems,[15] part of the tax on the company's profits is available to provide relief against the shareholders' own tax liability. The relief to the shareholder takes the form of a tax credit, the amount of which may be less than, equal to, or more than the shareholder's overall tax liability. If the tax credit exceeds this tax liability the excess may be payable to the shareholder. As this type of tax credit is an integral part of the imputation system of corporate income tax, any payment to the shareholders is treated as a repayment of tax and not as expenditure (compare the treatment of other tax credits described in §21).

33. As the tax credit under imputation systems (even when exceeding tax liability) is to be regarded as a tax provision, the question arises whether it should be deducted from individual income tax receipts (1110) or corporate income tax receipts (1210). In this Report, the full amount of corporate income tax paid is shown under 1210 and no imputed tax is included under 1110. Thus, the full amount of the credit reduces the amount of 1110 whether the credit results in a reduction of personal income tax liability or whether an actual refund is made because the credit exceeds the income tax liability. (Where, however, such tax credits are deducted from corporation tax in respect of dividends paid to corporations the amounts are deducted from the receipts of 1210.)

1120 and 1220 – *Taxes on capital gains*

34. These sub-headings comprise taxes imposed on capital gains, 1120 covering those levied on the gains of individuals and 1220 those levied on the gains of corporate enterprises, where receipts from such taxes can be separately identified. In many countries this is not the case and the receipts from such taxes are then classified with those from the income tax. Heading 1120 also includes taxes on gains from gambling.

2000 – *Social security contributions*

35. Classified here are all compulsory payments that confer an entitlement to receive a (contingent) future social benefit. Such payments are usually earmarked to finance social benefits and are often paid to institutions of general government that provide such benefits. However, such earmarking is not part of the definition of social security contributions and is not required for a tax to be classified here. However, conferment of an entitlement is required for a tax to be classified under this heading. So, levies on income or payroll that are earmarked for social security funds but do not confer an entitlement to benefit are excluded from this heading and shown under personal income taxes (1100) or taxes on payroll and workforce (3000). Taxes on other bases, such as goods and services, which are earmarked for social security benefits are not shown

here but are classified according to their respective bases because they generally confer no entitlement to social security benefits.

36. Contributions for the following types of social security benefits would, *inter alia*, be included: unemployment insurance benefits and supplements, accident, injury and sickness benefits, old-age, disability and survivors' pensions, family allowances, reimbursements for medical and hospital expenses or provision of hospital or medical services. Contributions may be levied on both employees and employers.

37. Contributions may be based on earnings or payroll ("on a payroll basis") or on net income after deductions and exemptions for personal circumstances ("on an income tax basis"), and the revenues from the two bases should be separately identified if possible. However, where contributions to a general social security scheme are on a payroll basis, but the contributions of particular groups (such as the self-employed) cannot be assessed on this basis and net income is used as a proxy for gross earnings, the receipts may still be classified as being on a payroll basis. In principle, this heading excludes voluntary contributions paid to social security schemes. When separately identifiable these are shown in the memorandum item on the financing of social security benefits. In practice, however, they cannot always be separately identified from compulsory contributions, in which case they are included in this heading.

38. Contributions to social insurance schemes which are not institutions of general government and to other types of insurance schemes, provident funds, pension funds, friendly societies or other saving schemes are not considered as social security contributions. Provident funds are arrangements under which the contributions of each employee and of the corresponding employer on his/her behalf are kept in a separate account earning interest and withdrawable under specific circumstances. Pension funds are separately organised schemes negotiated between employees and employers and carry provisions for different contributions and benefits, sometimes more directly tied to salary levels and length of service than under social security schemes. When contributions to these schemes are compulsory or quasi-compulsory (e.g. by virtue of agreement with professional and union organisations) they are shown in the memorandum item (refer to Section III.B of the Report).

39. Contributions by government employees and by governments in respect of their employees, to social security schemes classified within general government are included in this heading. Contributions to separate schemes for government employees, which can be regarded as replacing general social security schemes, are also regarded as taxes.[16] Where, however, a separate scheme is not seen as replacing a general scheme and has been negotiated between the government, in its role as an employer, and its employees, it is not regarded as social security and contributions to it are not regarded as taxes, even though the scheme may have been established by legislation.

40. This heading excludes 'imputed' contributions, which correspond to social benefits paid directly by employers to their employees or former employees or to their representatives (e.g. when employers are legally obliged to pay sickness benefits for a certain period).

41. Contributions are divided into those of employees (2100), employers (2200), and self-employed or non-employed (2300), and then further sub-divided according to the basis on which they are levied. Employees are defined for this purpose as all persons engaged in activities of business units, government bodies, private non-profit institutions, or other paid employment, except the proprietors and their unpaid family members in the case of unincorporated businesses. Members of the armed forces are included, irrespective of the duration and type of their service, if they contribute to social security schemes. The

contributions of employers are defined as their payments on account of their employees to social security schemes. Where employees or employers are required to continue the payment of social security contributions when the employee becomes unemployed these contributions, data permitting, are shown in 2100 and 2200 respectively. Accordingly, the sub-heading 2300 is confined to contributions paid by the self-employed and by those outside of the labour force (e.g. disabled or retired individuals).

3000 – *Taxes on payroll and workforce*

42. This heading covers taxes paid by employers, employees or the self-employed either as a proportion of payroll or as a fixed amount per person, and which do not confer entitlement to social benefits. Examples of taxes classified here are the United Kingdom national insurance surcharge (introduced in 1977), the Swedish payroll tax (1969–1979), and the Austrian Contribution to the Family Burden Equalisation Fund and Community Tax.

4000 – *Taxes on property*

43. This heading covers recurrent and non-recurrent taxes on the use, ownership or transfer of property. These include taxes on immovable property or net wealth, taxes on the change of ownership of property through inheritance or gift and taxes on financial and capital transactions. The following kinds of tax are excluded from this heading:

a) taxes on capital gains resulting from the sale of a property (1120 or 1220);

b) taxes on the use of goods or on permission to use goods or perform activities (5200); see §73;

c) taxes on immovable property levied on the basis of a presumed net income which take into account the personal circumstances of the taxpayer. They are classified as income taxes along with taxes on income and capital gains derived from property (1100);

d) taxes on the use of property for residence, where the tax is payable by either proprietor or tenant and the amount payable is a function of the user's personal circumstances (pay, dependants, and so on). They are classified as taxes on income (1100);

e) taxes on building in excess of permitted maximum density, taxes on the enlargement, construction or alteration of certain buildings beyond a permitted value and taxes on building construction. They are classified as taxes on permission to perform activities (5200);

f) taxes on the use of one's own property for special trading purposes like selling alcohol, tobacco, meat or for exploitation of land resources (e.g. United States severance taxes). They are classified as taxes on permission to perform activities (5200).

4100 – *Recurrent taxes on immovable property*

44. This sub-heading covers taxes levied regularly in respect of the use or ownership of immovable property.

- these taxes are levied on land and buildings;
- they can be in the form of a percentage of an assessed property value based on a national rental income, sales price, or capitalised yield; or in terms of other characteristics of real property, (for example size or location) from which a presumed rent or capital value can be derived.

- such taxes can be levied on proprietors, tenants, or both. They can also be paid by one level of government to another level of government in respect of property under the jurisdiction of the latter.
- debts are not taken into account in the assessment of these taxes, and they differ from taxes on net wealth in this respect.

45. Taxes on immovable property are further sub-divided into those paid by households (4110) and those paid by other entities (4120), according to the criteria set out in §26(b) above.

4200 – *Recurrent taxes on net wealth*

46. This sub-heading covers taxes levied regularly (in most cases annually) on net wealth, i.e. taxes on a wide range of movable and immovable property, net of debt. It is sub-divided into taxes paid by individuals (4210) and taxes paid by corporate enterprises (4220) according to the criteria set out in §26(a) above. If separate figures exist for receipts paid by institutions, the tax payments involved are added to those paid by corporations.

4300 – *Estate, inheritance and gift taxes*

47. This sub-heading is divided into taxes on estates and inheritances (4310) and taxes on gifts (4320).[17] Estate taxes are charged on the amount of the total estate whereas inheritance taxes are charged on the shares of the individual recipients; in addition the latter may take into account the relationship of the individual recipients to the deceased.

4400 – *Taxes on financial and capital transactions*

48. This sub-heading comprises, inter alia, taxes on the issue, transfer, purchase and sale of securities, taxes on cheques, and taxes levied on specific legal transactions such as validation of contracts and the sale of immovable property. The heading does not include:

a) taxes on the use of goods or property or permission to perform certain activities (5200);

b) fees paid to cover court charges, charges for birth, marriage or death certificates, which are normally regarded as non-tax revenues (see §9);

c) taxes on capital gains (1000);

d) recurrent taxes on immovable property (4100);

e) recurrent taxes on net wealth (4200);

f) once-and-for-all levies on property or wealth (4500).

4500 – *Other non-recurrent taxes on property*[17]

49. This sub-heading covers once-and-for-all, as distinct from recurrent, levies on property. It is divided into taxes on net wealth (4510) and other non-recurrent taxes on property (4520). Heading 4510 would include taxes levied to meet emergency expenditures, or for redistribution purposes. Heading 4520 would cover taxes levied to take account of increases in land value due to permission given to develop or provision of additional local facilities by general government, any taxes on the revaluation of capital and once-and-for-all taxes on particular items of property.

4600 – *Other recurrent taxes on property*

50. These rarely exist in OECD member countries, but the heading would include taxes on goods such as cattle, jewellery, windows, and other external signs of wealth.

5000 – *Taxes on goods and services*

51. All taxes and duties levied on the production, extraction, sale, transfer, leasing or delivery of goods, and the rendering of services (5100), or in respect of the use of goods or permission to use goods or to perform activities (5200) are included here. The heading thus covers:

a) multi-stage cumulative taxes;

b) general sales taxes – whether levied at manufacture/production, wholesale or retail level;

c) value-added taxes;

d) excises;

e) taxes levied on the import and export of goods;

f) taxes levied in respect of the use of goods and taxes on permission to use goods, or perform certain activities;

g) taxes on the extraction, processing or production of minerals and other products.

52. Borderline cases between this heading and heading 4000 (taxes on property) and 6100 (other taxes on business) are referred to in §43, §48 and §75. Residual sub-headings (5300) and (5130) cover tax receipts which cannot be allocated between 5100 and 5200 and between 5110 and 5120, respectively; see §28.

5100 – *Taxes on the production, sale, transfer, leasing and delivery of goods and rendering of services*

53. This sub-heading consists of all taxes, levied on transactions in goods and services on the basis of their intrinsic characteristics (e.g. value, weight of tobacco, strength of alcohol, and so on) as distinct from taxes imposed on the use of goods, or permission to use goods or perform activities, which fall under 5200.

5110 – *General taxes on goods and services*

54. This sub-heading includes all taxes, other than import and export duties (5123 and 5124), levied on the production, leasing, transfer, delivery or sales of a wide range of goods and/or the rendering of a wide range of services, irrespective of whether they are domestically produced or imported and irrespective of the stage of production or distribution at which they are levied. It thus covers value-added taxes, sales taxes and multi-stage cumulative taxes. Receipts from border adjustments in respect of such taxes when goods are imported are added to gross receipts for this category, and repayments of such taxes when goods are exported are deducted. These taxes are subdivided into 5111 value-added taxes, 5112 sales taxes, 5113 other general taxes on goods and services.

55. Borderline cases arise between this heading and taxes on specific goods (5120) when taxes are levied on a large number of goods, for example, the United Kingdom purchase tax (repealed in 1973) and the Japanese commodity tax (repealed in 1988). In conformity with national views, the former United Kingdom purchase tax is classified as a general tax (5112) and the former Japanese commodity tax as excises (5121).

5111 – *Value-added taxes*

56. All general consumption taxes charged on value-added are classified in this sub-heading, irrespective of the method of deduction and the stages at which the taxes are levied. In practice, all OECD countries with value-added taxes normally allow immediate deduction of taxes on purchases by all but the final consumer and impose

tax at all stages. In some countries the heading may include certain taxes, such as those on financial and insurance activities, either because receipts from them cannot be identified separately from those from the value-added tax, or because they are regarded as an integral part of the value-added tax, even though similar taxes in other countries might be classified elsewhere (e.g. 5126 as taxes on services or 4400 as taxes on financial and capital transactions).

5112 – *Sales taxes*

57. All general taxes levied at one stage only, whether at manufacturing or production, wholesale or retail stage are classified here.

5113 – *Other general taxes on goods and services*

58. This sub-heading covers multi-stage cumulative taxes (also know as 'cascade taxes') where tax is levied each time a transaction takes place without deduction for tax paid on inputs, and also those general consumption taxes where elements of value-added, sales or cascade taxes are combined.

5120 – *Taxes on specific goods and services*

59. Excises, profits generated and transferred from fiscal monopolies, and customs and imports duties as well as taxes on exports, foreign exchange transactions, investment goods and betting stakes and special taxes on services, which do not form part of a general tax of 5110, are included in this category.

5121 – *Excises*

60. Excises are taxes levied on particular products, or on a limited range of products, which are not classifiable under 5110 (general taxes), 5123 (import duties) and 5124 (export duties). They may be imposed at any stage of production or distribution and are usually assessed by reference to the weight or strength or quantity of the product, but sometimes by reference to value. Thus, special taxes on, for example, sugar, beetroot, matches, chocolates, and taxes at varying rates on a certain range of goods, as well as those levied in most countries on tobacco goods, alcoholic drinks and hydrocarbon oils and other energy sources, are included in this sub-heading.

61. Excises are distinguished from:

a) 5110 (general taxes). This is discussed in §54-55;

b) 5123 (import duties). If a tax collected principally on imported goods also applies, or would apply, under the law by which the tax is imposed to comparable home-produced goods, the receipts there from would be classified as excises (5121). This principle applies even if there is no comparable home production or no possibility of it (see also §65);

c) 5126 (taxes on services). The problem here arises in respect of taxes on electricity, gas and energy. All of these are regarded as taxes on goods and are included under 5121.

5122 – *Profits of fiscal monopolies*

62. This sub-heading covers that part of the profits of fiscal monopolies which is transferred to general government or which is used to finance any expenditures considered to be government expenditures (see §19). Amounts are shown when they are transferred to general government or used to make expenditures considered to be government expenditures

63. Fiscal monopolies reflect the exercise of the taxing power of government by the use of monopoly powers. Fiscal monopolies are non-financial public enterprises exercising a monopoly in most cases over the production or distribution of tobacco,

alcoholic beverages, salt, matches, playing cards and petroleum or agricultural products (i.e. on the kind of products which are likely to be, alternatively or additionally, subject to the excises of 5121), to raise the government revenues which in other countries are gathered through taxes on dealings in such commodities by private business units. The government monopoly may be at the production stage or, as in the case of government-owned and controlled liquor stores, at the distribution stage.

64. Fiscal monopolies are distinguished from public utilities such as rail transport, electricity, post offices, and other communications, which may enjoy a monopoly or quasi-monopoly position but where the primary purpose is normally to provide basic services rather than to raise revenue for government. Transfers from such other public enterprises to the government are considered as non-tax revenues. The traditional concept of fiscal monopoly has not been extended to include state lotteries, the profits of which are accordingly regarded as non-tax revenues. Fiscal monopoly profits are distinguished from export and import monopoly profits (5127) transferred from marketing boards or other enterprises dealing with international trade.

5123 – *Customs and other import duties*

65. Taxes, stamp duties and surcharges restricted by law to imported products are included here. Also included are levies on imported agricultural products which are imposed in member countries of the European Union and amounts paid by certain of these countries under the Monetary Compensation Accounts (MCA) system.[18] Starting from 1998, customs duties collected by European Union member states on behalf of the European Union are no longer reported under this heading in the country tables (in Part III of the Report). Excluded here are taxes collected on imports as part of a general tax on goods and services, or an excise applicable to both imported and domestically produced goods.

5124 – *Taxes on exports*

66. In the 1970s, export duties were levied in Australia, Canada and Portugal as a regular measure and they have been used in Finland for counter-cyclical purposes. Some member countries of the European Union pay, as part of the MCA system, a levy on exports (see note 18 to §65). Where these amounts are identifiable, they are shown in this heading. This heading does not include repayments of general consumption taxes or excises or customs duties on exported goods, which should be deducted from the gross receipts under 5110, 5121 or 5123, as appropriate.

5125 – *Taxes on investment goods*

67. This sub-heading covers taxes on investment goods, such as machinery. These taxes may be imposed for a number of years or temporarily for counter-cyclical purposes. Taxes on industrial inputs which are also levied on consumers [e.g., the Swedish energy tax which is classified under (5121)] are not included here.

5126 – *Taxes on specific services*

68. All taxes assessed on the payment for specific services, such as taxes on insurance premiums, banking services, gambling and betting stakes (e.g., from horse races, football pools, lottery tickets), transport, entertainment, restaurant and advertising charges, fall into this category. Taxes levied on the gross income of companies providing the service (e.g. gross insurance premiums or gambling stakes received by the company) are also classified under this heading. Tax revenues from bank levies and payments to deposit insurance and financial stability schemes are provisionally included here for the 2012 edition. The detailed classification is set out in paragraph 105.

69. Excluded from this sub-heading are:

a) taxes on services forming part of a general tax on goods and services (5110);

b) taxes on electricity, gas and energy (5121 as excises);

c) taxes on individual gains from gambling (1120 as taxes on capital gains of individuals and non-corporate enterprises) and lump-sum taxes on the transfer of private lotteries or on the permission to set up lotteries (5200);[19]

d) taxes on cheques and on the issue, transfer or redemption of securities (4400 as taxes on financial and capital transactions).

5127 – *Other taxes on international trade and transactions*

70. This sub-heading covers revenue received by the government from the purchase and sale of foreign exchange at different rates. When the government exercises monopoly powers to extract a margin between the purchase and sales price of foreign exchange, other than to cover administrative costs, the revenue derived constitutes a compulsory levy exacted in indeterminate proportions from both purchaser and seller of foreign exchange. It is the common equivalent of an import duty and export duty levied in a single exchange rate system or of a tax on the sale or purchase of foreign exchange. Like the profits of fiscal monopolies and import or export monopolies transferred to government, it represents the exercise of monopoly powers for tax purposes and is included in tax revenues.

71. The sub-heading covers also the profits of export or import monopolies, which do not however exist in OECD countries, taxes on purchase or sale of foreign exchange, and any other taxes levied specifically on international trade or transactions.

5128 – *Other taxes on specific goods and services*

72. This item includes taxes on the extraction of minerals, fossil fuels and other exhaustible resources from deposits owned privately or by another government together with any other unidentifiable receipts from taxes on specific goods and services. Taxes on the extraction of exhaustible resources are usually a fixed amount per unit of quality or weight, but can be a percentage of value. The taxes are recorded when the resources are extracted. Payments from the extraction of exhaustible resources from deposits owned by the government unit receiving the payment are classified as rent.

5200 – *Taxes on use of goods or on permission to use goods or perform activities*

73. This sub-heading covers taxes which are levied in respect of the use of goods as distinct from taxes on the goods themselves. Unlike the latter taxes – reported under 5100 –, they are not assessed on the value of the goods but usually as fixed amounts. Taxes on permission to use goods or to perform activities are also included here, as are pollution taxes not based upon the value of particular goods. It is sometimes difficult to distinguish between compulsory user charges and licence fees which are regarded as taxes and those which are excluded as non-tax revenues. The criteria which are employed are noted in §9–10.

74. Although the sub-heading refers to the 'use' of goods, registration of ownership rather than use may be what generates liability to tax, so that the taxes of this heading may apply to the ownership of animals or goods rather than their use (e.g. race horses, dogs and motor vehicles) and may apply even to unusable goods (e.g. unusable motor vehicles or guns).

75. Borderline cases arise with:

a) taxes on the permission to perform business activities which are levied on a combined income, payroll or turnover base and, accordingly, are classified following the rules in §78;

b) taxes on the ownership or use of property of headings 4100, 4200 and 4600. The heading 4100 is confined to taxes on the ownership or tenancy of immovable property and – unlike the taxes of 5200 – they are related to the value of the property. The net wealth taxes and taxes on chattels of 4200 and 4600 respectively are confined to the ownership rather than the use of assets, apply to groups of assets rather than particular goods and again are related to the value of the assets.

5210 – *Recurrent taxes on use of goods and on permission to use goods or perform activities*

76. The principal characteristic of taxes classified here is that they are levied at regular intervals and that they are usually fixed amounts. The most important item in terms of revenue receipts is vehicle licence taxes. This sub-heading also covers taxes on permission to hunt, shoot, fish or to sell certain products and taxes on the ownership of dogs and on the performance of certain services, provided that they meet the criteria set out in §9–10. The sub-divisions of 5210 are user taxes on motor vehicles paid by households (5211) and those paid by others (5212).[20] Sub-heading 5213 covers dog licences and user charges for permission to perform activities such as selling meat or liquor when the levies are on a recurring basis. It also covers recurrent general licences for hunting, shooting and fishing where the right to carry out these activities is not granted as part of a normal commercial transaction (e.g. the granting of the licence is not accompanied by the right to use a specific area which is owned by government).

5220 – *Non-recurrent taxes on use of goods and on permission to use goods or perform activities*

77. This section covers non-recurrent taxes levied on the use of goods or on permission to use goods or perform activities and taxes levied each time goods are used. It includes taxes levied on the emission or discharge into the environment of noxious gases, liquids or other harmful substances.

- Payments for tradable emission permits issued by governments under cap and trade schemes should be recorded here at the time the emissions occur. No revenue should be recorded for permits that governments issue free of charge. The accrual basis of recording means that there can be a timing difference between the cash being received by government for the permits and the time the emission occurs. In the national accounts, this timing gives rise to a financial liability for government during the period.
- Payments made for the collection and disposal of waste or noxious substances by public authorities should be excluded as they constitute a sale of services to enterprises.

78. Other taxes falling under heading 5200 that are not levied recurrently are also included here. Thus, once-and-for-all payments for permission to sell liquor or tobacco or to set up betting shops are included provided they meet the criteria set out in §9–10.

6000 – *Other taxes*

79. Taxes levied on a base, or bases, other than those described under headings 1000, 3000, 4000 and 5000, or on bases of which none could be regarded as being predominantly the same as that of any one of these headings, are covered here. As regards taxes levied on a multiple base, if it is possible to estimate receipts related to each base (e.g. the Austrian and German 'Gewerbesteuer') this is done and the separate amounts included under the appropriate headings. If the separate amounts cannot be estimated, but it is known that most of the receipts are derived from one base, the whole of the receipts are classified according to that base. If neither of these procedures can be followed, they are classified here. The sub-headings may also include receipts from taxes which

governments are unable to identify or isolate (see §28). Included here also are fines and penalties paid for infringement of regulations relating to taxes but not identifiable as relating to a particular category of taxes (see §15). A subdivision is made between taxes levied wholly or predominantly on business (6100) and those levied on others (6200).

A.6. Conciliation with National Accounts

80. This section of the tables provides a re-conciliation between the OECD calculation of total tax revenues and the total of all taxes and social contributions paid to general government as recorded in the country's National Accounts. Where the country is a member of the European Union (EU), the comparison is between the OECD calculation of total tax revenues and the sum of tax revenues and social contributions recorded in the combination of the general government and the institutions of the EU sectors of the National Accounts.

A.7. Memorandum item on the financing of social security benefits

81. In view of the varying relationship between taxation and social security contributions and the cases referred to in §35 to §41, a memorandum item collects together all payments earmarked for social security-type benefits, other than voluntary payments to the private sector. Data are presented as follows (refer section III.B of the Report):

a) Taxes of 2000 series.

b) Taxes earmarked for social security benefits.

c) Voluntary contributions to the government.

d) Compulsory contributions to the private sector.

Guidance on the breakdown of (a) to (d) above is provided in §35 to §41.

A.8. Memorandum item on identifiable taxes paid by government

82. Identifiable taxes actually paid by government are presented in a memorandum item classified by the main headings of the OECD classification of taxes. In the vast majority of countries, only social security contributions and payroll taxes paid by government can be identified. These are, however, usually the most important taxes paid by governments (refer section III.C of the Report).

A.9. Relation of OECD classification of taxes to national accounting systems

83. A system of national accounts (SNA) seeks to provide a coherent framework for recording and presenting the main flows relating respectively to production, consumption, accumulation and external transactions of a given economic area, usually a country or a major region within a country. Government revenues are an important part of the transactions recorded in SNA. The final version of the 2008 SNA was jointly published by five international organisations: the United Nations, the International Monetary Fund, the European Union, the Organisation for Economic Co-operation and Development, and the World Bank in August 2009. The System is a comprehensive, consistent and flexible set of macroeconomic accounts. It is designed for use in countries with market economies, whatever their stage of economic development, and also in countries in transition to market economies. The important parts of the SNA's conceptual framework and its definitions of the various sectors of the economy have been reflected in the OECD's classification of taxes.

84. There are, however, some differences between the OECD classification of taxes and SNA concepts that are listed below. They arise because the aim of the former is to provide the maximum disaggregation of statistical data on what are generally regarded as taxes by tax administrations.

a) OECD includes social security contributions in total tax revenues (§7 and §8 above);

b) there are different points of view on whether or not some levies and fees are classified as taxes (§9 and §10 above);

c) OECD excludes imputed taxes or subsidies resulting from the operation of official multiple exchange rates;

d) there are differences in the treatment of non-wastable tax credits

85. As noted in §1 and §2, headings 1000 to 6000 of the OECD list of taxes cover all unrequited payments to general government, other than compulsory loans and fines. Such unrequited payments including fines, but excluding compulsory loans can be obtained from adding together the following figures in the 2008 SNA

- value-added type taxes (D.211);
- taxes and duties on imports, excluding VAT (D.212);
- export taxes (D.213);
- taxes on products, excluding VAT, import and export taxes (D.214);
- other taxes on production (D.29);
- taxes on income (D.51);
- other current taxes (D.59);
- social contributions (D.61), excluding voluntary contributions;
- capital taxes (D.91).

A.10. The OECD classification of taxes and the International Monetary Fund (GFS) system

86. The coverage and valuation of tax revenues in the GFS system and the 2008 SNA are very similar. Therefore, with the exception of the treatment of non-wastable tax credits, the differences between the OECD classification and that of the 2008 SNA (see §84 above) also apply to the GFS. In addition the International Monetary Fund subdivides the OECD 5000 heading into section IV (Domestic Taxes on Goods and Services) and section V (Taxes on International Trade and Transactions). This reflects the fact that while the latter usually yield insignificant amounts of revenue in OECD countries, this is not the case in many non-OECD countries.

A.11. Comparison of the OECD classification of taxes with other international classifications

87. The table below describes an item by item comparison of the OECD classification of taxes and the classifications used in the following:

i) System of National Accounts (2008 SNA);

ii) European System of Accounts (1995 ESA);

iii) IMF *Government Finance Statistics Manual* (GFSM2001).

88. These comparisons represent those that would be expected to apply in the majority of cases. However in practice some flexibility should be used in their application. This is because in particular cases, countries can adopt varying approaches to the classification of revenues in National Accounts.

OECD Classification		2008 SNA	1995 ESA	GFSM2001
1000	Taxes on income, profits and capital gains			
	1100 Individuals			
	1110 Income/profits	D51-8.61a	D51A	1111
	1120 Capital gains	D51-8.61c,d	D51C,D	1111
	1200 Corporations			
	1210 Income/profits	D51-8.61b	D51B	1112
	1220 Capital gains	D51-8.61c	D51C	1112
	1300 Unallocable as between 1100 and 1200			1113
2000	Social security contributions			
	2100 Employees	D613-8.85	D61111	1211
	2200 Employers	D611-8.83	D61121	1212
	2300 Self-employed, non-employed	D613-8.85	D61131	1213
	2400 Unallocable as between 2100, 2200 and 2300			1214
3000	Taxes on payroll and workforce	D29-7.97a	D29C	112
4000	Taxes on property			
	4100 Recurrent taxes on immovable property			
	4110 Households	D59-8.63a	D59A	1131
	4120 Other	D29-7.97b	D29A	1131
	4200 Recurrent net wealth taxes			
	4210 Individual	D59-8.63b	D59A	1132
	4220 Corporations	D59-8.63b	D59A	1132
	4300 Estate, inheritance and gift taxes			
	4310 Estate and inheritance taxes	D91-10.207b	D91A	1133
	4320 Gift taxes	D91-10.207b	D91A	1133
	4400 Taxes on financial and capital transactions	D59-7.96d; D29-7.97e	D214B,C	1134:1161
	4500 Other non-recurrent taxes on property	D91-10.207a	D91B	1135
	4600 Other recurrent taxes on property	D59-8.63c	D59A	1136
5000	Taxes on goods and services			
	5100 Taxes on production, sale and transfer of goods and services			
	5110 General sales taxes			
	5111 Value-added taxes	D211-7.89	D211; D29G	11411
	5112 Sales taxes	D2122-7.94a; D214-7.96a	D2122D; D214I	11412
	5113 Other general taxes	D214-7.96a	D214I	11413
	5120 Taxes on specific goods and services			
	5121 Excises	D2122-7.94b; D214-7.96b	D2122C; D214A,B,D	1142
	5122 Profits of fiscal monopolies	D214-7.96e	D214J	1143
	5123 Customs/import duties	D2121-7.93	D2121; D2122A,B	1151
	5124 On exports	D213-7.95a	D214K	1152-4
	5125 On investment goods			
	5126 On specific services	D2122-7.94c; D214-7.96c	D2122E; D214E,F,G; D29F	1144; 1156
	5127 Other taxes on international trade and transactions	D2122-7.94d D29-7.95b D29-7.97g D59-8.64d	D2122F; D29D; D59E	1153 1155-6
	5128 Other taxes on specific goods and services			1146
	5130 Unallocable as between 5110 and 5120			
	5200 Taxes on use of goods			
	5210 Recurrent taxes			
	5211 Motor vehicle taxes households	D59-8.64c	D59D	11451
	5212 Motor vehicles taxes others	D29-7.97d	D214D; D29B	11451
	5213 Other recurrent taxes	D29-7.97c,d,f D59-8.64c	D29B,E,F; D59D	11452
	5220 Non-recurrent taxes			
	5300 Unallocable as between 5100 and 5200			
6000	Other taxes			
	6100 Paid solely by business			
	6200 Paid by other than business, or unidentifiable	D59-8.64a,b	D59B,C	1162

A.12. Attribution of tax revenues by sub-sectors of general government

89. The OECD classification requires a breakdown of tax revenues by sub-sectors of government. The definition of each sub-sector and the criteria to be used to attribute tax revenues between these sub-sectors are set out below. They follow the guidance of the 2008 SNA and GFSM2001.

Sub-sectors of general government to be identified

a) Central government

90. The central government sub-sector includes all governmental departments, offices, establishments and other bodies which are agencies or instruments of the central authority whose competence extends over the whole territory, with the exception of the administration of social security funds.Central government therefore has the authority to impose taxes on all resident and non-resident units engaged in economic activities within the country.

b) State, provincial or regional government

91. This sub-sector consists of intermediate units of government exercising a competence at a level below that of central government. It includes all such units operating independently of central government in a part of a country's territory encompassing a number of smaller localities, with the exception of the administration of social security funds. In unitary countries, regional governments may be considered to have a separate existence where they have substantial autonomy to raise a significant proportion of their revenues from sources within their control and their officers are independent of external administrative control in the actual operation of the unit's activities.

92. At present, federal countries comprise the majority of cases where revenues attributed to intermediate units of government are identified separately. Spain is the only unitary country in this position. In the remaining unitary countries, regional revenues are included with those of local governments.

c) Local government

93. This sub-sector includes all other units of government exercising an independent competence in part of the territory of a country, with the exception of the administration of social security funds. It encompasses various urban and/or rural jurisdictions (e.g. local authorities, municipalities, cities, boroughs, districts).

d) Social security funds

94. Social security funds form a separate sub-sector of general government. The social security sub-sector is defined in the 2008 SNA by the following extracts from paragraphs 4.124 to 4.126 and 4.147:

"Social security schemes are social insurance schemes covering the community as a whole or large section of the community that are imposed and controlled by government units. The schemes cover a wide variety of programmes, providing benefits in cash or in kind for old age, invalidity or death, survivors, sickness and maternity, work injury, unemployment, family allowance, health care, etc. There is not necessarily a direct link between the amount of the contribution paid by an individual and the benefits he or she may receive." (Paragraph 4.124).

"When social security schemes are separately organised from the other activities of government units and hold their assets and liabilities separately from the latter and engage in financial transactions on their own account they qualify as institutional units that are described as social security funds." (Paragraph 4.125).

"The amounts raised, and paid out, in social security contributions and benefits may be deliberately varied in order to achieve objectives of government policy that have no direct connection with the concept of social security as a scheme to provide social benefits to members of the community. They may be raised or lowered in order to influence the level of aggregate demand in the economy, for example. Nevertheless, so long as they remain separately constituted funds, they must be treated as separate institutional units in the SNA." (Paragraph 4.126).

"The social security funds sub-sector (of general government) consists of the social security funds operating at all levels of government. Such funds are social insurance schemes covering the community as a whole or large section of the community that are imposed by government units." (Paragraph 4.147).

95. This definition of social security funds is followed in the OECD classification with the two following exceptions which are excluded:

- Schemes imposed by government and operated by bodies outside the general government sector, as defined in §3 of this manual; and
- Schemes to which all contributions are voluntary.

Supra-national authorities

96. This sub-sector covers the revenue-raising operations of supra-national authorities within a country. In practice, the only relevant supra-national authority in the OECD area is that of the institutions of the European Union (EU). As from 1998, supra-national authorities are no longer included in the *Revenue Statistics*, to achieve consistency with the SNA definition of general government which excludes them. For example, income taxes and social security contributions collected by European Institutions and paid by European civil servants who are resident of EU member countries should not be included. However the specific levies paid by the member states of the EU continue to be included in total tax revenues and they are shown under this heading.

Criteria to be used for the attribution of tax revenues

97. When a government collects taxes and pays them over in whole or in part to other governments, it is necessary to determine whether the revenues should be considered to be those of the collecting government which it distributes to others as grants, or those of the beneficiary governments which the collecting government receives and passes on only as their agent. The criteria to be used in the attribution of revenues are set out in §98 to §101 which replicate paragraphs 3.70 to 3.73 from the 2008 SNA.

98. In general, a tax is attributed to the government unit that:

a) exercises the authority to impose the tax (either as a principal or through the delegated authority of the principal);

b) has final discretion to set and vary the rate of the tax.

99. Where an amount is collected by one government for and on behalf of another government, and the latter government has the authority to impose the tax, and set and vary its rate, then the former is acting as an agent for the latter and the tax is reassigned. Any amount retained by the collecting government as a collection charge should be treated as a payment for a service. Any other amount retained by the collecting government, such as under a tax-sharing arrangement, should be treated as a current

grant. If the collecting government was delegated the authority to set and vary the rate, then the amount collected should be treated as tax revenue of this government.

100. Where different governments jointly and equally set the rate of a tax and jointly and equally decide on the distribution of the proceeds, with no individual government having ultimate overriding authority, then the tax revenues are attributed to each government according to its respective share of the proceeds. If an arrangement allows one government unit to exercise ultimate overriding authority, then all of the tax revenue is attributed to that unit.

101. There may also be the circumstance where a tax is imposed under the constitutional or other authority of one government, but other governments individually set the tax rate in their jurisdictions. The proceeds of the tax generated in each respective government's jurisdiction are attributed as tax revenues of that government.

Levies paid by member states of the European Union

102. The levies paid by the member states of the EU take the form:

- VAT own resources; and
- Specific levies which include:

a) custom duties and levies on agricultural goods (5123);

b) gross monetary compensation accounts (5123 if relating to imports and 5124 if relating to exports); and

c) Steel, coal, sugar and milk levies (5128).

103. The custom duties collected by member states on behalf of the EU are recorded:

- on a gross of collection fee basis;
- using figures adjusted so that duties are shown on a 'final destination' as opposed to a 'country of first entry' basis where such adjustments can be made. These adjustments concern in particular duties collected at important (sea) ports. Although the EU duties are collected by the authorities of the country of first entry, when possible these duties should be excluded from the revenue of the collecting country and be included in the revenue of the country of final destination.

This is the specific EU levy that most clearly conforms to the attribution criterion described in §96 above. Consequently as from 1998, these amounts are footnoted as a memorandum item to the EU member state country tables (in Part III) and no longer shown under heading 5123. However the figures are included in the total tax revenue figures on the top line for all the relevant years shown in the tables.

104. The VAT own resources, which are determined by applying a rate not exceeding 1% to an assessment basis specified in the Sixth Directive,[21] are more of a borderline case. They have some of the characteristics of a transfer (they are not derived from a clearly identifiable source of funds that are actually collected) and some of a tax (the amount of the transfer is determined by the receiving sub-sector of government). In this publication they are not shown as a tax of the European Union (but as a tax of the EU member states), though the amounts involved are footnoted in the tables contained in Part IV.

A.13. Provisional classification of revenues from bank levies and payments to deposit insurance and financial stability schemes

105. The OECD have adopted the following interim approach to reporting revenue from bank levies plus deposit insurance and stability fees for the 2012 edition of *OECD Revenue Statistics*; The amounts should be recorded under category 5126.

- Compulsory payments of stability fees, bank levies and deposit insurance should generally be treated as tax revenues where the payments are made to General Government and allocated to the governments' consolidated or general funds so that the Government is free to make immediate use of the money for the purposes that it chooses. This principle would apply regardless of whether the Government is promising to make payments to guarantee the banks' customer deposits in some future contingency.
- If the compulsory payments are made to general government and placed in funds that are earmarked to be entirely channelled back to the sector of the economy that comprises the companies that are subject to the payment, they would still generally be treated as tax revenues on the grounds that the funds would be available for the government and would reduce its budget deficit, the fee is unrequited for an individual entity and the amounts raised could be unrelated to any eventual pay out to depositors or expenditure on wider support for the financial sector.
- Payments to made to the smaller long-standing schemes for insuring 'retail' deposits, where the payment levels are consistent with the costs of insurance should be classified as fee for service.
- Any payments which involve governments realising the assets of a failed institution or receiving a priority claim on its assets in liquidation in order to fund payments of compensation to customers for their lost deposits would be treated as a fee for a service as opposed to tax revenues.
- Compulsory payments that are made to funds operated outside the government sector and non-state institutions backed by the deposit takers and all payments to voluntary schemes should not be treated as tax revenues.

Notes

1. References in the OECD Interpretative Guide to Sections or Parts of "this Annex" refer to OECD (2015), *Revenue Statistics* 1965-2014, OECD Publishing, Paris.
2. All references to SNA are to the 2008 edition.
3. See section A.12 of this guide for a discussion of the concept of agency capacity.
4. It is usually possible to identify amounts of social security contributions and payroll taxes, but not other taxes paid by government.
5. If, however, a levy which is considered as non-tax revenue by most countries is regarded as a tax – or raises substantial revenue – in one or more countries, the amounts collected are footnoted at the end of the relevant country tables, even though the amounts are not included in total tax revenues.
6. Names, however, can frequently be misleading. For example, though a passport fee would normally be considered a non-tax revenue, if a supplementary levy on passports (as is the case in Portugal) were imposed in order to raise substantial amounts of revenue relative to the cost of providing the passport, the levy would be regarded as a tax under 5200.
7. There are practical difficulties in operating the distinction made by 1993 SNA.
8. A more detailed explanation of this distinction can be found in the special feature, "Current issues in reporting tax revenues", in the 2001 edition of the *Revenue Statistics.*
9. Sometimes the terms "non-refundable" and "refundable" are used, but it may be considered illogical to talk of "refundable" when nothing has been paid.
10. A different treatment, however, is accorded to non-wastable tax credits under imputation systems of corporate income tax (§32–34).
11. This is not strictly a true tax expenditure in the formal sense. Such tax expenditures require identification of a benchmark tax system for each country or, preferably, a common international benchmark. In practice it has not been possible to reach agreement on a common international benchmark.
12. Unless based on the profit made on a sale, in which case they would be classified as capital gains taxes under 1120 or 1220.
13. In some countries the same legislation applies to both individual and corporate enterprises for particular taxes on income.However, the receipts from such taxes are usually allocable between individuals and enterprises and can therefore be shown in the appropriate sub-heading.
14. For example, "...sufficiently self-contained and independent that they behave in the same way as corporations.......(including) keeping a complete set of accounts" (2008SNA, section 4.44).
15. In Canada – a country also referred to as having an imputation system – the (wastable) tax credit for the shareholder is in respect of domestic corporation tax deemed to have been paid whether or not a corporation tax liability has arisen.As there is no integral connection between the corporation tax liability and the credit given against income tax under such systems, these credits for dividends are treated, along with other tax credits, on the lines described in §21.
16. This may also apply where a scheme for government employees existed prior to the introduction of a general social security scheme.
17. In the 2008 SNA these are regarded as capital transfers and not as taxes (see section G).
18. This is the system by which the European Union adjusts for differences between the exchange rates used to determine prices under the Common Market Agricultural Policy and actual exchange rates. Payments under the system may relate to imports or exports and where these amounts are separately identifiable they are shown under the appropriate heading (5123 or 5124). In this Report, these amounts are shown gross (i.e. without deducting any subsidies paid out under the MCA system).
19. Transfers of profits of State lotteries are regarded as non-tax revenues (see also §64).
20. See §26(c) as regards this distinction.
21. At the Edinburgh Summit (1992) EU Member countries have decided to gradually reduce this percentage from 1.4 to 1, and to effectuate this reduction between years 1995 and 1999. During the period 1970–1983 this percentage also amounted to 1.

ANEXO A

Guía de interpretación de la OCDE

Índice

A.1. Clasificación de impuestos de la OCDE

1000 *Impuestos sobre la renta, las utilidades y las ganancias de capital*

- 1100 Personas físicas
  - 1110 Renta y utilidades
  - 1120 Ganancias de capital
- 1200 Sociedades
  - 1210 Renta y utilidades
  - 1220 Ganancias de capital
- 1300 No clasificables entre 1100 y 1200

2000 *Contribuciones a la seguridad social*

- 2100 Empleados
  - 2110 Sobre la base de la nómina
  - 2120 Sobre los ingresos gravables
- 2200 Empleadores
  - 2210 Sobre la base de la nómina
  - 2220 Sobre los ingresos gravables
- 2300 Trabajadores por cuenta propia o no empleados
  - 2310 Sobre la base de la nómina
  - 2320 Sobre los ingresos gravables
- 2400 No clasificables entre 2100, 2200 y 2300
  - 2410 Sobre la base de la nómina
  - 2420 Sobre los ingresos gravables

3000 *Impuestos sobre la nómina y la fuerza de trabajo*

4000 *Impuestos sobre la propiedad*

- 4100 Impuestos recurrentes sobre la propiedad inmueble
  - 4110 Hogares
  - 4120 Otros
- 4200 Impuestos recurrentes sobre la riqueza neta
  - 4210 Personas físicas
  - 4220 Sociedades
- 4300 Impuestos sobre sucesiones, herencias y donaciones
  - 4310 Impuestos sobre sucesiones y herencias
  - 4320 Impuestos sobre donaciones
- 4400 Impuestos sobre transacciones financieras y de capital

4500 Otros impuestos no recurrentes sobre la propiedad

4510 Sobre el patrimonio neto

4520 Otros impuestos no recurrentes

4600 Otros impuestos recurrentes sobre la propiedad

5000 *Impuestos sobre los bienes y servicios*

5100 Impuestos sobre la producción, venta y transmisión de bienes y prestación de servicios

5110 Impuestos generales

5111 Impuestos sobre el valor agregado

5112 Impuestos sobre las ventas

5113 Otros impuestos generales sobre los bienes y servicios

5120 Impuestos sobre bienes y servicios específicos

5121 Impuestos selectivos

5122 Utilidades de los monopolios fiscales

5123 Derechos de aduanas y otros derechos de importación

5124 Sobre las exportaciones

5125 Sobre los bienes de inversión

5126 Sobre servicios específicos

5127 Otros impuestos sobre el comercio y las transacciones internacionales

5128 Otros impuestos sobre bienes y servicios específicos

5130 No clasificables entre 5110 y 5120

5200 Impuestos sobre el uso de bienes y sobre el permiso para usar bienes y realizar actividades

5210 Impuestos recurrentes

5211 Sobre vehículos automotores: hogares

5212 Sobre vehículos automotores: otros

5213 Otros impuestos recurrentes

5220 Impuestos no recurrentes

5300 No clasificables entre 5100 y 5200

6000 *Otros impuestos*

6100 Pagados únicamente por empresas

6200 Pagados por otros distintos de las empresas o no identificables

Guía de interpretación de la OCDE[1]

A.2. Cobertura

Criterios generales

1. En la clasificación de la OCDE, el término "impuestos" se circunscribe exclusivamente a los pagos sin contraprestación efectuados al gobierno general. Los impuestos carecen de contraprestación en el sentido en que, normalmente, las prestaciones proporcionadas por el gobierno a los contribuyentes no guardan relación directa con los pagos realizados por estos.

2. El término "impuestos" no incluye las multas o sanciones pecuniarias no relacionadas con infracciones tributarias ni los préstamos obligatorios pagados al gobierno. La delimitación entre ingresos tributarios y no tributarios en relación con ciertas tasas y cargos se abordan en los §§ 9–13.

3. El gobierno general comprende la Administración central y los organismos que se hallan bajo su control efectivo, los gobiernos estatales y locales y sus respectivas administraciones, y ciertos regímenes de seguridad social y entidades gubernamentales autónomas, excluidas las empresas públicas. Esta definición del gobierno proviene del Sistema de Cuentas Nacionales (SCN) 2008;[2] en esa publicación, el sector del gobierno general y sus subsectores se hallan definidos en el capítulo 4, sección F, páginas 80-84 de la versión inglesa.

4. Los pagos obligatorios a autoridades supranacionales y a los organismos vinculados a ellas no se incluyen como impuestos desde 1998, con contadas excepciones; sin embargo, los derechos de aduana recaudados por los estados miembros de la Unión Europea en nombre de esta siguen registrándose como partidas informativas y se incluyen en los cuadros de países (parte III de la publicación Revenue Statistics de la OCDE), concretamente en la recaudación tributaria total del país en el que se cobran (véase el § 95). Por otra parte, en los países en los que la Iglesia forma parte del gobierno general, se computan los impuestos eclesiásticos, siempre que reúnan los criterios establecidos en el § 1. Además, habida cuenta de que los datos hacen referencia a las entradas que recibe el gobierno general, quedan excluidos los gravámenes abonados a órganos no gubernamentales, organismos de bienestar o regímenes de seguro social externos al gobierno general, y sindicatos u organizaciones profesionales, aun cuando dichos gravámenes sean obligatorios; sin embargo, los pagos obligatorios al gobierno general asignados a esos entes sí están incluidos aquí siempre que el gobierno no actúe como mero agente de estos.[3] Las utilidades de los monopolios fiscales se diferencian de las de otras empresas públicas, y se tratan como impuestos porque reflejan el ejercicio del poder tributario del Estado mediante el uso de prerrogativas monopolísticas (véanse los §§ 62–64), al igual que las utilidades percibidas por el gobierno por la compra y la venta de divisas a diferentes tipos de cambio (véase el § 70).

5. Los impuestos pagados por el gobierno (p. ej., contribuciones a la seguridad social e impuestos sobre la nómina pagados por el gobierno en su calidad de empleador, impuestos sobre el consumo en sus compras o impuestos sobre sus propiedades) no se han excluido de los datos presentados. Sin embargo, cuando ha sido posible identificar las cantidades de ingreso implicadas,[4] se han mostrado en la parte III, sección C, de la publicación Revenue Statistics de la OCDE.

6. La relación entre esta clasificación y la del Sistema de Cuentas Nacionales (SCN) se aclara en los apartados A.9 y A.11 infra.; dado que estas dos clasificaciones no coinciden en todos sus aspectos, en ocasiones, los datos presentados en las cuentas nacionales se calculan o clasifican de forma diferente a lo establecido en la presente guía y, aunque esas y otras diferencias se han mencionado en determinados casos (p. ej., en los §§ 13 y 26), no ha sido posible hacer referencia a todas ellas. Por otra parte, pueden darse asimismo ciertas disparidades entre la presente clasificación y la empleada internamente por algunas administraciones nacionales (véase el § 10), por lo que quizá las estadísticas de la OCDE y las nacionales no siempre concuerden; sin embargo, es más que probable que esas diferencias sean mínimas en lo que a la cuantía de ingresos se refiere.

Contribuciones a la seguridad social

7. Las contribuciones obligatorias a la seguridad social, tal y como se definen en el § 35, abonadas al gobierno general, se tratan aquí como ingresos tributarios, ya que, al tratarse de pagos preceptivos al gobierno general, se asemejan claramente a los impuestos. No obstante, pueden diferir de otros impuestos por el hecho de que la recepción de prestaciones de la seguridad social depende, en numerosos países, de que se hayan aportado las debidas contribuciones, aunque la magnitud de dichas prestaciones no tiene por qué estar supeditada obligatoriamente al importe de las contribuciones. Al tratar las contribuciones sociales como impuestos, se obtiene un mayor grado de comparabilidad entre países, aunque se han consignado en una categoría separada para poder distinguirlas en cualquier análisis.

8. Por el contrario, las contribuciones a la seguridad social voluntarias o no pagaderas al gobierno general (véase el § 1) no se tratan como impuestos, aunque en ciertos países, tal y como se indica debidamente en cada caso en las notas que figuran al pie de los cuadros, plantea dificultades el eliminar tanto las contribuciones voluntarias como algunos pagos obligatorios al sector privado.

Tasas, cargos a usuarios y licencias

9. Aparte de las tasas por licencia de vehículos, universalmente consideradas como impuestos, no resulta fácil distinguir entre las tasas y cargos a usuarios que deben tratarse como impuestos y las que no, ya que, aunque toda tasa o cargo se impone en conexión con un servicio o una actividad específicos, la intensidad del vínculo entre el derecho cobrado y el servicio prestado puede variar considerablemente, al igual que puede hacerlo la relación entre la cuantía de la tasa y el costo que supone proporcionar el servicio en cuestión. En todo caso, cuando el beneficiario del servicio pague una tasa claramente relacionada con el costo que supone prestar un servicio, puede inferirse que el gravamen tiene contraprestación y, de acuerdo con la definición reseñada en el § 1, no se considerará como impuesto. En sentido contrario, puede estimarse que el gravamen "carece de contraprestación" cuando:

a) el cargo exceda con creces el costo que supone prestar el servicio;

b) el pagador o sujeto pasivo del gravamen no sea el beneficiario del servicio (p. ej., tasas recaudadas de los mataderos para financiar un servicio proporcionado a los titulares de explotaciones agropecuarias);

c) el gobierno no proporcione un servicio específico a cambio del pago del gravamen, aun y cuando se emita un permiso en beneficio del sujeto pasivo (p. ej., cuando el gobierno concede licencias de caza, pesca o tiro que no otorgan el derecho a usar una zona específica propiedad del gobierno);

d) los servicios beneficien únicamente a los pagadores del gravamen, pero las utilidades recibidas por cada persona no guarden necesariamente proporción con sus pagos (p. ej., el gravamen sobre la comercialización de la leche que recae en los criadores de ganado lechero y que se utiliza para fomentar el consumo de la leche).

10. Pese a las anteriores consideraciones, en ciertos casos excepcionales la aplicación de los criterios plasmados en el § 1 puede resultar particularmente compleja. La solución adoptada –dada la conveniencia de uniformidad internacional y las cantidades de ingreso relativamente bajas implicadas por lo general– ha consistido en seguir la práctica dominante en la mayoría de las administraciones, en lugar de permitir que cada país aplique su propia visión sobre si estos gravámenes deben considerarse como ingresos tributarios o no tributarios.[5]

11. Seguidamente, se ofrece una lista de las principales tasas y cargos en cuestión, y su tratamiento normal[6] en esta publicación:

Ingresos no tributarios:	tasas procesales, permisos de conducir, tasas portuarias, tasas por expedición de pasaportes, licencias de radio y televisión cuando las autoridades públicas proporcionan el servicio de difusión.
Impuestos de la partida 5200:	permiso para realizar actividades tales como distribución cinematográfica; caza, pesca o tiro; suministro de instalaciones para actividades recreativas o de ocio o juegos de azar; venta de bebidas alcohólicas o tabaco; posesión de animales domésticos o uso de vehículos automotores; derechos sobre la extracción.

12. En la práctica, puede que no siempre resulte posible aislar las entradas tributarias de las no tributarias cuando estas se registran conjuntamente. En ese caso, si se considera que la mayoría de las entradas proviene de ingresos no tributarios, se tratará el importe total como tal; de lo contrario, esas entradas del gobierno se incluirán y clasificarán según las normas recogidas en el § 28.

13. En relación con la delimitación de los ingresos tributarios y no tributarios, se observan las dos siguientes diferencias entre la clasificación de la OCDE y la del SCN:

- El SCN considera un cierto número de gravámenes como impuestos indirectos si los abonan las empresas y como ingresos no tributarios si los satisfacen los hogares, una distinción obviada en la presente clasificación a la hora diferenciar entre ingresos tributarios y no tributarios.[7]
- La práctica dominante en la mayoría de las administraciones tributarias de la OCDE, un criterio empleado ocasionalmente en la presente clasificación para distinguir entre ingresos tributarios y no tributarios, no resulta pertinente a efectos del SCN.

Regalías

14. Las regalías percibidas por el derecho a extraer petróleo o gas, o a explotar otros recursos minerales, se consideran normalmente ingresos no tributarios, ya que son rentas de la propiedad procedentes de tierras o recursos del gobierno.

Multas y sanciones pecuniarias

15. Las entradas procedentes de multas y sanciones pecuniarias impuestas por el incumplimiento de normas vinculadas a un impuesto determinado, así como los intereses devengados por los pagos adeudados en relación con ese impuesto, se registrarán junto

con las entradas derivadas de dicho impuesto. Otros tipos de multas vinculadas a infracciones tributarias se clasificarán en la partida residual 6000. Las multas que no deriven de infracciones tributarias (p. ej., infracción de aparcamiento) o que no puedan vincularse a una infracción tributaria concreta no se tratan como impuestos.

A.3. Principios de registro

Criterio de devengo

16. Los datos recogidos en esta publicación relativos a los últimos años se han registrado predominantemente según el criterio de devengo, esto es, se han computado en el momento en que nace la obligación. En las notas que figuran al pie de los cuadros de países de la parte III del informe, se ofrece más información al respecto.

17. Sin embargo, los datos relativos a años anteriores han seguido registrándose principalmente según el criterio de caja, es decir, en el momento en que el gobierno recibió el pago. Por lo tanto, por ejemplo, los impuestos descontados por los empleadores en un año pero pagados al gobierno al año siguiente y los impuestos debidos un año pero liquidados el año después constan ambos en las entradas del segundo año. Las transacciones correctoras, tales como devoluciones, reembolsos y reintegros, se deducen de los ingresos brutos del periodo en que se realizan.

18. Los datos sobre ingresos tributarios se registran sin deducción de los gastos administrativos propios de la recaudación impositiva. De igual modo, cuando los recursos generados por un impuesto se emplean para subvencionar a miembros particulares de la comunidad, el subsidio no se descuenta del producto impositivo, aunque puede que el impuesto aparezca sin los subsidios en los registros nacionales de algunos países.

19. En lo que a los monopolios fiscales se refiere (5122), únicamente se incluye en los ingresos del gobierno el importe realmente transferido a este. Sin embargo, si cualquier gasto de los monopolios fiscales se considera gasto del gobierno (p. ej., gastos sociales emprendidos por los monopolios fiscales en beneficio del gobierno), se añadirán posteriormente con el fin de llegar a cifras de ingreso tributario (véase el § 62 infra.).

***Distinción entre disposiciones tributarias y disposiciones relativas al gasto*[8]**

20. Dado que la presente publicación aborda únicamente la actividad del gobierno desde el punto de vista del ingreso, sin tener en cuenta los aspectos relacionados con el gasto, resulta preciso realizar una distinción entre las disposiciones que rigen estos dos elementos. Por lo general, no existe dificultad alguna en diferenciar ambos aspectos, ya que los gastos operan en un ámbito externo al sistema tributario y sus cuentas, y se rigen por una legislación separada de la impositiva. En los casos de difícil delimitación, se emplea el flujo de caja para distinguir entre disposiciones tributarias y disposiciones relativas al gasto. En la medida en que una disposición incida en el flujo de pagos tributarios del contribuyente al gobierno, se entenderá que reviste un carácter tributario y se tendrá en cuenta en los datos recogidos en esta publicación. Cualquier disposición que no afecte a ese flujo se reputará como relativa al gasto y no se tendrá en consideración en la información plasmada en la publicación.

21. Las desgravaciones, exenciones y deducciones tributarias sobre la base imponible afectan claramente a la cantidad transferida al gobierno y, por ende, se consideran disposiciones de naturaleza tributaria. En el extremo opuesto, los subsidios o exoneraciones que no compensen la obligación tributaria y que estén claramente desvinculados del proceso de evaluación, no reducen los ingresos tributarios consignados en esta publicación. De particular interés en este ámbito resultan los créditos fiscales,

que son cantidades deducibles del impuesto liquidable (lo que los diferencia de las deducciones sobre la base imponible). Cabe distinguir dos tipos de créditos fiscales: los créditos fiscales no exigibles (a veces denominados desaprovechables), limitados al importe de la obligación tributaria y que, por ende, no pueden generar un pago de las autoridades al contribuyente; y los créditos fiscales exigibles (o no desaprovechables), que no están sometidos a dicho límite, de forma que toda cantidad que exceda la obligación tributaria puede abonarse al contribuyente.[9] Al igual que las desgravaciones, un crédito fiscal no exigible afecta claramente a la cantidad transferida al gobierno y, por ende, se considerará como tributario. La práctica seguida para los créditos fiscales exigibles[10] consiste en distinguir entre "el componente de gasto tributario"[11] que es la porción del crédito empleada en reducir o eliminar la obligación del contribuyente" y el "componente de transferencia", constituido por la parte que excede la obligación del contribuyente y que se paga a este. Al registrar los ingresos tributarios deberá restarse la parte equivalente al componente de gasto tributario, pero no la correspondiente al componente de transferencia. Además, las cantidades de ambos componentes deberán figurar como partidas informativas en los cuadros de países. Los países que no puedan diferenciar entre estos dos componentes deberán indicar si se ha restado de los ingresos tributarios el total de ellos y presentar las evaluaciones disponibles del valor que ambos representan. Para mayor información, consúltese la sección C de la parte I de la publicación Revenue Statistics de la OCDE, que examina el efecto de los diversos tratamientos de los créditos fiscales exigibles en la relación impuestos sobre PIB.

Calendario y ejercicio fiscal

22. Las autoridades nacionales cuyos ejercicios fiscales no coinciden con el año calendario deben presentar los datos, siempre que sea posible, sobre la base del año calendario, a fin de permitir el mayor grado posible de comparación con la información de otros países. Subsisten algunos países en los que los datos hacen referencia a los ejercicios fiscales; para ellos, los datos relativos al PIB utilizados en los cuadros comparativos corresponden igualmente a los ejercicios fiscales.

A.4. Criterios generales de clasificación

Principales criterios de clasificación

23. El desglose de las entradas fiscales en las diversas categorías (1000, 2000, 3000, 4000, 5000 y 6000) se rige en general por la base sobre la cual recae el impuesto: 1000, renta, utilidades y ganancias de capital; 2000 y 3000, remuneraciones, nómina o número de empleados (fuerza de trabajo); 4000, propiedad; 5000, bienes y servicios; 6000, bases múltiples, otras bases o bases no identificables. Cuando un impuesto se calcula sobre más de una base, las entradas que genera se distribuyen, en la medida de lo posible, entre las diversas categorías (véanse los §§ 28 y 78). Las categorías 4000 y 5000 no sólo cubren aquellos impuestos en los que la base tributaria está constituida por la propiedad, los bienes o los servicios en sí mismos, sino también ciertos impuestos afines; y así, por ejemplo, los impuestos sobre transmisiones patrimoniales se incluyen en la partida 4400,[12] y los impuestos sobre el uso de bienes y sobre el permiso para realizar actividades, en la 5200. En las categorías 4000 y 5000, se distingue en ocasiones entre impuestos recurrentes y no recurrentes: son impuestos recurrentes los que se recaudan a intervalos regulares (por lo general, anualmente), y no recurrentes, los que se imponen una sola vez (véanse los §§ 43 46, 49–50 y 76–77 para profundizar en las aplicaciones particulares de esta distinción).

24. La asignación de un impuesto a fines específicos no afecta a la clasificación de las entradas fiscales que genera. Sin embargo, tal y como se explica en el § 35 en relación con la clasificación de las contribuciones a la seguridad social, el hecho de que estas confieran un derecho a recibir prestaciones sociales es decisivo para la definición de la categoría 2000.

25. La forma en que se establece o recauda un impuesto (p.ej., mediante el uso de timbres) no afecta a su clasificación.

Clasificación de los contribuyentes

26. En ocasiones, se distingue entre diversas clases de contribuyentes. Esas distinciones dependen de cada impuesto.

a) Entre personas físicas y sociedades en relación con los impuestos sobre la renta y sobre la riqueza neta

La distinción básica aquí es que los impuestos sobre la renta de las sociedades (impuesto de sociedades), a diferencia de los impuestos sobre la renta de las personas físicas, gravan a la sociedad como entidad y no a sus propietarios, independientemente de las circunstancias personales de estos; la misma distinción se aplica a los impuestos sobre la riqueza neta de las sociedades y de las personas físicas. Los impuestos liquidados sobre las utilidades de las asociaciones y sobre la renta de las instituciones, tales como seguros de vida o fondos de pensiones, se clasifican siguiendo la misma regla, y así, se considerarán impuestos sobre las sociedades (1200) si se cargan a la asociación o institución como persona jurídica sin tener en cuenta las circunstancias personales de sus propietarios, o impuestos sobre las personas físicas en el caso contrario (1100). Por lo general, los impuestos aplicados a las sociedades y a las personas físicas se rigen por legislaciones diferentes.[13] La distinción realizada aquí entre personas físicas y sociedades no sigue la categorización por sectores entre hogares, empresas, etcétera, del Sistema de Cuentas Nacionales para las cuentas de ingresos y desembolsos. La clasificación del SCN requiere que ciertas empresas no constituidas en sociedad[14] se excluyan del sector de los hogares y vengan a sumarse a las empresas no financieras y las instituciones financieras. Sin embargo, el impuesto sobre las utilidades de esos negocios no siempre puede separarse del impuesto sobre la renta de sus propietarios o, como mucho, puede deslindarse sólo arbitrariamente. Por ello, no se ha intentado reproducir aquí esa separación, y la totalidad del impuesto sobre la renta de las personas físicas se ha recogido en un solo bloque, independientemente de la naturaleza del ingreso imponible.

b) Entre hogares y otros en relación con los impuestos sobre la propiedad inmueble

Esta distinción es la misma que la adoptada por el SCN para las cuentas de gasto del consumo final de los hogares y de producción. Se trata pues de diferenciar a los hogares como consumidores (esto es, excluidas las empresas no constituidas en sociedad), por una parte, y a los productores, por otra. Los impuestos sobre las viviendas ocupadas por los hogares, tanto a cargo de los propietarios-ocupantes como de los arrendatarios o de los arrendadores, se incluyen en los hogares, lo que coincide con la diferenciación que suele hacerse comúnmente entre los impuestos sobre la propiedad doméstica y los impuestos sobre la propiedad empresarial. No obstante, algunos países no se hallan en situación de operar esta distinción.

c) Entre hogares y otros en relación con las licencias de vehículos automotores

Se distingue aquí entre los hogares como consumidores, por una parte, y los productores, por otra, al igual que en las cuentas de gasto del consumo final de los hogares y de producción del SCN.

d) Entre empresas y otros en relación con los impuestos residuales (6000)

La distinción es la misma que en c), esta vez, entre los productores, por una parte, y los hogares como consumidores, por otra. Los impuestos recogidos en la categoría 6000 bien porque gravan más de una base tributaria, o bien porque su base no entra dentro del ámbito de ninguna de las categorías anteriores pero es identificable como imponible sobre los productores, y no sobre los hogares, se incluyen en "empresas". El resto de los impuestos de la categoría 6000 se imputan a "otros" o "no identificables".

Recargos

27. Las entradas procedentes de recargos relacionados con impuestos particulares se clasifican por lo general en base al impuesto correspondiente, ya sea el recargo temporal o no. Pero si el recargo posee una característica que lo califica para ser clasificada en una categoría diferente de la lista de la OCDE, las entradas generadas por el recargo se recogen en dicha categoría, separadas de las del correspondiente impuesto.

Entradas tributarias no identificables y partidas residuales

28. En un cierto número de casos, no logra determinarse que los impuestos pertenezcan enteramente a una categoría o partida de la clasificación de la OCDE y, en esos casos, se aplican las siguientes pautas:

a) Se conoce la categoría, pero no la forma de distribuir las entradas entre las diversas subdivisiones: las entradas se clasifican en la correspondiente partida o subpartida residual (1300, 2400, 4520, 4600, 5130, 5300 o 6200).

b) Se sabe que la mayor parte de las entradas procedentes de un grupo de impuestos (normalmente, impuestos locales) proviene de impuestos de una categoría o una partida particulares, pero algunos de los impuestos del grupo cuya cuantía no puede determinarse con exactitud pueden clasificarse en otras categorías o partidas: las entradas se consignan en la categoría o partida a la que pertenezca la mayoría de ellas.

c) No puede identificarse ni la categoría ni la partida correspondiente al impuesto (normalmente, local): el impuesto se incorpora a la partida 6200, a menos que se conozca que se trata de un impuesto sobre las empresas, en cuyo caso se incluye en la partida 6100.

A.5. Comentarios sobre ítems de la lista

1000 – *Impuestos sobre la renta, las utilidades y las ganancias de capital*

29. Esta categoría cubre los impuestos aplicados a la renta o a las utilidades netas (esto es, la renta bruta menos las deducciones permitidas) de las personas físicas y las sociedades, así como los impuestos a los que se someten las ganancias de capital de esos mismos sujetos pasivos, y las ganancias obtenidas en juegos de azar.

30. Se incluyen en esta categoría:

a) los impuestos que gravan predominantemente la renta o las utilidades, aunque recaigan parcialmente sobre otras bases; los impuestos aplicados a varias bases que no sean mayoritariamente la renta o las utilidades se clasifican de acuerdo con los principios establecidos en los §§ 28 y 78;

b) los impuestos sobre la propiedad aplicados a un ingreso presunto o estimado como parte de un impuesto sobre la renta (véase el § 43(a), (c) y (d));

c) los pagos obligatorios al fondo de contribuciones de la seguridad social impuestos sobre la renta que no confieran un derecho a prestaciones sociales; si esas contribuciones otorgan derecho a prestaciones sociales, se incluyen en la categoría 2000 (véase el § 35);

d) el producto de los sistemas integrados de impuestos sobre la renta de régimen cedular se clasifican como un todo en esta categoría, aunque algunos de los impuestos cedulares puedan basarse en la renta bruta y no tener en cuenta las circunstancias personales del contribuyente.

31. La principal división de esta categoría se efectúa entre los gravámenes a personas físicas (1100) y aquellos a sociedades (1200). A su vez, en cada partida, se separa entre impuestos sobre la renta y las utilidades (1110 y 1210) e impuestos sobre las ganancias de capital (1120 y 1220). Si algunas entradas no pueden atribuirse pertinentemente a la partida 1100 o a la 1200, o si no puede realizarse esta distinción en la práctica (p. ej., por falta de datos fiables sobre los receptores de los pagos de los que se deducen los impuestos con retención en la fuente), las entradas se incorporan a la partida 1300 como "no clasificables".

Tratamiento de los créditos fiscales en los sistemas de imputación

32. En los sistemas de imputación del impuesto de sociedades, los accionistas están exentos, total o parcialmente, de responder en concepto del impuesto sobre la renta por los dividendos abonados por la compañía a partir de la renta o de las utilidades sometidas al impuesto de sociedades. En los países con este sistema,[15] una parte del impuesto sobre las utilidades de la sociedad está disponible para exonerar a los accionistas de su propia obligación tributaria. La exoneración del accionista reviste la forma de un crédito fiscal, cuyo importe puede ser inferior, igual o superior al pasivo tributario total del accionista. Si el crédito fiscal excede al pasivo tributario, puede que ese exceso sea pagadero al accionista. Dado que este tipo de crédito fiscal es parte integrante del sistema de imputación del impuesto sobre la renta de las sociedades, cualquier pago a los accionistas se trata como devolución tributaria, y no como gasto (compárese con el tratamiento de otros créditos fiscales descrito en el § 21).

33. Puesto que en los sistemas de imputación el crédito fiscal (incluso cuando excede la obligación tributaria) debe considerarse como disposición tributaria, se plantea la cuestión de determinar si deberá deducirse de las entradas en concepto de impuesto sobre la renta de las personas físicas (1110) o de las entradas atribuibles al impuesto sobre la renta de las sociedades (1210). En este informe, la cantidad total pagada a título del impuesto sobre la renta de las sociedades se recoge en la subpartida 1210, y el impuesto no imputado en la subpartida 1110. Por lo tanto, la cuantía total del crédito se resta de esta última subpartida, tanto si el crédito da lugar a una reducción de la obligación tributaria por renta personal, como si se realiza un reembolso porque el crédito fiscal excede el pasivo tributario por este concepto. (No obstante, si los créditos fiscales se deducen del impuesto de sociedades por dividendos repartidos a otras sociedades, las correspondientes cantidades se descuentan de las entradas registradas en la subpartida 1210.)

1120 y 1220 – *Impuestos sobre las ganancias de capital*

34. Como su nombre indica, estas subpartidas engloban los impuestos sobre las ganancias de capital, ya de las personas físicas (1120), ya de las sociedades (1220), siempre que las entradas procedentes de estos impuestos puedan identificarse por separado. Ese no es el caso en numerosos países, y las entradas de estos impuestos se clasifican junto con las del impuesto sobre la renta. La subpartida 1120 contiene asimismo los impuestos sobre las ganancias obtenidas en juegos de azar.

2000 – *Contribuciones a la seguridad social*

35. Entran en esta categoría todos los pagos obligatorios que confieran un derecho a recibir una prestación social futura (contingente). Esos pagos suelen estar asignados al financiamiento de prestaciones sociales y, a menudo, se pagan a las instituciones del gobierno general que proporcionan dichas prestaciones. Sin embargo, esa asignación no forma parte de la definición de las contribuciones a la seguridad social y no es necesaria para que un impuesto sea clasificado en esta categoría, pero, para que un impuesto se incluya aquí, sí será preciso que confiera un derecho. Y así, los gravámenes sobre la renta o la nómina asignados a los fondos de seguridad social pero que no confieran el derecho a recibir prestaciones sociales quedan excluidos de la presente categoría y se registran bien entre los impuestos sobre la renta de las personas físicas (1100), bien junto con los impuestos sobre la nómina y la fuerza de trabajo (3000). Los impuestos que reposen sobre otras bases, como los bienes y servicios, no se consignarán aquí aunque estén asignados a prestaciones de la seguridad social, sino que se catalogarán según sus respectivas bases, ya que por lo general no otorgarán derecho alguno a prestaciones sociales.

36. Entre otras, se incluirán aquí las contribuciones a los siguientes tipos de prestaciones de la seguridad social: prestaciones y suplementos por seguro de desempleo; prestaciones por accidente, lesión o enfermedad; pensiones por jubilación, invalidez y supervivencia; ayudas familiares; reembolsos de gastos médicos u hospitalarios o prestación de servicios médicos u hospitalarios. Las contribuciones pueden recaudarse tanto de los empleados como de los empleadores.

37. Las contribuciones pueden tener como base bien las remuneraciones o la nómina ("sobre la base de la nómina"), bien la renta neta tras deducciones y exenciones por circunstancias personales ("sobre la base del impuesto sobre la renta"), y el producto de ambas bases deberá identificarse separadamente en la medida de lo posible. Cuando las contribuciones al régimen general de la seguridad social se basen en la nómina, pero las de grupos particulares (tales como los trabajadores por cuenta propia) no puedan evaluarse en función de esta base y se emplee en ese caso la renta neta como una aproximación de las remuneraciones brutas, las entradas seguirán clasificándose sobre la base de la nómina. En principio, esta categoría excluye las contribuciones voluntarias aportadas a los regímenes de seguridad social, que, cuando sea posible identificarlas de forma separada, se recogerán en la partida informativa sobre el financiamiento de las prestaciones sociales; sin embargo, en la práctica, estas aportaciones no siempre pueden desvincularse de las contribuciones obligatorias, en cuyo caso se incluirán igualmente en esta categoría.

38. Las contribuciones a los regímenes de seguro social no vinculados a instituciones del gobierno general, así como las aportaciones a otros tipos de sistemas de seguro, tales como planes de previsión o planes de pensiones, mutualidades u otros planes de ahorro, no se consideran contribuciones a la seguridad social. Los planes de previsión son acuerdos por los que las contribuciones de cada empleado y la parte correspondiente del empleador en nombre de aquél se conservan en una cuenta separada que genera interés, de la que pueden retirarse en circunstancias específicas. Por su parte, los planes de pensiones son regímenes organizados separadamente, negociados entres empleados y empleadores, que conllevan disposiciones sobre diversas contribuciones y prestaciones, a veces más directamente vinculadas a los niveles salariales y a la duración del servicio que en otros esquemas sociales. Cuando las contribuciones a esos regímenes son obligatorias o cuasiobligatorias (p. ej., en virtud de un acuerdo con sindicatos u organizaciones profesionales), se hacen constar en la partida informativa (véase la parte III, sección B, de la publicación Revenue Statistics de la OCDE).

39. Las contribuciones de los empleados del gobierno y de este con respecto a sus empleados a los regímenes de seguridad social incluidos en el gobierno general se clasifican en esta categoría. También se consideran impuestos las contribuciones de los empleados del gobierno a regímenes diferentes que puedan reputarse sustitutivos de los regímenes generales de seguridad social.[16] Por el contrario, cuando un régimen diferente no pueda considerarse sustitutivo de uno general y haya sido negociado entre el gobierno, en su papel de empleador, y sus empleados, no se estimará como régimen de seguridad social y, por lo tanto, las contribuciones a él no se tendrán como impuestos, aunque el régimen haya sido instaurado por la legislación.

40. Esta categoría excluye las contribuciones "imputadas", que corresponden a las prestaciones sociales pagadas directamente por los empleadores a sus empleados, antiguos empleados o personas a cargo de estos (p. ej., cuando los empleadores están legalmente obligados a correr con las prestaciones por enfermedad durante cierto tiempo).

41. Las contribuciones se dividen en tres partidas principales –empleados (2100), empleadores (2200) y trabajadores por cuenta propia o no empleados (2300)– y se subdividen posteriormente en función de la base que gravan. A efectos de la presente publicación, se entiende por empleados todas las personas contratadas en actividades de unidades empresariales, órganos gubernamentales, instituciones privadas sin ánimo de lucro u otro tipo de empleo remunerado, con excepción de los dueños de empresas no constituidas en sociedad y de los miembros no remunerados de sus familias. También se consideran empleados los miembros de las Fuerzas Armadas, independientemente de la duración y del tipo de su servicio, siempre que coticen a regímenes de la seguridad social. Por su parte, las contribuciones de los empleadores se definen como las aportaciones que estos realizan por cuenta de sus empleados a los sistemas de seguridad social. Si los empleados o los empleadores tienen la obligación de continuar cotizando a la seguridad social en el caso de desempleo de un empleado, esas contribuciones se muestran en las partidas 2100 y 2200, respectivamente, siempre que los datos lo permitan. En consecuencia, la partida 2300 queda reservada a las contribuciones abonadas por los trabajadores por cuenta propia y por quienes no se hallan incluidos en la población activa (p. ej., incapacitados o jubilados).

3000 – *Impuestos sobre la nómina y la fuerza de trabajo*

42. Esta categoría cubre los impuestos satisfechos por los empleadores, los empleados o los trabajadores por cuenta propia, ya como una proporción de la nómina, ya como una cantidad fija por persona, que no confieren derecho a prestaciones sociales. Como ejemplos de impuestos integrados en esta categoría, cabe citar la aportación al seguro nacional del Reino Unido (introducido en 1977), el impuesto sobre la nómina de Suecia (1969-1979) o la contribución al fondo de equiparación de la carga familiar e impuesto comunitario de Austria.

4000 – *Impuestos sobre la propiedad*

43. Esta categoría engloba los impuestos, recurrentes y no recurrentes, sobre el uso, la titularidad o la transmisión de la propiedad, lo que incluye impuestos sobre la propiedad inmueble y la riqueza neta, sobre el cambio de titularidad en la propiedad por herencia o donación, y sobre transacciones financieras y de capital. Quedan excluidas de esta categoría los siguientes tipos de impuestos:

a) los impuestos sobre las ganancias de capital procedentes de la venta de propiedad (1120 o 1220);

b) los impuestos sobre el uso de bienes y sobre el permiso para usar bienes o realizar actividades (5200): véase el § 73;

c) los impuestos sobre los bienes inmuebles gravados sobre la base de un ingreso neto presunto que tiene en cuenta las circunstancias personales del contribuyente: se clasifican como impuestos sobre la renta junto con los impuestos sobre la renta y sobre las ganancias de capital derivadas de la propiedad (1100);

d) los impuestos sobre el uso de la propiedad con fines residenciales, tanto si debe responder del impuesto el propietario como el arrendatario, siempre que la cantidad debida tenga en cuenta las circunstancias personales del usuario (ingresos, personas a cargo, etcétera): se integran en los impuestos sobre la renta (1100);

e) los impuestos sobre los edificios con una densidad máxima superior a la permitida; sobre la ampliación, construcción o modificación de ciertos edificios más allá de un valor umbral; y sobre la construcción de edificios: todos ellos se integran en los impuestos sobre el permiso para realizar actividades (5200);

f) los impuestos sobre el uso de la propiedad propia para fines comerciales especiales, tales como la venta de bebidas alcohólicas, tabaco o carne, o para la explotación de tierras (p. ej., impuestos sobre la extracción en Estados Unidos): se integran en los impuestos sobre el permiso para realizar actividades (5200).

4100 – *Impuestos recurrentes sobre la propiedad inmueble*

44. Esta partida comprende los impuestos con que se grava de forma regular el uso o la titularidad de bienes inmuebles.

- Estos impuestos gravan las tierras y los edificios.
- Pueden consistir en un porcentaje del valor tasado de una propiedad, basado a su vez en un ingreso por alquiler hipotético, en el precio de venta, en un rendimiento capitalizado o en otras características de la propiedad inmueble (por ejemplo, el tamaño o la ubicación) de las que quepa inferir un alquiler o un valor de capital hipotéticos.
- Estos impuestos pueden aplicarse a los propietarios, a los arrendatarios o a ambos. También pueden pagarse de un nivel de gobierno a otro en relación con los bienes bajo jurisdicción de este último.
- Para la evaluación de estos impuestos, no se tienen en cuenta las deudas y, en ese sentido, difieren de los impuestos sobre la riqueza neta.

45. Los impuestos recurrentes sobre la propiedad inmueble se subdividen a su vez en los pagados por los hogares (4110) y los abonados por otros sujetos pasivos (4120), de acuerdo con los criterios establecidos en el § 26(b) supra.

4200 – *Impuestos recurrentes sobre la riqueza neta*

46. Esta partida abarca los impuestos con que se grava periódicamente (por lo general, anualmente) la riqueza neta, esto es, los impuestos sobre un amplio abanico de bienes muebles e inmuebles, descontadas sus deudas. Esta partida se subdivide a su vez en los impuestos pagados por las personas físicas (4210) y los abonados por las sociedades (4220), de acuerdo con los criterios establecidos en el § 26(a) supra. Si existen cifras separadas para las entradas correspondientes a pagos realizados por instituciones, se añaden a la subpartida de las sociedades.

4300 – *Impuestos sobre sucesiones, herencias y donaciones*

47. Esta partida se divide entre impuestos sobre sucesiones o herencias (4310) e impuestos sobre donaciones (4320).[17] Los impuestos sobre sucesiones gravan el valor total de la sucesión o del caudal hereditario, mientras los impuestos sobre herencias se aplican a las cuotas recibidas por los causahabientes individualmente considerados o en función de la relación de estos con el difunto.

4400 – *Impuestos sobre transacciones financieras y de capital*

48. Esta partida incluye, entre otros, los impuestos sobre la emisión, transmisión, compra y venta de valores, sobre los cheques, y sobre transacciones legales específicas, tales como la validación de contratos o la venta de bienes inmuebles. La partida no incluye:

a) los impuestos sobre el uso de bienes y sobre el permiso para realizar ciertas actividades (5200);

b) las tasas abonadas en concepto de costos procesales o expedición de actas de nacimiento, matrimonio o defunción, que suelen considerarse como ingresos no tributarios (véase el § 9);

c) los impuestos sobre ganancias de capital (1000);

d) los impuestos recurrentes sobre la propiedad inmueble (4100);

e) los impuestos recurrentes sobre la riqueza neta (4200);

f) otros impuestos no recurrentes sobre la propiedad o la riqueza (4500).

4500 – *Otros impuestos no recurrentes sobre la propiedad*[17]

49. Esta partida cubre los gravámenes sobre la propiedad que, a diferencia de los impuestos recurrentes, se recaudan una sola vez. Se divide en impuestos no recurrentes sobre la riqueza neta (4510) y otros impuestos no recurrentes sobre la propiedad (4520). La subpartida 4510 contiene los impuestos que se recaudan a fin de hacer frente a gastos excepcionales o de redistribuir la riqueza. Por su parte, la subpartida 4520 comprende los impuestos que gravan los incrementos de valor de la tierra, debido, por ejemplo, a permisos para su desarrollo concedidos por el gobierno general o a la provisión por parte de este de instalaciones locales adicionales; cualesquiera impuestos sobre la reevaluación del capital; y aquellos impuestos gravados una sola vez sobre determinados tipos de propiedad.

4600 – *Otros impuestos recurrentes sobre la propiedad*

50. Aunque este tipo de impuestos rara vez se dan en los países miembros de la OCDE, esta partida incluye los impuestos sobre bienes tales como ganado bovino, joyas, ventanas y otros signos externos de riqueza.

5000 – *Impuestos sobre los bienes y servicios*

51. Se incluyen en esta categoría todos los impuestos y derechos sobre la producción, extracción, venta, transmisión, arrendamiento y entrega de bienes, así como sobre la prestación de servicios (5100), y también los impuestos aplicados al uso de bienes y al permiso para usar bienes o realizar actividades (5200). Por lo tanto, esta categoría comprende:

a) los impuestos acumulativos de etapas múltiples;

b) los impuestos generales sobre las ventas aplicados, ya sea en la fabricación/producción, ya sea en la venta al por mayor o al por menor;

c) los impuestos sobre el valor agregado;

d) los impuestos selectivos;

e) los impuestos sobre las importaciones y exportaciones de bienes;

f) los impuestos sobre el uso de bienes y sobre el permiso para usar bienes o realizar ciertas actividades;

g) los impuestos sobre la extracción, el procesamiento o la producción de minerales y otros productos.

52. Los casos de difícil delimitación entre esta categoría y la categoría 4000 (impuestos sobre la propiedad) o la partida 6100 (otros impuestos pagados únicamente por empresas) se tratan en los §§ 43, 48 y 75. La partida 5300 y la subpartida 5130, ambas residuales, incluyen, respectivamente, las entradas tributarias que no hayan podido clasificarse entre las partidas 5100 y 5200 o entre las subpartidas 5110 y 5120.

5100 – *Impuestos sobre la producción, venta, transmisión, arrendamiento y entrega de bienes, y la prestación de servicios*

53. Esta partida comprende todos los impuestos aplicados a transacciones de bienes y servicios por las características intrínsecas de estos (p. ej., valor, peso del tabaco, graduación de las bebidas alcohólicas, etcétera) a diferencia de los impuestos determinados por el uso de bienes o por el permiso para usar bienes o realizar actividades, que entran dentro del ámbito de la partida 5200.

5110 – *Impuestos generales*

54. En esta subpartida, se incluyen todos los impuestos, aparte de los derechos de importación y exportación (5123 y 5124, respectivamente), que gravan la producción, el arrendamiento, la transmisión, la entrega o la venta de un amplio abanico de bienes o la prestación de una gran variedad de servicios, independientemente de que sean de producción nacional o importados, o de la etapa de producción o de distribución en la que recaigan. Por ende, comprende los impuestos sobre el valor agregado, los impuestos sobre las ventas y los impuestos acumulativos de etapas múltiples. A las entradas brutas generadas, se añaden las entradas por ajustes fronterizos en concepto de esos impuestos cuando se importan bienes, y se restan las devoluciones de dichos impuestos cuando se exportan bienes. Esta subpartida se divide a su vez en los epígrafes 5111, impuestos sobre el valor agregado; 5112, impuestos sobre las ventas; y 5113, otros impuestos generales sobre los bienes y servicios.

55. Suelen plantearse dificultades de delimitación entre esta subpartida y la dedicada a los impuestos sobre bienes y servicios específicos (5120) cuando los impuestos se aplican a un gran número de bienes, como, por ejemplo, en el caso del impuesto sobre las compras del Reino Unido (abolido en 1973) o el impuesto sobre mercancías de Japón (abolido en 1988). De acuerdo con las respectivas perspectivas nacionales, el antiguo impuesto sobre las compras británico se ha clasificado como impuesto general (5112), mientras el desaparecido impuesto sobre mercancías japonés se ha incluido entre los impuestos selectivos (5121).

5111 – *Impuestos sobre el valor agregado*

56. Todos los impuestos generales al consumo cargados sobre el valor agregado entran dentro de este epígrafe, independientemente del método de deducción y de las etapas en las que recaiga el impuesto. En la práctica, todos los países de la OCDE con este tipo de impuestos permiten que todos los intermediarios, excepto el consumidor final, se deduzcan inmediatamente los impuestos sobre las compras e imponen tributación en todas las etapas. Para algunos países, puede que se incluyan en este epígrafe otros impuestos, tales como los aplicados sobre actividades financieras y de seguros, o bien porque las entradas que generan no pueden identificarse separadamente de las procedentes del impuesto sobre el valor agregado, o bien porque se considera que forman parte de este último, aunque esos mismos impuestos puedan clasificarse diferentemente en terceros países (p. ej., como impuestos sobre servicios específicos (5126) o impuestos sobre transacciones financieras y de capital (4400).

5112 – *Impuestos sobre las ventas*

57. Se clasifican aquí todos los impuestos generales aplicados a una sola etapa, ya sea en la fabricación/producción, o en la venta al por mayor o al por menor.

5113 – *Otros impuestos generales sobre los bienes y servicios*

58. Este epígrafe comprende los impuestos acumulativos de etapas múltiples (también conocidos como "impuestos en cascada"), en los que el impuesto se aplica cada vez que se realiza una transacción sin deducción del valor del impuesto pagado sobre los insumos, así como los impuestos generales al consumo cuando estos combinan elementos de los impuestos sobre el valor agregado, sobre las ventas o en cascada.

5120 – *Impuestos sobre bienes y servicios específicos*

59. Se incluyen en esta subpartida los impuestos selectivos, las utilidades generadas y transferidas por los monopolios fiscales, y los derechos de aduana y otros derechos de importación, así como los impuestos sobre las exportaciones, las transacciones de divisas, los bienes de inversión y las apuestas, y los impuestos especiales sobre los servicios que no formen parte de uno de los impuestos generales de la subpartida 5110.

5121 – *Impuestos selectivos*

60. Los impuestos selectivos son impuestos que se aplican a productos particulares o a un abanico limitado de productos, que no pueden clasificarse ni en 5110 (impuestos generales) ni en 5123 (derechos de aduana y otros derechos de importación) ni en 5124 (impuestos sobre las exportaciones). Pueden imponerse en cualquier etapa de la producción o la distribución, y suelen determinarse por referencia al peso, la graduación o la cantidad del producto, aunque, en ocasiones, también en función del valor de éste. Se incluyen, por lo tanto, en este epígrafe, los impuestos especiales sobre, por ejemplo, el azúcar, la remolacha, los fósforos o el chocolate; los impuestos a tasas impositivas variables sobre una cierta gama de bienes; y los impuestos que gravan en la mayoría de los países los productos derivados del tabaco, las bebidas alcohólicas, y los aceites de hidrocarburos y otras fuentes de energía.

61. Los impuestos selectivos se distinguen de:

a) los impuestos generales (5110): abordado en los §§ 54 y 55;

b) los derechos de aduana y otros derechos de importación (5123): si un impuesto recaudado principalmente sobre los bienes importados también se aplica, o podría aplicarse, de conformidad con la misma ley que establece el impuesto, a bienes comparables producidos en el país, las entradas de dicho impuesto se clasifican como impuestos selectivos (5121); este principio rige incluso cuando no existan productos nacionales comparables ni la posibilidad de que se produzcan (véase el § 65);

c) los impuestos sobre servicios específicos (5126): el problema se plantea en relación con los impuestos sobre la electricidad, el gas y la energía, que se consideran impuestos sobre los bienes y se incluyen en el epígrafe 5121.

5122 – *Utilidades de los monopolios fiscales*

62. Este epígrafe comprende la parte de las utilidades de los monopolios fiscales transferida al gobierno general o usada para financiar gastos considerados como gastos del gobierno (véase el § 19). Las cantidades implicadas se registran cuando se transfieren al gobierno general o cuando se usan para gastos considerados como gastos del gobierno.

63. Los monopolios fiscales reflejan el ejercicio del poder tributario del gobierno mediante el uso de prerrogativas monopolísticas. Se trata de empresas públicas no financieras que ejercen un monopolio, en la mayoría de los casos sobre la producción o la distribución de tabaco, bebidas alcohólicas, sal, fósforos, cartas de juego, productos derivados del petróleo y productos agrícolas (es decir, sobre el tipo de productos susceptibles de estar sometidos, alternativa o adicionalmente, a los impuestos selectivos del epígrafe 5121), con el fin de recaudar ingresos para el gobierno que en otros países se obtienen gravando las operaciones que sobre dichos bienes efectúan las unidades empresariales privadas. El monopolio del gobierno puede intervenir en la etapa de producción o, en el caso de los establecimientos de licores propiedad del gobierno o bajo control de éste, en la etapa de distribución.

64. Cabe distinguir los monopolios fiscales de los servicios públicos, tales como el transporte ferroviario, la electricidad, los servicios de correos y otras comunicaciones, que pueden gozar también de una posición monopolística o cuasimonopolística, pero cuyo fin primero suele ser la prestación de servicios básicos y no la obtención de ingresos para el gobierno; las transferencias de esas otras empresas públicas al gobierno se consideran ingresos no tributarios. El concepto tradicional de monopolio fiscal no llega a abarcar las loterías estatales, cuyas utilidades se consideran, en consecuencia, ingresos no tributarios. Las utilidades de los monopolios fiscales se han separado de las de los monopolios de importación y exportación (5127) transferidas de juntas de comercialización u otras empresas dedicadas al comercio internacional.

5123 – *Derechos de aduana y otros derechos de importación*

65. Se incluyen aquí los impuestos, derechos de timbre y sobrecargas limitados por ley a los productos importados, así como los gravámenes sobre los productos agrícolas importados impuestos en los países miembros de la Unión Europea y las cantidades satisfechas por algunos de esos países a tenor del sistema de montantes compensatorios monetarios (MCM).[18] Desde 1998, los derechos de aduana recaudados por los Estados miembros de la Unión Europea en nombre de ésta ya no se registran en este epígrafe en los cuadros de países (parte III de la publicación Revenue Statistics de la OCDE). Quedan excluidos aquí los impuestos recaudados de las importaciones como parte de un impuesto general sobre los bienes y servicios, así como los impuestos selectivos aplicables tanto a bienes importados como a bienes de producción nacional.

5124 – *Impuestos sobre las exportaciones*

66. En los años 1970, los derechos de exportación se aplicaban en Australia, Canadá y Portugal como una medida de carácter regular, y en Finlandia se han utilizado con fines contracíclicos. Algunos países miembros de la Unión Europea pagan un gravamen sobre las exportaciones, en el marco del sistema MCM (véase la nota a pie de página 18 en el § 65). Cuando las cantidades recaudadas son identificables, se integran en este epígrafe, que no incluye, sin embargo, las devoluciones de impuestos generales al consumo, de impuestos selectivos o de derechos de aduana sobre los bienes exportados, que se deducirán de las entradas brutas de 5110, 5121 o 5123, según corresponda.

5125 – *Impuestos sobre los bienes de inversión*

67. Este epígrafe cubre los impuestos sobre los bienes de inversión, tales como la maquinaria. Estos impuestos pueden cargarse por un cierto número de años o temporalmente con fines contracíclicos. No se incluyen aquí aquellos impuestos sobre los insumos industriales que recaen también en los consumidores (p. ej., el impuesto sobre la energía en Suecia, que se clasifica en 5121).

5126 – *Impuestos sobre servicios específicos*

68. Todos los impuestos sobre el pago por servicios específicos, tales como los impuestos sobre las primas de seguro, los servicios bancarios, los juegos de azar y las apuestas (p. ej., carreras de caballos, quinielas de fútbol, lotería), el transporte, las actividades recreativas o de ocio, los restaurantes y la publicidad, entran dentro de este epígrafe. También se clasifican aquí los impuestos sobre el ingreso bruto de las empresas que prestan el servicio (p. ej., primas de seguro o apuestas brutas recibidas por una empresa). Los ingresos tributarios procedentes de gravámenes bancarios y pagos a sistemas de seguro de depósitos y de estabilidad financiera se han incluido provisionalmente en este epígrafe para la edición de 2012. La clasificación detallada figura en el Anexo A.

69. Se excluyen de este epígrafe:

a) los impuestos sobre servicios que formen parte de un impuesto general sobre los bienes y servicios (5110);

b) los impuestos sobre la electricidad, el gas y la energía (5121, impuestos selectivos);

c) los impuestos sobre las ganancias de las personas físicas en los juegos de azar (1120, impuestos sobre las ganancias de capital de las personas físicas o de las empresas no constituidas en sociedad) y los impuestos fijos sobre la transferencia de loterías privadas o sobre el permiso para crear loterías (5200);[19]

d) los impuestos sobre los cheques y sobre la emisión, transmisión o compra y venta de valores (4400, impuestos sobre transacciones financieras y de capital).

5127 – *Otros impuestos sobre el comercio y las transacciones internacionales*

70. Este epígrafe abarca los ingresos percibidos por el gobierno por la compra y la venta de divisas a diferentes tipos de cambio. Cuando el gobierno ejerce poderes monopolísticos para obtener un margen entre los precios de compra y de venta de divisas superior al que sería necesario para cubrir los costos administrativos, el ingreso generado constituye un gravamen obligatorio impuesto en proporciones indeterminadas tanto sobre el comprador como sobre el vendedor de divisas. Es un equivalente común de los derechos de importación y exportación cargados en un sistema con tipo de cambio único o de un impuesto sobre la compraventa de divisas. Al igual que las utilidades de los monopolios fiscales o de los monopolios de importación y exportación transferidas al gobierno, representa el ejercicio de las prerrogativas monopolísticas con fines fiscales y, por lo tanto, se incluye en los ingresos tributarios.

71. El epígrafe engloba asimismo las utilidades de los monopolios de importación y exportación, que, sin embargo, son inexistentes en los países de la OCDE; los impuestos sobre la compraventa de divisas; y cualesquiera otros impuestos que recaigan sobre el comercio o las transacciones internacionales.

5128 – *Otros impuestos sobre bienes y servicios específicos*

72. Este epígrafe incluye los impuestos sobre la extracción de minerales, combustibles fósiles y otros recursos agotables de yacimientos de propieddad privada o de otro nivel de gobierno, así como cualesquiera otras entradas no identificables procedentes de impuestos sobre bienes y servicios específicos. Los impuestos sobre la extracción de recursos agotables suelen traducirse en un importe fijo por cantidad o peso, pero también pueden adoptar un valor porcentual. Los impuestos se registran en el momento de extracción de los recursos. Los pagos por extracción de recursos agotables de yacimientos propiedad de la unidad de gobierno que recibe el pago se clasifican como alquiler.

5200 – *Impuestos sobre el uso de bienes y sobre el permiso para usar bienes o realizar actividades*

73. Esta partida incluye los impuestos aplicados al uso de bienes a diferencia de los impuestos sobre los propios bienes. Al contrario que los impuestos de este último tipo (registrados en la partida 5100), los impuestos considerados aquí no se basan en el valor de los bienes, sino que suelen revestir la forma de importes fijos. Los impuestos sobre el permiso para usar bienes o realizar actividades entran asimismo en esta partida, como, por ejemplo, los impuestos sobre la contaminación que no se basan en el valor de bienes particulares. En ocasiones, resulta complejo distinguir entre cargos obligatorios a los usuarios y tasas de licencia que se consideran como impuestos y aquellos que quedan excluidos por reputarse como ingresos no tributarios; los criterios de deslinde empleados se explican en los §§ 9 y 10.

74. Aunque el título de esta partida menciona el "uso" de bienes, es posible que sea el registro de la propiedad, y no el uso, lo que dé lugar a la obligación tributaria, y que los impuestos contenidos aquí se apliquen más al hecho de ser titular de ciertos animales o bienes (p. ej., caballos de carreras, perros y vehículos automotores) que al uso que se hace de ellos, o que recaigan incluso en bienes inutilizables (p. ej., vehículos automotores o armas inservibles).

75. Se plantean casos de difícil delimitación con respecto a:

a) los impuestos sobre el permiso para realizar actividades empresariales que parten de una base combinada de renta, nómina o volumen de ventas, que se clasifican de acuerdo con las normas del § 78;

b) los impuestos sobre la propiedad o el uso de la propiedad de las partidas 4100, 4200 y 4600; la partida 4100 se dedica exclusivamente a los impuestos sobre la titularidad o la posesión de bienes inmuebles y, a diferencia de los impuestos de la partida 5200, recaen siempre sobre el valor de la propiedad; los impuestos sobre la riqueza neta (4200) y otros impuestos recurrentes sobre la propiedad (4600) se circunscriben al hecho de ser titular de propiedades, y no al uso de activos; se aplican a grupos de activos, y no a bienes particulares; y están en todo caso relacionados con el valor de los activos en cuestión.

5210 – *Impuestos recurrentes*

76. La principal característica de los impuestos consignados aquí es que se recaudan a intervalos regulares y se cobran por lo general según una cantidad fija. En términos de ingresos, el elemento más importante está constituido por los impuestos por licencia de vehículos, aunque también integran esta subpartida los impuestos sobre los permisos de caza, pesca o tiro o sobre la venta de ciertos productos, así como los impuestos sobre la propiedad de animales domésticos y sobre la prestación de ciertos servicios siempre que estos reúnan los criterios establecidos en los §§ 9 y 10. Los epígrafes en que se divide la partida 5210 son: los impuestos sobre vehículos automotores pagados por los hogares (5211) y los satisfechos por otros sujetos pasivos (5212);[20] por su parte, el epígrafe 5213 abarca las licencias a propietarios de animales domésticos y los cargos a usuarios por el permiso de realizar actividades, tales como la venta de carne o de bebidas alcohólica cuando los gravámenes se imponen de forma recurrente, así como las licencias generales periódicas de caza, pesca y tiro cuando el derecho a emprender esas actividades no se otorga como parte de una transacción comercial normal (p. ej., la concesión de la licencia no implica el derecho a usar una zona específica propiedad del gobierno).

5220 – *Impuestos no recurrentes*

77. Se incluyen aquí los impuestos no recurrentes aplicados sobre el uso de bienes y sobre el permiso para utilizar bienes o realizar actividades, así como los impuestos aplicados cada vez que se utilizan los bienes.

- Entran en esta subpartida los impuestos sobre la emisión o liberación en el medio ambiente de gases y líquidos nocivos y otras sustancias peligrosas. Los pagos por permisos negociables de emisión expedidos por los gobiernos en el marco de programas de límites máximos y comercio de emisiones deberán registrarse aquí en la fecha en que se produzcan las emisiones. No se computarán ingresos por los permisos que los gobiernos expidan a título gratuito.
- El registro según el criterio de devengo implica que habrá una diferencia temporal entre el momento en que el gobierno reciba el pago por los permisos y el momento en que se produzca la emisión. En las cuentas nacionales, esta diferencia genera un pasivo para el gobierno durante ese periodo.
- Se excluirán los pagos efectuados por la recogida y eliminación de desechos o sustancias nocivas por parte de los poderes públicos, ya que constituyen una venta de servicios a las empresas.

78. También se incluyen aquí otros impuestos que entren dentro del ámbito de aplicación de la partida 5200 y que no se recauden recurrentemente. Por lo tanto, quedarán comprendidos los pagos únicos por permisos para la venta de alcohol o tabaco o para la creación de centros de apuestas, siempre que cumplan los criterios de los §§ 9 y 10.

6000 – *Otros impuestos*

79. Esta categoría recoge los impuestos que reposan en una o varias bases diferentes de las descritas en las categorías 1000, 3000, 4000 y 5000, o en bases que no puedan considerarse predominantemente las mismas que las incluidas en esas categorías. En relación con los impuestos de base múltiple, si es posible estimar las entradas relacionadas con cada base (p. ej., el impuesto Gewerbesteuer en Alemania y Austria), las cantidades desglosadas se repartirán en las correspondientes categorías. Si no pueden calcularse los valores por separado, pero se sabe que la mayoría de las entradas proceden de una base determinada, el total de estas se atribuirán de acuerdo con dicha base. Si no puede seguirse ninguno de estos procedimientos, las entradas se clasificarán aquí. Las diversas partidas de esta categoría podrán incluir asimismo el producto de impuestos que los gobiernos no puedan identificar o aislar (véase el § 28). Se incorporan asimismo aquí las multas y sanciones pecuniarias pagadas por el incumplimiento de normas tributarias, pero no imputables a una categoría particular de impuestos (véase el § 15). Esta categoría se subdivide entre los impuestos pagados completa o principalmente por las empresas (6100) y los abonados por otros sujetos pasivos (6200).

A.6. Conciliación con las cuentas nacionales

80. Esta sección de los cuadros reconcilia el cálculo de la recaudación tributaria total realizado por la OCDE y el total de todos los impuestos y contribuciones sociales pagados al gobierno general tal y como figuran en el registro de las cuentas nacionales de cada país. Cuando el país es miembro de la Unión Europea (UE), la comparación se establece entre el cálculo de la recaudación tributaria total realizado por la OCDE y la suma de los ingresos tributarios y contribuciones sociales registrado en la combinación del gobierno general y de las instituciones de los sectores de la UE de las cuentas nacionales.

A.7. Partida informativa sobre el financiamiento de las prestaciones sociales

81. A la vista de la variedad de relaciones entre la tributación y las contribuciones a la seguridad social y de los casos mencionados en los §§ 35–41, se ha previsto una partida informativa que recopile todos los pagos asignados a las prestaciones tipo de la seguridad social, aparte de los pagos voluntarios al sector privado. Los datos se presentan de la forma siguiente (véase la parte III, sección B, de la publicación *Revenue Statistics* de la OCDE):

a) Impuestos de la categoría 2000.

b) Impuestos asignados a las prestaciones de la seguridad social.

c) Contribuciones voluntarias al gobierno.

d) Contribuciones obligatorias al sector privado.

Los §§ 35–41 ofrecen las debidas orientaciones para efectuar el desglose entre las rúbricas (a) a (d).

A.8. Partida informativa sobre impuestos identificables pagados por el gobierno

82. Los impuestos identificables realmente pagados por el gobierno se presentan en una partida informativa, desglosados según las principales categorías de la clasificación de impuestos de la OCDE. En la vasta mayoría de los países, sólo pueden identificarse las contribuciones a la seguridad social y los impuestos sobre la nómina satisfechos por el gobierno, que, sin embargo, suelen ser los gravámenes más importantes liquidados por los gobiernos (véase la parte III, sección C, de la publicación *Revenue Statistics* de la OCDE).

A.9. Relación de la clasificación de impuestos de la OCDE con el Sistema de Cuentas Nacionales

83. El Sistema de Cuentas Nacionales (SCN) pretende proporcionar un marco coherente para registrar y presentar los principales flujos relacionados con la producción, el consumo, la acumulación y las transacciones con el exterior de una determinada zona económica, por lo general, un país o una región destacada de un país, y, en este sentido, los ingresos del gobierno constituyen una importante parte de las transacciones registradas en todo sistema de cuentas nacionales. En agosto de 2009, la versión final del SCN 2008 se publicó conjuntamente por cinco organizaciones internacionales: la Organización de las Naciones Unidas, el Fondo Monetario Internacional, la Unión Europea, la Organización para la Cooperación y el Desarrollo Económicos, y el Banco Mundial. La publicación está diseñada para ser empleada en países con economías de mercado, sea cual sea su estadio de desarrollo económico, así como en países en transición hacia economías de mercado. Las principales partes del marco conceptual y las definiciones de los diversos sectores económicos del SCN se han plasmado en la clasificación de impuestos de la OCDE.

84. Sin embargo, existen ciertas diferencias, reseñadas seguidamente, entre la clasificación de impuestos de la OCDE y los conceptos del SCN, debidas a que la finalidad de la clasificación de la OCDE consiste en lograr la máxima desagregación posible de los datos estadísticos en relación con lo que, por lo general, las Administraciones tributarias consideran como impuestos. Y así:

a) la OCDE incluye las contribuciones a la seguridad social en la recaudación tributaria total (véanse los §§ 7 y 8 *supra.*);

b) los puntos de vista sobre la calificación de algunos gravámenes y tasas como impuestos son diferentes (§§ 9 y 10 *supra.*);

c) la OCDE excluye los impuestos imputados o los subsidios procedentes de la aplicación de múltiples tipos de cambio oficiales;

d) los créditos fiscales exigibles se tratan de forma diferente.

85. Tal y como se ha apuntado en los §§ 1 y 2, las categorías 1000 a 6000 de la lista de impuestos de la OCDE cubren todos los pagos sin contraprestación al gobierno general, aparte de las multas y los préstamos obligatorios. Esos pagos sin contraprestación, incluidas las multas pero excluidos los préstamos obligatorios, pueden obtenerse añadiendo los siguientes valores del SCN 2008:

- impuestos sobre el valor agregado (D211);
- impuestos y derechos sobre las importaciones, IVA no incluido (D212);
- impuestos sobre las exportaciones (D213);
- impuestos sobre los productos, IVA e impuestos sobre las importaciones y exportaciones no incluidos (D214);
- otros impuestos sobre la producción (D29);
- impuestos sobre la renta (D51);
- otros impuestos corrientes (D59);
- contribuciones sociales (D61), excluidas las contribuciones voluntarias;
- impuestos sobre el capital (D91).

A.10. Relación de la clasificación de impuestos de la OCDE con el sistema de estadísticas de finanzas públicas del Fondo Monetario Internacional

86. La cobertura y la valoración de los ingresos tributarios en el sistema de estadísticas de finanzas públicas (EFP) y en el SCN 2008 son muy similares. Por lo tanto, a excepción del tratamiento dado a los créditos fiscales exigibles, las diferencias entre la clasificación de la OCDE y la del SCN 2008 (véase el § 84 *supra.*) son de aplicación igualmente al sistema de EFP. Además, el Fondo Monetario Internacional (FMI) escinde la categoría única 5000 de la OCDE en dos categorías distintas dedicadas a los impuestos nacionales sobre bienes y servicios (114) y a los impuestos sobre el comercio y las transacciones internacionales (115). Esto refleja el hecho de que, mientras estos últimos impuestos suelen generar insignificantes cantidades de ingresos en la zona de la OCDE, ese no es el caso en la mayoría de los países no pertenecientes a la Organización.

A.11. Comparación de la clasificación de impuestos de la OCDE con otras clasificaciones internacionales

87. El cuadro siguiente recoge una comparación ítem por ítem entre la clasificación de impuestos de la OCDE y las clasificaciones empleadas en:

i) el Sistema de Cuentas Nacionales (SCN 2008);

ii) el Sistema Europeo de Cuentas (SEC 1995);

iii) el *Manual de estadísticas de finanzas públicas* del FMI (MEFP 2001).

88. Estas comparaciones representan equivalencias que podrán aplicarse en la mayoría de los casos. Con todo, deberán emplearse con cierta flexibilidad, ya que, en casos particulares, los países pueden adoptar enfoques diferentes para la clasificación de los ingresos en las cuentas nacionales.

Clasificación de la OCDE		SCN 2008	SEC 1995	MEFP 2001
1000	Impuestos sobre la renta, las utilidades y las ganancias de capital			
	1100 Personas físicas			
	1110 Renta/utilidades	D51-8.61a	D51A	1111
	1120 Ganancias de capital	D51-8.61c,d	D51C,D	1111
	1200 Sociedades			
	1210 Renta/utilidades	D51-8.61b	D51B	1112
	1220 Ganancias de capital	D51-8.61c	D51C	1112
	1300 No clasificables entre 1100 y 1200			1113
2000	Contribuciones a la seguridad social			
	2100 Empleados	D613-8.85	D61111	1211
	2200 Empleadores	D611-8.83	D61121	1212
	2300 Trabajadores por cuenta propia o no empleados	D613-8.85	D61131	1213
	2400 No clasificables entre 2100, 2200 y 2300			1214
3000	Impuestos sobre la nómina y la fuerza de trabajo	D29-7.97a	D29C	112
4000	Impuestos sobre la propiedad			
	4100 Impuestos recurrentes sobre la propiedad inmueble			
	4110 Hogares	D59-8.63a	D59A	1131
	4120 Otros	D29-7.97b	D29A	1131
	4200 Impuestos recurrentes sobre la riqueza neta			
	4210 Personas físicas	D59-8.63b	D59A	1132
	4220 Sociedades	D59-8.63b	D59A	1132
	4300 Impuestos sobre sucesiones, herencias y donaciones			
	4310 Impuestos sobre sucesiones y herencias	D91-10.207b	D91A	1133
	4320 Impuestos sobre donaciones	D91-10.207b	D91A	1133
	4400 Impuestos sobre transacciones financieras y de capital	D59-7.96d; D29-7.97e	D214B,C	1134:1161
	4500 Otros impuestos no recurrentes sobre la propiedad	D91-10.207a	D91B	1135
	4600 Otros impuestos recurrentes sobre la propiedad	D59-8.63c	D59A	1136
5000	Impuestos sobre los bienes y servicios			
	5100 Impuestos sobre la producción, venta y transmisión de bienes y prestación de servicios			
	5110 Impuestos generales			
	5111 Impuestos sobre el valor agregado	D211-7.89	D211; D29G	11411
	5112 Impuestos sobre las ventas	D2122-7.94a; D214-7.96a	D2122D; D214I	11412
	5113 Otros impuestos generales sobre los bienes y servicios	D214-7.96a	D214I	11413
	5120 Impuestos sobre bienes y servicios específicos			
	5121 Impuestos selectivos	D2122-7.94b; D214-7.96b	D2122C; D214A,B,D	1142
	5122 Utilidades de los monopolios fiscales	D214-7.65e	D214J	1143
	5123 Derechos de aduanas y otros derechos de importación	D2121-7.93	D2121; D2122A,B	1151
	5124 Sobre las exportaciones	D213-7.95a	D214K	1152-4
	5125 Sobre los bienes de inversión			
	5126 Sobre servicios específicos	D2122-7.94c; D214-7.96c	D2122E; D214E,F,G; D29F	1144; 1156
	5127 Otros impuestos sobre el comercio y las transacciones internacionales	D2122-7.94d D29-7.95b D29-7.97g D59-8.64d	D2122F; D29D D59E	1153 1155-6
	5128 Otros impuestos sobre bienes y servicios específicos			1146
	5130 No clasificables entre 5110 y 5120			
	5200 Impuestos sobre el uso de bienes y sobre el permiso para usar bienes y realizar actividades			
	5210 Impuestos recurrentes			
	5211 Sobre vehículos automotores: hogares	D59-8.64c	D59D	11451
	5212 Sobre vehículos automotores: otros	D29-7.97d	D214D; D29B	11451
	5213 Otros impuestos recurrentes	D29-7.97c,d,f D59-8.64c	D29B,E,F; D59D	11452
	5220 Impuestos no recurrentes			
	5300 No clasificables entre 5100 y 5200			
6000	Otros impuestos			
	6100 Pagados únicamente por empresas			
	6200 Pagados por otros distintos de las empresas o no identificables	D59-8.64a,b	D59B,C	1162

A.12. Atribución de ingresos tributarios por subsectores del gobierno general

89. La clasificación de la OCDE requiere un desglose de los ingresos tributarios por subsectores del gobierno general. Seguidamente, se establecen la definición de cada subsector y los criterios que deben emplearse para atribuir los ingresos tributarios entre ellos, que siguen las orientaciones del SCN 2008 y del MEFP 2001.

Identificación de los subsectores del gobierno general

a) Gobierno central

90. El subsector del gobierno central incluye todos los departamentos, oficinas y establecimientos del gobierno, así como otros órganos que constituyen organismos o instrumentos de la autoridad central, cuya competencia se extiende a todo el territorio, con excepción de la administración de los fondos de seguridad social. En consecuencia, el gobierno central tiene la facultad de someter a tributación a todas las unidades residentes y no residentes que emprendan actividades económicas en el país.

b) Gobierno estatal, provincial o regional

91. Este subsector está compuesto por unidades intermedias del gobierno que ejercen su competencia a un nivel inferior al del gobierno central. Incluye a todas las unidades que operan independientemente del gobierno central en una parte del territorio de un país que engloba numerosas pequeñas localidades, con la excepción de la administración de los fondos de seguridad social. En los países unitarios, puede considerarse que los gobiernos regionales tienen una existencia separada, en la que cuentan con la suficiente autonomía como para recaudar sus ingresos de fuentes bajo su control, y sus funcionarios son independientes del control administrativo externo en el ejercicio de las actividades de la unidad.

92. En la actualidad, los países federales representan la mayoría de los casos en los que los ingresos atribuidos a unidades intermedias del gobierno se identifican de forma separada. España es el único país unitario en ese caso; en el resto de los países unitarios, los ingresos regionales se computan junto con los de los gobiernos locales.

c) Gobierno local

93. Este subsector incluye todas las demás unidades del gobierno que ejercen una competencia independiente en parte del territorio de un país, con excepción de la administración de los fondos de seguridad social. Engloba varios entes urbanos o rurales (p. ej., autoridades locales, municipios, ciudades, delegaciones, distritos).

d) Fondos de seguridad social

94. Los fondos de seguridad social forman un subsector separado del gobierno general. El SCN 2008 define el subsector de la seguridad social según lo expuesto en sus puntos 4.124 a 4.126 y 4.147, citados seguidamente:

> "Los regímenes de seguridad social son sistemas de seguros sociales que cubren a la comunidad en su conjunto o a amplios sectores de la misma, y que son impuestos y controlados por unidades del gobierno. Los sistemas abarcan una gran variedad de programas, y ofrecen prestaciones en dinero o en especie por vejez, invalidez o muerte, supervivencia, enfermedad y maternidad, accidentes de trabajo, desempleo, ayudas familiares, asistencia sanitaria, etc. No existe necesariamente una relación directa entre la cuantía de la contribución pagada por un individuo y las prestaciones que este pueda recibir." (punto 4.124)

"Cuando los sistemas de seguridad social se organizan por separado de las demás actividades de las unidades del gobierno, mantienen sus activos y pasivos separados de estas últimas, y realizan operaciones financieras por cuenta propia, se califican de unidades institucionales, que reciben el nombre de fondos de seguridad social." (punto 4.125)

"Las cantidades recaudadas y pagadas por contribuciones y prestaciones de la seguridad social pueden modificarse deliberadamente con el fin de alcanzar determinados objetivos de la política del gobierno que no tengan relación directa con el concepto de la seguridad social como sistema destinado a ofrecer prestaciones sociales a los miembros de la comunidad. Pueden aumentarse o disminuirse, por ejemplo, con el fin de influir en el nivel de la demanda agregada de la economía. No obstante, mientras se mantengan como fondos constituidos por separado, han de ser tratados, en el SCN, como unidades institucionales diferentes." (punto 4.126)

"El subsector de los fondos de seguridad social [del gobierno general] está conformado por los fondos de seguridad social que operan en todos los niveles del gobierno. Dichos fondos son sistemas de seguros sociales que cubren a la comunidad en su conjunto o a amplios sectores de la misma, y que son impuestos por unidades del gobierno." (punto 4.147)

95. La clasificación de la OCDE sigue esta definición de los fondos de seguridad social con las dos siguientes excepciones, por las se excluyen:

- os sistemas impuestos por el gobierno pero administrados por órganos externos al sector del gobierno general, tal y como se ha definido en el § 3 de este manual, y
- los sistemas en los que todas las contribuciones son voluntarias.

Autoridades supranacionales

96. Este subsector engloba las operaciones de recaudación fiscal de autoridades supranacionales dentro de un país. En la práctica, la única autoridad supranacional que cabe tener en cuenta en la zona de la OCDE es la que conforman las instituciones de la Unión Europea (UE). Desde 1998, las autoridades supranacionales no se incluyen en *Revenue Statistics*, a fin de ser coherentes con la definición que el SCN da del gobierno general, que las excluye. Por ejemplo, los impuestos sobre la renta y las contribuciones a la seguridad social recaudados por instituciones europeas y pagados a empleados públicos europeos que residen en países miembros de la OCDE no deberían incluirse. Pese a todo, ciertos gravámenes específicos pagados por los Estados miembros de la UE siguen incorporándose a la recaudación tributaria total y, en ese caso, se muestran bajo esta denominación.

Criterios de atribución de los ingresos tributarios

97. Cuando un gobierno recauda impuestos y los transfiere, en todo o en parte, a otros gobiernos, es necesario determinar si esos ingresos se imputarán al gobierno recaudador que los distribuye a otros en forma de donaciones, o si se atribuirán a los gobiernos beneficiarios para los que el gobierno recaudador actúa como mero agente, recibiendo el producto de los impuestos y transfiriéndolos posteriormente. Los criterios de atribución de los ingresos se establecen en los §§ 98–102 siguientes, y siguen lo dispuesto en los puntos 3.70 a 3.73 del SCN 2008.

98. Por regla general, un impuesto se atribuye a la unidad de gobierno que:

a) ejerce la facultad de aplicar el impuesto (como entidad principal o a través de la autoridad delegada por la entidad principal), y

b) puede a su discreción establecer y modificar la tasa del impuesto.

99. Cuando un gobierno recauda impuestos para y en nombre de otro, y este último tiene la facultad de aplicar el impuesto y establecer y modificar su tasa impositiva, entonces el gobierno recaudador actúa como agente de este, y el impuesto se reasigna. Cualquier cantidad retenida por el gobierno recaudador como cargo por la recaudación deberá tratarse como pago por un servicio. Cualquier otra cantidad retenida por el gobierno recaudador, por ejemplo, en el marco de un arreglo de coparticipación de impuestos, deberá tratarse como una donación corriente. Si se delegó al gobierno recaudador la autoridad para establecer y modificar la tasa impositiva entonces las cantidades recaudadas deberán tratarse como ingresos tributarios de este gobierno.

100. Cuando diferentes gobiernos establecen conjuntamente y por igual la tasa de un impuesto y el uso de los recursos, sin que ninguno de ellos tengan la autoridad final y exclusiva, entonces los ingresos tributarios se atribuyen a cada gobierno según la proporción de recursos que le corresponda; si el acuerdo permite a una unidad del gobierno ejercer el control final y exclusivo, entonces todos los ingresos tributarios se atribuirán a dicha unidad.

101. También puede ocurrir que un gobierno tenga la autoridad constitucional o de otra índole de aplicar un impuesto, pero que otros gobiernos establezcan individualmente la tasa de ese impuesto en sus jurisdicciones; los recursos generados por el impuesto en cuestión en la jurisdicción de cada gobierno se atribuirán como ingresos tributarios a los respectivos gobiernos.

Gravámenes satisfechos por los Estados miembros de la Unión Europea

102. Los gravámenes satisfechos por los Estados miembros de la Unión Europea (UE) revisten la forma de:

- recursos propios por IVA, y
- gravámenes específicos, entre los que se incluyen:

a) derechos de aduana y gravámenes sobre los bienes agrícolas (5123),

b) montantes compensatorios monetarios brutos (5123 en relación con las importaciones y 5124 en relación con las exportaciones), y

c) gravámenes sobre el acero, el carbón, el azúcar y la leche (5128).

103. Los derechos de aduana recaudados por los Estados miembros de la UE en nombre de esta se registran de la siguiente forma:

- sobre la base de un coeficiente de recaudación bruta;
- ajustando los resultados, siempre que sea posible, de forma que esos derechos se muestren en relación con una base de "destino final", por oposición a la base de "país de primera entrada"; estos ajustes atañen particularmente a los derechos colectados en importantes puertos (marítimos); aunque los derechos de la UE se perciben por las autoridades del país de primera entrada, siempre que sea posible cabrá excluir esos derechos del ingreso del país recaudador e incluirlos en el ingreso del país de destino final.

Este es el gravamen específico de la UE que más claramente se ciñe al criterio de atribución consignado en el § 97. En consecuencia, desde 1998, las cantidades en relación con este gravamen se registran como partida informativa en los cuadros de países de los Estados miembros de la UE (en la parte III de la publicación Revenue Statistics de la OCDE) y no se integran ya en el epígrafe 5123. Sin embargo, se incluyen en las cifras de recaudación tributaria total de la línea superior para los años correspondientes mostrados en los cuadros.

104. En cuanto a los recursos propios por IVA, que se determinan aplicando una tasa no superior al 1 por ciento a una base cuya evaluación viene dada en la Sexta Directiva,[21] se trata ciertamente de un caso de más difícil delimitación, ya que estos recursos reúnen ciertas características de una transferencia (no nacen de una fuente claramente identificable de fondos realmente recaudados) y ciertas otras de un impuesto (la cantidad de la transferencia viene determinada por el subsector del gobierno receptor). En esta publicación, no se consideran un impuesto de la Unión Europea (sino un impuesto de los Estados miembros), aunque las cantidades implicadas se indican al pie de los cuadros de la parte IV de la publicación Revenue Statistics de la OCDE.

A.13. Clasificación provisional de los ingresos tributarios procedentes de gravámenes bancarios y pagos a sistemas de seguro de depósitos y de estabilidad financiera

105. La OCDE ha adoptado el siguiente enfoque provisional para el registro de los ingresos procedentes de gravámenes bancarios, así como de seguro de depósitos y tasas de estabilidad para la edición 2012 de la publicación *Revenue Statistics* de la OCDE. Los importes deberán consignarse en el epígrafe 5126.

- Los pagos obligatorios de tasas de estabilidad, gravámenes bancarios y primas de seguro de depósitos se tratarán por lo general como ingresos tributarios cuando se abonen al gobierno general y se asignen a los fondos consolidados o generales de este, de forma que el gobierno pueda utilizar libre e inmediatamente el dinero para los fines que elija. Este principio se aplicará independientemente de que el gobierno prometa revertir esos pagos para garantizar los depósitos de los clientes de los bancos en caso de necesidad futura.
- Si los pagos obligatorios se abonan al gobierno general y se destinan a fondos afectados exclusivamente a volver al sector de la economía que engloba a las sociedades sujetas a dichos pagos, éstos seguirán considerándose ingresos tributarios dado que los fondos estarán disponibles para el gobierno y podrán reducir su déficit presupuestario, que la tasa no conlleva contraprestación para una entidad individual y que las cantidades recaudadas no tienen relación con cualquier pago posterior a los depositantes o cualquier gasto realizado como medio de respaldo más amplio al sector financiero.
- Se clasificarán como tasa por servicio los pagos que deban aportarse a sistemas permanentes más reducidos para garantizar los depósitos de "particulares" cuando los niveles de pago concuerden con el coste del seguro.
- También se clasificarán como tasa por servicio, y no como ingreso tributario, los pagos que impliquen que el gobierno ejecute los activos de una institución en quiebra o tenga un derecho prioritario sobre la liquidación de activos de esta con objeto de financiar los pagos de compensación a los clientes por la pérdida de sus depósitos.

No se tratarán como ingresos tributarios los pagos obligatorios destinados a fondos externos al sector de gobierno y a instituciones no estatales respaldadas por los tomadores de depósitos, ni los pagos hechos a sistemas voluntarios.

Notas

1. Las referencias en la Guía de interpretación de la OCDE a las secciones o partes de "este reporte" se refieren a OCDE (2015), *Revenue Statistics* 1965-2014 (Estadísticas tributarias 1965-2014), Publicaciones de la OCDE, París.
2. Todas las referencias al SCN deberán entenderse hechas a la edición de 2008.
3. Véase el apartado A.12 de la presente guía para el análisis del concepto de agente.
4. Por lo general, es posible identificar la cuantía de las contribuciones a la seguridad social y de los impuestos sobre la nómina, pero no otros impuestos asumidos por el gobierno.
5. Sin embargo, si un gravamen considerado como ingreso no tributario en la mayoría de los países se califica de tributario –o permite recaudar sustanciales ingresos– en uno o más países, las entradas en concepto de dicho gravamen se indican en las notas que figuran al pie de los cuadros de países, pero no se incluyen en la recaudación tributaria total.
6. Obsérvese, no obstante, que los nombres pueden dar lugar a confusión. Por ejemplo, aunque una tasa sobre los pasaportes se trataría normalmente como ingreso no tributario, si se impone un gravamen suplementario sobre los pasaportes (como en el caso de Portugal) con el fin de conseguir un ingreso sustancialmente mayor que el costo que supone proporcionar el pasaporte, dicho gravamen deberá considerarse como un impuesto sobre el uso de bienes (5200).
7. Existen ciertas dificultades prácticas para llevar a cabo la distinción operada por el SCN 1993.
8. Para una explicación más detallada de esta distinción, consúltese el estudio especial sobre cuestiones de actualidad en relación con el registro de los ingresos tributarios Current issues in reporting tax revenues, en la edición 2001 de Revenue Statistics.
9. En ocasiones, se emplean asimismo los términos "no reembolsable" y "reembolsable", pero puede parecer ilógico hablar de "reembolsable" cuando no se ha pagado nada.
10. Con la excepción del diferente tratamiento dado a los créditos fiscales exigibles en los sistemas de imputación del impuesto sobre sociedades (§§ 32–34).
11. No se trata aquí de verdaderos gastos tributarios en sentido formal, ya que tales gastos requieren que se identifique un sistema tributario de referencia para cada país o, mejor si cabe, una referencia internacional común y, en la práctica, no se ha logrado acuerdo sobre esta última.
12. A menos que se basen en la plusvalía obtenida con la venta, en cuyo caso se clasificarían como impuestos sobre las ganancias de capital, en las subpartidas 1120 o 1220.
13. Con todo, algunos países aplican la misma legislación a ambos en impuestos particulares sobre la renta, aunque las entradas procedentes de dichos impuestos suelen ser fácilmente atribuibles a uno u otro caso y pueden, por lo tanto, consignarse en la debida partida.
14. Por ejemplo, "[...] que son suficientemente autónomas e independientes y se comportan como si fueran sociedades [...] (incluido en el hecho de llevar) conjuntos completos de cuentas" (SCN 2008, 4.44).
15. En Canadá, país en el que se considera que rige un sistema de imputación, el crédito fiscal (no exigible) para el accionista nace en relación con el impuesto nacional sobre sociedades que se reputa haber pagado, tanto si ha surgido una obligación tributaria para la sociedad como si no. Habida cuenta de que no existe una conexión íntegra entre la obligación tributaria de la sociedad y el crédito concedido en relación con el impuesto sobre la renta en esos sistemas, los créditos por dividendos se tratan, junto con otros créditos fiscales, según lo descrito en el § 21.
16. Esto puede darse, por ejemplo, cuando ya existía un régimen para los empleados del gobierno previo a la introducción de un régimen general de seguridad social.
17. En el SCN 2008, se consideran transferencias de capital y no impuestos (véase el apartado G).
18. Mediante este sistema, la Unión Europea ajusta las diferencias entre los tipos de cambio empleados para determinar los precios de la política agrícola común (PAC) y los tipos de cambio reales. Los pagos realizados en este sistema pueden estar relacionados con importaciones o exportaciones y, cuando ha sido posible identificar por separado las respectivas cantidades, se han mostrado en el correspondiente epígrafe (5123 o 5124). En el presente informe, esas cantidades se han consignado en valores brutos (esto es, sin deducir ningún subsidio otorgado en el marco del sistema MCM).
19. Las transferencias de las utilidades de las loterías del Estado se consideran ingresos no tributarios (véase el § 64).
20. Véase el § 26(c) en relación con esta distinción.
21. En la Cumbre de Edimburgo (1992), los países miembros de la UE decidieron reducir paulatinamente este porcentaje del 1.4 al 1, entre los años 1995 y 1999. Durante el periodo 1970-1983, este porcentaje también fue de 1.

OECD PUBLISHING, 2, rue André-Pascal, 75775 PARIS CEDEX 16
(23 2016 13 3 P) ISBN 978-92-64-25191-5 – 2016

www.ingramcontent.com/pod-product-compliance
Lightning Source LLC
Chambersburg PA
CBHW061208240926
51846CB00006B/1148